CHILDREN OF CHE
Childcare and Education in Cuba

Karen Wald

Foreword by Hal Z. Bennett

Ramparts Press
Palo Alto, California 94303

Library of Congress Cataloging in Publication Data

Wald, Karen.
    Children of Che.

    Includes bibliographical references and index.
    1. Child welfare — Cuba.   2.   Education, Cooperative
— Cuba.   3.   Child health services — Cuba.   4.   Rehabili-
tation of juvenile delinquents — Cuba.   I.   Title.
HV747.C9W34   362.7'097291   76-25414
ISBN 0-87867-064-5
ISBN 0-87867-065-3 pbk.

Photo credits: *Bohemia* magazine, pp. 21, 268t, 280; Kathinka
van Dorp, p. 382; Indochina Friendship Committee, p. 374;
Mayra A. Martinez, pp. 1, 328, 332; Mark Sheldon, p. 59; Venceremos Brigade, pp. 385, 388; Joaquin Vinas, pp. 44, 45, 273;
all others by the author.

Published by Ramparts Press, Palo Alto, California 94303.

Library of Congress Catalog Card Number 76-25414
ISBN 0-87867-064-5 (cloth)
ISBN 0-87867-065-3 (paperback)

Glossary

albergue	Home, house serving as a dormitory.
auto-servicio	Self-service, a program in which students clean up after themselves, do kitchen and maintenance work in their school.
becado	Scholarship student.
bohío	Primitive hut in rural area made of crude materials, generally only consisting of walls, door and roof.
compañero	Friend, companion, comrade.
campesino	Peasant farmer, farmworker.
casitas	Doll houses, playhouses.
círculos infantiles	Literally, children's circles. Childcare centers.
corrales	Large collective playpens.
educadoras	Educators, the teaching personnel in childcare centers.
empleadas	Employees, non-teaching personnel in schools and dormitories.
guajiro	A person who lives in the mountains, a peasant.
guerrillero de la enseñanza	Teaching guerrillas; a program in which primary school students elect to become teachers, begin practice teaching.
hogares maternos	Maternity homes where women from remote areas can go during late pregnancy and receive adequate medical care.
hogares de recuperación nutricional	Homes for nutritional recuperation.
huerto, huerto escolar	Garden, orchard, school garden.
internado	Student who lives in school; a school where students receive room and board.
jardines	"Children's gardens," playgroups similar to nursery schools, unstructured, with minimal facilities.
latifundista	Large landowner, generally an absentee landlord.

madres combatientes	Mother combatants for education; a program in which mothers not working outside the home give concrete assistance to the schools.
madres acompañantes	A program in which mothers accompany their young hospitalized children.
padrino	Sponsor (generally of *círculo* or school).
recibidora	"Catcher," "receiver" — untrained midwife.
solar	Urban living unit of single rooms built around an alley or courtyard. Each room houses a family.
vago	One who doesn't work or study — a parasite.

ANAP	*Asociación Nacional de Agricultores Pequeños*; National Association of Small Farmers
CDR	*Comité de Defensa de la Revolución*; Committee for the Defense of the Revolution
CJC	Centenial Youth Column, a work-study program for youths not in school
CNC	*Consejo Nacional de Cultura*;National Council on Culture
CTC	*Central de Trabajadores de Cuba*; Cuban Workers Central Organization, encompasses all trade union activity
EJT	*Ejército Juvenil de Trabajo*; Army of working youth
FAR	*Fuerzas Armadas Revolucionarias*; Revolutionary Armed Forces
FEEM	*Federación Estudiantil de Enseñanza Media*; Middle level Student Federation
FEU	*Federación de Estudiantes Universitarios*; University Student Federation
FMC	*Federación de Mujeres Cubanas*; Federation of Cuban Women
ICAIC	*Instituto Cubano de Arte e Industria Cinematográfica*; Cuban Institute for Art and Cinema
ICAP	*Instituto Cubano de Amistad con los Pueblos*; Cuban Institute of Friendship with the Peoples
MINSAP	*Ministerio de Salud Pública*; Ministry of Public Health
UJC	*Unión de Jovenes Comunistas*; Union of Young Communists
UPC	*Unión de Pioneros de Cuba*; Union of Cuban Pioneers

Contents

Foreword

Closing Castro's Cuba to U.S. citizens in 1961 was but one of many infamous blunders in our relationship to that country. At the very least, had we been free to visit Cuba we would have witnessed the evolution of a people emerging from the chaos of revolution and poverty, toward a proud and orderly way of life. We would have witnessed the birth and the growing pains of an infant who is now an adult.

No one will dispute that the place to begin building a new society is with the children. If we could have witnessed the evolution of Cuban society in the years immediately following the revolution, we might have seen that process unfolding there. This book offers important insights into how it unfolded, and why. Hopefully, it will help us appreciate those early years which we were prevented from witnessing first hand.

It is essential, now that we are free to travel to Cuba, to have a perspective about what's happened there. It would be easy to jump to the conclusion that what we see there now was there all along, and that the only difference between pre-Castro Cuba and now are the faces in the President's convoy. It would be easy, in other words, to overlook the tremendous accomplishments of the *Cuban people* under Castro's leadership.

Some familiarity with pre-revolutionary Cuba, however, reveals that more than the faces have changed. It isn't a matter of changing the rulers; the Cuban people have gone from *being ruled*, to being themselves the rulers. From the start, the revolutionary government has made it a point to give the people the tools they need to do this. To make this a continuing process, the focus has had to be on the children.

If the focus on children in Cuba has been stressed by that country's leadership, it has been done in a way that is probably unique in the history of revolution. The goals, as well as the educational methods, are clear expressions of the Cuban leadership's understanding of the complexities of the human problems they face in creating a revolutionary society in the midst of underdevelopment.

How, for example, do you communicate complex social and political concepts to a people who are largely pre-literate? You can either take advantage of that lack of skill and move the masses toward your own ends with hypnotic demagoguery; or you can provide the people with the education and skill to begin making their own choices. The Castro administration has clearly chosen the latter route.

Health care, nutritional education, housing, general education, and jobs through which the worker can experience self-worth are perhaps obvious necessities in a society which calls itself humane. And yet, how many political systems neglect these basic human needs? It will be interesting, as travel between Cuba and the United States resumes, to compare our own accomplishments and neglects in these areas with the same in modern day Cuba.

Oscar Lewis (author of *The Children of Sánchez*), who was perhaps our most popular Cuba-watcher, argued that one of the most difficult problems faced by emerging countries is the dynamic of what he called "the culture of poverty." Over the years, or centuries, a group of people, living in extreme poverty, develops a culture of its own, a set of behavioral traits, or, if you will, *skills,* to best cope with their lot in life.

Nearly fifteen years ago, as a teacher in a childcare center in the center of a large, urban housing project, I had my white, middle-class sensibilities thoroughly jarred by the way people lived in that poverty-stricken environment. Up to that time, I had perceived poor people as being pretty much like myself, except with less money to spend. What I was suddenly forced to see was that poverty had its own set of rules, thrusting upon the poor a set of values so different from mine that I was left with the feeling of having been launched off onto another planet. Very little of what I had learned in my life seemed applicable to this society of poverty into which I had been thrust.

In extreme poverty, anxiety about the basic necessities of life — food, shelter, and physical well-being — dominate one's every waking hour. Diseases of malnutrition and overcrowding mark the children, most often with scars which don't heal but which they carry into adulthood. Ever-present anxiety, frustration, malnutrition, and disease eat away at peoples' souls, resulting in constant irritability and impatience. And more often than not a child grows up in an environment that is brooding, violent, and without hope.

This is the kind of poverty the great majority of Cuban people suffered during the years before the Revolution. While Batista and his generals, surrounded by parasitical hangers-on who controlled all branches of the government, army and police, worked hand-in-hand with the Mafia to bleed the cities dry, largely absentee landlords reaped huge profits from the Cuban sugar cane crops. Not only were the farm workers — upon whom the landlords depended — paid less than meagre wages, but their poverty and lack of marketable skills kept them that way, as though that condition was part of a deliberate plan. Sick and dying children were commonplace in a countryside that knew no doctors or hospitals. In the cities, the poverty of the workers took the form of appalling, overcrowded slums, hunger and ignorance, petty crime, prostitution, and begging.

This was the Cuba of the 1950s. It was a social and economic dead end, and for most of Cuba's people there was little or no room for change. One did well just to survive the physical reality of his or her dismal, day-to-day existence. To break clear, to find enough energy to change one's lot, either individually or collectively, required something like a miracle — or a revolution. The physical environment itself, and the economic and political interests which maintained it, had to change before the people who suffered within it could even dream of finding the personal resources to make positive changes in their lives.

Poverty is a powerful force, shaping one's life long before birth, sometimes generations before the point of conception. Changing the society that is molded by that force requires an effort that must go far beyond the more obvious self-interests of a single person or group of people, and must capture the imaginations of huge numbers of people. Moreover, the effort must go beyond lies and half truths, and must bore into the hearts of each and every person involved.

In reading Karen Wald's description of children growing up in today's Cuba, the reader cannot help but find areas in which the Cuban leadership has kindled a light which now burns brightly in the hearts and minds of the people. One is convinced that the culture of poverty is being turned around by the Cuban people themselves, under Castro's administration.

The Revolutionary Government has made impressive changes in the material conditions of peoples lives. More important, it has set in motion a process which changes the very nature of the human beings growing up within the new society. Human dignity, pride, and a new freedom to choose a fulfilling way of life, are dominant themes in today's Cuba. Nowhere can this be more clearly seen than in the childcare centers and the schools.

That doesn't mean, however, that professional educators from the United States will immediately see the value of the changes taking place. Sophisticated educators, raised in middle class or upper middle class, suburban U.S., and educated at universities dominated by people like themselves, have, in recent years, developed a cynicism about what we now call *traditional education.* Rote learning and respect for the teacher's authority have been replaced by a wide variety of theories and practices aimed at motivating students to explore on their own and express themselves *from within.* The teacher's authority has been replaced by faith in each student's desire for self-betterment through self-expression.

To this kind of person, the educational methods employed in Cuba today might seem archaic. Such methods might easily fall prey to short-sighted criticisms of our modern educators. However, the critic who fails to examine the exact context in which that education takes place, at the same time that he or she is examining the methods employed, is bringing the distortion of his or her own bias to that criticism.

Knowing how difficult it is for a person outside Cuba to give a relevant assessment of the changing society of that country, Wald has let the Cuban people themselves — especially the children who are both the products and makers of the Revolution — tell their own story. From them we learn how Castro's administration has, by trial and error at times, developed ways to meet the needs, as well as the natural limitations, of the people it serves. If there is any one word which describes the approach of this government, it is "pragmatic." When one method fails, or falls short of its goal, another is quick to replace it, until something is found which *does* work. If authority is to be respected, it must do something to show itself worthy of that respect — at least in the majority of cases.

One point is abundantly clear: Cuban children today don't need "gimmicks" or special innovative forms of education to lure them into the schools and keep them there. They are only one generation away from the abject poverty that kept their parents and their parents' parents down for so long. The young person in Cuba today is motivated to learn basic skills (and social history, I might add) because it is being demonstrated daily that this education is a way out of poverty. It is a way to change one's life and make it better. It is a tool with which to build an alternative to poverty, with all its concommitant physical and emotional ramifications.

That is not to say there is no innovation in Cuban education. On the contrary, education in Cuba is profoundly innovative. But it is of a wholly different nature than what we've become accustomed to here. Having first redefined the goals of education — both in terms of the class interests it was to serve and the type of human being they wanted to develop — the Cuban leadership began experimenting with as great a variety of forms as their continued state of economic underdevelopment permitted.

Where non-traditional teaching is concerned, the Cubans employ some interesting and highly successful work-study programs, which might serve as models to us in the United States. Even very young children are given jobs in gardens or fields as part of their school curriculum, jobs through which they can experience how it feels to do something valuable both for themselves and for the community in which they live. Because agricultural production is so important to the Cuban economy, this early education has more abstract things to teach than the simple planting, nurturing and harvesting of the plants; it teaches a certain reverance both for the farming and for the people who choose to make agriculture their lives. In addition, it should be noted, Cubans are trying to amass enough technical education to help them get their country out of a stage of underdevelopment.

I believe it is important for all of us, from both ends of the political spectrum, from radicals to conservatives, to develop a clear perspective about how social change occurs. To those who preferred to see Cuba as a Utopia created in a few months following the Revolution, there is the necessity to see the hard work that has gone, and which continues to go, into making that country work for all its people. To those who would argue that revolution serves no purpose, or a negative purpose, there is the necessity to see that sometimes the stranglehold of a leadership which either does not care or does not know how to reach the people, must be broken.

As the ban on travel to Cuba is lifted, more and more people from the United States will have the opportunity to judge for themselves what the Cuban revolution has done, or not done, for the Cuban people. It is a shame, however, that we could not be witness to that cultural revolution in its earlier stages. One hopes that books like this one will help fill in between the lines, to remind us all that creating a better society, a society responsive to all its people, is not so much an act of magic as it is a continuing process of dedicated labor.

Hal Z. Bennett
Author of *No More Public Schools*

Gracias

Just about everything going on in Cuba today is a collective process. That is especially true when you are trying to write a book describing the Revolution. The problem in trying to draw up a "thank you" list enumerating all the people who helped produce this book is that it's impossible to know where to begin — or end. Certainly many people whose names deserve to be listed here will be left out. At best this should be considered a partial listing of the many individuals, organizations and institutions who collectively helped create this book, and to whom I owe my thanks.

THE CHILDREN The ones who sang, laughed, wrote compositons, drew pictures, danced, gave me lectures on Cuban history and international politics, taught me Spanish (and so much more!) — and who showed me that a true revolution can create new people, who in turn can create a better world. They *are* the book, because they are the Revolution.

THEIR PARENTS, THEIR TEACHERS, THEIR GUIDES The families all over Cuba: Margaret Randall and Robert Cohen and their children, Gregory (Goyo), Sara, Ximena and Anna. Enrique (Kiko) Bueno Silverio and his cousin María de los Angeles Reina (Maruchy), whose comments inspired this book, and their families, who became like my own family while I was there. Yolanda, Landa and Diana Tamara. Nicolás and Dara, who gave me Elvira and Alina. Pedro, Jean and Ilmi. María Carla, Raulito and Carlita. Julio Machado and Julio Cesar.

THE LEADERS OF THE REVOLUTION The ones who fought to make the Revolution possible and the ones who do the daily work to help it survive, the ones who make the New Children possible. The people from all the ministries and organizations, the schools and the *círculos*, the polyclinics and hospitals, the Children's Salon at the National Library and The National Council on Culture, The Union of Pioneers (especially Pampín) and the *Instituto de la Infancia* (Haydee, Elba). The people who invited me, arranged my travel and accommodations, helped plan my itinerary. Carlos Rafael Rodríguez and Migda, his secretary, who opened many doors for me. Edmundo; Georgina; Rizo; Machín; Rafael and Silva, who helped me climb Pico Turquino, and Mario, a Party official from Oriente who not only cleared the way for all my visits but drove us to the mountains in his jeep; Carlos Ciaño and everyone from ICAP; Pablo, Pedro Borroto and the others who drove me where I needed to go, and who were always so much more than drivers; the men and women who work at the Habana Libre, Habana Riviera and Hotel Nacional, and many of the people who live there (Domingo, the exile families — especially the children from Brazil).

THE NEWSPAPERS AND MAGAZINES Bohemia (Angel Guerra and Manolito, for, among other things, giving me access to their archives and copying old photos for me); *Juventud Rebelde* (Jorge López, and Landa); *Granma; La Revista Cuba; Pionero; Prensa Latina (Direct from Cuba);* and *Santiago,* the magazine of the University of Oriente.

THE MANY PHOTOGRAPHERS in Cuba and the U.S. who generously contributed photos to add depth and variety to my collection. The Cuban photographers who urged me to take my own pictures, developed and printed them, and taught me how to do better. Karen Kerschen and John Clements who gave many hours of their time printing and developing my film when I came back to California.

THE PEOPLE AND RESOURCES of the Center for Cuban Studies, Cuba Resource Center (*Cuba Review*), North American Congress on Latin America (NACLA), Venceremos Brigade. The many, many people who helped me prepare my slide show and videotape on Cuban children, and all those whose comments on viewing these helped me in writing the book.

ALL THE PEOPLE WHO HELPED with transcribing and translating, including Pedro González and Yolanda Gómez in Havana, and Maritza in Berkeley. (All conversations and interviews in this book were conducted in Spanish.) Doctors Pastor Cabrera, Linda Morse and Richard Fine, for their comments on the medical section and their helpful comparisons to the way things are here. The Centro Infantil de la Raza, and the people who took care of my children so that I could write. Nina Serrano, Gail Dolgin, Lincoln Bergman, Nancy Stein, Hal Bennett, Beatriz Pesquera, Debbie Begel and Kathinka van Dorp, whose comments and contributions, editing and inspiration were indispensable at key points during the seven years it took to produce *Children of Che*; Russ Stetler, without whose editing and encouragement it would still be a 500-page manuscript sitting on a shelf.

ONCE AGAIN, THE CHILDREN Including my own children, who provided new insights as I was writing, a new way of looking at the world.

Gracias a todos.

1

Being Born

1953:
A REVOLUTION AND A BABY ARE BORN

On a hot summer night the soft moans of a woman in labor could be heard in a small *bohío* (hut) high up in the Sierra Maestra mountains. Her cries drifted out of the wood-and-palm-leaf hut into the heavy night air, then were absorbed by the mountains and jungle-like plants that grew everywhere. A small kerosene lamp threw dark shadows against the walls of the *bohío*; outside, a full moon and bright stars lit up the sky and the countryside.

Yolanda Suárez was a simple mountain woman. She had spent her life in the Sierra Maestra, at the southernmost tip of Cuba's Oriente Province. Like her husband, she had eked out a bare living from the earth; raising animals, growing coffee, somehow surviving. During the cane-cutting season Alexis — whom she had married when they were both sixteen — went down to the flatlands where for a few months he could earn some money by working fourteen or sixteen hours a day on the sugar plantations. But money was never enough to last through the long "dead" season when there was no cane to cut. Now in their early thirties, Yolanda and Alexis looked as though they were past fifty.

The hard life had taken its toll on their children, too. Although this was Yolanda's fifth pregnancy, she had only one living child, Rafaelito, who now wandered naked around the *bohío* as his mother tossed and turned in the agony of giving birth. Two of her other pregnancies had resulted in miscarriages; her malnourished body simply couldn't sustain another life. Another child, a little girl, had been born two years before, only to die in her third month, belly swollen, eyes dull, worn away by the diarrhea that accompanies gastroenteritis. Her parents looked on helplessly as their baby died.

There were no doctors or hospitals in the Sierra Maestra. There weren't even roads. When Alexis went down the mountain he traveled over time-worn footpaths, suitable only for people and sure-footed horses and mules. A certain resignation was written into the faces of the mountain people when it came to matters of sickness, life and death. This was the way things had always been and would always be.

When Rafaelito was born three years earlier, Yolanda had had the help of a *recibidora* — the *campesino* (peasant) equivalent of a midwife, but with little of the knowledge or expertise of traditional midwives. As her title indicated, the job of the *recibidora* was to catch or receive the baby as it came out. She knew nothing of hygiene or medicine. The symbol of her trade was a long, hard fingernail on one hand, used to rupture the water bag that enveloped the fetus if it didn't break of its own accord. Fortunately, there were no problems with the birth of Rafaelito. He was a strong, sturdy little boy with a healthy desire to come into the world and stay in it.

Now he looked confused as his mother cried and moaned. He didn't understand what was happening, and he looked to his father for reassurance.

But Alexis could offer him none. The baby was early and there was no one to help. Alexis sat on a hand-hewn wooden chair, awaiting the outcome. Finally, with a gasp, Yolanda pushed out the head of her little girl. Alexis went to help bring the baby out, cut the cord, and clean up the mess. Yolanda lay on the bed, panting and exhausted, as her husband went out into the hot night to seek a woman neighbor who lived a few miles away. He would ask her to come stay with them and help his wife for a few days, until she was back on her feet and ready to take on her normal household chores.

Far away, the city of Santiago was celebrating the traditional summer carnival that night. Men and women masqueraded in colorful costumes, drank beer and danced in the streets. It was the 26th of July, 1953, and something else was being born, something which would change the life of Yolanda and Alexis and open up a whole new world to the little girl who was born in the mountains, the little girl they named Celia.

Cuba was giving birth to the Revolution which would climax its hundred years of struggle to be free and independent of all foreign powers — free of absentee landlords, exploitation and misery. While Yolanda cried and struggled to bring a new life into the world, a handful of men and women in a farmhouse near Siboney were planning to enter Santiago and capture the Moncada Fortress, the second-largest military garrison of Batista's regime.

The attack on the Moncada was the idea of Fidel Castro Ruz, a young lawyer who had tried unsuccessfully to challenge in the courts the Batista dictatorship's abuse of the Cuban constitution. When all legal means failed, Fidel gathered together a group of young men and women who were willing to risk everything to free their people from centuries of oppression by foreign powers and corrupt governments. The rebels hoped to take over the city of Santiago by capturing the Palace of Justice, the Moncada Fortress and the hospital. Then they would take over the radio station and broadcast an appeal from Santiago to the rest of the island, calling for insurrection throughout the country, reading their political and social program to the people.

Militarily, the attack on the Moncada was a disaster. Unfamiliar with the city streets, some of the young rebels got lost. Without the element of suprise they had counted on, outnumbered more than ten to one and armed only with .22 calibre rifles, most were easily captured. The majority of those captured were later shot — murdered — when an indignant Batista gave orders that he wanted ten rebels shot for every soldier who'd been killed in the fighting. Some of the prisoners, such as Abel Santamaría, the second-in-command to Fidel, were tortured before they were killed.

The attack on the Moncada was meant to be a new birth for the Cuban people. When Haydee Santamaría, one of the participants in the assault, spoke to students at the University of Havana many years later, she described it that way. By then she had watched the Revolution grow and develop. In the process she had lived through many more battles, including *Playa Girón* (the Bay of Pigs). But the assault on the Moncada was different, special, she told the students — like the birth of your first child:

> When my son was born there were difficult moments, moments like those any woman goes through when she is going to have a child, very difficult moments. The pain was tremendous, pain enough to tear out one's insides; and on the other hand there was the strength to keep from crying out or screaming or cursing. When you have a pain like that you curse and yell and scream. And why is a person strong enough to keep from screaming and cursing when there is pain? Because a child is coming. In those moments I found out what Moncada was.

Haydee came to see the Moncada in the light of the birth of her first child. On the 26th of July, 1953, as Celia was being born in the Sierra Maestra, young rebels were dying at the Moncada, and those who survived the attack watched their dreams die along with their brothers. Haydee, calling that the "sorrow greater than any other," asked, "How was it that we didn't curse and weep and lose our serenity? We believe that only because of the coming of something grandiose (like the coming of a child) can a person stand that much grief."

The "something grandiose" that Haydee, Fidel and the other combatants dreamed of that night was the Cuban Revolution. It took a long time to reach maturity. Many more lives were lost before the triumph of the rebellion on January 1, 1959. But because of that Revolution, when Celia herself gave birth to her first child twenty years later, she did not do so alone and in pain in a dirt-floored *bohío*, far from medical care, crying in pain.

In 1973 I was visiting Cuba for the fourth time. My first stay in Cuba — eight months in 1969 — was spent working at *Tricontinental* magazine, translating, editing and sometimes writing articles. But although I thought of myself as a writer, I found myself unable to write about the Cuban Revolution when I returned home to California. It was too complex; I'd learned too much in my eight months there — enough to know how little I, or any foreigner, could really understand the process of the Revolution.

It was on my second trip in 1970 that some conversations with Cuban schoolchildren gave me the idea that the words of the children could make a very interesting book. What better way to write about the Cuban Revolution than to let the Cuban people tell their own story? And what better people than this new generation that was creating, and being created by, the revolutionary process? I asked for and quickly received permission to come back for an extended period of time, to travel, meet and interview children all over the island.

The first phase of this work, in 1970-71, produced an abundant amount of material. But I was still unable to put it all together. My interviews showed what today's generation of Cuban children is like — but it didn't show how they got that way. In 1973 I returned once more, to amplify and update my earlier material. By now I was pretty familiar with many aspects of the Cuban Revolution; I knew a lot of people, places and institutions in Cuba.

But there was one difference on this trip that affected my attitude in many subtle ways, and produced an entirely new set of experiences.

This time, when I went, I was pregnant.

Many pre-revolutionary *bohíos* were not this well made.

1973:
A NEW KIND OF LIFE, A NEW KIND OF BIRTH

APRIL The polyclinic I found near my hotel was an old, Spanish-style house on a residential street in Vedado. An open porch ran the length of the front of the building; open doors led into a large reception room. As I went to the information desk I could see rows and rows of files and records behind a counter. The walls, floors and stairway seemed to be made of marble.

I explained that I was an *extranjera* (foreigner), would be visiting Cuba for several months, and was three months pregnant. The woman behind the desk looked suprised. There are special clinics set up for foreign guests, and every hotel has a medical staff and pharmacy. But, wanting to see how Cuban women experience pregnancy and childbirth, I'd asked a friend to direct me to her neighborhood polyclinic. Now I stood waiting, while the information clerk checked to see if I could just walk in off the street like that. The answer was apparently yes, because she soon directed me upstairs to the maternity section of the clinic.

I passed by several examining rooms and a nurses' station, then joined a number of other women — in varying stages of pregnancy — on the balcony which, like the porch below, ran the length of the house and served as a waiting room.

It was here that I met Celia. She was six months pregnant, her belly already beginning to jut out distinctly, and she seemed to know her way around the clinic and its routines. When I appeared confused about where to go, she took me under her protective wing. "Is this your first child?" she asked. I nodded yes. "Don't worry," she reassured me. "Here, everyone takes good care of you." She began telling me about what her first few months were like.

"Are you tired a lot? Are you nauseous? You have to rest a lot and take care of yourself, you know." I kept nodding my head. Some of the other women joined in the conversation: "They'll send you to the dentist right away," said a small woman with her brown hair pulled back in a pony-tail. "The baby's bones and teeth need a lot of calcium; if you are not drinking enough milk, the baby can take the calcium from your teeth." "You have to go, too," added another woman, tall, black and very, very pregnant. "Don't think you can skip it because you don't like dentists. The dentist will send a report back here, and if you don't go, you'll have to answer to the nurse when you come back for your next visit."

The women began recounting their various experiences with the dentist. I sat and listened, watching their faces and hands move as

Children are born in modern facilities today.

they talked. Celia was a medium-sized woman, with copper-colored skin and thick, shiny black hair. She looked like many of the women I had seen in the mountains of Oriente. But there was a subtle difference that I couldn't put my finger on. "Maybe it's just because she lives in the city," I thought.

When it was my turn to be examined, Celia led me through a door, back to the cool shadows of the old house. The nurse-receptionist began filling out a card with my medical history, took my weight, pulse and blood pressure, then sent me into another room for a pelvic exam. The doctor was a short *mulata* woman in her mid-forties. After she examined me and told me I was doing fine, I complained of constipation. She said she'd have the nurse give me a prescription for some medication. "Do you have any other problems or questions you want to ask?" Her look and tone encouraged my questions. We talked for a while, then I went back into the nurses' ante-room.

"Your diet is very important now," the nurse explained, and she asked what I was eating. I told her I was living at the hotel, and had meat, vegetables, milk and fruit every day. Two other women were in the room, one being weighed, the other having her blood pressure taken. Both listened with interest as I described my diet. The older one nodded in apparent satisfaction.

"It's good that you are getting a balanced diet. Here, before the Revolution, we didn't even know what a balanced diet was."

"Even if we knew, who could afford it?" interjected the younger one, a slight woman with wispy blond hair. "Nobody ate meat or drank milk in those days."

"Nobody but the rich," agreed the older woman. "My mother never ate beef in her whole life. On special occasions, like a Saint's Day or christening — because they were very religious in those days — someone might kill a pig, and everyone would eat roast pork. Those were special feasts! But we never even knew why we were unhealthy. We thought God made rich people with better bodies than poor people! No one ever heard the words 'calcium,' 'proteins,' 'vitamins.' When the Revolution started giving milk to all the children, and weekly rations of meat to every family, we first learned the true value of these foods. Some children didn't like milk at first — all they had ever had to drink was coffee!"

"That's why all polyclinics have social workers and nurses who visit people's homes, and explain all about nutrition and hygiene," remarked the nurse who had just finished filling out my chart. "Here, you keep this," she said, handing me the cardboard card with little boxes to be checked each month for weight, blood pressure, belly size, lab reports, etc. "It's your responsibility to bring it with you to the lab and to each clinic visit." I took the card with surprise, and looked at it. In the clinic in California, I was never even informed about my blood pressure and lab reports unless I specifically asked. Here it was taken for granted that I was an active participant in this process, not just a passive "patient." I felt more important, being entrusted with my medical record, although it struck me as silly to feel that way.

I left thinking, "There's a lot more to this Revolution than I had realized. Being pregnant here is going to be a very interesting experience."

MAY   When I returned the next month, I saw four or five of the same women I had talked with last time, and two or three new ones. Celia wasn't there; but she came in about five minutes later.

This time the waiting period passed all too quickly, and before I knew it my turn had come, and I had to leave the excited conversation of the women. I wanted to talk more with them — especially with Celia, my first benefactor. I decided to wait around after my check-up.

Celia was still waiting her turn when I came out, so I sat down in an old rocking chair next to her, and we began to talk. She had, as I suspected, been born in Oriente. "High up in the Sierra Maestra mountains," she told me, "in a little dirt-floored *bohío*, surrounded by pigs and chickens." She said it with a wry smile, but something in her face and her voice suggested the pain and misery of those years.

That was how I learned about Yolanda and Alexis, and the anguish of birth in those years before the Revolution. Celia, the baby who was born that night in 1953, was almost twenty years old now — "I'll celebrate my twentieth birthday on July 26th, when the whole country is celebrating," she told me. She was five and a half years old when the Revolution triumphed. "The rebel soldiers set up clinics in the mountains even while the fighting was still going on," she remembers. "Afterwards, they sent us teachers. Later, people from the Party came and talked to people in our region; they convinced us to move closer together, so they could build roads and put in electricity for us. They gave us materials and built sturdy houses for us. Then, when about six families had moved into this little village, they began building a school. Now the school has grown, with more and more families moving together, and we have stores, a polyclinic, and there'll even be a childcare center next year."

I asked what the people do for a living. "Well, most people still grow some of their own food — *plátanos, boniato, yuca* — and raise hogs, but that's mostly a supplement now. The *campesinos* in our area have collectivized, and grow coffee together, which they sell to the State.

I was curious about Celia's life since she left the mountains, but as I was about to ask, the nurse called her name. "I have to go for my check-up now," she said, half-apologetically. "Maybe we'll be able to talk some more the next time."

JUNE Now I had come to look forward eagerly to my clinic appointments, not just to see how my baby was progressing, and ask the questions that kept coming up — but to continue my conversations with Celia. She was there ahead of me this time — also interested in talking some more, I thought. When I sat down beside her, Celia asked how I was feeling. I told her I felt much better this month, not as tired, and never nauseous any more. "Enjoy it while you can," she told me, "because when you get into the last months, you start getting tired again. This *bebito* weighs so much and is kicking me so hard that I can't get any sleep at night." Her brown hands were folded over her belly — large now in her eighth month. She smiled as a sharp kick caused her blouse to jump. "See what I mean? He gets mad when I talk about him that way."

"Do you want it to be a boy?" I asked, responding to her use of the male pronoun. "No, it really doesn't matter to me. I had an older brother whom I loved very much. His name was Rafaelito. He was killed two years ago during a *gusano* (counter-revolutionary) raid on a coastal village in Oriente. He was working in a fishing commune. If the baby's a boy, I'll name him Rafaelito.

"But a girl would be nice, too. She could help me, we could be good friends as she grows up. And she can be so many things now. It's not like before, when the girls just stayed at home or worked in the fields of their husbands and fathers.

"My husband doesn't care whether it's a boy or girl, either. He just wants a healthy baby."

"What does your . . . ?"

"What does my husband do?" She asked my question for me. "He's a technician in a sugar mill. He studies ways to improve the cane, and also how to make other useful products from the cane by-products. He studied at the University of Santiago."

She seemed to anticipate my next questions, too. "I was a student there, too — that's how we met. Then, when he graduated and was given work in Havana, we decided to get married and come here together. I have one more year at the University of Havana. I'm studying biochemistry. But I'll probably teach for a while, rather than do research. We still need a lot more teachers."

"Won't having the baby interrupt your studies?" I asked.

"Not very much. It's good timing. The baby will be born next month — early I hope. I could go back to school at the end of September if I want, if there's room in the childcare center. Otherwise I'll only miss one semester."

Just then I felt a movement inside my belly. "My baby's started kicking now," I told Celia happily. "Just wait, it gets worse," she warned, but she smiled, remembering how exciting it was the first time she felt her baby move inside her. "You'll be starting childbirth classes this month," she told me. "We have *parto sin dolor* here — prepared childbirth — so women don't have to go through the agony that our mothers did. They had natural childbirth then too. But there was nothing natural about it. That just meant they had no medical attention, no hygienic conditions, no medications or oxygen in case something went wrong. Now over 90 percent of the children are born in hospitals or maternity clinics — and twice as many live as before.

"My husband and I went to see some films about childbirth. One was called *Sin Dolor* (Without Pain) and the other one *Atención Pre-natal* (Pre-natal Care). They explained everything about the growth of the fetus, and how your body changes during pregnancy. They even showed a woman giving birth. They answered a lot of questions we had.

"At first my husband wasn't too convinced about this method. In Cuba men usually didn't have much to do with childbirth — except in cases like with my parents, who were alone in the mountains and sometimes didn't have any help. My husband thought all this breathing and excercising was just a way to get your mind off the pain — a kind of self-deception. But after we went to a few classes, and saw the films, he felt much better about it. Now he's really glad our baby will be born that way."

My exam was shorter this visit. After the routine weight and blood pressure measurements, my belly was measured, and we talked some about my diet. My weight gain was fine; the doctors in this clinic didn't seem to have any fixed preconceptions about how much weight I was allowed to gain, as long as I was eating the right things. We talked about the prepared childbirth classes, and the results of my lab work. By now I was beginning to feel like an old pro.

JULY The weather was oppressively hot as I walked over to the polyclinic for my fourth visit, and I was sweating as I climbed the old marble stairs. On the balcony, women were sitting fanning themselves with newspapers. Several were bunched together, talking animatedly about something in the newspaper. I walked over and sat down near them, conscious of my swollen belly as I sat.

They were talking about the proposed maternity law which was being discussed throughout Cuba that summer. Under its provisions, the already ample, free maternity care would be extended. Working women would receive six full days or twelve half days off from work, with pay, during their pregnancy, for medical and dental visits. They would get six weeks paid leave before the baby was born, with a two-week leeway for late births, and twelve weeks after the birth, also with pay. Those expecting multiple births would be able to stop work two weeks earlier.

But the law didn't stop here. Each working mother would be given one day off a month during her child's first year to take the child in for medical check-ups. And, if she didn't want to return to work right away, she could be given unpaid leave till the end of the child's first year, with automatic rights to return to the job she had before.

Carmen, a woman who had once told me how her daughter marched in the May First Parade, was very excited about the new law. "When Carmencita was born, I had to quit my job at the textile factory," she said. "I quit when I was five months pregnant, and didn't go back till Carmencita was in kindergarten. Everybody was upset with me — my husband, my neighbors, the women in the Women's Federation . . . "

"You see, during the past years we've been trying to involve more and more women in the labor force," interrupted Isabel, who was very active in the Women's Federation. "We've been trying to explain to the women — and their husbands — how important it is for the Cuban economy, and for their own development, for them to get out of the house and get involved in productive work."

"Lots of women joined the work force," added a small, brown-skinned woman I hadn't seen before, "But so many dropped out each year that it almost canceled out the gains.

"It wasn't that the women weren't conscious of the need for their work. Most of them would have liked to remain working. But when you have children to take care of, and a house to clean, and have to wait on the *colas* (lines) at the food store — well, it all piles up. Pretty soon you start to think: 'It's a fulltime job just taking care of my house and family.' Then one of your kids gets sick, and you have to miss a few days from work. Or you find that you're pregnant. So you drop out.''

"And besides," added a young black woman who looked just barely pregnant, "we'd be in there working every day, then doing our 'second shift' at home at night, and watching the men getting all the work merits, being chosen vanguard workers, being chosen for the Party, becoming Work Heroes. But they could never be such 'heroes' if we weren't there cooking their meals, cleaning their clothes, watching the kids while they went to meetings or did voluntary overtime or productive work on Sundays — and soaking in all the glory."

"But that's starting to change now," said Isabel. "After our Congress of Women Workers last year we began to implement some changes. We set up a 'shopping bag plan,' so that women who work could drop off their grocery bag and list at the store in the morning and pick it up full when they come home at night, without waiting in line. And we proposed that just being a working mother be a work-merit, so we'd have equal status with the men at our work-places. And there'll be more changes soon."*

"This one is going to make a big difference," offered Carmen, pointing to the article about the new maternity law in the newspaper she was reading. "I'm on the list for this new baby to go to our *círculo* (childcare center), since I'm working at the textile plant again, but I was already starting to worry about the days missed for doctors' visits. My husband and I were just talking about when I should stop work, and whether I would stay out a long time, like I did with Carmencita.

"My husband is in the Party, and he felt really strongly that I should be setting an example in our neighborhood committee and in the Women's Federation by not dropping out of work. And it's true, I was really miserable during the years I was just staying home and doing housework, and watching my friends doing interesting jobs, jobs that were useful to the Revolution."

By now Celia had joined our group. She had listened intently to the first few minutes of conversation. Now she added: "A lot of other things are changing, too. There are more laundries, more

---

*Isabel was right. In 1975 after much sometimes heated discussion throughout the nation, a Family Code was enacted into law which attempted to institutionalize many of the socialist family relationships women were beginning to push for in 1971-73. According to this, working men and women are expected to share the work of the household and childrearing. See more on the Family Code on pages 254-257.

workers' cafeterias, more *círculos* for our children. All of these things, plus this new law, will make it easier for us to have children and continue being a part of the productive life of our Revolution." (I noticed a special inflection on the word "our".)

"But even that's not enough," insisted the young black woman. "Look, I'm a revolutionary, and I'm going to keep working. All these laws are good, and we're going in the right direction. But we can't be satisfied with just that. Women are going to have to take their full place in this Revolution — and that means the men are going to have to make some changes, too. Give up some of their privileges. Share our work load with us if we're going to share the country's work load with them."

Several heads nodded in agreement; then the women returned to looking over the many provisions of the new law. "Do you think there'll be any trouble in getting this law passed?" I asked. "No, how could there be!" several responded, almost in chorus. "If any of the all-male work centers don't understand the importance of this law, someone from the Women's Federation will go out there and talk to them about it," explained Isabel. "Everyone should be able to see how helping working women is better not just for the women, but for the whole country, and for the unborn children."

"You see, everything changes when you're making a Revolution," Celia elaborated. (I remembered the clinic nurse using almost the same words the day of my first visit.) "The Revolution is changing the women, and the women in turn are changing the Revolution.

"The children change most of all — they're born without any of our handicaps, the remnants of the past that we all carry with us. And that's not separate from the way they're born: better nutrition, better care while they're still inside their mothers' bellies, and from the moment they open their eyes to look up at the Cuban sun. This Revolution is about children; it's for children. They are the people of the twenty-first century that Che talked about; they're the builders of the future. And if it's going to be a better future than our parents ever dared dream of, we have to give them a better beginning."

2

An Aside on Women

This is a book about children, but one related discussion cannot be cut short or omitted: that of the lives of the women. The historic struggle of women in Cuba — which is continuing today — has been the theme of various books and films.* It would be

---

*Films put out by the Cuban Film Institute (ICAIC) include several which are available in the United States, notably *Lucia, With Cuban Women,* and *Alicia.* A number of others, both feature films and documentaries, available only in Cuba, focus on women in the Revolution or in Cuban history.

Books and articles on Cuban Women are too abundant to list here. Partial bibliographies are contained in Nelson P. Valdés and Edwin Lieuwen, *The Cuban Revolution, A Research Study Guide (1959-1969)* (Alburquerque, U. of New Mexico Press, 1971), pp. 168-69; and in Nelson P. Valdés, "A Bibliography on Cuban Women in the Twentieth Century," reprinted from *Cuban Studies Newsletter,* vol. 4, no. 2, June 1974. The latter, which has thirty-one pages of listings, is more extensive. Its annotations, however, reflect the editor's political-intellectual bias against the Revolution, so should be taken with a grain of salt. (Valdés dismisses as too sympathetic, for example, Margaret Randall's *La Mujer Cubana Ahora* — also available in English — which is probably the single most important book portraying revolutionary Cuban women written by a North American author.)

Among the materials not listed by Valdés and worthy of attention are: Pamphlet: *La Mujer de Hoy en America Latina,* published by the Cuban Women's Federation, 1972; *La Mujer en la Revolución Cubana*, compiled by the Unión de Periodistas de Cuba, 1972; Fidel Castro, speech of Nov. 29, 1974 at closing session of Second Congress of FMC, "The Revolution has in Cuban Women Today an Impressive Political Force," pamphlet published in English by Instituto Cubano del Libro, Editorial de Ciencias Sociales, La Habana, 1974; reprints of the Family Code of 1974, available from the Center for Cuban Studies, New York, N.Y.

Cuba Review, vol. IV, no. 4 (Dec. 1974), which contains the above speech by Castro along with an introductory article by Margaret Randall, "Women's Con-

dishonest to claim that anything more than the most superficial view of this complex history could be undertaken here. But to make the comments of women and children throughout this book understandable, and to place them in their historical context, we must say a few words about the role of women in Cuba's past.

Although degrees of exploitation have varied, women in most societies since the beginning of recorded history have been placed in unequal, and generally inferior, roles. It is important to point out though, that "recorded history" is essentially that of class society, in which the subjugation of women was just one aspect — albeit an important one — of the class oppression of those who did not own the land or the tools of their work. This does not mean that there has been something biologically inherent in the nature of men and women that has enabled the one to dominate the other. There is in fact ample evidence to the contrary.

Studies of Cuban history prior to the invasion of the Spaniards in the late fifteenth century indicate that the Guanajatabey, Siboney and Taino peoples of that island lived in communal societies often referred to as "primitive communism," in which land was communally owned and cultivated, and crops distributed equally among all the people. In such primitive societies, according to many anthropologists and historians, women occupied a central and equal place, boys and girls were cared for collectively and equally.

What Frederich Engels argued in *The Origin of the Family, Private Property and the State* appears to have been true of Cuba: the introduction of private property (with the arrival of the Spanish *conquistadores*) and a land-owning, slave-holding class capable of acquiring great wealth initiated the change from a primitive matriarchal society such as described above to one in which women became the property of their husbands. Monogamy became an essential aspect of this relation both because of the Catholic and Moorish traditions the Spaniards brought with them and — more

tinuing Struggle for Liberation," *Cuba Review,* vol. IV, no. 2 (1973) "Women in Transition."

In addition, the Cuban magazines *Mujeres* and *Bohemia* are available in select bookstores in certain cities in the United States. These provide the reader with a broad view of the range and scope of activities, struggles and problems relating to women in the Cuban Revolution. Marta Rojas and Mirta Rodríguez Calderón, *Tania, La Guerrillera Inolvidable,* Instituto del Libro, Habana, 1970 (also available in English).

importantly — because of the new economic relationships they set up. A man who accumulated great wealth expected to pass it on to his sons — and needed to know for sure who his sons were.

The male supremacist attitudes brought by the Spaniards were complemented by similar beliefs held by many of the African peoples the Spaniards later kidnapped and brought to the New World as slaves. But these attitudes are likely outgrowths of, and secondary to the systems of economic relationships. It should not be thought, however, that these standards existed only for the wealthy who had property to pass on. The values adopted by this class were imposed on all of the enslaved, colonized and exploited peoples they ruled during the centuries of class society. When the Revolution triumphed in 1959, all Cuban women suffered to some degree from the double discrimination of being colonized and, as women, being considered inferior within the oppressed people.

The discrimination differed in form and content among rural and urban women, and women of different classes, but all women were affected by it in one way or another, just as all Cuban men were in some way affected by Spanish and U.S. economic and political domination of their country. Capitalism (which followed feudalism in Cuba just as the U.S. rule followed Spanish domination) left its mark on all strata and segments of Cuban society. It was for this reason that Vilma Espín, the president of the Cuban Women's Federation (FMC) has said "For us, the liberation of women cannot be separated from the liberation of all of society."

The roles that Cuban men and women had been forced to play during the years prior to the Revolution cast them into certain stereotypes. Man was supposed to be strong, virile, protective and dominant; the woman was in turn passive, silent, obedient, virtuous and motherly. The man's duty was to go out and earn an income for his family; the woman's was to keep his house and bear his children. The fact that Cuba's economic reality kept many of the Cuban peasants and workers — the majority of the people — from being able to fulfill these roles did little to abolish the "ideal"; rather, it caused frustration, hostility, humiliation, and the break-up of families.

Woman's place was in the home, and she was thus dependent on the man — her father or husband. In the cities, a girl of the upper and middle classes was thought to need only that education required to make her "ladylike" and "cultured" . . . a good wife and mother. Employment opportunities were limited, even for women of this class. If a young woman should have a little education and training and for some reason be without male support, she could perhaps become a teacher, a clerk in a U.S.-owned store, a secretary or nurse. But most women in the cities were poor and uneducated; when left on their own, many had little choice but to become domestic servants or prostitutes. Thousands of Cuban women were forced into these degrading professions before the Revolution. Education, which was most often private, was rarely available to the working-class girl. Even if she did manage to get some training, sexual discrimination kept most women out of most jobs. With a large portion of the Cuban male population out of work all or most of the year, who was going to hire a woman? And when women *were* hired for difficult, low-paying jobs, their wages were even lower than those of their male counterparts doing the same work.

People in the countryside had some difficulty fulfilling the traditional stereotypes imposed on them, too. In the mansions of the *latifundistas* (plantation owners) the woman could be pampered and spoiled, guarded and protected. But over 90 percent of the rural people were peasants. The wives and daughters of small farmers and agricultural laborers shared some of the field work; tended the animals; and like their working-class sisters in the cities, washed, cooked, cleaned house and cared for the children. When left on their own, they were sometimes forced by the threat of starvation into the cities, where they, too, were often left with the choice of becoming a maid or a prostitute.

An incredibly cynical double standard existed, a double standard imposed by poverty and foreign domination. On the one hand, a proper young lady in Cuba was put on a pedestal: she did not go out at night without a chaperone; she was a virgin until she married and faithful to her husband (who was seldom faithful to her) forever after. She was a possession, an adornment, a wife, a mother. On the other hand, left alone or forced to feed a large family on scant earnings, the Cuban woman was swept off her pedestal, put to work in the casinos, the streets, the bars, or in rich folks' homes as a servant. But in neither case was she considered part of the productive or political life of the country.

There were significant exceptions, of course, throughout Cuba's long history. The exceptional women fought or carried messages, prepared food and clothing for the rebel army in the nineteenth century War of Independence against Spain. They joined the underground and organized strikes to overthrow the Machado dictatorship in the 1930s. They were guerrilla fighters and clandestine members of July 26th movement.*

Cuban women fought not only for the independence of their country, but for women's rights as well. Feminist strains of the movement appeared as early as the nineteenth century; the agitation for women's suffrage that swept the middle classes of the West in the 1920s and 1930s affected Cuba as well. The drive for better conditions for women was not limited to the upper classes, however. Small groups of women — many inspired by the October Revolution in the Soviet Union — began to push for the rights of working-class women. Partly as a result of all this agitation, the progressive constitution enacted in 1940 included equal rights for women.

But, like so many other aspects of that constitution, these rights remained essentially on paper, never backed up by any legislation or enforcement. At the triumph of the Revolution, most Cuban women were still living in oppressive, degrading or semi-feudal conditions, economically as well as socially.

As can be seen from the conversations throughout this book, all of this had begun to change when I visited Cuba. Prostitution had been abolished and the women who had been forced into this profession retrained for other work. Equal pay for equal work had been established throughout the island. All Cuban children, male and female, attended compulsory education through the age sixteen, and the doors to technical, vocational, artistic and liberal arts schools of higher education were open to all. Economic independence and an easing of the divorce laws enabled Cuban women to choose with whom they wanted to live on the basis of feelings rather than economic necessity and social pressure. This was greatly assisted by the decision of the Revolution that the health and educational needs of the children were the responsibility of the whole society, not just of individual parents.

---

*The role of women has been abundantly documented in the books by Margaret Randall, cited above. See also Victoria Ortiz, *The Land and the People of Cuba*, J. P. Lippincott, 1973, and *Haydee Habla del Moncada* (La Habana: Instituto del Libro).

The Cuban Revolution, spurred by the Women's Federation, began a massive campaign to get women out of the house and involved in the political and productive life of the country. This was a complex task. Women — and men — had to be freed from the age-old belief that women's place is in the home. And part of this involved assuring the women that *this* time they would not be exploited as part of the reserve labor force, but would be working for their own self-fulfillment as well as to develop the Revolution.

But attitudes don't change as rapidly as the economic reality, even if economics underlie the attitudes. In 1969 Cubans could laugh at the peasant farmer in the film *Lucía* who could barely tolerate allowing his wife to learn to read and write, and flew into a rage when she wanted to go out to work — not because his super-macho ideas were so outmoded, but because they all *remembered* themselves, their fathers, sons, brothers, husbands or neighbors reacting in the same way. It wasn't until 1971 that Cuban women really began talking seriously about the "double shift" they performed when expected to do housework and childcare after a full day's work in the factory, fields or office. 1973 saw the first real push to end this, with special compensatory rights for women workers and the promulgation of a Family Code that stated, for once and for all, that men and women who chose to marry or live together were equally responsible for all aspects of the household and family they created.

The situation of women changed noticeably from my first visit in early 1969 to my second in 1970-71. It had changed even more by 1973. And now, in the late seventies, it is undergoing even more changes — and much of what is written here will be outdated by the time it is read, if the revolutionary process continues at the same pace.

This book gives some glimpses into the life of Cuban women, and how it is changing for the women and especially for their daughters, but it is only a slice of life taken from two or three specific time periods. This little aside is to help put the comments and remarks in the rest of this book in some historical context, understanding that it was different the day before, and will certainly be very different tomorrow.

3

Spreading Consciousness

HAVANA

Like most foreigners, my first contact with Cuba — and therefore with Cuban children — was in Havana. Havana is the Big City, the seat of government, the center of cultural and intellectual activities. Developed as a port and commercial city by the Spaniards and converted into a vice den as well by the North Americans, Havana is like a huge, inflated head on a scrawny, scarecrow body. Prior to the Revolution, the most valued goods and services — from books and toilet paper to fine restaurants and luxury apartments, from schools and hospitals to diaper pins and carburetors — were to be found in Havana. In Havana the people ate well; in the provinces they starved. In Havana they went to the theatre, the ballet, concerts; in the provinces many people had never seen a motion picture. For Cubans, Havana was the hub of the universe.

Havana was also, unfortunately, the part of Cuba where you could find most heroin, prostitutes, gambling casinos, bars, foreign tourists, Batista's secret police, graft and corruption. In Old Havana you could see children begging the tourists for a few pennies, girls barely into their teens offering to sell their bodies, alcoholics lying in the gutters.

It was the Cuban countryside — the mountains, the provinces — which first rose up in arms as the guerrillas slowly drove the Batista forces out. Although there were always strikes, protests and clandestine activities in the cities, the liberation of Havana —

the flight of Batista — was the last step in the revolutionary war.

After the triumph of the rebellion, the new government instituted a policy whereby the poorest sectors of Cuba — the rural and mountainous areas — would be the first to receive the benefits of the Revolution. The new clinics, schools, houses would first be built in those areas where people had suffered the most and fought the hardest.

But that didn't mean that there were no changes to be made in Havana. Havana could not remain the top-heavy, super-rich and super-corrupt metropolis that it had been. Somehow Havana had to be brought into line with the rest of the country.

The first time I arrived in Cuba the port and the streets of Havana bore huge signs announcing the Tenth Anniversary of the triumph of the rebellion — January 1, 1969. The Revolution had had ten years to begin making changes. What were the children like, those who were under ten, those who had grown up in a revolutionary society?

The first Cuban child I met was six-year-old Carlita, the daughter of one of my co-workers at *Tricontental* magazine, where I was working as a translator and sometimes editing. Before coming to Cuba I had been working as a reporter covering political trials in California. Carlita came into the office one day as I was editing an interview with a black political prisoner (an imprisoned leader of the Black Panther Party) for publication in *Tricontinental.* Seeing a picture of the prisoner on my desk, she wanted to know who he was and whether he was here in Cuba, too. When I explained to Carlita that this man was considered by many a political prisoner, and had been in prison in the United States for a year and a half, she exclaimed: "In prison for a year and a half!?! Why haven't you freed him yet??!!"

Much later, after I had seen first-graders reading newspaper accounts of urban guerrillas in Brazil, had watched a children's adventure program about the Tupamaros on television, and had listened to primary school children tell me of the bold events of Cuba's own long independence struggle, I began to expect such questions from Cuban children. At the time, though, I was left staring at Carlita, my mouth wide open, and with no words of explanation coming to mind.

It wasn't long before I learned that Carlita was, rather than exceptional, a very typical Cuban child. For soon I met Elvira and Alina, seven-year-old friends who lived in the Miramar section of Havana. Miramar was formerly a rich suburb of The City, the home of North Americans, government officials, and the Cuban upper class. Now most of these palatial homes have been abandoned by their former owners — many of whom fled to Miami — and have been converted into schools and dormitories, childcare centers, and embassies.

Elvira is the *mulata* daughter of a black Cuban film-maker and a Bulgarian artist. Before the Revolution strict racial segregation in both jobs and housing would have prevented Elvira's family from living in a place like Miramar.

I first decided to interview Elvira in the fall of 1970. The decision was prompted during a visit with Elvira's parents, Nicolás and Dara, friends I had known since my first trip to Cuba in late 1968, when Elvira was a curly-headed five-year old with big eyes and a shy smile.

On this night we were sitting in Nicolás and Dara's living room, talking with several friends from the neighborhood. The discussion focused on the then-recent election of Salvador Allende, Chile's first socialist president, and the possible reaction by other Latin American oligarchies and military dictatorships. The conversation became almost a game, guessing which two Latin American dictatorships would get together to gang up on Chile. "It will be Uruguay and Brazil," suggested one. "No, it will be Bolivia and Argentina," guessed another.

Then Elvira, who had been sitting silently on the floor playing with her toys, looked up. "It really doesn't matter which it is," she said with her seven-year-old wisdom. " 'Cause in the end, it'll be the United States that comes out ahead."

A few weeks later, with her parents' permission, I went back to "interview" Elvira. Her friend Alina was visiting that day, so instead of going through a list of prepared questions, I decided just to turn my tape-recorder on and record their conversation. Our talk covered a wide range of topics, with the two girls sometimes agreeing, often interrupting, contradicting or arguing with one another. The scene of our "interview" moved from Elvira's parents' bedroom, to the living room, to a small balcony overlooking the street. It lasted for several hours, interrupted by periods in which we played with paper dolls or listened to music on Nicolás and Dara's record player.

I had told the girls I wanted them to teach me about Cuba. Elvira asked if anyone had told me about the life of Camilo. I told her no. "And of Che?" Again my answer was negative. "Not any of the martyrs?" she asked in surprise.

"No. Who are they?"

"Camilo, Che, Van Troi — no? — Martí, Almeida, Maceo . . . " she rattled off, throwing in one Vietnamese, two heroes of the nineteenth century War of Independence against Spain, and one member of the Cuban Central Committee who had fought in the Revolutionary war (and was still living) along with the martyred Camilo Cienfuegos and Che Guevara. I soon learned that Elvira had very little sense of time or space, but a very solid sense of Revolution. She knew her revolutionary history; it was just that she sometimes mixed up centuries and continents, or rather, mixed them all together to form one revolutionary whole. At one point she began: "I'll tell you something about Vietnam . . . " Without pausing or seeming to change the conversation she continued, "When Fidel was in Mexico, preparing to launch the *Granma*, and Che — who was not Cuban, who was Argentinian, but very revolutionary, and Camilo . . . " She went on, soon including Antonio Maceo, a general of the War of Independence, and eventually summed up: "The Vietnamese don't fight for pleasure. They fight so the people can be happy, so the people won't be poor, just like we fought in Cuba — and so the people can have houses, and schools, and all the things we have now."

She hadn't really forgotten that she was "telling me about Vietnam." It was just that her understanding of Vietnam was based on her understanding of the history of her own country. The most natural, logical progression then, in telling me about Vietnam, was to talk about Cuba's own wars of liberation.

They had started my lesson in Cuban history during the period when Fidel and other rebels were in Mexico, making preparations to re-initiate the revolutionary war after the initial failure of the Moncada attack. Now Alina informed me:

"When they were in Mexico, Fidel said, 'If we set out, we'll arrive, if we arrive, we'll enter, and if we enter, we'll win.' When Fidel left the country after he was freed from prison, he swore that he would be back by the end of 1956, and this time he'd win. And that's why if they weren't in Cuba before the end of the year they wouldn't be martyrs; but they got there before the year was over so that's why they were martyrs."

I understood at this point that to them the term "martyrs" was interchangeable with "heroes" or "revolutionaries". But Elvira couldn't let it go at that.

The two children told me about the landing of the *Granma*, and how so many of the rebels had died when they were met by waiting Batista troops and in the later battles in the Sierra Maestra.

"But, look, Che didn't die in the Sierra Maestra," Elvira informed me.

"He died in Bolivia," Alina added.

"Yes, because look, Che had a lot of courage — Camilo, too, who was one of those who survived the *Granma* landing, and Fidel too, and Almeida. Only twelve survived."

"Only twelve altogether," agreed Alina.

By this time we had moved into the living room, and I looked out at the street from the small balcony while the two girls played with paper dolls. When I first met Elvira's parents they were living in a *solar* — two small rooms off an open courtyard in an old, Spanish-style building. Now they were living in a spacious, modern apartment in a four-unit building in the formerly rich suburb of Miramar. I wondered if Elvira was conscious of her changed surroundings, and aware that there were others in Cuba still living in *solares* and *bohíos*.

At first I wasn't sure how to pose the question, so I began by asking Elvira to describe her house for me. "It has three bedrooms," she told me. "I have my own room. It has a little balcony, air-conditioning (but it's broken), a kitchen, a bathroom, it has furniture, paintings on the walls . . . " I asked if she lived in such a fine, big apartment because her family was rich. She assured me they weren't rich. This led us into a discussion of wealth, rich and poor.

I found the children more sophisticated than many adults I know when discussing the question of all people being equal. Alina explained that one person could have more things than another, more possessions, but as people they were and should be equal.

Getting back to the subject that started this conversation, I asked if there were people who lived in houses poorer than theirs. Although the housing shortage still existed, and the children clearly had friends who still lived in the old housing, they chose to stress the positive side, "They are building houses of concrete, just like this one, for all the people in our country who have houses made of sticks, because the hurricanes could come and endanger them and blow their houses away."

The problem of housing was being met by construction brigades. Groups of workers from offices, factories or farms formed volunteer brigades to construct houses, schools, clinics and childcare centers, while their fellow workers made up for the work of the absent volunteers. Although most of these workers had never done construction work before, they learned very quickly under the direction of regular construction workers. The entire city of Alamar — housing sixty thousand people, and including a number of schools, factories, childcare centers, food-markets, laundries, a water purification plant, etc. — was being built in this way.

From talking about housing we got into the subject of life in Cuba in general; then they began telling me about the subjects they studied in school. Once I started to laugh when Alina demanded of Elvira: "What are you eating, Elvira? Paper? Elvira, it's bad to eat paper. Paper is full of germs. . . "

Elvira retorted, "It is not."

"It is, too."

"No it's not — it's been boiled," declared Elvira, triumphantly.

"It has not; if you boil paper it would all come apart."

Alina's superior manipulation of facts won out.

I was amused by this dialogue, but even more so because I knew where it was coming from. Both Elvira and Alina had gone to childcare centers (known as *círculos infantiles*) until they were six years old. In the *círculos* a tremendous stress is placed on cleanliness. Children are bathed one or twice a day, and all items the children use are boiled to assure sterility. How many times had these children been told, "Don't put that in your mouth — it's dirty. It has germs on it"? How often had they heard *asistentes* or *círculo* workers discuss whether something was clean enough to give the children, whether it had been "boiled"?

One of the first things that interested me in Elvira was her awareness of what was happening around the world. This came up over and over again as we talked.

Alina told me she had some friends in Cuba who were Americans, from the United States. I asked if the United States was a socialist or capitalist country, and she replied: "Neither; it is imperialist." Then added, "Not the country, the government. The country is socialist, the people there are socialist, but the government is imperialist."

I asked if that meant there was a liberation struggle going on there. Alina didn't know if there was a struggle or a "movement" in the United States, but Elvira quickly chimed in: "It's my turn! There are movements there. There is a movement against the war [in Vietnam] and I don't know what else."

I asked what else they knew about the United States. They told me there was racism there. Alina tried to explain racism, but Elvira, who is very proud of her blackness, stated, "You don't know how to explain it." Alina, slightly flustered, said, "The, the whites, white people like us . . . "

"Are you white?" asked Elvira in surprise.

"I'm neither white nor black," replied Alina, "Now, racism means . . . I don't know how to explain it well, but . . . "

"Do you want me to explain it?" offered Elvira, and Alina acquiesced.

"Racism is when some white is protesting against some black, saying 'You blacks look like coal' and other nasty things . . . "

"Yeah, that's racism," agreed Alina.

Elvira elaborated further: "Racism also is when a person says 'I don't like blacks, I don't like anything about them, they don't have straight hair like we do . . . ' "

Elvira told me that "half the United States is imperialist." I wasn't quite sure what she meant. I asked her a lot of questions about how she imagined life in the United States, and she seemed to think life there was OK. "Then why did you tell me it was bad?" I asked.

"Because they exploit the good countries."

"But you think life in the United States is OK?"

"So-so. It's not so bad, because half the people are good and a few are bad. Did you come to Cuba to exploit Cuba?" she asked suddenly.

"No," I answered, taken by surprise by her question.

Elvira shows that individuality and spontaneity are not lost in Cuba.

"Then, half the people are bad, the other half good," she declared, certain that I had proven her point.

The girls were quite serious about their commitment to fight for their country. "If right now, at this moment, it was announced on the radio that we were being attacked," Alina told me, "it would be clear what I would have to do, because this is my country, and I have to defend it."

I asked what they would do if some *gusanos* from Miami wanted to invade Cuba. "We'd kick them out!" replied Elvira ferociously. "We'd grab a rifle and we'd kill them."

The two girls were as filled with love for "poor and exploited peoples of the world" as they were filled with anger and hatered for those they described as "racists" and "imperialists." Alina told me sorrowfully of the terrible conditions of the schools in Vietnam. "There are planes dropping bombs all the time, and the children have to go to school in caves."

"When they don't, their schools get blown to smithereens," added Elvira.

"They have to use leaves for writing pads," noted Alina, "because they don't have any paper."

"I'd like to go to Vietnam and bring them supplies," Elvira confided. "I'd bring them notebooks and pencils."

For Cuban children, the characteristics of internationalism and

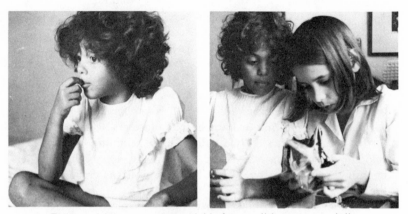

Elvira and Alina can move quickly from politics to paper dolls.

revolutionary heroism that they learn about in school, TV, movies and magazines are personified by real-life heroes. The ones they most commonly talk about are Argentinian-born Ernesto Che Guevara, and German-Argentinian "Tania" Bunke, both of whom fought and died in the guerrilla war in Bolivia.

"Tania *la Guerrillera* was a simple woman, a revolutionary, also very brave," Elvira told me. "She had a lot of courage. She fought together with Che, and she died fighting." It was clear Elvira admired this woman a lot. Both girls said if given the chance, they would do the same thing as Tania.

"Isn't it really hard to fight in a guerrilla war?" I asked.

"No," replied Elvira.

"Yes," answered Alina. "But I'd do it anyway."

I asked them why Cuban children think so much of Che. Elvira answered: "The good thing about Che is that he is a revolutionary who fought in many countries, like Argentina, Cuba, Bolivia and other countries I can't remember because there are too many."

It was time for Alina to go home for dinner. By now, we had talked about Cuban history, a little of Cuban life today, and about other countries and struggles in the world. I had developed a pretty strong image of these children of the Revolution. I wondered what image they had of themselves and of their future roles in the Revolution. After Alina left, I asked Elvira a final question: "What do you think is the role of women in the Revolution?"

"The duty of a woman in the revolution is to work, to study hard," Elvira told me. "Especially to study, when she is little, before she grows up, to study a lot of things."

I asked if there was any difference between the role of the woman and the man in the revolution; she told me no. She also said there was no difference at all between a man and a woman, except that one was male, masculine, and the other was female, feminine — which simply ment that one was a man and one a woman. Pressed for the characteristics of "masculine" and "feminine," she at first said she didn't know, they were the same. Asked by her mother how she knew if someone was a boy or a girl, she responded "By the 'peepee,' and by the hair."

"And in school, are boys smarter than girls, or girls smarter . . ."

"What the . . .!!" she replied indignantly. "The boys are less intelligent; the smarter ones are the girls. All the boys want to do is play during recess, that's all."

I asked about sports, and she said boys and girls were the same — neither one was better than the other. At first she said that girls were better than boys in productive work, because "the boys never like to carry anything." But she felt that boys were better in some types of work — like swimming, being a lifeguard. She agreed boys were probably better in baseball, " 'cause girls don't play it much." But they are both the same in shooting. "I love shooting," she exclaimed. "Bring me a pistol and I'd go 'pow, pow, pow,' and play *pistolero* [gunslinger]."

Elvira felt men could work in childcare centers, but wasn't sure at first if they could or should be nurses. But women could be fishermen, or even the captain of a ship. When I asked if a woman could be a pilot she replied: "Sure, a woman can be anything!"

Elvira and Alina weren't the only children I met in Havana. During the period from 1969 through 1973 I came to know hundreds of children whose home was the Big City. Some of them lived in comfortable, fairly modern apartments like Elvira's. Some lived in antiquated *solares* — their families crowded into one- or two-room spaces off a single, narrow alley. Many lived in the old Spanish-style stucco houses which alternate with Havana's skyscrapers and modern apartment buildings.

Elvira and Alina were firmly committed to the Revolution. Most children I encountered were — whether in schools, in the streets, in their homes or in the parks. It came as a shock to me, in fact, the first time I encountered a child who did *not* talk like a typical revolutionary child. But I found that these children, too, were part of the revolutionary process. And it was important to learn how they got that way, and how they changed, as it was to learn about the children who were more integrated into the Revolution.

I learned most about the children when I spent time at their schools, sitting in their classrooms, observing their daily activities, sharing meals and games with them, talking with them during recess. In this way I began to get a real sense of how children live, learn and develop in Cuba.

My first lesson was from the Bernardo Domínguez National School.

The Bernardo Domínguez School, which I visited in 1971, wasn't on my planned agenda of activities. It was simply on the route between my hotel and the nearest bus stop. Often as I went by the children would be playing out in the yard of the old stone house that served as their school. Spotting my foreign clothes, they would talk to me over the fence as I walked by. Finally one day I went in to talk to the principal, to ask if I could spend some time visiting the school.

In the next few weeks, I learned a great deal from the first through sixth graders of the school. The time I spent in their classes, their lunch and recess periods, their school trips, gave me a better idea of the day-to-day life of Cuban school-children. What struck me most was the new kind of consciousness I found among these children. It was a consciousness revealed in many little ways. The growing sense of friendship and confidence in me that they showed, and their ways of showing it: through gifts of books (poems about Che); of pins (earned by family members for being outstanding workers, or given to the children by other foreign visitors); inviting me to their homes; and, finally — the highest level of *compañerismo* shown to me — inviting me to go with them, their families and their neighbors to do voluntary agricultural work one Sunday. For one whole Sunday, on hands and knees, getting covered with Cuba's rich red earth, I picked potatoes with about a dozen of the ten- and eleven-year-olds from Bernardo Domínguez. I realized afterwards that I would never have the same, offhand attitude toward potatoes again, and that now I understood — as I hadn't before — how this activity made the world of work and production real for Cuban children.

The Bernardo Domínguez children, at my request, put down on paper many of the ideas we had talked about in the classroom, the schoolyard and the fields. They wrote compositions. The two fifth grades got together, and between us we came up with a list of topics which the students could write about. (They could add others if they wanted.) This was going to be an emulation.* I had about a dozen political buttons from the United States with various slogans: "Power to the People," "Free the Soledad Brothers," etc. They were in great demand, but I had too few to give to everyone. I had already decided against giving them arbitrarily to my "friends" and "favorites" among the children. The fifth graders decided they could "earn" them through an emulation. After they wrote the compositions at home, the two fifth grades met together again, and each read his or her composition aloud. The other students jotted down notes, and when all had read, a girl was asked to read off her list of those she thought best. After each selection the other students were asked whether they agreed or disagreed, and why. "I didn't like the focus of her composition." "I didn't like the content." "The point he made was correct, but I didn't like the way he expressed it." "I didn't like the examples she used." "There's nothing wrong with it, but there were others I thought were better." "I didn't like it because it jumps around a lot — it begins with one idea, then goes off into another. There's no order." These were some of the criticisms voiced. Those who liked a particular composition had a chance to defend it.

*An emulation is a socialist form of competition in which each tries to "win" not by beating the others but by meeting a standard which others can achieve as well.

After agreement was reached on five of the original list of suggestions, other students raised their hands to name the compositions they liked best. At the end, eleven were chosen, and each child came up to have a button pinned to his or her shirt collar.

Then some of the students suggested that their teachers should receive buttons too. When they were pinned on, the children burst into loud cheers and applause.

The Bernardo Domínguez school could have been any school on any street in any city in Cuba. Later, I made several trips to more "special" schools: the *internados*.

The *internados* are scholarship schools, where children selected on the basis of need live in the school all week, going home Saturday afternoon and returning to school Sunday night. They are not only provided with free room and board and school uniforms; they also have the additional influence of living in a collective environment all week long. Added to this, their surroundings are generally better than those of most Cuban families, since the scholarship schools are often located in the mansions of those who left Cuba, or are new, modern structures built in spacious areas provided by the Revolution.

Although these children could be considered in some ways "privileged," I didn't encounter noticeable differences between them and the children who went to the regular public schools or the *semi-internados*.

At a school in the suburb of Marianao the kindergarten children were listening to a story when I entered and sat down at the back of the room. Seated in a circle on the wooden floor, with light pouring in from windows that lined two sides of the room, the children seemed fascinated by the story. Soon I recognized the tale as one from my own childhood: "The Little Red Hen." The story told how the little red hen kept asking the other barnyard animals who was going to help her plant the corn, weed the fields, harvest the grain, cook the bread. Each time the other animals said, "Not I," and she was left to do it alone with her chicks. Finally, when she asked, "Who's going to help me eat the bread?" all the other barnyard animals were more than willing. But this time she said no — she and her chicks had done all the work, so they would eat the bread.

Following the story the children began to discuss it with the teacher. After several other questions she asked them: "What part of the story did you like best?" A number of hands shot up. She called on one boy who was waving his arm frantically. "What I liked best was the part where she says, 'Those who don't work don't eat!'" he pronounced gleefully. At first I thought that was a rather harsh comment, wondering what would happen to all the people in the United States who couldn't work or were out of jobs if this policy were in effect. Then I realized that he was of course referring to able-bodied people — like the characters in the story — who simply don't *want* to work. Since there is no unemployment in Cuba, it seemed perfectly reasonable to this child to expect those who eat the food to share the work.

After wandering through a number of classes and dormitories located in a series of suburban houses, I stopped to speak with a group of sixth graders. These older children, too, were sitting around in a circle. I asked them to tell me what the most important thing in Cuban life is. They named four things: to study, to help in the sugar harvest, to form the "New Man," and to develop the country. We began to discuss each of these.

The comments recorded here are a composite of those made by many different students.

Estudio.   Here we educate children so we can defend our country, to serve our country and other countries, too. Education is equal for everyone. Everyone studies. In other countries families have to pay so their children can study. We're making schools all over, not just for children but for the parents who didn't have a chance to study before. We learn all about the sugar harvest. Our people learn to help the other peoples of the world. Struggling people in other countries don't have this chance.

The *Zafra* (sugar harvest).   Every day we advance more than before. The entire population is working for a bigger harvest this year. It's not just the Cubans who cut the cane, but people from the United States, Vietnam, Korea, and others have participated. We thought it was really good that they wanted to help develop our country. In the United States since the people are subjugated by their government, they can't carry out these activities. They want to see Cuba, since Cuba before was subjugated by its government and now it's liberated. They want to struggle like others have — Che, Frank País, Camilo and other martyrs who died not just for their own peoples but others as well. One of the really important things about the harvest this year is how people from all over have come to help us, and how we all worked hard together so we could get out from underdevelopment.

Hombre Nuevo (The New Man). Before Che left Cuba to help the people of Bolivia gain their independence, he wanted to mold the children so they would be as José Martí had described — so they would be like the "New Man" — people who work and study and fight for their country, and sacrifice themselves for the good of all the people and the future generations. To do this we have to mold the children who are now studying into this image, little by little, and then they'll mold their children.

We're different from our parents and grandparents because they lived in a different epoch. To go to school, to have food or clothes, they had to have money.

I'm glad my parents were poor. Because things are very different now — things are changing now — and perhaps if they hadn't been poor, they wouldn't be able to understand what's going on.

Economic Development. An underdeveloped country has only one product, and doesn't have all the resources and equipment that other countries have. We're underdeveloped because we depend on only one product to exchange — sugar. Now we're trying to produce more products. But we don't have all the mechanization that a country like the USSR has. Since we were under the yoke of another country before the Revolution, we couldn't develop our own industry. Now that we're free we can develop ourselves.

Riding down the mountain for a medical checkup.

ORIENTE

As far from Havana as you can get, and still be on the island of Cuba, and as different as day and night, is Oriente Province. Havana is in the northwest; Oriente is the extreme southeast. Havana is the seat of government, the Big City, the center of urban culture; Oriente is rugged mountains, barren plains, people and places isolated and independent for centuries.

Oriente has a history of rebellion dating back to when the native population of Cuba fought against the Spanish *conquistadores*. Black slaves kidnaped from Africa followed this tradition, as did the *criollo* Spanish-Cubans who wanted independence from Spain in the nineteenth century.

Where the mountains slope down to the sea in Oriente there is a large natural bay, where the port city of Santiago was founded. It was there I met María de los Angeles — "Maruchy". Maruchy was one year old when Fidel and the 26th of July guerrillas declared their victory over the Batista regime in Santiago de Cuba, before marching triumphantly into Havana. Her parents worked with the July 26th Movement.

Maruchy lives and goes to school in this historic city, capital of the province of Oriente. Santiago, with its colonial-era fortresses and castles, its narrow cobbled streets and old Spanish buildings, was one of the urban centers of the resistance against the Spanish monarchy in the 1800s. Food, clothing and supplies for the *independentistas* of the Mambi Army were gathered in the city and smuggled to the rebels.

On July 26, 1953 Santiago was the site chosen by Fidel for the attack on the Moncada Garrison, the second largest military base of the Batista dictatorship. It was during his trial for that attack, in the Santiago Palace of Justice, that Fidel made his powerful plea before the court, which became known as "History Will Absolve Me." In his speech Fidel declared that the ruling Batista dictatorship, and not he and his fellow rebels, was guilty of violating the Cuban Constitution and the basic rights of humanity.

Fidel and other imprisoned survivors of the Moncada attack were released from prison after much public pressure. They went to Mexico, to prepare to launch the struggle anew. Meanwhile, the 26th of July Movement grew and spread in Santiago and throughout the island. Three years after the historic attack, the rebels were ready to launch the armed struggle once again. The landing was to take place in a remote part of Oriente; the rebels in the city were prepared to "welcome" their invading comrades with a massive uprising in the city of Santiago, led by schoolteacher Frank País. (The uprising didn't occur because of the belated, abortive landing of the *Granma*, which left only a handful of rebels to begin the fighting in the mountains in December 1956.)

After two more years of fighting, on January 1, 1959, Fidel Castro proclaimed the creation of the revolutionary government in the city hall of Santiago.

If Cuban children are being molded and formed by the revolutionary ideals of their new government, they are also affected by the history, traditions and conditions of the place in which they live. Maruchy, heir to a long tradition of hardship and rebellion, was brought up in Holguín and Santiago, in Oriente Province. She knew from her parents, aunts and uncles, and grandparents of the poverty and fear in which the tenant farmers and urban poor lived before the revolution. From them, and from her schoolbooks, she knew that at every stage, brave men and women had fought against the oppressive conditions of their lives.

Because that fight had succeeded, she learned, there was a

chance for the Cuban people now to put an end to poverty, discrimination and exploitation, and in the process to create new men and women, human beings developed to their full potential. The New Socialist Man the Cubans were striving for had been described by Che Guevara, and his selfless example in Cuba and around the world serves as an inspiration for Cuban children.

Maruchy, child of Santiago, incorporates the characteristics of the New Man and Woman to a degree I found as impressive as it was startling. She was unlike any children I had known in the United States: more aware of the world around her, genuinely concerned about the needs and desires of other peoples, yet, still a child. It was through conversations with Maruchy, and her cousin Kiko (who was a military cadet), that I finally decided that the best way to write something meaningful about the Cuban Revolution was through the thoughts and the actions of the children.

I met Maruchy in a motel overlooking the city of Santiago when she was eleven years old. She was with her cousin Kiko from Camagüey, who was vacationing there with his aunt. Maruchy's parents work for ICAP, the Cuban Institute of Friendship among Peoples, whose job is to make all arrangements for foreign visitors. I was with several other North Americans who came to see the 26th of July Carnival in Santiago.

Maruchy stirred the interest of one of the other women in our group when she told us she was going to be a doctor when she grew up. "I always wanted to be a doctor," recalled the woman, a little sadly. "But everyone always told me I'd have to be a nurse."

We invited Kiko and Maruchy to come talk to us in our rooms after dinner. When they came, we talked for hours; mostly about themes *they* brought up: the war in Vietnam, racism in the United States, political trials, repression, Cuba before the Revolution, etc. Their comments presented a fascinating view of how Cubans saw the world — and especially the United States — in relation to Cuba and to the values they'd been taught at home and in school. At one point Maruchy observed: "If you changed presidents, and the new president ended racism, and pulled out of Vietnam, and ended all the little wars the United States has going on all over the place — they would kill him."

After a pause she added, "And everyone saw what happened to those two boys and two girls [referring to the Kent State students killed by the National Guard during an antiwar protest]. If you're against the war in your country, they'll kill you."

Later, she queried: "What did your government think of the Venceremos Brigade [North Americans who went to Cuba to help with the sugar harvest] coming here? They didn't like having you break the blockade, did they?"

Although her opinion of the U.S. government was pretty low, she showed no hostility towards us. "The children in my class at school thought all Americans were bad," she told us. "I explained to them that it wasn't the American *people* who were bad, but the government. But they didn't understand. Then the teacher came in, and told them how people can be our friends even though their government is bad. She gave the example of black people in the United States struggling against the government. Then they understood."

I was only in Cuba for a few weeks, for the 26th of July celebration, when I met Maruchy and Kiko. But spurred on by that conversation, I arranged to go back and spend more time with children from all over the island. One of my first stops was Santiago.

On this visit I learned a lot more about the young girl who had taught me so much about the Revolution. Sitting on the back patio of her pastel-colored ranch-style stucco house, we talked about a lot of things. María de los Angeles was twelve then, and had finished primary school. She told me that she liked school a lot, especially mathematics and physics. "Because physics is the study of the phenomena that occur in nature, and I like math because it's very complicated, and I like difficult things — there is a lot to learn and each day you learn more." There were some things she didn't like about school, though — the students who don't behave themselves, "because they interrupt classes, they don't let us study and then we suffer on the exams." I asked why she thought some students behaved badly. "Because they don't like school, classes or the teacher. There are only a few students like this — none in my class. They are the ones who are older — seventeen or eighteen years old, and are still in the seventh grade. They're losing their love for school; they're not children any more; they've been in this same grade for many years, and they don't like school or studying. But in my class everyone is pretty good."

Maruchy

On our first meeting Maruchy said she wanted to be a doctor when she grew up; this time she told me she wanted to study foreign languages and become an interpreter, to work for ICAP like her parents. She said she would like to work with foreigners, getting to know their customs, how they live and what their countries are like. Like most children her age, she will probably change her mind many times before she is grown up.

Maruchy is very much like twelve-year-old girls anywhere. Her favorite games are "playing school" and "playing house." When she plays house, "We play with dolls, dress them, bathe them, and make food, just like in a real house, but just for fun." When playing school, "I'm the teacher and the other younger kids are the students." Maruchy's favorite toys are her dolls, kitchen sets, hair dresser set — and chess.

She likes to watch TV; her favorite programs are "The Mambises" — "because it relates to the history of Cuba during the war of independence against Spain, and I want to know about it." — and "The Count of Monte Cristo." (Most kids in Santiago named these two programs as their favorites.) What she likes best on the radio are musical programs — all kinds of music, but especially "modern."

All Cuban children are encouraged to participate in sports. Maruchy's favorites are volleyball, gymnastics and basketball. Baseball, although it is Cuba's national sport, doesn't interest her. She's aware that Cuba has won the world championship in baseball; she says that's because "the players are very good and Cuba always has to set an example."

Like many children, Maruchy often goes to the store to buy food for the family, and so has experienced waiting in lines. She didn't seem to object to this, though, and explained that the reason there are lines is because "the stores are small, there are few clerks, and lots of people." When asked why there was rationing, she replied, "so that everything there will be shared by everyone."

We began to talk of other subjects. At one point I asked her whether she felt children should always obey their parents. Like most Cuban children, her first response was "yes", but when pressed: "Any child, but not any parent. All children should obey their parents, but there are parents who don't pay much attention to their children, so these children see that their parents aren't taking good care of them, and they don't obey." Her answer reminded me of a similar conversation, in a school in Havana, where the children told me that if adults treat children badly, and don't respect them, then the children are entitled to stand up for themselves, to speak back — that they are only required to show respect to people who show respect for them.

Maruchy has been the "detachment leader" in her class, which means "to help the teacher, to review the notebooks, maintain discipline, and clean the classroom, direct political acts." The best student is chosen for this responsibility by the other students.

To Maruchy, "a leader should be first in everything, to always be an example in all aspects, especially be a good revolutionary and participate in all the tasks of the Revolution." On a local town level, leaders are "to help the people and take care of things." The most important functions of the CDRs* are "to keep watch on the block so that no counter-revolutionary acts are committed"; also "to give vaccinations to the people who live on their blocks, to prevent sickness."

---

*Neighborhood "Committees for the Defense of the Revolution."

Of Fidel as a leader; Maruchy commented, "He is a magnificent leader . . . .He thinks that we all should be equal and that we should all have the same things, and that no one is better than others." Other leaders she looks up to: "Celia Sánchez, Haydee Santamaría and Vilma Espín. Celia Sánchez is a *compañera* who praticipated in the revolutionary movement. Haydee took part in the attack on the Moncada Fortress and they killed her brother. Vilma Espín is the president of the Cuban Women's Federation."

Maruchy admired the internationalism of Che Guevara and Tania Bunke. She read both Che's diary and a book about Tania. What she liked about these books "is that they are people who fight for the freedom of their people and other countries." The only United States radical whose name was familiar was Angela Davis.

I asked: "What has impressed you most in your life?"

"The triumph of the Revolution."

I asked Maruchy her view of the role of a woman in the Revolution. She responded, "The role of the woman in the Revolution is that she should carry out all the tasks that the Revolution gives her, to be revolutionary before everything else, to work the same as the man, — clearly, some jobs women can't do, but the majority she can."

"Do you think there are differences between men and women, in study, productive work, sports?" I continued.

"No. But maybe in sports — like weight-lifting. But in the majority there is no difference."

"Do you think men could and should work in childcare centers?"

"No, because men can't behave like women, since men can't be mothers like women can with the children."

"Do you think that in the future, when the socialist man exists, the New Man, that they ought to know how to take care of children, too?"

"Yes."

"Do you think a woman can be a fisherman?"

"Sure, why not?"

"Captain of a ship?"

"That too."

"Airplane pilot?"

"That too."

Maruchy has an air of confidence about her unusual in a twelve-year-old. There were very few questions I could put to her which she had difficulty answering. She seems always ready to deal with the unusual. One question I had on my list was made up by a ten-year-old boy in Havana. It asked: "How would you feel if you were asked to become the director of a poultry farm?" Maruchy, without hesitation replied: "Very happy."

Her answer caught me by surprise. "What would you do?" I asked.

"Direct it. You get some kids, and you give them boxes to collect the eggs that the hens lay, then every morning they sign a book and then you give each one a few boxes and then the hens have little pipes where they let their eggs fall and then the kids go collecting from each little tank, carrying the little boxes — you can only carry two in your arms — and then they bring them to the storeroom and look for empty ones."

The Moncada: The Revolution kept its promise to turn fortresses into schools.

TURNING FORTRESSES INTO SCHOOLS

In the nineteenth century Cuba's apostle of Independence, José Martí, wrote of a future when Cubans would run their own country, free from outside interference. Then Cuba could focus all its energies on developing its resources for its own people, who would live in peace and harmony. It was Martí — a teacher as well as a poet, writer and leader of the struggle for independence — who called for a new society in which the people would "turn fortresses into schools."

Throughout the years of Spanish colonial rule, and the pseudo-republic which followed in its wake, fortresses proliferated in Cuba. With the triumph of the Revolution, this trend was reversed. All over the island, the military garrisons of the Batista regime were converted into schools and hospitals. Perhaps the most symbolic change of all took place in Santiago, where the Moncada Fortress was turned into the 26th of July School City.

The first time I visited the Moncada it was to see the section which had been made into a museum. Room after room of larger-than-life photos depicted the fighting, the bloodshed, the sacrifice that took place there. I looked with amazement at the collection of .22 calibre rifles — appearing more like toys than weapons of war — which the rebels had used to launch their attack.

As I was leaving the museum, feeling the heaviness of history all around me, I suddenly smiled as I heard the light voices of children laughing and playing. "It must be a school trip to the museum," I thought. But I soon learned that this wasn't a class trip to the Moncada — the Moncada *is* their school.

I wondered what it must feel like to go to school every day in a place so steeped in history. Is it overwhelming? Awesome? Or do the children just take it for granted, forget the past that happened here? Each morning, as the children listen to the national anthem, paying momentary tribute with their silence to the soldiers who fell here, passersby and nearby housewives stop and watch. For the people of Santiago, the gunshots and spilled blood are still vivid.

But the children can't remember — they were born long after the revolution, and it could be supposed that the memories are left to the adults and the stones of Santiago.

The following material answers that supposition. Here are answers of the students of the July 26th School City (as the Moncada Fortress is now called) to questions posed by Martha Parada and Sonnio Moro*, professors of History and Letters at the University of Santiago. The first and second graders responded orally, the older ones in writing.

FIRST AND SECOND GRADE CHILDREN

What happened here on the 26th of July?
What happened here is that they caught the people who were running with Fidel, because they were with Fidel attacking the Moncada from different places, from other places, a lot of places.
And what else?
They made them prisoners and put them in tiny rooms like this and they didn't give them water or food and they beat them, and whipped them and tore their shirts. . .
Did this happen a long time ago?
Uff! A long time. Maybe three months.
Who took part in the attack?
Fidel.
Why did Fidel attack?
Fidel attacks the Yankees. He doesn't attack children.
Why does Fidel attack?
Fidel attacked so that the Cuban children could be happy.
Is Fidel a friend of yours?
Yes.
Who is Fidel? If he came here, how would you know him?
Fidel is a strong, fat man.
And a brave revolutionary.
He's got a beard.
How come this school didn't keep on being a fort?

---

*Published in *Santiago*, the magazine of the University of Santiago, No. 11, June 1973. In June of 1973 I spent several afternoons interviewing the children there. Although my questions were slightly different, the overall content of the replies was basically the same.

Because Fidel attacked the Moncada and then they captured Fidel and made him a prisoner; then Fidel left when they let him go and he wrote a book and went to Mexico. And Fidel came with a group of men, with Camilo and Che, then they got together and landed in the yacht *Granma* and Batista saw the *Granma*. Then they began to climb the hills — Fidel and the group of men — and then they fought in the Sierra, and when they won, then the Revolution won, and then Fidel came here and turned this into a school.

Do you know why there are going to be celebrations here the 26th of July?

Yes. Because on the 26th of July we're going to attack the Moncada.

Do the children attack it with guns?

No, not with guns, because then you could be in the middle and then they shoot and you could get killed. We attack with pencils and notebooks.

You told me the children here are revolutionary. What do you do?

I study.

Read and write.

Study. Study a lot. Not miss school.

When you are bigger, what will you do to keep being revolutionary?

Me. . . to keep being revolutionary we have to be. . . doctors, to work in hospitals, in nurseries, planting foods, sugar cane . . . and . . . go cut cane every Sunday. This is what helps us become men.

If Fidel came here and asked what you were doing, what would you say?

Studying.

The children talked more about the various martyrs of the attack on the Moncada, whom they knew by name, sometimes because they had seen pictures of them and heard stories about them, sometimes because their group or section was named after a particular hero. They also knew about Batista:

He was a bad man.

Batista was bad and he exploited the Cuban people.

He was a tyrant.

CHILDREN FROM THE THIRD TO SIXTH GRADE

Can you tell us what is the Revolution?
Revolution is your life and death.
For us Revolution is to study.
The Revolution is to learn.
The Revolution is a creative people.
It's the happiness of children, men and women.
The Revolution is to have absolute independence, to do everything communally, to produce for all.
The Revolution is the liberation of all people. Cuba already has a real Revolution, that's why other people follow Cuba's example.
The Revolution is work, anti-racism, anti-imperialism, solidarity, jobs, study, socialism, communism.
The Revolution is the rebellion of a people against imperialism, the struggle, the sacrifice to get a country out from exploitation.
What was there in this place before the triumph of the Revolution?
Before the Revolution what there was in this place was one of the most powerful fortresses the tyranny had.
Here before the triumph of the Revolution there was a horrible fortress of the tyranny which only knew to torture and kill those who desired freedom.
There were some very cruel men who didn't like the Revolution and their chief was Fulgencio Batista.
What happened here before 1959?
There was misery and hunger and exploitation of man by man.
Before '59 Cuba was governed by Batista, who was only interested in enriching himself.
There were bad men and then Fidel and a group of men organized to get them out of here.
Many Cubans shed their blood to see Cuba free and independent.
Why did Fidel attack a fortress twenty years ago?
Fidel attacked the fort twenty years ago to put into practice the ideals of José Martí and to wipe out exploitation.

This was the second biggest fortress of the Batista tyranny, that's why Fidel attacked it.

What do you do to be a revolutionary child?

To be a revolutionary child you have to go to school every day, to learn a lot of things, like Martí.

What I do to be a revolutionary child is to be studious, good and a Pioneer.

You have to get good grades and be a Pioneer so Fidel can trust in the new generation.

To be a revolutionary child you have to study in school, participate in the activities of the CDR, and defend Cuba from whatever possible aggression.

What do you like best about the History of the Moncada Museum at the front of the school?

What I like best is where there are children in a circle singing happily because the Revolution has triumphed.

The most emotional part is when Fidel, Camilo, and Che are seen all together reunited when the Revolution triumphed.

What I like best is the last part, where you see the Revolution already won, where they are building houses for the *campesinos.*

What would you like for your school to do or be?

What I want for my school is to keep moving forward in the educational part until we reach socialism in education of all Cuban children.

GETTING OUT OF THE CITIES:
THE CHILDREN OF THE MOUNTAINS

Until now all my encounters with children had been with those living or going to school in the cities. Even the children of Santiago, I supposed, who were less "cosmopolitan," and had less contact with foreigners and modern urban culture, must still know more about the Revolution, the changes in Cuba, and the outside world than children who lived in remote mountain areas.

The Revolution talks of bringing all the benefits of the Revolution to the people of the mountains, to the *guajiros* and *campesinos* who suffered the most under all previous regimes. How had this been put into practice? And how had it affected the children? The only way to find out was to go to the Sierra Maestra, and talk to the children there.

The Sierra Maestra, Cuba's largest mountain range, in the heart of Oriente province, is known as "the cradle of the Revolution." It was here that twelve men from the boat named *Granma*, led by Fidel Castro, landed in 1956. They came to launch a revolutionary war against the Batista dictatorship and the U.S. corporations and crime syndicate which owned and controlled Cuba. They came to the Sierra Maestra because they knew they would find allies among the people who lived here.

The Sierra Maestra has a long history of rebelliousness — a rebelliousness common to the entire province of Oriente. It was in Oriente that the Spanish conquerors first met the resistance of the Indians, the original inhabitants of the island. Here the Indian Chief Hatuey was burned at the stake, and his people annihilated by the Spaniards, because of their resistance to this foreign occupation.

When the Spaniards had killed all the Indians, and needed someone to do the work in the plantations and mines, they brought black slaves from Africa in through the ports of Oriente. It was to the refuge of the Sierra Maestra mountains that rebellious escaped slaves fled. There they set up their own independent colonies where no Spaniard dared set foot.

In 1868, it was in Oriente that rebelliousness against Spanish rule of Cuba reached its peak, and was expressed in the War of

Independence. People of Oriente, mountain people, made up a large part of the Mambí Army which, armed only with sticks and machetes, defeated the Spanish troops.

There was another reason, besides its history, why Oriente, and especially the Sierra Maestra, was considered fertile ground for the 26th of July guerrillas. As Spaniards, then North Americans, took over the island of Cuba, they built it up for their own benefit. They constructed a few large cities and towns in various parts of the country, cleared land for huge plantations called *latifundias*, and dug mines. The riches from the work done by the black, brown and creole Cubans on these plantations and in these mines went to the people who lived in the cities, or went back to Spain or the United States. The people who did the work, who lived in the countryside or the mountains, never saw the benefit of their labor or the rich resources of the island.

In the mountains, there was no electricity, no running water, no stores, no schools or hospitals. There were no roads to bring supplies in or to provide a means of communication to the "outside world" for these people who had no telephones, radios or newspapers.

The mountain people were cut off from the rest of the world. Even if they had had schools and books, hospitals, clinics and medical supplies — which they didn't — no doctors, nurses or teachers wanted to travel to, let alone live in, these remote areas. It was a privilege of the wealthy in Cuba to go to school and become doctors or teachers. The people who received a professional education reserved their abilities for members of their own class, for the wealthy people who lived in the cities and towns. They did not want to give up their comfortable life in the cities to go live and work in the mountains.

So the people of the Sierra Maestra grew up without learning to read and write. Their culture was passed down in songs and stories, from parents to children. They grew whatever food they needed, raised chickens and hogs when they could, and learned to survive from what the jungles and forests of the mountains had to offer.

When they got sick, the mountain people treated each other with herbs and folk medicines. Sometimes, when someone was very ill — a sick child, a badly injured man, a mother having difficulty giving birth — the mountain people would try to get the sick person some medical help. They would carry the sick one down the rugged mountain paths on their backs or shoulders, to a point at the foot of the mountains overlooking the sea. There they would wait, hoping to flag down a passing ship which could take them to a city with a hospital or at least a doctor. If a ship didn't come in time, or if the captain didn't feel like stopping, the sick man, woman or child died there on the shore, waiting for help.

Today, when you drive along the rough mountain road built by the Revolution, you can look down at various points along the coast and if you look very closely, you can see the scores of tiny graves in each makeshift cemetery.

If you drive a little farther, to where the road dips down to the coast, you'll arrive at the village of Ocujal, where the Revolution has built a new hospital.

When you set out to climb the Sierra Maestra mountains, the last village with electricity and direct communication to the outside world on the southeast side is Ocujal. The town is spread out on a little pocket of land with the blue-green waves of the Caribbean on one side and the mountains of the Sierra Maestra on the other. Ocujal has a store, a restaurant, a hospital and a school, where students from the surrounding mountains as well as from the village study.

Marlene is a student in the school in Ocujal. The school has two classrooms and two teachers for first through sixth grade. There are ten students in Marlene's classroom, studying in grades one through three.

The subjects taught in Marlene's school are the same as those taught in schools throughout the island: math, science, Spanish, penmanship, ...

Marlene says her favorite is mathematics, "because you learn more." The subject she likes least is penmanship, "'cause it's real hard to do."

Her favorite games are dolls and baseball.

I asked Marlene what she wanted to be when she grew up.

"A medical doctor," she answered.

"A general practitioner or a specialist?"

"General practitioner."

"Why do you want to be a doctor?"

"To care for all the sick people in Cuba."

The mountain school that Marlene attends has a different schedule from the city schools. The year begins in January and ends in September — harvest time. The children go out to the fields during the autumn months and help their parents harvest the crops.

Before the Revolution, when the mountain people were scattered throughout the Sierra Maestra, there were no schools. Now, the Revolutionary Government encourages families to move together into small towns or settlements, so that sturdy houses, with electricity and plumbing and floors can be built, along with schools, clinics and stores.

I visited Marlene in a sunny blue concrete house where she lived with her parents and four brothers. There was a small generator behind their house. At night her father went out and turned it on, and the house lit up like a firefly. Soon you could see about a dozen bright lights between the sea and the hills.

Inside the house, we ate a dinner of pork, rice, beans and *plátano.* Marlene told me that she and her brothers wash, cook, clean house and help take care of the pigs and chickens.

Once a month the ICAIC traveling crew brings films to Ocujal. Marlene's favorite movies are the cartoons. She doesn't like war movies. But she does like to watch boxing ("men punching each other"), wrestling and shooting. She likes Che "because he fights a lot; he freed Cuba, and he fought in Bolivia, where they killed him."

On some aspects of the struggle, however, Marlene is not quite so clear. She couldn't tell me the difference between a capitalist and a socialist country, between a revolutionary and a counterrevolutionary (except that one is "good" and the other "bad"). She thinks Che is Bolivian, and she identifies Tania, who fought and died with Che in Bolivia, as "Nguyen Van Troi's wife." (Van Troi was a Vietnamese hero, executed for attempting to assassinate Robert McNamara). But she knew who Van Troi was, that Vietnam was fighting the United States (although she didn't know why) and that "Vietnam will win."

Marlene is interested in the United States and would like to see it, although she acknowledges that the kind of people who go there are "older people who aren't revolutionaries," and thought that it "might be dangerous for her to go to a capitalist country."

Although she is only nine years old, Marlene — perhaps because she comes from a family with four boys — has very decided views about the role of women. Girls are smarter than boys in school, she told me, better in sports, productive work, "and everything." A revolutionary woman should work — doing "anything, everywhere." Marlene does voluntary work with her school, planting onions and working in the tree nursery along the slopes of the mountain behind the town.

The highest mountain of the Sierra Maestra is Pico Turquino. It was at the top of Turquino that Fidel's rebel band regrouped after the landing of the *Granma*. More than sixty-four hundred feet high, it looks down through the clouds at ruggedly beautiful forested slopes reaching down to the sea. From the top of the mountain it seems as though you can look out over all of Cuba. Certainly you can easily spot anyone approaching from any direction. It was for this reason that it was a perfect spot for the guerrillas to regroup and to launch their operations.

Today Pico Turquino has become a symbol. What it takes to

Although hospitable, the mountain children were reserved with strangers.

make the arduous climb is *esfuerzo voluntad* — will power — the same thing it takes for people to rebel successfully against a brutal dictatorship and take power into their own hands. Soldiers, students, new doctors, teachers all make the rugged climb anywhere from one to five times, symbolically demonstrating their willingness to go anywhere and suffer any hardship for the Revolution.*

To get to know the children of the mountains, I knew I had to climb Turquino, too.

When I set out to climb Pico Turquino, the children I met were very shy and wary of this stranger from the North who said she was going to climb their mountain. The impression I had from Marlene, and from the young girls in Las Cuevas who served us coffee the morning we set out, was that life in the mountains, although it had clearly improved a great deal since Batista days, was still quite different from life in the cities. The children seemed less talkative, and less aware of events going on outside their community and outside their country than the city children.

But when I descended the mountain, the situation had changed. Without my having realized it, I was now a new person. The children who had watched me with some doubt when I set out, now looked with different eyes at the *gringa* who had climbed Pico Turquino. They gathered around me on the steps of their schoolhouse at dusk, gazed at me curiously and began to talk. As we talked, I turned on my tape-recorder. It recorded the voices of Tonito, age eleven; Eva, age seven; Asela, eleven; Juan, thirteen, and Luís, nine. Two others listened but didn't speak except when the children answered all together. Most of them said they were Pioneers, most had climbed Turquino — or claimed to — at least once.

For the first time, I didn't use my prepared notes and questions; we just talked.

Karen: Where do you live?

Tonito: In the Caves of Turquino [a tiny "village" of about six
    houses and a school at the foot of the path that goes up the
    mountains].

---

*For many years the teacher training institute was located up in these mountains. Only recently, in the interest of training greater numbers of teachers, was it moved to a more accessible location.

K: Have you ever been to Santiago? What's it like there?

T: Yes. It's a very pretty city.

K: Would you rather live here in the mountains, or in Santiago?

T: I'd rather live here, but Santiago is nice to visit.

K: Why do you like it better here.

T: Because there's a lot of food. [Scarce food supplies are rationed to make sure everyone gets enough. In the cities, people are limited by their ration cards to what is available in the stores. In the mountain and countryside, people can grow their own in addition to the ration].

The children were intrigued by my tape recorder. They told me they had never seen one before. Tonito told me he had been given a scholarship to study to be a forestry specialist. I asked if that meant he was going to live in the mountains when he grew up. He said no, it meant that he would give classes in another school, to teach other people about forestry.

We began to talk about the Pioneers.

K: What is a Pioneer?

Alesa: It means to be a well-educated child, to study a lot, and to pay attention to the teacher.

K: Are most of the children in your school Pioneers?

Chorus: Yes.

A: Almost all.

K: What's the difference between a revolutionary and a counter-revolutionary?

T: It's a very big difference.

A: Revolutionaries love their country and if on some occasion they have to fight, they fight. And the *gusanos*, what they do is betray their country.

K: Who are the *gusanos*?

Eva: The counter-revolutionaries.

K: And where are they?

Luís: In the United States?

K: And why are they there?

L: Because they can't come to Cuba; we don't let them.

I began to realize that these children had just as deep a sense of patriotism as the children of the cities. I wondered if they also had a strong sense of history and regional pride.

K: Did the Cuban Revolution begin in the mountains?

Chorus: Yes!

K: Where?

Chorus: Right here in the Sierra Maestra.

K: Is this the most revolutionary part of Cuba?

A: Yes.

K: What is Havana?

A: A province of Cuba.

K: What else?

A: The capital of Cuba.

K: Is the government in Havana?

T: (emphatically) No, it's all over Cuba.

K: I'm going to Ocujal. Is that very far?

R: Yes, it's far.

K: Do you go to Ocujal a lot?

T: No, just when someone's sick. There's a hospital there.

K: Does ICAIC show movies here?

T: Yes, a truck comes twice a month.

K: What movies have you seen?

T: So many I can't remember.

K: Do you remember what picture you liked best?

T: Yes, the one about the war.

K: And you?

A: The cartoons.

K: Is there TV or radio?

A: There's radio.

K: What programs do you get?

T: Radio Havana, Radio Revolution. I like the music programs the best.

Later, we began to talk about a favorite theme of Cuban children: Che.

K: What did Che do?

A: He fought for freedom.

K: Just for the freedom of Cuba?

A: No, for other countries too.

K: What other countries?

A: I don't remember.

K: Where did Che fight?

Juan: In Bolivia.

K: And what happened?

T: They killed him there.

K: Would you also go to Bolivia?

J: Yes.

K: Who else fought in Bolivia, besides Che?

J: Inti, Coco, Joaquín and Tania.

K: Who was Tania?

A: A very outstanding guerrilla fighter.

K: Is Cuba a socialist country?

E: Yes.

K: Does anyone know anything about the United States?

E: No.

K: Would you like to visit my country?

L: No.

K: Why not?

L: Because I can't.

K: (To other children) Would you like to visit it?

J: Me, yeah.

K: Could you visit the United States now?

J: No.

K: Are there some differences between Cuba and the United States?

E: Yes.

J: Racism. For example, now in the United States there is a mass of black people who the whites think are worthless, they don't have anything to do with them.

K: Is there racism in Cuba?

J: No. There was, before the Revolution.

T: Now we don't see things the way we did before the Revolution.

J: Racism is bad. Because you can't have some people valued more than others. Everyone has to be the same.

K: How do you imagine the life of children in the United States?

J: That for a while they go to classes and for a while hang around, and then, when they're bigger, they get sent to fight in Vietnam, Cuba and other countries, so that they can't be happy. And the Cuban children are different, wherever they are they are free and educated until they are grown.

K: Did you tell me that children of the United States study, or not?

J: Yes, they study, when they're little and all that.

K: Then what is the difference between you and them?

J: It's not the same as here, because wherever the United States

The children became more open and friendly after we descended the mountain.

children go they don't find freedom, and we go anyplace and are free.

K: Are there any of those children who don't want to fight against Cuba?

J: Yes, there are some who feel they are revolutionaries and they come to Cuba, but not to fight.

This was 1971, when the war in Vietnam was still very much on people's minds. But here in this remote mountainous region, only recently made aware of the rest of Cuba, I wondered how much children could have heard and thought about Vietnam, a country thousands of miles away.

K: How do you picture the children of Vietnam?

J: The children of Vietnam study in caves because of the bombers.

K: And why are those planes over there?

J: To take away the Vietnamese people's land.

K: But why do you think the Yankees want to fight against a country like Vietnam?

J: They have a little piece that they took from Vietnam, and the other part belongs to the Vietnamese, but they are fighting with this little piece to see if they can grab the rest of the land so that all of Vietnam will belong to them.

K: Do you have any idea who will win in Vietnam?

J: The Vietnamese.

K: Why will the Vietnamese win?

J: Because as long as they have been fighting the Vietnamese have won one battle after another, many battles, and they shoot down a lot of planes.

K: Is Vietnam a small country?

J: No, it's big, but it's littler than the United States.

K: And is Cuba big or small?

J: Small.

K: Did Cuba fight against the Yankees?

J: No, Cuba fought against Batista, and before that the Spanish.

K: What was Batista like?

J: He was bad. He didn't have ideas like Fidel; all he wanted was to exploit the people.

K: What does "exploit" mean?

J: To exploit is to take the people and leave them without work and the people can hardly eat and when the workers work he gives them a penny if he wants, if not he doesn't give them anything and they work without being paid anything, they work for nothing.

K: Did the struggle [against Batista] take place here in the mountains?

J: Yes.

K: What happened here in the mountains?

J: What happened is that Fidel got together with a group in Mexico (Raúl, Almeida, Che and others) and they came here to the mountains to fight against Batista. They came in a boat.

K: What was the name of the boat?

J: I don't remember. What I do know is they landed at Las Coloradas, and a guide brought them here to the mountains and they began to fight. Then after some months thousands of men began to climb up here to fight against Batista and that's why they won and Batista had to leave.

K: Were Batista's troops here?

J: Yes.

K: What did they do here?

J: They got scared and went running out.

K: Were the people of the mountains on the side of Batista or Fidel?

J: They were on Fidel's side.

K: Why?

J: Because Fidel came to find freedom for Cuba, to make our country free, and Batista, no. Batista had the country enslaved.

K: And do they still support Fidel?

J: Yes.

K: Have things changed a lot here?

J: Yes, it's changed in a million ways.

K: What things have changed?

J: Before they didn't bring us shoes nor clothes, and now they bring us shoes, good pants, and lots of things. Before they didn't bring us anything.

K: Was the hospital in Ocujal there before the Revolution?

J: No. The Revolutionary Government built it when they won.

K: And the school?

J: The Government built that, too.

K: Did your mama go to school when she was a little girl?

J: No because there weren't any schools; there wasn't any way to get to them.

K: Did she say anything to you when they built the school here?

J: Yes, she said she was really glad because now I'd have a chance to learn to read and write and become educated. She said I should study real hard, because an educated people can't be fooled and taken advantage of the way people are when they don't have any education.

K: Did she say anything about the hospital?

J: At first she cried. She said she was happy that we wouldn't have to go through what they did when she was little. She said a lot of people would still be alive if that hospital had been built then. One time when we passed the hospital she told me that this is what the Revolution was fought for, and if anyone ever tried to take it away from us, we'd all have to pick up guns and fight to keep it.

4

Sound Bodies

In Cuba it seemed the most natural thing in the world to combine care for children's bodies with day care, education, and the formation of the New Man and Woman. Over and over I heard educators talk about the *integral* education of the *whole* human being. What could be more logical, then, than to begin at the beginning: with the diet of the mother while the child is in the womb, the vaccinations and immunizations while at the childcare center, check-ups, proper diet, physical activity while in school?

But getting back to the United States I had to be reminded that here all these parts of the whole are compartmentalized. Pre-natal care. Nutrition. Hygiene. Doctors. Dentists. Childcare. School. The childcare centers are places to store your child while you work; schools teach children to read, write, and (hopefully) become productive citizens. Health care is the business of parents and pediatricians.

Yet here, too, everyone from militant community groups (generally in the Third World communities) to educational researchers have talked about the links. The educators talk about the cycle of poverty, poor health and nutrition, failure at school — leading to another generation of poverty. The activists do something about it, organizing "Breakfast for Children" programs and free health clinics. Community struggles brought hot meals to some childcare centers and schools. But the remedies all still lie outside the institutions of education and learning.

In Cuba the entire well-being of the child is considered part of the responsibility of the whole society. That society then sets up the institutions to safeguard the child's health: polyclinics, pediatric hospitals, visiting nurses, mobile medical units, and health programs in the schools and the *círculos* themselves. Even the mass media become involved, with advice columns to parents in newspapers and magazines, posters and billboards reminding parents to take advantage of the various medical services available for their children. In every neighborhood, the Committees to Defend the Revolution (CDR) go door-to-door during immunization campaigns. The Cuban Women's Federation (FMC) is actively involved in community health programs.

Some of the impetus for this focus on total medical care lies in the bitter memories of Cuba's semicolonial past, which exacted a high price in human lives prior to 1959. Economic underdevelopment, which resulted as much from a semi-feudal latifundia system as from the foreign domination which forced Cuba into a single-crop economy, took its heaviest toll on the children. With sugar cane as Cuba's dominant crop, the vast majority of rural workers were employed only four months of the year. The pay for such work was so low that few could save enough to provide adequate food, clothing and housing for their families, let alone the more costly luxuries of medical care and education.

Malnutrition, rickets, decayed teeth, swollen bellies, and early infant death due to acute diarrhea were the more evident results of this system among the rural population. Sanitary conditions in these areas were infamous, hygiene unknown. The few public hospitals dispersed around the island were too far away for most peasants and mountain people to get to, and had too few pediatric beds and other facilities when they did. Access to these State hospitals, which were always filled to overflowing, had to be bought or begged from some powerful local politician at the price of the patients' votes. Those elected in this way perpetuated the system for their own gain.

Given these conditions, infant mortality and childhood deaths from preventable and curable diseases were astronomical. "The exact figures will probably never be known," explained Dr. Julio López of the William Soler Pediatric Hospital, "because in those days no national records were kept, and no one kept track of how many poor people died. They just died and were buried."

Cuba was not alone in this situation; it was endemic throughout Latin America. Fidel Castro pointed it out in his Second Declaration of Havana, when he compared the road the Cubans had set out on to the sorry plight of most of Latin America:

. . . In this sad picture we cannot forget the helpless, uncared for children. America's* children who have no future. While America has a high birth rate, its death rate too is high. The death rate among children under one year of age reached 125 per thousand a few years ago in 11 countries . . . . By contrast, the average death rate among infants in 102 countries of the world was 51 per thousand. In [all of] America . . . 74 children in each thousand die sadly, forsakenly during the first year of life. There are Latin American countries in which this figure mounts in certain sections to 300 per thousand.

Thousands upon thousands of children under seven die of unbelievable ailments — diarrhea, inflamation of the lungs, malnutrition, hunger; thousands upon thousands die of other diseases without hospital care or medicine; thousands upon thousands are walking about crippled by endemic cretinism, malaria, trachoma and other ills brought about by contamination, lack of water and other necessities.

Ills of this type enchain the nations of America where thousands of children are dying. They are the children of pariahs, children of the poor and of the petty bourgeoisie whose life is hard and whose resources are few. The statistics . . . are horrifying . . . .

The summary of this nightmare which torments America from one end to the other is that in this continent of almost 200 million human beings, two thirds of whom are Indians, Mestizos, Blacks, are those who are discriminated against . . . in this continent of semi-colonies there die of hunger, of curable diseases or of premature old age some four persons per minute, some 5,500 per day, two million per year, some 10 million each five years.

These deaths could be easily averted, but nevertheless they continue. Two thirds of Latin America's population lives briefly, and lives under the constant threat of death . . . .

*"America" is used by most Cubans to refer to what people in the United States call "South" or "Latin America." When referring to the United States, they say "*North* America" or "the U.S."

Today, almost two decades later, the situation in most of Latin America has not changed a great deal. Six Latin American countries have infant mortality rates of between 70 and 91 per thousand live births; eight others have between 45 and 69 deaths per thousand.

The Cubans were aware of why so many of their children were dying. Economic exploitation, and doctors who didn't want to travel to rural areas; the one-crop, big-plantation system, and not enough money to buy food and medicine; ignorance of proper nutrition and hygiene, and no transportation to get to the hospital.

An elderly woman once told a reporter of the difficulties getting medical care and ambulance service for herself and her children before the Revolution. She described having to bribe and bully an ambulance driver to take her critically ill child to a hospital in Havana, after begging a local politician to supply the needed gasoline.

She concluded her narrative, "Have you noticed the beautiful ambulances we have now? And they're at the service of whoever needs them."

I didn't realize the full significance of this story (which I noticed in the daily newspaper *Juventud Rebelde* while I was in Havana in 1973) until I was back in the United States and talking to a doctor who works in San Francisco's General Hospital. "Where do the ambulances come from now?" asked Doctor Richard Fine. "Who is authorized to call for them?"

"Why, the ambulances are run by the hospital," I replied, thinking that was obvious. "And a person who is too sick to go to the polyclinic or emergency room alone can simply call the hospital and ask to have an ambulance sent. Even in a non-emergency, if transportation is a problem, an ambulance will pick up a patient."

"You know, hospitals here don't have ambulances," Dr. Fine explained. "They're run by private ambulance services, or by the local public health department. And it's often very difficult to get service, especially in the poor and Third World communities. Sometimes you have to argue over the phone with some health department bureaucrat to convince them to send an ambulance. I've seen cases in San Francisco where the 'public' ambulance service was called to a residence and, once there, the driver refused to take the patient, saying 'You're not sick enough. Take a bus or cab.' After they were already there!

"Of course the private ambulance services will generally pick up anyone who can afford to pay their price, " Dr. Fine went on. "After all, they're getting paid sixty dollars plus three dollars a mile for each trip. It can cost up to one hundred fifty dollars to go to the hospital by ambulance in San Francisco."

Until I talked with Dr. Fine and other health workers, I had thought of Cuba's vast improvement in health care only in comparison to its past or to other underdeveloped countries. I had not thought of comparing Cuba's health system to that in the U.S., because materially, scientifically and technologically we are still far ahead of Cuba. Those who can afford it can usually get the best medical care in the world. Cuban doctors pointed out that despite great advances, they still do not have the resources to bring all the most modern medical attention to all their people.

What struck me in talking with Dr. Fine is that the crucial difference between Cuba and U.S. medical services is in their commitment to bring these services to all the people. Despite our technological advantage, Cuba's delivery of health care to *all* of its citizens puts our own medical delivery system to shame.

In all parts of Cuba older people had sad and bitter tales of the lack of medical services before the Revolution. Some of the more interesting tales came, not from patients, but doctors.

The older doctors — those who have stayed on with the Revolution — remember the situation during the years of the "Republic" prior to 1959.

The William Soler Children's Hospital is on the outskirts of Havana. The hospital is a big, modern, light and airy building with a scenic view of green hills, palm trees and the distant skyline of Havana. It was named after a fifteen-year-old boy who was cruelly tortured, then killed, by Batista's secret police. The boy had been a courier for the clandestine movement in the city and the 26th of July guerrilla fighters. He was rounded up when Batista's forces made a sweep of all "suspects" whom they believed to be linked with the 26th of July movement, torturing and murdering all of them. Almost all children's hospitals in Cuba, I learned, were named after children who died in the revolutionary struggle.

Dr. Julio López, one of the administrators of the hospital, is tall, thin, black, with a youthful face and countenance that are belied by the grey flecks in his hair. He remembers very well the Cuba that existed before the Revolution: the lack of medical care for the poor and the racial discrimination against the blacks and mulattos who comprise the bulk of the Cuban population.

Blacks, he told me, had a very difficult time getting apprenticed to surgeons and specialists after graduating from medical school. Apprenticeship was the only way a young doctor could become a specialist.

At the time Dr. López was having such difficulty getting apprenticed, there were only a thousand doctors working in all Cuban hospitals — less than one sixth the number working in Cuban hospitals today. The remainder were working in private practice. Today, three fourths of Cuba's doctors do work in hospitals. Many of the remainder practice in rural areas.

"Before the Revolution," Dr. López told me, "all the best specialists were in Havana. A child who was sick anywhere in Cuba had to be sent to Havana to receive treatment. The policy of the Revolutionary Government is the opposite — it's to *de*centralize. Specialists are sent to work in the various provincial hospitals, reversing the former situation in which 65 percent of them resided in the capital city. Now everyone in need of medical care has the possibility of receiving it in his or her own local area.

"The creation of new medical schools in Santiago (Oriente Province) and Santa Clara facilitated this decentralization," he explained. "Doctors and professors of medicine who had formerly been concentrated in Havana went out to these provinces to teach in the medical schools. Once the medical schools began graduating doctors, each area then had its own supply of medical personnel.

"Before the Revolution," Dr. López observed, "there was one children's hospital in all of Cuba — in Havana, of course. Havana also had two general hospitals which had children's wards, and each province had one such general hospital. These state-run hospitals were badly neglected, but the private ones were exorbitant, and who — before the Revolution — had the money to pay for them? The best-trained doctors, of course, preferred to work in the more modern, better equipped private institutions rather than the state-run provincial hospitals. So the poor were left to the handful of really dedicated doctors, and those who were too ill-trained to be able to get jobs in the private hospitals."

Dr. López continued his explanation: "It wasn't only that the state-run hospitals were ill-equipped and under-staffed in Batista's time. It was the attitude of the doctors toward the patients. At the Calixto García Hospital, for example — a huge medical complex in Central Havana — there were four hundred ninety-six doctors to attend the patients. But of these, only one hundred eleven were paid staff members. The rest were men connected with the medical school of the university, and viewed the patients as objects on which to experiment and learn. After the Revolution triumphed it took us a while to change from the idea that 'the patient exists for science' to 'science is to serve the patient.' Before the Revolution, private doctors went to the general hospital, studied the diseases of the patients there, and then used the knowledge they acquired, not to treat the poor patients in the general hospital, but for their wealthy clients in the private hospitals."

The lack of medical care for the poor took an especially heavy toll among the children. "Before the Revolution 63 percent of the recorded deaths of children (and how many thousands must have died with no records kept at all?) occurred outside of hospitals, without the patients ever having had the possibility of receiving the medical care which might have saved them.

"Today, according to carefully kept records of births and deaths, that number has dropped to one percent.

"Since the previous government didn't keep such records, the exact infant mortality rate can never be known," the pediatrician continued. I thought about Yolanda's babies dying in the Sierra Maestra, with no one to know or care except her family. "But in 1961 the Revolutionary government began keeping such records," Dr. López's voice brought me back to the present. "The post-Revolutionary infant mortality rate has gone down to 27.4 per thousand, and we expect to have it under twenty by 1980.* That compares to ninety-five per thousand in Haiti, Cuba's nearest Caribbean neighbor, and eighty-two per thousand in Guatemala.

"In countries with more advanced medicine and more resources," he acknowledged, "the figure of course is lower. In the United States it's already well under twenty deaths per thousand, and in Sweden the figure is lower still." He didn't mention that in the

---

*Preliminary figures for 1976 showed infant mortality down to 22.8/1000.

United States, the richest nation in the world, there are pockets of poverty where the infant mortality rate equals or exceeds that of many Latin American countries.

Jonathan Kozol, well-known Boston educator, pointed out in *Free Schools* (New York: Bantam Books, 1972): "Black children in the United States have approximately twice the chance of dying in the first twelve months of life as white children born in the same section of the nation on the same day." At a time when the national average was about twenty per thousand live births, the infant mortality rate was approximately fifteen per thousand in white surburban neighborhoods, but in black communities like Harlem, Watts and Newark the figure seldom ran lower than thirty or thirty-five. Chicago's West Side ghetto had a rate of thirty-eight deaths per thousand in 1972. Kozol contended that the figure in some areas frequently ran as high as fifty per thousand, and that "there are also a number of Northern ghetto census tracts in the United States in which the infant mortality rate exceeds one hundred per thousand."

The death rate for women in the act of giving birth is six times higher for black women than for white women in the Deep South. A significant part of maternal and infant deaths, Kozol contends, whether in the South or in Northern ghettos, is part of the phenomenon known as "excess mortality" — unnecessary deaths produced by poverty and neglect, of "gross medical injustice, both created and maintained by the surrounding white and middle-class population which derives direct and measurable advantage from the unjust allocation of available resources."

Dr. López wasn't the only doctor I met who recalled the deplorable state of public health care in Cuba before the Revolution. Although most doctors at that time came from the upper class, and fled the shores of Cuba with other members of their class after the Revolution, a number of older doctors who had practiced before could still be found. (Perhaps not suprisingly, many of those I encountered were black, although I could not generalize and say that most of those who stayed were non-white.) In Santiago de Cuba I met Dr. Varán, also tall, thin, black, and dedicated to the principle of medicine for the people. A friend had introduced us because Dr. Varán was known as a storyteller, a man with a million anecdotes.

Over lunch, he began to tell me of some of his early experiences as a doctor. He had graduated from medical school in 1959 — the year the Revolution triumphed. He thus had the unique mixture of pre-Revolutionary medical training with post-Revolutionary internship and practice.

"I graduated in 1959," he began. "At that time many doctors in Cuba graduated without ever having seen a birth, without ever having seen a child be born. I was one of those, and since I was afraid of everything having to do with childbirth, and knew I was going to practise rural medicine, I went to a hospital to learn.

"I did about forty or fifty deliveries in the maternity hospital on Linea [in Havana]. Then I thought I knew everything about obstetrics and I took off for the countryside. I began to work in a cooperative in Camagüey Province. There in the country I assisted many women. But one day, shortly before I was to return to carry out some promises, and satisfied because until then I hadn't had any problems and none of my patients had died, I was called on to attend to a lady who was about to give birth."

Dr Varán went on to describe, in humorous fashion, the shock he experienced when the baby he was to help deliver began to come out buttocks first.

Being very nearsighted, and never having seen a breech-birth before, the young doctor at first believed the woman was giving birth to a deformed monster!

On closer inspection he was able to determine the real nature of the situation, and successfully assisted in the difficult birth.

Dr. Varán explained, "What's interesting about it is that it came about because doctors used to graduate without ever having seen a birth. I had heard about transverse positions, but I thought they were just stories, until I was presented with one in that manner. Luckily, that *campesina* had very good pelvic proportions and helped me a lot and the little girl was born immediately, so we could solve the problem. But it all came about because of the combination of my bad vision and my faulty diagnosis."

Other doctors told similar stories. Dr. Pedro González was practicing in Santiago when I met him in 1973. He'd had long experience working in Oriente Province.

"When I first graduated from medical school I'd never given an injection," Dr. González told me, echoing the words of Dr. Varán. "The first time I had to give one, in an emergency situation, I didn't know what to do, where to put it. I was a specialist, but I'd had no practice. Studying medicine at that time was often a politically related privilege — you got into medical school because you knew some powerful politician. The type of student who went to medical school didn't want to get his hands dirty. He just wanted a profession in which he would earn a lot of money. The schools obliged, never making him do anything but read books and attend lectures. The first time I went to a house to help a woman give birth I almost lost the child."

Both doctors made it clear that this kind of near-tragedy — averted only by luck — could not come about today. Dr. González explained: "Today medical students begin working in a hospital during their first year of study. There is a constant combination of practice with study. When our doctors graduate, they are fully prepared to practice medicine."

Dr. Varán was more specific: "Every fourth-year medical student studies obstetrics and gynecology for a period of time, during which you have to attend no less than forty births. Then, during your internship, whether or not you are going into obstetrics or gynecology, you have to spend three months in that field, delivering babies. Those who will specialize spend another month. Now all those who graduate have sufficient experience to confront any kind of gynecological or obstetrical problem."

Some of the health problems Cuban's faced were the result of too few doctors, with inadequate training. Others came from outright neglect of the poor. The problems inherited from years of medical neglect weren't wiped out overnight, as I learned from the experiences recounted by these doctors. Not only were the doctors handicapped by an inferior medical education aimed at serving wealthy patients in urban settings, but poor nutrition and hygiene had already had serious effects on much of the population, and these could not easily be counteracted. Although this neglect had its greatest effect on today's adults, children still suffered from this previous neglect and hardship during the first years after the triumph of the Revolution.

Doctors told me of incidents where rural peasants trusted superstition above medicine — or feared vaccination was a form of chemical brainwashing.

There were reasons why the country people tended to distrust doctors at the beginning of the Revolution. They had rarely been able to count on the services of these white-coated city-dwellers before. When they had, they were often treated with disdain, or duped by quacks and dishonest practitioners. In Dr. Varán's words, "Before the Revolution all the land that this cooperative was part of belonged to one man, who was a doctor. Once a year he rode horseback around all his farms, wearing a stethoscope with a very long rubber hose. *Campesinos* with sick children would approach him. Without getting off his horse, the 'doctor' would lean over, toss the end of the stethoscope to the mothers and tell them 'Put it over there on your child's chest . . . ' That's how he did his diagnosis, from the back of a horse.

"When I was a child," remembered Dr. Varán, "my little sister was very sickly, with constant colds. We were very poor. We sent to the *Casa de Socorros* (a type of public assistance first aid station that provided minimal medical services for the poor) for the visiting doctor. These visiting doctors were the least qualified, the most out-dated there were, and since they were useless for anything else and they had to earn a living, they attended to us, the poor.

"Anyway, one of these doctors came out and diagnosed my sister as having double bronchial pneumonia, and then prescribed a whole series of medicines that were only sold at Díaz' Pharmacy, prepared by Díaz himself.

"These were fake medicines, placebos, like sugar-water, not real medicines. This happened a lot when I was a child. A doctor would prescribe one particular type of medicine which you could only get at one certain pharmacy, which happened to belong to his cousin or friend, and who would pay him back a certain percentage of the cost of the medicine."

Given these conditions, it wasn't surprising that the *campesinos* the doctors encountered during their first years in rural medical service after the Revolution felt little confidence in the doctors. "But slowly, after the Revolution, this changed," Dr. Varán told me. "Until this time, when someone on the old La Ignacia Farm — now the Manuel Sangüili Cooperative — would get sick, his neighbors would immediately begin collecting money among themselves to pay for the funeral services. They thought that the only result of sickness was death. When young rural doctors began appearing in different zones at the beginning of the Revolution, the population of these zones didn't believe they could solicit their services, and that they'd come any place, at any hour, under any circumstances. They just didn't trust them.

"But these doctors put their feet in the water, rode horseback, etc. Little by little the people realized that the doctor was the forerunner of the Revolution in the countryside, and this was an immense factor for change. Then the respect and love the *campesinos* felt for their doctors was incredible."

The children who have been born since the triumph of the Revolution never had to deal with these conditions. For them, medical care is a basic human right which they inherit by the fact of their birth.

Dr. Pedro González, a middle aged pediatrician who works for the childcare centers in Santiago, spoke of the changes he had encountered. Cuba is predominantly rural, but Oriente Province has the additional problem of being the most mountainous region. The medical problems common to all of Cuba existed and were intensified in this area; so the changes were the most radical.

"In Oriente there was a heavy population spread out in the mountains, without roads or any form of communication to tie them together — places like Gran Tierra. Civilization never reached there. In Maisí the people were living in caves. People in this area were forgotten by all previous governments, left to survive on their own however they could.

"To attack the problems of Gran Tierra required a total effort by the revolutionary government on all fronts. Roads and electricity were brought in; a small rural hospsital was built, and two primary schools that the children scattered around the region could live in during the week. The people of the region were given contact with the 'outside world' through nurses, teachers and others who came into the area to work with them.

"At that time parasitic infections and malnutrition were rampant. Sometimes it wasn't even a matter of lack of food, but just ignorance of the basic nutritional requirements of children. No one had ever bothered to explain to them.

"In this regard, the creation of schools, and then childcare centers (there are now five) did more than educate the children and provide them with the essential medical and nutritional care — they also taught the parents how to feed their children properly. Now there are almost no cases of malnutrition or parasites in Gran Tierra.

"Gran Tierra is an extreme case," Dr. González went on, "but similar problems existed throughout our province, and were combated in similar ways. Childcare centers and schools took on the responsibility of seeing that children were properly fed, and vaccinated against contagious diseases. Then the Committees for the Defense of the Revolution became involved in the vaccination program in a massive way, and wiped out first polio, then tetanus, by seeing that every single child was vaccinated.

"Improved education of the people, and better early diagnosis led to the elimination of many diseases and many causes of infant mortality. In persistent cases of malnutrition youngsters are sent to special nursing homes in the area. Sometimes the problem comes from premature birth or early disease, such as gastro-enteritis. When the problem is ignorance of nutrition on the part of the parents, we teach them.

"The process of improving the health in our area is integrally tied to all other aspects of the Revolution. The beginning of emancipation of women and their incorporation in the work force led to the creation of the *círculos infantiles*, which led to better health care for the children. By the time they are six years old and ready for school, the youngsters in the *círculos* have had a complete, integral education and health care that prepares them to fulfill all their responsibilities in school.

"All the institutions in the country — of the women, the workers, the Party, the youth, the Ministry of Public Health — all contribute in some way to the childcare centers, and thus to the preventive medical care of the children."

Dr. Julio López described the overall pattern of health care for Cuban children, beginning with the care of the pregnant woman. "Pregnant women are encouraged to go to the doctor at the slightest sign of trouble," he told me. "Women are divided into two medical groups, those with normal pregnancies and those with problems. The best qualified obstetricians are assigned to attend the women with problems. A woman with a problem pregnancy is also visited by a nurse twice a month, to make sure she is taking all the medications prescribed to her, keeping all her medical appointments, etc.

"The second part of the plan to reduce infant mortality centers on creating better conditions in the maternity hospitals. Part of this plan involves increasing the number of medical attendants. Another aspect is specialization among the nurses, with special training given in obstetrics, pediatrics, etc. The specialized nurses then work all the time in their particular field, and are thus more capable of dealing with problems by noting symptoms in their early stages, and knowing how to treat the problems.

"This program of course includes increased specialization among the doctors, so that it can always be pediatricians, rather than general practicioners, who attend newborn babies."

Before the Revolution the vast majority of babies were born at home — and most homes were shacks, *bohíos* or city slums. Today 99.3 percent are born in medical units: maternity hospitals or *hogares maternos* (maternity homes). Women from remote mountain or rural areas are brought to maternity homes a month before they are born, so that medical care can be promptly available to them.

Before, a large percentage of Cuban children died every year from malnutrition, gastroenteritis, whooping cough, diphtheria, polio, malaria and other preventable diseases. Today, most of these have been wiped out, and the others have been greatly reduced.

The main unit responsible for delivery of health care to the Cuban population is the polyclinic. The whole country is divided into medical units. The smallest unit, encompassing thirty thousand persons, is the polyclinic. (In rural areas, where people are more spread out, the polyclinic serves from twelve thousand to fifteen thousand people.)

A typical city polyclinic has a pediatrician, an obstetrician-gynecologist, an internist and a dentist. The number of doctors of each kind depends on the population of the area.

More than 80 percent of medical problems are solved at this level. If they can't be, the patient is sent to the regional medical unit, generally a hospital with specialists. More complicated problems go to the provincial hospital, where the best specialists and special equipment are located.

When a healthy child leaves the hospital after birth, the medical department sends the records of mother and child to the polyclinic in the area where the mother lives. The polyclinic then sends a nurse to visit the mother and child, as part of the overall preventive medical care program. The nurse will discuss hygiene, nutrition, and sanitation with the parents; a worker specially trained in the field of sanitation will also visit the home and check overall cleanliness, conditions of pets, presence of insects, conditions of the water supply, etc.

In the case of premature babies under the normal birth-weight, or infants with other problems, the records are sent to the polyclinic even before the mother and child leave the hospital, so the nurse

Center for Visually Handicapped: Needed medical care is integrated with general education.

can go to the house immediately and be available to help with any special problems.

During this first visit the nurse sets up a schedule of visits with the doctors at the polyclinic, to begin within ten days. The polyclinic begins keeping records of the baby's weight, size, vaccinations, etc.

If the child goes to the *círculo*, his/her medical attention continues there. Otherwise the polyclinic continues to be responsible. A commission of public health, made up of representatives of the local CDR, FMC (Women's Federation), CTC (trade union council), ANAP (Association of Small Farmers), Poder Local (local government), the Cuban Communist Party and the Young Communists, works in conjunction with the polyclinic. This commission provides a two-way flow of information: the mass organizations tell the polyclinic what problems are bothering the people in their zone, such as particular medical problems, the hours the polyclinic serves the public, etc. The polyclinic lets the people know, through these popular organizations, of various health campaigns and preventive measures.

The CDRs and FMC each have special departments within their organizations working in the health area. These community workers are especially important in reaching people who don't receive their medical care through school or work. They have played a vital role in each immunization campaign.

The preventive medicine program for children begins with vaccinations shortly after birth. During the first year all Cuban babies receive immunizations against tuberculosis, tetanus, diphtheria, whooping cough, and typhoid. Every Cuban child, by the age of six, has received the Sabin oral anti-polio vaccine, distributed door to door by the CDRs. In this way Cuba became one of the first countries in the world to eliminate polio totally. Dr. López told me that when Dr. Sabin visited Cuba, he told doctors there that his vaccine was being put to the best use in Cuba of all the countries in the world, because of the program of systematic mass distribution.

The polyclinics have a sick-and-well-child program, with highest priority going toward lowering the infant mortality rate. The regular program of clinic and home visits in the child's first year, coupled with the work of the *circulos* and the mass organizations, has been very effective in this regard. But gastroenteritis, the stomach and intestinal disease that kills most babies in underdeveloped countries, is still a problem they are constantly combating. Doctors Roa Ochoa and Paul Riverón of the Ministry of Public Health (MINSAP), who gave me much of my background information about health care in Cuba, stressed that the principal medical problems come from living conditions: poor hygiene, lack of education. The home visits play an especially important part in teaching parents how to keep their children healthy by helping them understand the need to boil water and milk in homes without refrigerators, and other precautionary measures.

The polyclinics try to serve an educational role for the children as well as the parents. With diseases such as diabetes and asthma it is felt that the earlier a chid understands the disease and learns to deal with it, the better. Diabetic children learn to inject themselves, asthmatics how to use a respiratory apparatus. To facilitate this, these children are taken to a special camp at the beach during their vacation. There they both play and learn, together with other children suffering from the same disease. The diabetic children learn how to prepare the insulin, to tell when they need it, and to give themselves their injections. The children with asthma learn various breathing exercises. This educational program begins in simple stages, with explanations about the disease and its treatment, when the children are five. They usually begin taking an active part in their own treatment when they are seven.

As Cuban medical schools turned out more and more doctors — making up for the deficit caused by those who fled the country and surpassing the previous number — more health services have become available to the people. In 1973 the polyclinics began a program of home visits for sick children. The polyclinic has a list of symptoms they check when a parent calls in, to ascertain if the problem calls for a home visit. Vomiting, high fever, coughing, and diarrhea are the most common symptoms. It is felt that most cases that don't require hospitalization can best be dealt with at home.

A pediatrician from a new, very modern-looking polyclinic in an older section of Havana took me with him on his visits one afternoon.

Our first stop was at a small, old stucco house filled with children, relatives and neighbors. There was a small puppy playing on the floor. The two youngest children — six months old and two years old — were in a bedroom which they apparently shared with their parents. Two older children were playing just outside the door.

The infant had a rough, red throat, a rash and a fever which the mother hadn't been able to lower with aspirin. No appetite. In response to the doctor's questions she said the baby had not had any diarrhea or vomiting. The pediatrician diagnosed measles after a brief examination

The two-year-old also had a fever, was coughing and crying a lot, with the beginnings of a slight rash. The doctor made the same diagnosis, prescribing medicine for both children. He also prescribed medicine for an ear infection he had detected in his examination of the infant.

Addressing the mother, the doctor explained that the medications weren't to eliminate the measles, which would have to run their course, but to alleviate some of the side effects: aspirin for the fever, cough syrup, etc. He spoke to her a little longer about the care of the children while they were sick, then we left for the next house call.

The second visit took us to an older barrio. There were no gardens in front of the houses like in the first neighborhood. We approached an old apartment building with rows of doors facing an open courtyard. It began to rain as we climbed the stairs and walked along a narrow outdoor walkway to number sixteen. There we encountered Alejandro, nine months old, with black hair and dark eyes. He had a red throat and a slight fever, which his mother said she had lowered with aspirin, but she didn't want to continue giving it to him. After examining the boy the pediatrician prescribed some suppositories for the fever and some throat syrup, asked the mother to watch for other symptoms.

A neighbor came in, greeted the doctor familiarly, and began asking questions about her child. I looked around the apartment as they talked. It was small, but clean and bright. The crib was in the front room, which also served as living room, with a TV, couch, table, armchair and two rocking chairs. It also held a refrigerator which apparently didn't fit in the small kitchen I could see in back. There seemed to be two other rooms in the rear.

The area around the crib was decorated like a nursery, with a net full of children's toys suspended over the crib. Alejandro looked happy and alert, apparently not feeling the effects of his illness at this moment. He walked around the inside of his crib, watching the adults. "Show how we clap our hands for Fidel," his mother prompted. Alejandro laughed, clapped his hands. The doctor and I smiled, sat sipping strong, sweet Cuban coffee the woman had offered us as we waited for the rain to let up.

While we waited the mother showed me Alejandro's health card, on which were recorded all his medical visits and vaccinations since birth, along with a record of his size and weight at each visit. She told us she was waiting for the *círculo* in her neighborhood to open in a few weeks, so she could return to work. "Meanwhile" she said, "I have a copy of the *círculo's* schedule of meals, naps and activities. Alejandro — and I — are keeping on this schedule, so he'll be ready to enter the *círculo* without any problems of readjustment." She told me she had first thought of getting a copy of the schedule just to orient her own program with him, since this was her first child, and only later realized that this would speed up the child's transition into the *círculo.*

On the way back he explained that parents are just now getting used to the idea that they can simply call the polyclinic and arrange to have the doctor visit their sick children the same day. Many still tend to head for the nearest emergency room at the first sign of illness. Through general meetings of the neighborhood committees and Women's Federation, however, more parents are learning of this service and are beginning to use it.

There are times, of course, when children have diseases or injuries too serious for the polyclinics. In this case, the regional pediatric hospital — often via an emergency room or polyclinic — takes over the care of the child.

The first pediatric hospital I visited was the William Soler in 1971. Two years later I visited the Central Havana Children's Hospital. Although in very different settings, the two hospitals had a great deal in common: bright, pleasant surroundings, dedicated medical personnel and staff, and a program called *madres acompañantes.*

The mother-companions program was initiated especially for mothers of young infants suffering from diseases such as gastroenteritis. Psychologists have told the doctors that when a child is sick the mother's warmth and attention are most needed. "A sick child doesn't understand all these white-clad people poking things into him, moving her, handling him," explained Dr. López at the William Soler Children's Hospital. Dra.* Elcira Fernández expressed the same idea at the Central Havana hospital: "When I first practiced medicine the mother was not permitted to stay in the hospital with the child; now I can't imagine having a young child in a hospital without the mother close by. This system helps the parents, the children, and the doctors and nurses. When parents and relatives bring a child here, they are worried and nervous. Staying close by, they feel calmer, and so do the children. Children accompanied by a parent or relative cry less, and are calmer, more confident when having to deal with things like shots, medicine, oxygen tents, etc."

Dr. López described the program as a "double educational process. In the hospitals we have meetings and programs to teach the mothers how the children get sick, how to prepare the food, clean the diapers, etc. We also teach them everything about the care and treatment of their particular disease. That serves to re-educate the medical personnel who care for the children when we have to explain everything to the parents."

A nurse at Central Havana, Berta Castellón, credited the mothers with very concretely assisting the medical staff. "Mothers know their children better than anyone else. They know what symptoms the child had before they brought him in, and how the child usually behaves. They are the first to notice changes for better or worse."

Dra. Fernández added, "We try to answer all the questions the mothers ask us, and to give them thorough explanations. On the other hand, they give us vital information about the child's reactions which greatly assists us in our work.

"For instance, if we have a child who is critical, when we get to the ward to see that child, the first thing we do is ask the mother how she finds the child. If the mother says that the child is better, in the majority of cases we can be sure that the child is better. If on the other hand a mother whose child had been improving tells us the child had a relapse, we take that very seriously. The mother knows the child intimately and if a child behaves unusually, the mother recognizes that immediately.

Doctora, the Spanish feminine form of the word doctor.

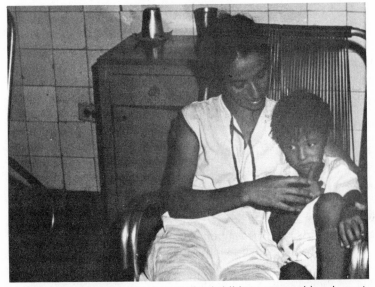

Mothers who stay with their hospitalized children are considered a part of the medical team.

"If a mother calls a nurse during the middle of the night with some problem, the nurse almost always calls the doctor. The doctors always rush up, because we know from past experience that when a mother calls it is because the child needs the doctor. In the past this would have been impossible; the doctor would resent being called in the middle of the night. But we feel, on the contrary, that this is very helpful in allowing us to make an expedient diagnosis and adopt the proper measures."

"When we decide to discharge a child, we ask the mother if she thinks the child can go home, if she thinks the child is well enough. Usually, when we think the child can be discharged, the mother is of the same opinion."

Doctora Fernández also described some of the activities carried on in the hospital to make the children feel more at home, such as the celebration of holidays like Mother's Day or International Women's Day with cultural activities and special meals, and activities on the children's birthdays.

Mothers I spoke with in this hospital felt very strongly that the *madre-acompañante* program was an important part of their children's medical care. Ceylán, a twenty-seven-year-old mother of two, was at the hospital with her youngest daughter. The child had been born prematurely, and had allergies, asthma and recurring respiratory problems. When the parents found the child gasping for breath the night before, Ceylán rushed the child to the hospital.

"The doctors examined her right away, and gave her oxygen. They admitted us to the hospital, because they felt she could get better treatment here than at home. They gave her a lot of attention right away. They always give a lot of attention to all the children, but I could see their special concern when we got here last night. She got treatment right away, and began to get better. And I began to feel better, too."

Ceylán told me this was the third time she'd had to bring her infant to the hospital. Before she'd been treated for diarrhea and gastroenteritis; the second time for an allergic reaction to milk. "They've always treated me and my child very well. Here she has all the care she needs to find out what her problems are and what will be done to make her better."

Ceylán was convinced that her presence provided more than just emotional support for her child.

"Here, I'm contributing with my knowledge of the child. I'm helping the doctor with information about my child, and helping my child emotionally. The mothers here take care of our children; we feed them, change their diapers, take them out for some sun, entertain them.

"Mothers here also receive very good care; all the facilities of the hospital, clothes to change into, a place to bathe, three meals a day. When we get tired, or need to do some errands, some other family member takes our place."

Ceylán told me that the doctors always carefully explain to the mothers what is going on, what kind of treatment the child is receiving and why, "to make sure the mother isn't frightened, not knowing what is being done to her child."

Ceylán had only been in the hospital for twenty-four hours this visit. The next woman I spoke to had been there ten days, accompanying her seven-month-old son who was suffering from high fever and convulsions. "When we came in he was so sick we thought he would die. Now," she smiled, "he's almost all better. He looks as though he'd never been sick."

She attributed his improvement to the rapid attention he'd received from the doctors and nurses. "They gave him medicines to control the convulsions as soon as we came in. The fever persisted, and they ran all kinds of tests, but the results were all negative. At first they thought the convulsions were the result of the fever. But after twenty-four hours the fever subsided but the convulsions reappeared. This alarmed the doctors, and they continued watching and treating him. After forty-eight hours he'd improved considerably, and now you can see he's almost well."

I asked about the mother's participation at the hospital.

"When we arrived I was able to tell the doctor everything that happened till that time. I explained how the convulsions came, all the details. The hospital assigned a special, round-the-clock nurse who stayed with me all night watching the child.

"When the convulsions returned after twenty-four hours I saw the early signs and, since I'd seen them before, I was able to warn the nurse immediately. Aside from this I think his recovery has been due to the fine care they've given him here."

Although only a young child before the Revolution, this mother recalled: "I remember that to put a child in the hospital one had to have connections. Even if the child was dying they wouldn't take him in. Not everyone could get medicine, either. Years ago, I wouldn't have been able to save my child."

Dra. Elcira Fernández and the nurse Berta had accompanied me on parts of my tour of the hospital. Afterwards we talked about what I'd seen, and the reactions of the mothers. Noting that many of the mothers pointed out the warm attitude of hospital personnel, I asked if new personnel were given special instructions regarding this.

"Yes," she told me. "We notice that when a new group of medical students arrive they often complain that some mother is too anxious or calls too much. They don't yet realize that the mother's constant calling is almost always justified.

"The main orientation we give them is in respect to treating the patients humanely. In the past we had seen how, even when patients received all the medication they needed, their families would still feel the treatment was unsatisfactory, because the doctor was rude to them or some such thing. It came from an attitude that the doctor is always right. We tell the students that when mothers have questions about their children's care, they are generally right. Even if at first one thinks that she is making too much of it, it usually turns out that the mother was right.

"One of our first tasks at the beginning of the Revolution was to get rid of the old sense of 'professionalism,' and the class distinction that used to exist between doctors and nurses, and between them and the orderlies and attendants. We try not to make any distinctions or give any privileges. Today's medical students not only work in hospitals as observers and assistants — they also spend time cleaning the floors, changing sheets and bedpans. We have to know that every single job in the hospital is vital to the health of the patients, and we all depend on each other. If the person responsible for keeping the rooms clean and the equipment sterile falls down on the job, the best surgical training isn't going to prevent the patients from getting infections.

"Because we have that kind of training, you see a cooperative attitude not only among doctors, but among nurses, staff and the children's parents."

Dr. López pointed out another aspect of the *madres acompañantes* program. "Perhaps even more important than the comforting role of the parent with a sick child is the direct concern this produces among the doctors for the children's families," he commented. "The well-being of a child means even more to a doctor when you have personal contact with the child's family. The work of the doctor, nurses and attendants is a personal, not a mechanical thing. And if the child should die, the parents know it is not because of lack of concern on the part of the doctor and the staff.

"You know," he mused, "it's said that doctors get accustomed to death, and that is one of the biggest lies in the world." He went on to talk about a number of cases in which the human bonds between the hospital staff and their young patients were especially strong. "And with children who have incurable diseases, like leukemia, we try to give them everything they want," he added. "If they ask for an elephant from India, we try to get it." He spoke of one child, close to death, whose greatest wish was to be a *Pionero* (member of the mass children's organization). "All the kids in his class came to the hospital," Dr. López recalled, "to have an official ceremony making him a *Pionero*."

The same feelings were expressed by nurses and other hospital staff. In the wing that houses leukemia patients the medical personnel were especially interested in the fact that I was from California. About a month before Cuban newspapers had published a letter written by an unhappy Cuban woman who had gone with her husband to California, taking their nine-year-old son with them. "The little boy was suffering from leukemia," one of the nurses told me. "We had been taking care of him here at William Soler. We were giving him the life-saving drug Rubidomycine. We still don't have a cure for leukemia," she observed, "but Rubidomycine has helped prolong the lives of many of our patients, while doctors all over the world are looking for a cure."

But when the parents of young Omar took him out of Cuba, they were no longer able to get the medicine for him. In Spain, where they landed first en route to the United States, they were told that Spanish hospitals didn't stock the drug because so few patients could afford the cost of this life-prolonging medicine. Shortly after they arrived in California the little boy died. "His mother wrote to us," another nurse added, "recalling the constant, free and loving attention her child had gotten in Cuba, and wondering why she had left."

"We were all very attached to Omar," an orderly commented. "Everyone in the hospital tried to convince his parents not to take him out. But they thought everything would be better in the United States. So they took him away, to die in a strange place, thousands of miles away, without the friends, the love and the care that the Revolution would have given him."

A friend later asked me if it hadn't been very sad and depressing going through a pediatric hospital, seeing so many sick and injured children. I was a little surprised to realize it hadn't been. Both pediatric hospitals were bright, pleasant places. The strongest impression I had was of sunlight pouring through the window-lined halls and stairways of William Soler, of the brightly-colored paintings of Vietnam at the entrance of the Central Havana hospital. Children's murals lined many of the walls, and toys filled many of the rooms. Children with their mothers nearby were generally playing happily or resting quietly.

The only place I heard children crying was in the wing for children with gastroenteritis, mostly infants crying for their food. The only really sad place in the whole hospital was the section for badly burned children. Even in the accident ward, where some children had both tiny legs in casts, suspended in the air by pulleys, the children had such an air of self-assurance, of being well-cared-for, that the feeling was of encouragement, not depression.

Even in the best hospital environment, problems still exist, as Dr. López pointed out. One of these is "hospitalism," a psychological state that children sometimes get into if they remain in a hospital too long. "Some become totally indifferent and withdrawn," he said, "and others become super-active and aggressive. You have to make sure to give these children a lot more attention." he stressed. "More toys, more personal contact. Older children who are hospitalized for a long period generally don't have a parent living here with them; sometimes it's necessary to arrange for the parents to spend more time here."

The intensely human and personal approach was what distinguished each hospital I visited from the ones I had experienced in the U.S. As Dr. López walked around the William Soler Hospital his relation with hospital workers, nurses, doctors and patients wasn't one of authority, but of comradeship—marked by warm smiles, arms on shoulders, and by children who smiled as he came into their rooms, reached up to hug and kiss him as he passed by their beds.

The daily care provided by the polyclinics, assisted by health programs in the *círculos* and schools, and the intensive care offered in the children's hospitals throughout Cuba were impressive, especially as contrasted to the situation that existed just a short time before, and that still exists throughout most of the underdeveloped world. But this isn't the extent of the health services offered to the Cuban people. Special nursing homes and facilities exist in all parts of the island for children with special problems ranging from eye impairments to mental retardation.

It was in these areas that I learned once again that Cuban care is exemplary not just for poor countries but compared to the United States as well.

In Oriente I visited a center for "nutritional recuperation." The first *Hogar de Recuperación Nutricional* was founded in Holguín, in 1968. Now there are twenty such centers throughout the province of Oriente. The center in Santiago had been functioning three years when I spoke with the staff there. "At first, most of our cases resulted from the parents' lack of education," explained the director of the Hogar. "Mothers fed their children improper foods, failed to give them milk, meat and eggs. They didn't understand when the doctors told them to do this. *Their* mothers never had milk, meat of eggs to give their children, so even when these became available to everyone, the mothers didn't know what to give their babies, what foods they needed at what age.

"When children suffered the ill-effects of poor nutrition, we brought them to these *hogares* and fed them properly, gave them vitamins and sunbaths, until their weight reached a normal level. At the same time we had classes for the mothers, teaching them about nutrition and hygiene and how to prevent diseases.

"Now most of the children who are here are suffering from gastroenteritis and other early infancy diseases, although there are still a few cases due to ignorance."

The *hogares* (homes) are generally caring for between twenty and thirty children, who may stay anywhere from one to three months. In explaining the unique benefits of the *hogares,* the director pointed out that before, such children went to a hospital, where their condition improved. But as soon as they were well, they were simply returned to their homes, and many of these babies died because the conditions at home had not changed. The *hogar* provides the educational supplement to the dietary program.

"Before the Revolution such children just died and were buried," the director pointed out. "Now, even if parents are unaware of the problem, the visiting nurses from the polyclinics will notice if a child is malnourished and will send such children to the polyclinic, which may refer them to the *hogar.*"

Although gastroenteritis is the cause of the malnutrition which sends many infants to the *hogares*, only healthy infants are cared for in these homes. Infants with contagious diseases are sent first to the hospital, and only after successful treatment are they referred to a *hogar* for recuperation. Infants who show sufficient weight gain in the hospital are simply sent home. In these cases the parents will receive obligatory classes from the hospital or local polyclinic.

So important does the Revolution consider the parents' knowledge of proper nutritional and medical care of their children, that the parents are given a "test" when the child is ready to go home, with a doctor or nurse asking questions to make sure they are really ready to care for the child properly. When the child is released, the polyclinic is informed. Visiting nurses will then go to the child's home regularly for the next three months.

Although the mothers do not live in the *hogares* with the children, every effort is made to make sure the children do not become "institutionalized." In addition to regular visits by the mother, there is at least one adult to every ten children in the *hogar*. The one we visited had five nurses. The children are played with a lot to keep them alert and mentally healthy. Some of their time each day is spent in outdoor *corrales* (playpens).

When a baby is brought in the mother fills out a history of the infant, what it has been fed, etc. A chart is made out with the mother's age, child's weight at birth, number of children, father's salary, mother's diet during first three months of pregnancy, etc. The child is weighed every day in the center, and the weight is duly recorded on the chart, which is checked every day. If the baby's weight drops at any time the doctor is called immediately.

The doctor checks the child's progress chart every day. In addition to the weight the chart records such items as "child didn't want to eat today," "playing more actively," etc.

I asked why there wasn't an attempt to create conditions in the *hogares* for the mothers to accompany the children as they do in the pediatric hospitals. The director told me that the constant attention of the mother is not so necessary here, since these children are healthy — their only problem is that they are malnourished. Being in the *hogar* is similar to being in a *círculo infantil*, but with special dietary conditions.

The Home for Nutritional Recuperation was located in Vista Alegre, a once wealthy suburb of Santiago. Like the other suburbs of Havana, this had been the exclusive domain of the rich before the Revolution. When many of these left Cuba, they left behind fine old homes and estates, which the Revolution put to use to serve the needs of the poor people of the region.

Driving out of the city, we next visited a home for physically and and mentally retarded children. Set in a woodsy location, the estate looked like the summer vacation spot that some wealthy city dweller once enjoyed: rustic cabins, well-furnished inside, surrounded by lawns and rich tropical plants and trees, set well back from the road.

My formal introduction to the home was presented by a young woman seated behind a desk in one of the cabins. "The children here are those with severe brain damage or cerebral palsy, children whose neurological illness leaves them unable to speak, or to walk, or mentally retarded.

"The children in this institution are those who, in addition to these physical and mental problems, have serious social problems as a consequence of their parents' social development. Here we give them physical therapy, physiotherapy as well as neurological and pediatric care."

After this brief explanation, we began to walk around the buildings and grounds accompanied by a nurse and staff member. I wondered about the nature of the "social problems" that had been described. This became clear as they explained further which children were here, and the assistance given them and their families.

"The children who are here either have some possibility of improvement with therapy, or, because of a social problem at home, have no one to care for them there," the young woman continued.

"Children whom the neurologists determine to be 'incurable' are actually better off at home, if there is someone to care for them. But in many cases, the parents are separated, and the mother cannot work if she must stay home all the time to care for a seriously ill or retarded child. If the mother can care for the child, she is taught how to conduct the various therapy treatments at home.

"Those children who can actually learn and improve are brought here whether or not there are problems at home. The home care, and the treatment of 'incurables' here, is basically to help them become somewhat self-sufficient in their daily living — to learn to sit, walk, feed, and perhaps wash and dress themselves."

As we talked we approached a group of nurses and children sitting on the lawn. Some of the children were playing, one attempting to walk, several simply sat cuddled next to some nurse or assistant. I felt depressed by the sight of so many severly retarded children — perhaps fifteen in this area — but the young women who worked with them seemed in good spirits, smiled and laughed with the children.

"A social worker is here permanently, to work with the parents of these children. She visits their homes, explains how to treat the children, how to modify their surroundings so they can function at home. There are schools for parents to explain why the chidren are retarded, what their possibilities are.

"One important function of her work is to help relieve the parents' guilt feelings. The feelings produced by having a retarded child often lead to divorce and other marital problems."

The children in this home were between the ages of two-and-a-half and ten years. Their therapy includes "work-therapy": learning to walk holding onto parallel bars or walkers for the younger children. "School" consists of a blackboard on which the teacher draws simple things like houses and flowers, and teaches the children to recognize them. Most of the toys are brightly colored; there's a toy piano which the children can play. Almost all of these children must be fed by the nurses and assistants.

The program is drastically different from what existed before. Prior to 1959 there was no specialized care for such children. Until 1973, the only such home was in Havana. Although this provided good care and therapy for the children, it severely broke up the families from the other provinces, since most couldn't visit the children very often. By 1973 the Revolution had created provincial centers, where parents could visit three times a week. Children also can go home on weekends if they don't live too far away and if there are proper conditions for them at home. Eight of the children at this center — more than half — regularly go home on weekends.

Those children not involved in a rigid training-therapy program also go on vacations, to the beach, etc., with their parents.

During the time spent in the institution the children are also taken on outings and excursions, rather than kept cloistered in the *hogar.*

Although these children can eventually learn to take care of themselves, it is unlikely that they can reach a level of social productivity. Nevertheless, the Revolution invests a great deal of time and resources in them.

MINSAP, the Ministry of Public Health, besides providing therapy and care, uses radio, TV, magazines and newspapers to educate the public, to change the attitudes and ideas which have existed about mental retardation.

SOMETIMES NO CARE AT ALL IS BETTER

I didn't realize the full import of what Cuba was doing for the mentally retarded until someone pointed out how different it is in the United States. To me, the program sponsored by MINSAP, contrasted to a time when there simply was no care at all for mentally retarded children, was a significant enough improvement to be worth noting. When I read of conditions in some of the institutions for the mentally retarded in this country, I began to wonder whether perhaps the children who were left at home with no assistance from the State weren't better off than those sent to institutions where they suffered and died from total neglect.

When Dr. Wilkins slid back the heavy metal door of B Ward, building No. 6, the horrible smell of the place staggered me. It was so wretched that my first thought was that the air was poisonous and would kill me. I looked down to steady myself and saw a freak: a grotesque caricature of a person lying under a sink on an incredibly filthy tile floor in an incredibly filthy bathroom. It was wearing trousers, but they were pulled down around the ankles. It was skinny. It was twisted. It was lying in its own feces. And it wasn't alone. Sitting next to this thing was another freak. In a parody of human emotion, they were holding hands. They were making a noise. It was a wailing sound that I still hear and that I will never forget. I said out loud, but to nobody in particular, "My God, they're children."

Wilkins looked at me and said, "Welcome to Willowbrook."

The above passage was written by ABC-TV news reporter Geraldo Rivera, describing his first visit to Willowbrook State School for the mentally retarded in New York. Rivera had gotten interested in the story when a young doctor who had been trying to organize parents to demand better conditions for their children was fired from Willowbrook. Willowbrook at that time had a staff of less than a third of the minimum number necessary to give the children the most minimal care. A state freeze on hiring combined with governmental cuts of funding for the mentally retarded had combined to produce the agonizing scenes Rivera witnessed.

After an intensive campaign in which more than two and a half million television viewers witnessed the horrors perpetrated against the mentally retarded in the name of the people of the state of New York, Rivera had to admit that, despite some token changes that would slightly alleviate conditions for a few patients for a short time, everything remained basically the same.

I became aware of places like Willowbrook when Dr. Richard Fine was looking at my notes on the *hogar* in Oriente. He pointed to a passage where I had more or less taken for granted as the minimal care provided all such children: that the children regarded as "incurable" (unable to become socially productive, working citizens) were simply taught to become self-sufficient in their daily living "to learn to sit, walk, feed and perhaps wash and dress themselves."

Seeing that I didn't understand what was special about this, he handed me a copy of Rivera's "Willowbrook: A Report On How It Is And Why It Doesn't Have To Be That Way," opened to page 46. I read:

> Inside A Ward, I asked [Dr.] Wilkins to describe what was going on. "Many of the profoundly retarded children aren't capable of feeding themselves. We have no staff to train them in a systematic way to use utensils to feed themselves. This can be done, but what is happening here is the result of our inadequate staff. You take a bowl of food you've made into a mush-like substance with a big spoon and you ladle it into the mouths. In these buildings where the kids can't feed themselves, there are so few attendants that the average feeding time per child — and it's been timed — is three minutes."
>
> "How much time would be needed to do the job adequately?"
>
> "The same amount of time that your children and my children would want to have for breakfast."
>
> "What is the consequence of three minutes per child per meal?"
>
> "The consequence is death from pneumonia."

Dr. Wilkins explained to Rivera that rapid force-feeding can cause death by food clogging the windpipe and choking the child to death, or by food entering the lungs setting up a chemical pneumonia. He added that more children die at Willowbrook from pneumonia than from any other cause.

The director of Willowbrook, asked about children dying as a result of the shortage of attendants, admitted it happened, but rarely. Asked to define "rare" he answered: "Perhaps three or four deaths a month."

Given this kind of treatment in the wealthiest country in the world, the intensive care given to the mentally retarded in Cuba took on new meaning for me. It wasn't just that Cuba had made progress over its sorry past, or that it was way ahead of other underdeveloped countries. I began to see that the Cuban system of health services for its children could be taken as an example for us here.

The people of Oriente, who rarely had seen a doctor before the Revolution, now not only had hospitals and polyclinics, but centers for specialized care all over the province. It was here, too, that the *Hogar Materno*, maternity home, was originated, as a way to get women from the mountains to give birth under safe and hygienic conditions. The Cuban "midwives" used to have as their trademark a long, hard nail on one finger, one woman told me. "When your nine months were up, the midwife would use that long nail to break the membrane of your waterbag, and begin to extract the baby! And it never occurred to them to even wash their hands."

The time spent in the maternity homes also allowed the medical staff to try to break through some of the old superstitions many rural women had about child-raising (such as a taboo against eggs), and to teach them elementary nutrition and hygiene. "Before," a doctor told me, "women in the rural zones, who'd had many children, often gave birth prematurely. The babies would be sick and underweight, many came down with diarrhea and would die. The *hogares de recuperación nutricional* (homes for nutritional recuperation) were set up to combat this problem, but at the maternity homes we try to create the conditions to prevent it in the first place."

It was in Oriente, too, that I saw an interesting corollary to the program of combating tuberculosis. This disease, the scourge of working and poor people around the world, once filled Cuba's TB hospitals to overflowing. Now, although not completely eliminated, the number of cases has been drastically reduced. With fewer medical facilities and resources taken up combating the disease itself, the Revolution is now able to pay special attention to the corollary problems which affect families when a member has tuberculosis.

Overlooking the Santiago Bay, surrounded by tropical trees and swept by fresh sea breezes, sits a large old wooden house. This is where children of TB patients are cared for, anywhere from six months to a year or two when necessary. The children range from six to fourteen, and attend school from nursery through fifth grade. (Because most of these children are from rural areas they are often several grades behind in their studies.)

These children are not sick themselves; they simply come from a home where one member has been hospitalized with TB, and have been diagnosed as having low resistance to the disease.

Before the Revolution such children generally ended up in the TB wards with their parents, or begging in the streets. Such children most often died in their homes, without ever receiving treatment.

Now, as soon as a parent is hospitalized with TB, any children who might be susceptible to the disease are sent to a home like this one. Here they have special diets, including meat, fish or chicken twice a day. The sea air provides additional iodine. The children are attended daily by a pediatrician and have regular dental care.

The life in this home is almost idyllic. Children get up in the morning, exercise, breakfast, and attend classes till lunch. After lunch they nap till three o'clock, have a snack, and play until the evening. Their play often involves going to the beach or on outings around Santiago. In the evenings they bathe, read collectively, have dinner, then nap briefly. Later they may read or watch TV or a movie brought regularly to the home by ICAIC, the Cuban Film Institute.

Clothes, food, books and toys are provided for the children. A seamstress on the premises makes them each special outfits to wear on their excursions. Some of the workers here told me that although some children are a little sad and homesick when they first get here, the abundant attention and ideal conditions soon dispel that. Many more are sad to leave when it is time to return home.

Social workers from the institution visit the children's homes before they return, check to see what health or hygiene problems might exist. Children receive visits from some family member the last Sunday of every month.

Although most children eventually return home after their stay here, there are of course some cases in which the parent dies. In those cases the children are offered scholarships to any school that interests them.

Homes like these made me realize that lowering infant mortality, while perhaps the first priority in Cuban medical care, is only one small part of the overall health care for children. The better quality and quantity of medical care that all children now get, the better education of the people, the growing acceptance of the norms and standards recommended by medical personnel, the widespread use of preventive medical measures, the prompt attention given

Mentally retarded children receive abundant care from trained medical assistants.

to sick children (which requires first of all that the parents be ready to take their children to the doctor at the first sign of trouble), and the progressive improvement of the nutritional level of the children all contribute to the drastic reduction in the number of infant deaths each year.

The technical aspects of Cuban pediatric care are not unique, in general, when compared to similar care in developed countries (although it is quite exceptional when compared to all other under-developed countries). What is unique is the delivery of this medical care to the entire population. In 1973 the Public Health Ministry was involved in setting up national norms among pediatricians all over the country, so that the children in the mountains would have exactly the same advantages as children in Havana — with the emphasis going towards the mountains.

At the same time the Children's Institute, which combines the work, experience and research of every field of study related to children, has been carrying on a nation-wide Growth Study. Dr. Alonso, one of those in charge of coordinating the massive study which will record the development of every Cuban youth from birth to nineteen years, described the project:

"We believe the change in physical measurements of the human body reflects the growth and development of the country. A poor, underdeveloped country is marked by high illness and mortality rates, small body size. As the country grows, so does its people. We can demonstrate this through the changes recorded in the size and weight of children at birth and as they develop. What we are saying is that human beings reflect the conditions they live in not just in a social, but also in a concrete, physical sense. England is the only other country in the world that has tried a similar undertaking.

"Why do we want to measure our population? Prior to this Cuba — like most other Latin American countries — used U.S. or Mexican standards of human measurement. The 'correct' height, weight, growth rate and development patterns for children were based not on our own cultural and physiological reality, but on that of other, more 'advanced' countries which happened to have those measurement standards.

"This was very artificial, since the height, weight and motor development of a child in Santiago de Cuba was not likely to be the same as that in New York City. So the Children's Institute is engaging in a study of all Cuban children which, when finished, will provide us with a guide to standard growth which reflects our own reality.

"There are numerous uses for such a study. One, as I mentioned, is that it is a reflection of the economic growth of our country. Another very important reason is that it is an expression of the health of our people, and can be used for further improvements in the health field. In addition, there are industrial uses — also linked to our people's well-being — for such measures. Setting up norms for clothes sizes, the measurements of desks and chairs for our school children, sports equipment, etc. We hope to learn some more in the field of proper nutrition for our youngsters from this study. The possible uses are innumerable."

Talking with Dr. Alonso I was once again reminded of how inextricably children's health care, nutrition, growth and development are linked with all other aspects of the Revolution.

Still, some people might wonder why, with such massive public health programs, the schools need to be involved. One answer is that it facilitates periodic check-ups and vaccinations, which are carried out in the childcare centers and schools. But perhaps the best example of this inter-relation between education and physical well being of the child can be seen in a school like the Centro Especial de Oftalmología Infantil.

The Centro is a primary school. It is also a treatment center for children with visual problems. The stated reasons for founding such a center are simple:

> The loss of vision in children has been the object of investigation by ophthalmologists all over the world, and is also of great concern to parents who fear their children may lose vision in one or both eyes. This loss of vision is in many cases recoverable with systematic medical treatment which, for various reasons, is often not carried out.
>
> Among these causes:
>
> 1. Children don't want to keep one eye covered since, in almost all cases, the eye covered is the healthy one, so that the weak eye will be exercised.
>
> 2. When an eye is kept covered the children don't want to attend school because they become objects of their classmates' curiosity. They can't see the blackboard well, they miss lines when copying, etc.
>
> 3. When they must go to the Pediatric Hospital for their eye treatment they miss school.
>
> 4. Sometimes children can't get to the Pediatric Hospital for daily eye treatment because their parents both work and there's no one to take them.
>
> All of these difficulties lead to the following consequences:
>
> 1. The vision in one or both eyes is diminished or lost.
>
> 2. Loss or diminished vision leads to falling behind in school.

Yolanda Marrero, the *directora* of the Centro, located in the Vedado section of Havana, added this clarification:

"All of the children here have visual problems. Some of them were so bad that they had to feel things to know what they were like. Here they will spend a few years, combining school and treatment, and learn to see, so they can be completely reintegrated into their regular school life.

"Before, they almost all had problems at school. They couldn't see the board. If they went to the hospital for treatment they missed school and fell behind. Many of them became behavior problems. Children who can't see well get restless, they get up and move around, they become bored and start playing with their neighbor in the next seat. Sometimes they get into fights, or become very withdrawn, because other children make fun of their glasses or eye patches. At home and on the street they have problems, too.

"Here, everyone is the same. They all wear glasses, they all have eye patches (even those who don't need it). The teachers are ones whom the Ministry of Education has specially prepared to handle conduct problems in a sympathetic way.

"The building is specially constructed to aid the children in seeing, with special lighting, desks, books, etc. There are never more than sixteen children in a class and each one gets individual attention."

We walked around visiting the various classrooms. I saw adjustable desks that could be moved to different heights in accord with each child's visual needs, tilted, raised or lowered to facilitate reading. The books, and the lettering on the blackboard, were extra-large. Paintings on the walls were brightly colored and of complex designs.

The school has a music salon, complete with piano and record player, and a clinic infirmary which deals with all normal health care, plus vaccinations and monthly pediatric check-ups.

Treatment for their visual problems is part of every child's daily routine — just like going to one more class. We went into some of the "treatment" rooms on the second floor. The first room we entered was dark. A little girl with pigtails and one eye covered was sitting on a chair facing a wall. Three widely spaced letters were projected onto the white wall. An electronic light was flashed into one eye, then the child was asked to look at a letter. I asked the little girl what happens. "You see a circle of light around where the letter was," she told me, "and a smaller black circle covers the letter." I tried it, and saw the same visual image. When the lights were back on you could see the letter with a faint circle around it.

Doctora Marrero explained that this is the first stage of treatment for most children, and generally lasts some three to four months.

The next stage, when the child has recovered his or her vision to the point where they can read letters at six meters, they are shown an inverted E. The E is moved around and the children are asked to indicate with their hands which way the E is going.

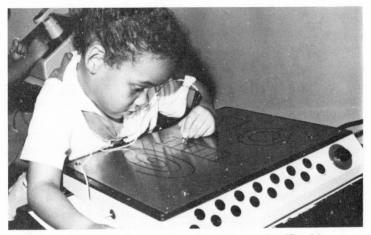

Eye-hand coordination training with modern scientific aids.

In the *ortóptica* department children begin working with more sophisticated apparatus. One piece of equipment looks like a two-lens microscope. It is aimed at improving focusing ability. A different picture is placed before each lens. One may have a dog house, the other a dog. The child must move a lever until the dog is in the dog house. The exercise is repeated until the child is able to see the dog in the dog house at the correct point.

A variation on this is to show two identical pictures — such as two bunny rabbits — and ask the child whether there is one or two. The object is to fuse them together. Another game-type exercise aims at eye, ear and hand coordination. The child takes a pen and traces the lines on a metal sheet, forming pictures, letters and shapes. The machine buzzes when the pen goes off the line.

There are other machines aimed at improving visual coordination, and a test involving red and green lenses in the glasses to determine whether the child is using both eyes. Looking at red, green and white lights, the child will see only colors if he or she is using only the eye covered by a colored lens.

All of the exercises are in the form of games, some fun, most challenging, that can interest the children and keep them from getting bored with the exercises.

School is not limited to classes and exercises. A complete children's library, visual displays, puppet shows and songs and skits are provided for and by the children. They celebrate the national holidays, births and deaths of heroes and martyrs just like all other schoolchildren. On my second visit there they were celebrating a week about José Martí and Ho Chi Minh. Pictures, clippings from magazines, and compositions written by the children lined the walls and bulletin boards. The children have their own unit of Pioneers, and compete in emulations with other schools. They all take part in sports activities, and work in a small flower and vegetable garden on the grounds of the school.

Perhaps the most interesting aspect of the *Centro* is how the children arrive here. Sometimes it is on the initiative of a parent and an ophthalmologist, or on the recommendation of a polyclinic. But very often a teacher has been the first to spot the child's problem. An agressive child, an indifferent child, a child with "conduct problems," a child who would be termed "hyper-active" in United States schools and be given tranquilizers, or considered "bad" and be punished, is given a physical and psychological evaluation at a *Centro de Orientación Diagnóstico.* A team of doctors, psychologists, psychiatrists, and social workers tries to determine, after a thorough study and examination of the child and the family, what is the cause of the child's behavior. It is in this way that many physical problems, such as visual impairment, are uncovered at a very early age (prior to eight years old), when the child can still receive successful treatment.

"This is one of the reasons," explained Dr. Riverón from MINSAP, "why we feel that all aspects of a child's education are totally and inextricably linked with that child's overall health care.

"Teachers as well as medical workers are taught the relation between a child's state of health and a student's ability to do well in school. When our teachers see behavior problems, or students falling behind in classes, they look for physical reasons as well as psychological ones. And, on the other hand, they take a special interest in seeing that the children are fed properly, get the proper exercise, receive all their immunizations, and that they begin to learn how their own bodies work. They see the child as a whole person, not just a mind to feed data into."

5

New Children Begin
in the Círculos

Life had begun to change for the Cuban people in 1959. Centuries of domination by foreign powers had ended. There were the beginnings, too, of an end to misery, degradation and other characteristics of a colonized people which had marked most of the Cuban population for generations. Within the first few years the Mafia was gone, and with it the gambling casinos, dope dens, vice rings and whorehouses. The Revolution began to offer full employment to men who had spent eight months of the year out of work and four months struggling to feed themselves and their families on pennies a day. Although the handful who had benefited from the previous status quo, and many others who were afraid of what the revolutionary changes would bring, left the country or attacked the Revolution, for most of the Cuban people, in cities and countryside, the changes were welcome.

But while revolutionary changes affected every person in Cuba, there were two categories of people who were especially affected. Women, who had shared the poverty and degradation of the colonial and neo-colonial periods with their men, had been subjected to additional hardships and humiliations. For them, the Revolution would have to go beyond the steps it was taking for *everyone*. There would have to be a special revolution for the women.

The children are the other special category. Not because children necessarily suffered more than adults (although children's suffering always evokes more sympathy than that of their parents), but because

children are the future of the Revolution; the ones whom the Revolution is being made for and, ultimately, the ones whom it will be
made by.

In Cuba, as in most other countries, the two are interrelated. As
in most societies, women in Cuba have always been responsible for
raising the children. Most of Cuba's women belonged to the agricultural or industrial working class by family origin, employment or
marriage. What they had known in their lives was hardship, and
hard work (when work was available). That, and discrimination
and humiliation at the hands of the North Americans and the small
Cuban bourgeoisie. And sickness, hunger, lack of education. Trying
to get a job and trying to survive, trying to keep their children alive.
This was the life they knew. This was the life they would try to
prepare their children to cope with.

There were two reasons why the Revolution had to change the
lives of Cuban women profoundly. One was for the sake of the
women themselves, to enable them to become happier, healthier,
more productive and more complete human beings. The other was
for the children — because it remains true in Cuba that women are
the primary molders and teachers of the new generation. The goal of
the Revolution was to provide such conditions that a new human
being would be formed. If the women were to create this new, revolutionary generation, they themselves had to change.

And for this to become possible, someone had to take care of
their children.

For this to happen, women had to be freed from the home —
both physically and psychologically. They needed to go to school,
be trained for jobs, become an active part of the revolutionary
process.

So when the Revolution was just an infant — scarcely more
than a year old — it conceived the idea of childcare centers. The
original idea of the centers, suggested by the Federation of Cuban
Women (FMC), was announced by Fidel Castro in 1960 as a means
of freeing the woman from the home. But it was immediately seen
that, beyond this, such centers would enable children to grow up
in a new, collective environment that could help instill the goals
and values of the Revolution in the new generation. This soon
became the major reason for the childcare centers — even more
important than the initial, and continuing purpose of enabling

women to leave their children in a safe environment while working or studying.

What were these "new people" the Revolution was trying to create? Many of the ideas were formulated by Ernesto "Che" Guevera, hero of the Cuban Revolution, who talked of creating a society which would produce the New Man, the Socialist Man, the Man of the Twenty-first Century.*

Trying to get a grasp of how Cubans understand the term New Man, I spoke with a group of teachers and *asistentes* who worked in the new childcare centers. "What is it you want the new children to be like?" I asked them. "What are the characteristics, behaviors and attitudes you are trying to create in them?"

The answers came out quickly at first, then more slowly and thoughtfully.

"We want them to have a sense of solidarity and collectivity with the people around them."

"They shouldn't be selfish; they should be able to identify with the group, even though each one retains his or her own individual character. They should know that we all work together to produce what we have, and that we then all share the things we have created."

"Work should be seen as something fulfilling and rewarding; not just something you have to do to stay alive."

"They should respect all kinds of work, if that work serves the Revolution — serves the people. They should understand that the cane cutter plays just as useful a role in our society as a surgeon."

"We want our children to have strong personal and moral characters; to be intellectually curious and demanding; to be creative."

"They should also have a strong sense of individual responsibility; working with a group should never mean submerging yourself in the group, or abdicating responsibility."

---

*The women's movement in Western countries has become particularly sensitive to the use of the term "man" when referring to men and women. For this reason, I try whenever possible in this book to refer to "new people" or "new children," etc. But it would be a dishonest re-writing of history to attribute this more advanced thinking about the use of vocabulary to Che Guevara, almost five years before it became part of women's consciousness in other parts of the world. Almost everyone who has ever read, studied or known Che Guevara insists that he fully intended the inclusion of women and children in his term New Man. For these reasons, I will continue to use the term, when appropriate, and hope that readers who are normally sensitive to such usage will understand it in its proper time and context.

"The fruits of their labor should be generously shared, not just with all the working people of this country, but with all the peoples of the world who need the things we produce."

"We want our children to have a sense of solidarity and identification with other peoples of the world: the working people of all countries, the people struggling for independence — even the people in capitalist countries, as long as they are not the ones who exploit or oppress others."

This is an impressive list of characteristics, and would clearly require the work of the whole society, as well as the most creative minds within the society, to develop them in the new generation of Cuban children. This was one of the initial purposes of the childcare centers, known as *círculos infantiles*. Clementina Serra, director of the National Program of Childcare Centers and member of the Central Committee of the Cuban Communist Party, told North American writer Margaret Randall:

"The childcare program has two main objectives: to liberate women so they can become an active part of the productive work force, and to aid in the social development of the children. Both objectives are very important, but the formation of the child is primary. The principle pursued in the childcare centers is to form the child completely — a healthy, strong, well-developed child, culturally prepared, politically clear, with just ideas — the child for the new society, children who will replace today's workers.

"The main focus of the *círculos* is the formation of the New Man and New Woman, with their own concepts. We want an individual, we don't want a mass of people who all think alike and accept everything. On the contrary, we want each one to have his or her own personality. But the fundamental thing that we want is that he or she be a person capable of creating the new society and of feeling happy in that new society.

"What is the new society? One where there is no exploitation of man by man, in which everyone has the same opportunities, where humanity becomes a mass of sisters and brothers, not enemies. One where there is not the kind of competition to get ahead so that one puts out his foot to trip the one behind, but rather that we all help each other. Where, as Che said, the pain of one is the pain of everyone, and an injustice to one hurts all of us. That is what we mean by the New Society.

The leaders of the Revolution did not think producing this society would be an easy task, but they were confident it could be done. "The present is struggle, the future is ours" they proclaimed on billboards seen throughout the countryside. But it was clear that if this was to be real, children would have to be a very high priority in every sense. This concept has been put into practice so thoroughly that one author who wrote about Cuban childcare centers, titled his book *Children ARE the Revolution.* [emphasis added]*

The Federation of Cuban Women set up the National Program of Childcare Centers, and took responsibility for developing and staffing these centers. The idea of *círculos infantiles* was born — but where to put them? Cuba was still a very poor country, with not enough building materials to provide decent housing for all those millions who needed it in the first years of the Revolution. Where were they going to get materials to construct childcare centers?

The answer was first provided by using the urban and suburban mansions and estates of wealthy landowners, businessmen and professionals who fled the country after the Revolution triumphed. Old fortresses of the Batista tyranny, as José Martí had once predicted, were converted into schools and childcare centers. Later, workers formed the idea of volunteer construction brigades. These microbrigades are made up of thirty workers from any work center where the rest of the workers are willing to pitch in and fulfill the quota of the volunteers while they are building schools, housing, hospitals and childcare centers.

First through the old methods, then the new ones, childcare centers began appearing all over the Cuban landscape. Remote areas that had not even known a road before now have modern childcare facilities.

But finding or building the *círculos* was only half the problem; the other half was staffing them. Male workers were out of the question. Every able-bodied man of working age was needed to fulfill the jobs vital to the economy and defence of Cuba. Even if this were not true, it was simply inconceivable to Cubans in 1961 that men could perform the role of caring for children, which had always been done exclusively by women. Centuries of poverty

*Marvin Leiner, *Children Are the Revolution* (New York: Viking Press, 1974).

and exploitation, plus a U.S.-induced drain of skilled workers and professionals after the Revolution, left Cuba with an under-populated and uneducated work force. There *were* enough non-working women to fill the jobs at the childcare centers, but few of these had any education or training.

This left the Revolutionary Government with a dilemma. They wanted as many women as possible to be free to go to school or to work, to become actively involved in the life of the country. This meant providing childcare facilities at the earliest possible date. But to create "new children for the new society" would require extensive training of the women who would work with these children. The FMC had as its initial goal that all childcare workers have at least a sixth-grade education, and then attend a comprehensive childcare course. A realistic appraisal of the human and material resources at hand soon taught them that this wasn't possible. Education was a luxury simply not available to most working class and peasant girls before the Revolution. The women who were now eager to serve the Revolution and to care for children did not have a sixth-grade education. But many of them had worked as maids and governesses in the homes of the wealthy, and brought with them a rich experience of caring for their own and others' children, and a love for the Revolution that was for the first time freeing them of the drudgery and humiliation of their former lives. Fidel suggested that these women who had been caring for the children of the rich could instead be caring for the children of their own compañeras.

So the *círculos infantiles* began in 1961, often in makeshift centers in converted mansions, with women who had not been through sixth grade, but had diligently studied modern and scientific methods of childcare in special crash courses. Since none of the women had the required level of special training to be considered *educadoras* (educators), the first *círculos* were completely staffed by *asistentes* (assistants). Today, every *círculo* has at least one *educadora*. In the near future, nearly all *círculo* workers will be *educadoras*.

The women who started out staffing the *círculos* were tremendously dedicated, hardworking women. They spent lunch hours, evenings and any free time they had studying, to upgrade their educational level and make them even better prepared for their new position of responsibility in the society. At times, such as during the Bay of Pigs invasion in April of 1961, their commitment has meant fighting to protect the children. One week after the first *circulos* were opened, the one in Ciudad Libertad was bombed during that abortive invasion. Women who had just learned to care for children now found they must also learn how to shoot.

A STEP TOWARD THE FUTURE

The *circulos infantiles* have come a long way since those early days. Alongside the older women educated in the hardships of life under Batista are young women brought up and educated by the Revolution. And joining the Women's Federation and the National Program of Childcare Centers in preparing *circulo* workers and programs is the *Instituto de la Infancia:* the Children's Institute.

Formed in 1971, the Children's Institute has three main objectives:

1. To integrate all children's institutions, the *circulos infantiles,* other local children's homes (orphanages, homes for children with special problems, children with social problems at home ranging from disease to divorce to imprisonment, homes for the mentally or physically retarded), along with the Ministry of Public Health.
2. To prepare the personnel who work in the *circulos infantiles,* in two ways:
   (a) advanced training for present workers (those who began before the new schools were set up) and
   (b) formation and training of new workers.
3. The Children's Institute is responsible for carrying out research concerning all aspects of child development up to the age of five. It coordinates all related organizations and institutions with professionals of various specialties, pedagogy, biology, psychology, sociology, anthropology, pediatrics, etc.

LEARNING HOW TO TEACH NEW PEOPLE

If the *circulo* workers were to raise a new, socialist generation they themselves must be "new people," with the characteristics described by Che at least a goal, if not an accomplished fact. To carry this out, new schools for educators (*Escuelas de Educadoras*) were built in Havana, Las Villas and Oriente provinces.

The Schools for Educadoras began in 1970, open to young women with an eighth grade education.* Most of the students are fourteen to eighteen years of age, and follow a program that is a combination of basic high school and specialized vocational training. Although some women up to the age of twenty-five, who were previously forced to interrupt their education are enrolled in the schools, the preference is for younger women to work with young children. Young women with more than an eighth grade education can attend, beginning at a higher level, and attending special seminars in addition to the regular program.

The high school courses include mathematics, Spanish literature and expressive reading, physics, history, chemistry, biology, geography and political education. In addition to this there are cultural education courses such as art, music, dance and gymnastics. They also study health and hygiene (i.e., bodily functions) and food and nutrition.

Pedagological study includes child psychology, pedagogy, and methodology of teaching math, science and artistic expression. Examples of what they are taught in these various "methodology" courses are:

— in math, how to develop notions of size and space in three, four or five year olds;

— in science, stress on teaching the children to know their environment through games and stories. They try especially to enable the educators to answer questions about "why does this do that?" Taking care of plants and animals is one of the approaches taught in this section.

— in education, they learn about children's literature, including adaptation of stories for children of different ages; how to ask questions; to accompany a story with pictures or objects appropriate

---

*Although the beginnings of a powerful women's movement which was to alter radically Cuban consciousness about men's and women's roles was already in its infancy in 1970, tradition combined with Cuba's unique economic situation still meant no one was yet seriously considering men for this work. Some of the Institute workers I spoke to in 1973, however, did express concern about the small number of men working with the young children, and indicated they hoped it would soon be possible to have male teachers in the *círculos*.

to each age group so the children can understand and be interested in the story.

The students do manual work, and learn how to teach children to perform simple manual work such as gardening. Teaching work as an integral part of the children's lives will become one of the important roles of the women building the new generation.

Che, the man and the symbol, is taught as a central figure in many *educadora* classes. He is used to introduce basic political concepts, to talk about Latin America, and to point out the characteristics of Che — collectivity, selflessness, internationalism — which they will hope to pass on to the children. The teachers, in their turn, use Che as a frequent example when talking to the children.

Each year of the four-year course the student increases her links with the childcare center. During the first year she spends one week at the *círculo,* observing, seeing how it functions, helping with cleaning up, but not working as an educator.

During the second year she spends one week of each semester at the *círculo.* She begins to make observations based on the psychology and pedagogy she has learned. She begins to carry out some tasks.

Che Guevara with family and neighbor children.

In the third year she spends one month of directed teaching practice each semester, and begins working directly with the children, applying what she has learned in school. She is in turn observed by the women of the *círculo infantil* and by her professors.

In the fourth year she works in the *círculo* the whole year. She is responsible for a group of children, and directs their activities. This is still a program of directed studies, and she has weekly meetings on Saturdays to discuss questions arising out of her work, special problems, and ways to improve her work. During this year she also learns to familiarize herself with the various equipment she'll use in her work, and how to lead the children in garden work.

During all the four years the majority of students live in dormitories at the school. But the similarity to American college students ends there. Rather than leading a cloistered life while acquiring an education, Cuban students are encouraged always to combine practice with theory, work with study. An *educadora* does not begin putting into practice what she knows about childcare when she graduates; she combines practical work experience with her studies.

I asked Hilda and Angela, two *compañeras* from the Children's Institute if there weren't at times conflicts between the older, more traditional and less-educated *asistentes* and the new, young, theoretically trained *educadoras*. They said no such conflicts had arisen nor did they expect them. "The older women are very dedicated to their work and to the Revolution," one explained, "and are very willing to accept new concepts taught by the Revolution." "Besides," added the other, "they can usually understand and agree with the new concepts." She gave the example of the changing concept of the man's role in the house. "A few years ago, little boys were discouraged from playing with household and kitchen toys in the *círculo,* because the *asistentes* thought these were 'girls' toys'. But that idea is changing in the society as a whole; as more and more women work, men are expected to share in some of the housework. So when the *educadoras* suggest that the boys can play with these toys, the *asistentes* agree, because they don't see a conflict in the role of a boy playacting that he's the father in the household, doing his share of the work. But before they would have thought that he was playing the mother."

I asked the *compañeras* what they considered the most essential aspect of the training the *educadoras* received. After much thought they told me: "Developing in the *educadoras* the ability to answer questions in a revolutionary way, and to set a revolutionary example for the children."

ENOUGH FOR ALL

From a small beginning, when an underdeveloped, newly-liberated Cuba was struggling to get enough facilities and staff to care for some of the country's children, the revolution in childcare has come a long way. By 1973 childcare was provided for over fifty thousand children from forty-five days to five years old, with three adults caring for every twenty-five children. Cuba, which had no public childcare before the Revolution, now spends a larger percentage of its national wealth on childcare than almost any other country in the world. Its goal for 1980 is completion of *círculo infantil* facilities for one hundred fifty thousand children. By comparison, in the United States only six states provide some form of support for pre-kindergarten programs, and only eight states require school districts to offer kindergarten to all who want it! (Federal and state-funded childcare has been cut back drastically as the economic recession has continued through the 1970s.) The total population of New York City is approximately the same as that of Cuba — nine million — but in New York only eighteen thousand children were enrolled in daycare programs at the start of the seventies, and even that small number has since been reduced. U.S. pre-schools do not provide the total care offered Cuban children: meals, clothing, shoes, complete preventive-medical and dental care, absolutely free, as well as pre-school education.

But Cuba still is far from reaching the goal it has set for itself. Despite the huge resources put into the program and the impressive enrollment figures compared to the United States, less than 10 percent of the women who wanted to work and enroll their children in *círculos* were able to do so in 1973. The Children's Institute expected to have staffed facilities for all of the women waiting by 1978 — but by this time, they added, hopefully many more women would want to be incorporated into the productive workforce. Because there is still a limited number of childcare centers, they are available only to the children of working parents who have no one else to care for them. In the more distant future, however — as Cuba succeeds in its battle against underdevelopment — they hope to have enough *círculos* for *all* children, whether or not their mothers work. This represents a focus on the childcare center as the primary agent for creating the "New Man" in Cuba, above and beyond its role of liberating the mother to work and study (although it is still hoped that eventually all women will be working or studying).

The focus on the childcare center as a place to educate and mold new generations, rather than to function simply as a caretaking facility was made evident in the struggle that took place over the development of various alternative forms of childcare centers in the late 1960s and early 1970s.

The initial form of childcare center was the *círculo infantil,* which was designed to provide complete health and nutritional care as well as developmental programs for infants and educational activities for pre-school youngsters.

Later, a secondary, more limited type of childcare was offered for older pre-school children. The new centers were known as *jardines infantiles.* The idea for the *jardines* came, I think, from a variety of sources. First, it was obvious that there simply weren't enough facilities for fully equipped and fully staffed *círculos infantiles* to meet the ever growing demand. The *jardines* circumvented this problem by using more minimal facilities and staff. In general, the *jardines* were operated in a small park, with a playhouse for eating, napping and some indoor games. Two women watched approximately twenty to thirty children who spent their time in more or less free play. The adults were there to see that the children shared the toys, to give them ideas for new games or activities, and to supervise their meals and naps and keep them clean.

The *jardines* did not care for infants, since they did not have the staff, facilities or hygienic conditions required. Although children received periodic check-ups, there was no full-time medical staff, nor a complete program of vaccinations and preventive medicine as is conducted in the *círculos.* There were also no structured learning activities.

To some people — including several Western osbservers — this lack of structured activity was in fact a blessing. To them, the *jardines* represented a way of letting children have freer expression

Collective living begins in the *corrales.*

in a less structured environment than the *círculos,* where all activity
except the free play periods is directed. Some parents and educators
felt that not all children adapt equally well to the more structured
environment of the childcare centers, and looked to the *jardines* as
an alternative. Queens College, New York, Professor of Education
Marvin Leiner, who spent a year observing the *círculos* and *jardines*
in 1969, went further to argue that the unstructured environment of
the *jardines* was more conducive to fostering the free and creative
thinking necessary to revolutionaries, and found the *círculos* re-
pressive in this regard.

But Leiner was forced to admit that most of the parents and
educators who advocated the "free play" policy of the *jardines*
came — as he did — from the former professional and upper middle
classes. Some of the aspects he most disliked — structured learning,
emphasis on cleanliness and hygiene, etc. — were those that found
strong support among the masses of working-class parents whose
children attended the *círculos.*

Leiner and other "progressive" educators have raised the question,
"Why does a three- or four-year-old need to know how to read
and write?" A broader look at Cuban society, the underdevelop-

ment and scarcity of teaching personnel, would provide them with the answer. Fifteen and sixteen-year-olds are teaching school full-time. Does Leiner really need to ask, given this situation, why Cubans are anxious to prepare their youngsters to acquire as many skills as possible, at the earliest possible date? The children in the *circulos* do not, of course, learn to read and write like first or second graders. What they are given are the basic skills which will enable them to move faster into this kind of learning when they enter the regular school system. Given the years of backwardness Cuba has had to overcome to give its population a decent standard of living, it's not really so surprising that the majority of the parents prefer this kind of directed learning to four or five years of "free play" — an indulgence that can really only be afforded by the wealthier sectors of an affluent society.

I think it is fundamentally mistaken to view Cuban childcare in isolation from the rest of the revolutionary and educational process. The fact that pre-school children in Cuba learn to develop a strong sense of order and internal discipline is what enables them to be given so much responsibility as soon as they reach primary school. Children who have simply engaged in "free play" the first five years of their life may, perhaps, be very "creative," but they are unlikely to be handed the reins of a mass children's organization and be told: "Here, this is yours. You can lead and organize. You can set out your own goals, analyze your own work." It is this leadership that is developed in the children during their primary school years, I believe, that enables the adult leaders of the Revolution to have confidence in the youth taking over and maintaining and developing the revolutionary tradition. Yet this would be impossible without the basis laid in the childcare centers.

The childcare centers were created to aid working-class women in a working-class society. Given the shortage of resources and labor, it might have been tempting for the Revolutionary government to provide additional childcare by increasing the number of *jardines.* But this would have negated the other, and equally important purpose of the childcare centers: the formation of children who would take part in the building of this new society. The leaders of the Women's Federation, the *círculos infantiles,* and the revolutionary

*See Jonathan Kozol's *Free School* for the limitations of non-structured schooling on poor children in an affluent society.

government made the decision that this could best be done under the conditions provided by the *círculos*. In 1971 they began to phase out the *jardines*, incorporating them into the *círculos* program. Some aspects of the *jardines* — such as inter-aging and more free play periods — became part of the *círculos* program. But directed activities and directed learning remained dominant.

By 1975, Cuba boasted a total of 652 childcare centers — with an enrollment of 54,382 children of 49,805 working mothers. Under an ambitious plan now in operation, a minimum of four hundred new *círculos* are to be built by 1980—when the projected enrollment will be one hundred sixty thousand children of over a hundred thousand working mothers.

GLIMPSING THE CIRCULOS

Having learned the basic goals of the childcare program, its historical development, and the preparation of its personnel, I next wanted to find out how these goals are put into practice. Two other *compañeras* from the Children's Institute — Haydee and Elda — took me to several childcare centers in Havana province, then put me in contact with others in Oriente. The *círculos* I visited included ones in the city, in the suburbs, and in a remote fishing village. All of them provided the same clean, colorful facilities, the same educational programs, the same medical care for the children. Yet each one was different, each center had its own "personality." I began to see what Clementina Serra meant when she talked about creating unique individuals within a collectivity.

My talks with the directors, *educadoras*, nurses and *asistentes* at the various *círculos* provided a picture of daily life at the childcare centers.

One childcare worker told me: "When children are brought to the *círculo* as infants, they adapt to the patterns of life and behavior here as they grow. But when a new child is brought in at two, three or four years — like Manolito over there — they bring all their old habits from home, and have a lot of adapting to do." She had motioned to a little boy who looked about two and a half years old, and had his thumb firmly fixed in his mouth. "The new arrivals like Manolito," she went on, "are generally the only child, or the youngest child in the family. In either case, they are used to having everything given to them. When Manolito first came here, we didn't try to change him immediately. His mother accompanied him for the first few days, until he was used to the place.

"At first he just spent an hour or so here: getting to see the house and grounds, the people who work here and the other children. He didn't share in any of the collective activities like lunch or snacks.

"His mother stopped coming after the first few days, but even then we let him bring his favorite toy or blanket from home. This is only his second week here. New children can wear their own clothes, have their own bottle or pacifier. We always accede to the children's wish to cling to something familiar from home in the beginning."

The woman motioned to little Manolito, who was now sitting in a circle with other toddlers of his age, playing some kind of game. His thumb was forgotten as he clapped his hands with the other children. "As the child begins to adapt to the group, he begins taking part in collective activities. Then we slowly remove the things that he's brought from home, until finally he doesn't bring any. Manolito doesn't bring anything from home anymore, although as you see he still sucks his thumb sometimes when he feels a little insecure.

"He's already being socialized by his interaction with the group of children his own age, and with the *asistentes* and *educatoras*. Collective games like the one he's playing, and the sharing of toys, is an important first step in this process."

Not all children who enter the *círculos* have to overcome old habits from home. Some infants begin their life in the childcare centers when they are only forty-five days old. The youngest infants are cared for in a separate room, each in his/her own crib, each fed separately by the *asistentes'* who wear hygienic masks and gowns. When the babies are a little older, they may be put in playpens in a room full of other children. In a sense these babies' socialization begins as soon as they enter the *círculo,* for they can see and hear the presence of other babies, being cared for just as they are cared for.

The real socialization/collectivization begins when the infants are old enough to sit, stand and/or crawl. At that age they are put in the *corrales.* A *corral* is a large playpen, the length of a small room, made of wood and raised from the floor on wooden legs, so the children are looking out at the world, not up at it. The *corral* isn't a place to put children to get them out of the way. It is where they begin learning to develop their visual, manual, motor and verbal abilities, and to begin interacting with other children as well as adults.

For instance, an *asistente* or *educadora* will say to a child in the *corral*: "Pepito, bring me the ball." When pepito has learned this, through repetition and trial and error, he is told: Give the ball to Carmen." If Pepito succeeds at giving the ball to Carmen, Carmen is subsequently asked to give it back to Pepito. The children very soon begin to learn to play together with the ball and other toys.

A number of other such games are devised, some using bells, flutes or other instruments to teach the infants to look for and identify sounds. As the babies get older, and learn to walk, they are encouraged to walk up and down a ramp leading into the *corral.*

At this stage, all activities are collective: bathing, changing, napping, even eating. The children old enough to sit up by themselves, but not old enough to feed themselves, are put in double feeding tables. When they can feed themselves, the children are fed at long tables in the dining room.

There is heavy emphasis on hygiene at every level in the *círculo,* but especially so for the infants and toddlers. Infant toys are always washable, so they can be cleaned after a child has placed the toy in

Eating is a shared experience at the double feeding table.

his or her mouth, and before another child does so. All items that can be boiled are sterilized regularly. All children are bathed every day.

The emphasis on hygiene in the *círculo* is accompanied by teaching the importance of cleanliness to the children and by educational sessions for the parents. (This is true of nutrition, too.) Before the Revolution very few Cuban parents knew anything about hygiene or nutrition. In rural and city slum areas, they also seldom had proper facilities to put this knowledge into practice. Very few homes had running water; almost none had hot water or sanitary toilet and bathing areas. The diseases that destroyed the lives of so many infants and young children could often be attributed to these lacks, along with improper diet. The *círculos* saw it as part of their function to provide for the immediate hygienic and nutritional needs of the children, and teach the parents who had the means to do so to apply this in the home as well. The more long-range goal of the Revolution was to see that all families did have the proper conditions for meeting their children's nutritional and hygienic needs.

When children are big enough to leave the *corrales* they begin playing games with other children, in play areas inside and outside the house. They learn to put away their toys as soon as they can walk, to dress and undress themselves by age three. Sometimes they are aided in this by playing games which involve buttoning and unbuttoning, opening and closing things.

Toddlers learn to use clay, paint, listen to music (and dance if they wish), and work in the gardens, first watering and pulling weeds, later doing all the work of the garden.

On a typical day, after breakfast the children go out to play together in groups. Interpersonal (one-to-one) play generally begins around age three, but younger children are often seen imitating the older ones in this. Most of the games are aimed at muscular development, but many are also aimed at developing a collective spirit. The children are generally grouped according to age, with groups of up to ten children playing for twenty or thirty minutes in one game area. Groups of different ages get together to play. Although they do this naturally on their own, the practice is encouraged by the *educadoras* and *asistentes*, so that the younger children will learn language, habits and attitudes from the older ones. When young children have older brothers or sisters whom they want to follow or stay with in the *círculo*, this is permitted. Because of this interaction it is not unusual to see one-to-one play occur among children as young as eighteen months to two years old.

As the children get older there is greater emphasis on learning through games and other creative activities. The *círculos* follow a weekly program prepared by the National Direction of *Círculos Infantiles* and the Children's Institute. There are specific activities for each day and each week for thirty-five weeks. The *asistentes* or *educadoras* are encouraged to try to follow the schedule as closely as possible, and review the week's activities each Saturday. The women know what the children are supposed to learn in a given period; if the children do not seem to have a good grasp of that material, the *educadora* or *asistente* will repeat it.

Many of these activities are aimed at developing verbal skills. Most common is storytelling. This is also aimed at developing certain attitudes and habits in the children. Very young children might be told a story about an animal, a flower, or a person. Through the story they are taught what care this object needs, where it lives, what it does, and what characteristics it has. Puzzles, poems, songs, rhymes and word games are used in the same way.

Adivinanzas is another game aimed at developing verbal skills. The *educadora* will say to the children: "It bathes me . . . I drink it . . . it's good for plants . . . What is it?" The children guess water. If the children have a hard time guessing, more clues are given. In this way mental as well as verbal development is stimulated.

Puppets and play-acting are also used to help children develop verbal skills. Two or three children talk via the puppets, making up their own dialogue. Often the children themselves are dressed up in costumes.

Some games are always aimed at getting the children to know each other. In a *círculo* outside of Havana I watched and listened to three- and four-year-olds playing a name-game "Who ate the cake?" The rhythmic chanting was a close approximation of "Who ate the cake?" "Tony," "Who me?" "Yes you." "Couldn't be." "Then who?" "Patricia . . . " I was especially struck by this game because I rememberd playing it as a child, and more recently hearing a group of nine- and ten-year-olds in California play it. The difference was that we didn't use names — we used numbers. "Who stole the cookies from the cookie jar?" "Number one." "Who me?" "Yes you." "Couldn't be." "Then who?" "Number two . . . " I wondered whether children who played games with names didn't have a different view of life and people from ones who learned to call each other by numbers.

Through games children begin learning political consciousness, collectivism, internationalism, love of work and love of country.

A shortage of supplies has meant that *asistentes* and *educadoras* have constantly been "inventing" ways to make new toys and games for children. To teach colors, cardboard tubing was used. Each tube was fashioned into the figure of a person, painted a different color. Children would use the tubes like dolls or hand-puppets, having dialogues between Mr. Blue and Ms. Red, between Dr. Yellow and Plant Manager Green, etc.

Originally, each *círculo* had to scrounge for whatever materials it could find, or those that the parents or *padrinos** could supply. Now, each regional area has a unit which prepares the various toys, games and other materials used by the *círculos*. Many of these are made by simply utilizing scrap material, too. But they are distributed equally to all the childcare centers. In the fishing village of Batabanó I saw many of the same toys and games as those I saw in the suburbs of Havana.

Learning in the *círculos* includes hygiene and bodily functions. The children are taught a healthy respect for bathing and cleanliness. Many childcare centers in the United States will not take children before they are toilet trained. In the Cuban *círculos* toilet training is considered just one more part of the learning process. It generally begins when the child is between eighteen months and two years old. The women from the Children's Institute told me there is a marked tendency for the younger children in the *círculo* naturally to imitate the older ones. When they begin to talk, they will often start asking to "go make peepee or caca." Haydee noted with a smile that sometimes the toddlers will ask to "go" even when they don't really have to — just because they want to be doing what the big kids do.

In learning table habits the influence of the older children is also

---

*Padrinos is a term used to denote a work center, neighborhood committee, or section of the Women's Federation which sponsors each *círculo*. *Padrinos* take part in many activities at the centers and provide material assistence when needed.

visible. Older children often teach the younger ones how to hold a spoon or fork.

Overall, the *círculos* manage to overcome whatever problems they encounter. The dining areas are quiet, orderly, happy places. You never see children throwing food — although you do sometimes see children "helping themselves" off other children's plates. In this case the *asistentes* only intervene to make sure the other child is getting enough to eat and giving up his/her portion willingly.

Up to this point, the nature of childcare in Cuba doesn't seem very different from that available in many other places, even in the United States. It is similar to such facilities in poorer communities of our country in that it has to deal with a scarcity of materials, and must improvise a lot. It differs from these in that there is national coordination in attempting to supply all the centers equally from this scarce supply. And it differs even more in that the really vital things: food, staff, and medical care, clothing — are provided for all the children at all *círculos;* and all children of working parents *can* attend, free of charge — limited only by the temporary lack of facilities and trained personnel. Providing such care is seen as a national priority.

The teaching of verbal and motor skills is basically the same as that practiced around the world.

What is different is the way the children are socialized, the way they are taught to relate to work, to each other, and to other peoples of the world. The political and social consciousness of Cuban children begins in the childcare centers.

LIVING COLLECTIVELY

At first I thought Cuban children learned their distinctive behavior in the schools. After spending time in the *círculos infantiles* and with the people from the Children's Institute, I realized that this socialization takes place partly in the home and largely in the childcare centers. Collective consciousness begins the moment an infant or toddler is introduced to the childcare center. For those who begin at forty-five days, their earliest recollection is a sharing of experiences: other babies are napping, eating, being bathed, changed and cuddled all around them every day. Each stage of their development — learning to hold toys, learning to crawl, learning to sit up, to eat — is accompanied by other children learning to do the same things at the same time, and other older children who are already doing those things.

For children introduced to the *círculo* at a later stage, the process of collectivization is more gradual since, as has been pointed out, they often have to overcome the habits and attitudes of being an only or youngest child at home. If the child does not yet walk, his/her first experience of living together with other children may be in the *corral*. A toddler entering the *círculo* may learn that living with other children means playing games with them, eating with them, taking naps or having snacks when they do.

But it is not just the fact of having a lot of children cared for collectively that develops their collective consciousness. Children in nursery schools — even progressive ones — in this country do not come out so free of aggressive competitiveness and selfishness as the children in the Cuban *círculos* do. There are specific techniques — learning experiences, games, attitudes and examples of the teachers — which foster this collectivism.

One of these is the collective birthday party. The birthday of every child in the center is celebrated — together with the birthday of every other child born in that month. Clementina Serra described the collective birthdays: "Each month, in each *círculo,* we celebrate the birthdays of all the children born in that month. The birthday party is held at the *círculo,* with the participation of the parents, who make cake and bring sweets and ice cream. There is a special meal that day. Sometimes we bring clowns; other times older children sing; other times we bring actors. This is very good and the parents like it a lot because the children learn to collectivize their own birthday parties.''

The state provides for birthday parties for children not in *círculos*, too. All scarce items — including many foods — are controlled by ration cards known as *libretas,* by which a family can purchase those items allotted to it in a given time period. The *libreta* takes into consideration children's birthdays, however; and on those days the parents can buy party decorations, a big cake and beverages — soda and beer or *malta* — enough for family, friends and neighbors. They can also reserve sections of the public parks, and have clowns come entertain. Although the extended family and all the neighbors generally join in the festivities, these birthdays are not collective in the way the children's in the *círculos* are, because all the festivities are for one child.

Attempts at collectivization in the *círculos* aren't just matters of convenience — the simplest way to care for large numbers of children. As Clementina Serra explained: ''The collective life of the child among other children is very important. The child who is raised alone at home, an only child, misses something. It's hard to raise an only child properly. In a larger family the collective of other little brothers and sisters helps in the formation of each child. In the *círculos,* living with other children, black and white, the child learns how to work together with them, to play with toys without breaking them, and to share them. If there's only one ball, it has to be shared.''

Traveling to the *círculos* with the *compañeras* from the Children's Institute I began to see how this desire to collectivize the life of the children is put into practice. When we saw babies in the *corrales,* they explained the functions of the *corrales* as an early experience in living and playing together. We saw that *asistentes* and *educadoras* not only taught the babies in the *corrales* how to pick up toys, but how to share them with the other babies. One of the women told me, ''You see a great deal of affection and concern for each other among the children in the *corrales.* If Sarita cries, Pedro will pat her head and try to console her. If Eddy hits Carmen, and Carmen doesn't hit him back, some other child will respond, either by hugging Carmen, or protesting. Very small infants are generally in separate cribs or playpens, but they can begin in the *corrales* as early as two months.''

Another form of early socialization is the double feeding table. As soon as the child can sit up — generally around eight months — s/he is placed in the double feeding table. This is an oblong table with cut-outs at either end with seats for children. The *asistente* sits along the side halfway between the two children and feeds first one, then the other, then the first. Eating in that way becomes a collective activity. Each child knows s/he has to wait for the other to get a spoonful before s/he gets his/her next spoonful. As with everything else, there are regular feeding schedules: those fed earliest at the first meal of the day are fed earliest throughout the day, so they don't start crying from hunger while others are being fed.

Taking baths is done collectively too, with some children getting undressed while others are bathing and still others are getting dried and dressed.

But in 1973, this collectivity did not yet extend between the sexes. The reason, as in so many other things, had something to do with underdevelopment: the educational and cultural backward-ness that the Revolution inherited along with economic scarcity. When the American writer Margaret Randall was talking to *círculos* director Clementina Serra, she was told that bathing was the only activity *not* shared by boys and girls. "Why not?" asked Margaret. "Because then the children would begin asking questions," was the response. "But I would think that would be a good idea!" exclaimed Margaret. "Then the children could learn about those things natu-rally." "It would be a good idea," agreed Clementina Serra, "if we had the kind of teachers who could answer their questions."

When Margaret told me this story, I realized how much under-standing a writer from an "advanced" country like the United States had to bring to a study of Cuba. Now that it was pointed out, I could envision the kind of red-faced embarrassment a woman from the countryside, with almost no formal schooling, would feel when confronted with such a question. Certainly no one would have dis-cussed a topic such as male and female genitals during her childhood. By 1975, the first teachers were graduating from the four-year childcare teacher training schools. Today, hopefully, the childcare workers are prepared to answer such questions.

Games provide one of the best sources of socialization for chil-dren. A child is first taught how to grasp and play with a ball; then how to play with another child, then with larger groups so they can

begin collective games. Even apparently individual play — like working with clay, or painting — becomes a collective activity in the *círculos.* Each child makes whatever s/he wants. Afterwards there is a collective discussion about what the children have made, which the children think are best, and why. Then the children who did the "best" explain how they made them. Later, children who did "well" are mixed with children who did not do so well. The *asistentes* try never to have tables with all children who did well, or all who did not. There is great emphasis on children learning from each other and helping each other.

Children are rewarded by being praised for good work, and chosen as "outstanding" in that activity. The *directora* of one *círculo* explained that children who do exceptionally well are kept from feeling elitist by the emphasis on sharing skills and knowledge and helping each other and by varying activity so everyone has a chance to be chosen as "outstanding." *Asistentes* or *educadoras* work especially with children who don't seem to excel in any activity. If they notice some child has not been chosen *destacado* for some time, they will switch to some activity that they know s/he does well in. At the same time, they praise children more for helping others to learn than they do for the mere fact of being *destacado*.

Just as children analyze and praise each other's work and activities, they also criticize one another. When Pedro told the teacher: "Raulito threw some clay out the window" he wasn't regarded by the others as a little snitch. Criticism is done openly and publicly, and children feel it is their responsibility to correct the behavior of one of their group who is misbehaving, just as it is their responsibility to help teach someone who is learning slowly. This becomes especially important later on in school, and sets the groundwork for the spirit of emulation — cooperative, non-competitive attempts to do the best work — among adult workers.

Many of the play areas in the *círculos* are designed to encourage group play. In one childcare center we saw different areas of the two-story house set up as a hairdresser (or barber shop), a clinic, a doll house, and for a kind of water game. Each area game required two or more people to play.

Pulling weeds is fun, yet gives a sense of accomplishment.

The children are very early taught a sense of collective responsibility for their childcare center. "This is your center, you should help keep it clean and in good repair" seems to be an attitude prevalent throughout the *círculos.* Children learn to put away their clothes and playthings in their own cubby holes, or in the areas where they are kept, as soon as they learn to walk! If the center is for everybody, everybody shares in its pleasures, and everybody shares in its work.

WORKING CHILDREN IN A WORKING COUNTRY

Equally important as the sense of collectivity in the socialization process of children in Cuba is the love of work, and respect for working people. The love for work also begins in the *círculos.* The need for this is inherent in the type of society Cuba is trying to build and the state of its economic development.

The place to begin, of course, is at the beginning. Clementina Serra asserts: "Children should learn love of work, not have the idea that they've got to have someone to sew for them, be their maids, take care of them. The children have to learn to do these things for themselves and to be able to help the others."

In the new society Cuba hopes to break down the ancient divisions between manual and intellectual labor by encouraging all people to learn and perform a variety of skills and trades, until all of the more odious jobs are eliminated by mechanization. They want to create integral human beings, children who relate to the food they eat as the producers of that food. The childcare centers and the schools play a key role in developing this positive attitude towards work. The children who start attending the *círculos* at three or four years of age bring some of these attitudes with them. They learn it first from their parents, who at this stage must be workers in order for the children to be enrolled in the *círculo.* They also see the love of work and respect for working people in the society around them: on TV, in movies, on billboards, at neighborhood meetings. They see their parents, relatives and neighbors do voluntary work on weekends, and know that the highest praise in Cuban society goes to the best workers.

The *circulos* try to perpetuate and develop these attitudes in the children systematically in games and educational activities. In most *círculos* the children have a small garden plot. The children plant, weed, water and harvest the vegetables and fruits which they will later eat. In their daily activities, the children learn to clean up after themselves and put things away.

Love of work is also incorporated in the teaching of other verbal and motor skills. In the series of weekly educational materials distributed to all the *círculos* by the Children's Institute are picture cards and puzzles involving work and workers. One learning game shows a picture of a carpenter with a saw, then another picture of the carpenter without the saw. The children are to guess what tool is missing; in this way they learn the carpenter's tool, and can be led naturally into a discussion of what the carpenter does. This series of pictures features all different kinds of work common in Cuba.

The most direct contact with the workers outside their own center is through the *padrinos*. Every childcare center is *apadrinado* (sponsored) by a work center. The men and/or women of the work center "adopt" the *círculo*; they help provide scarce resources, build things for the center, visit the children on collective birthdays and other holidays. The children are taken to visit their *padrinos'* work centers, where the workers and teachers talk to them about how the work from the place relates to their lives. For instance, in a furniture factory the workers will show the children how to make a chair. They will explain that this chair is like one the children will sit on at home or in the *círculo,* or in school when they are bigger. They explain how and why the children should care for the chair. In this way children are taught to respect what the workers do.

I visited the remote village of Batabanó, where the childcare center is, as might be expected, sponsored by the fishing combine, the town's main industry. Most of the children of this *círculo* know that their fathers are fishermen, and their mothers work at the combine which treats and preserves various kinds of sea food, crustaceans, etc. Although this *círculo* is located at the far end of Havana province, it looks like the ones in the city: a large, rambling, airy and cheerful structure, with facilities for infants, toddlers and pre-schoolers, including a large vegetable garden. But the main industry of this village permeates the *círculo,* and lets you know you are in a fishing town in a number of ways. When you walk into one

Fishing is a way of life.

room, you see crayon drawings that the children did — a large number of them featuring fishing boats of assorted sizes and colors. Out in the play-yard, children are scrambling over and around a wood and net fishing boat built by their *padrinos*. On the walls and on the shelves you can see strange and interesting objects that the fishermen found in the sea and brought to the *círculo* to show the children. For these children, fishing isn't something they will learn about in school; it's a way of life.

Cuban children are made aware of workers in a way they never are in the United States. Hilda and Angela of the Children's Institute commented that when children have a collective birthday, they see that the kitchen workers — the people who prepare and serve their meals — are taking part in this collective birthday by preparing a special meal, a cake, etc. When they see workers bringing supplies into the *círculo*, they don't take this for granted, but are encouraged to see these workers as their friends, people whose work is helping them.

The ideas and attitudes the children see and hear all around them are concretized by their teachers. The *educadoras* talk to the children about what work their parents do; they ask if they went out to do voluntary work over the weekend; they tell them about the National Heroes of Labor. This is very deeply ingrained in the consciousness of the young women who are educating the children. In one *círculo* I asked how children are taught about heroes. I was thinking of guerrilla and independence fighters, such as José Martí, Antonio Maceo, Che Guevara, etc. But in Cuba the term "heroes" today means *work* heroes, so the young *educadora* responded: "The children know their parents work, do militia duty, etc. So here we teach them that some people do extra work, such as cutting cane, and they are work heroes. On May 1, Workers Day, we explain that those men and women on the platform with Fidel are the most distinguished workers in the country."

It was only when I specifically asked about other kinds of heroes (who are more often referred to as "martyrs" in Cuba) that she added: "Those who fought in liberation struggles are also heroes. We teach the children that these are people just like us who have made an extra effort."

When children indicate that their parents went out to do voluntary work over the weekend, the *educadoras* ask them if they know what kind of work they did, and why. Sometimes they relate it to the work the children do themselves in their garden.

POLITICALLY CONSCIOUS FOUR YEAR OLDS

Cubans as a whole (even those who have left the country, oddly enough) are a fiercely patriotic people. The very youngest children know something about the history of their country, the heroes and martyrs, and that Cuba is a socialist country "where there is no privilege — everybody is treated the same." Children are taught to love their flag, and the men and women who have fought and died to make Cuba free. Clementina Serra observed: "In our society we educate children about those who have given their lives for the Revolution, first to be free from Spain and then from imperialism. We do this according to the age of the children, sometimes through songs, sometimes through drawings. Of course, we're still limited in materials, but we're working on this. We substitute one thing for another. If we don't have paints or brushes, we make them ourselves."

In the childcare centers the children are taught, according to their age group, a little about the political history of their country, through the use of symbols such as the flag, and historic dates, and heroes who have fallen, such as Maceo and Marti in the War of Indepence against Spain, and Camilo and Che from more modern times. They celebrate national holidays and learn what they are about. At one *circulo* they told me that on May Day the streets around the center are closed off and the children march in a May Day parade, just as the adults do. The children are dressed up as workers in various trades. In July, when the country celebrates its summer carnival, the children have their own week of carnival. For all holidays the children have their equivalent of what the adults are doing. This makes them feel important, and part of what is happening throughout the country.

Cuban children are made to feel that they are very special people. In the United States there is Mother's Day and Father's Day. Cuba celebrates Children's Day. Each year there is a week-long Children's Celebration (*Jornada de la Infancia*) in which children from the *círculos* and primary schools participate. One of the functions of these activities is to involve the children in the life of the country, and vice versa. The children do paintings, write poems, perform pageants, plays and folk-dances, go on outings and excursions. In 1973 the billboard seen throughout the country announcing the *Jornada de la Infancia* was a blow-up of a drawing done by a five-year-old boy. A gallery in downtown Havana featured paintings by the children; its opening was attended by the national press and members of the Cuban Central Committee, including Vilma Espín, head of the Women's Federation and the Children's Institute. Children preformed at a large downtown theatre (also attended by high-ranking government officials and international guests). In one of the skits, the children acted out parts of the July 26, 1953 assault on the Moncada.

Political education for Cuban children isn't just a matter of learning about history or current events — it involves creating in the children the kind of consciousness and characteristics the Revolution wants the future generations to have. Foremost in teaching this is the example of Che. The *educadoras* teach the children about Che's life; what he did, how hard he worked, what characteristics he possesed that the children may want to imitate. Older children in Cuba talk about Che all the time. Even the young ones are familiar with his face, know he fought to liberate Cuba, and died struggling to free other peoples in Latin America. Talking to children in any part of Cuba, the outstanding characteristics you learn about Che are his selflessness and his internationalism.

But Che is only the leading example of a number of internationalist fighters the children learn about. Another whom they speak about quite often is Tania (Tamara Bunke), a woman who was part of the revolutionary guerrilla band that fought and died with Che Guevara in Bolivia. For little girls, Tania, known as "the unforgettable guerrilla," is an especially important model for what they can aspire to as revolutionaries. Born in Argentina and raised in East Germany, Tania offered her services to the Cuban Revolution. There she lived and worked until she joined the guerrilla forces of Che Guevara and the Bolivian National Liberation Army (ELN) which was trying to free Latin America from neo-colonial domination. All Cuban children sing, chant or pledge "We shall be like Che." But I've known many little girls who have added, "Or like Tania."

THE LITTLEST INTERNATIONALISTS

Because love of freedom is the underlying concept on which patriotism is taught to Cuban children, the children in the *círculos* are taught to love all the peoples of the world, and to seek their freedom. In the *círculos* when the children learn about their flag, which represents the Cuban people, they are also taught that the flags of different countries represent the people of those countries, people who are struggling (as in Vietnam, Laos or Cambodia, or in Chile or Angola), people "who don't have what you have," people from socialist countries "who are our brothers and sisters." When a delegation from another country comes to visit the *círculo*, the children are all given flags of that country, and taught a little bit about the dress and customs of the people who live there.

Internationalism, like working class consciousness, is something that Cuban children grow up with. They see it all around them, on billboards, TV, in movies, in the songs they sing and in the stories they hear. In the *círculos* they play games like "The Children of the World" which encourage them to learn about other people. The songs they learn are often about Vietnam, or Chile, or another country in which Cuba is especially interested because of the struggle going on there.

When *educadoras* try to teach the children about internationalism, they do so in a very simplified way. "We teach them that they are children who live in this country, Cuba, and therefore they are Cubans. Other children like them live in other countries, they have different customs, clothes, music, food, flags, etc."

There are regular relations with various foreign embassies, and with children from other countries who are resident in Cuba. There is an exchange of dances, presentations and games, with an emphasis on getting to really know the people of other countries, to feel "they are just like me." In the "Children of the World" game the Cuban children portray children from other countries. "I'm from Mexico — I'm Mexican." The *educadoras* try not to go too deeply into the differences, but instead stress the aspect of "these are children just like you, with different clothes and language."

Many *círculos* are named after other countries, or martyrs from other countries, such as the *Círculo Infantil Vietnam Heróico*

(Heroic Vietnam). In this case, they learn more about that particular country or struggle. During my visits in 1971 and 1973 the children were learning about Vietnam, its history and its struggle. They were taught that another country was trying to take over its land and that the people were fighting to have the things the Cuban people have already won: *círculos,* food, clothes, houses. Later, the same reasons were given for Cuba's great effort in support of Angola's struggle against foreign intervention.

The children I saw often dressed up in the costume of other countries, with Vietnam again the favorite. Sometimes the children acted out a battle between the Vietnamese and U.S. soldiers. Other times they played at how the Vietnamese children went to school in caves, to avoid the bombs.

Because Cuba is a small country, ruled for centuries by foreign powers, and engaged in a battle for economic development following its successful liberation struggle, the Cuban people feel a very strong sense of identity with peoples around the world in similar situations. The friendship for the Vietnamese people which is transmitted to the children from the adults is a very natural one, and is emotional as much as intellectual. Perhaps that is why the children respond so eagerly.

Manifestación norteamericana
contra el imperialismo.
René

6

New Schools

"An educated people is a free people."
— José Martí

The childcare centers have been able to start the process of creating new people for the new society. They teach the children to live, play and work collectively. Children learn that things are produced through work; they go to workplaces and meet workers, so they learn to love and respect work and working people. By teaching the children the history of their country's struggles for independence, the *círculos* begin creating a love for their country among the children. And by extending this to other peoples, the *círculos* begin fostering a sense of internationalism.

This process has just begun when the children leave the childcare centers at five and six years of age. It must be continued in the schools if the children are to become the men and women Che dreamed about. But Cuba did not have an abundance of schools when the Revolution came to power. Education was simply not a priority of the Batista regime, and very little money was allocated to school buildings, teachers salaries, and educational materials. To go to school in those days you had to pay — tuition, books, papers, pencils and sometimes bribes. Most families in Cuba didn't have the money to buy shoes and proper clothes for their children, let alone pay the additional expenses of going to school.

Rural schools were almost nonexistent, with the exception of one-room schools in palm-roofed *bohíos,* taught by dedicated teachers who paid for the children's books and pencils — and sometimes their shoes and meals — out of their meager salaries. The expensive boarding schools were the only "alternative" for children in areas without schools.

The result of all this can be seen in the statistics. In 1959 two thirds of Cuban children did not attend school — either because they lacked money or clothes, or because there were no schools in their regions. Of those who attended, few got past the first three grades. Forced to drop out of school to work or beg, or simply because there wasn't enough money to send them, only one out of every twenty Cubans had a sixth-grade education before the Revolution. One out of four was totally illiterate (one out of three in the countryside).

The problem was not, oddly enough, lack of trained teachers. In that year twelve thousand teachers were unemployed — unable to teach the children, who so badly needed to learn — because the Batista government had been unwilling to pay them.

Cuba was not alone in this situation. Throughout Latin America children suffered the same fate at the hands of indifferent regimes. Fidel Castro described their plight in his Second Declaration of Havana in 1962:

> . . . . As to educational matters, it is infuriating to think of the depths of ignorance from which America suffers. While in the United States persons over fifteen have an average of eight or nine years of schooling, in the Latin America which they have plundered and harvested, this same age group averages less than one year's instruction. It is even more infuriating to learn that in some countries only 20 percent of children between five and fourteen are in school, while 60 percent are in school in those countries where the standard [of living] is higher. That is to say that over half of Latin America's children are not going to school.
>
> But the grief mounts as we discover that those in the first three grades comprise more than 80 percent of all who are enrolled, and that in the sixth grade the student body varies between six and twenty-two pupils of each hundred who had started out in the first. Even in those countries which believe they take good care of their children there is an average 73 percent loss between first and sixth grades. In Cuba it was 74 percent before the Revolution. In Colombia, with its "representative democracy" it was 78 percent. And if we look at the countryside, only 1 percent of children, under the best of circumstances, get as far as the fifth grade in schooling.

Upon investigating the causes of this disastrous absence from school, one reason explains it: the economy of misery. Lack of schools, lack of teachers, lack of family resources, child labor . . . . It all boils down to imperialism and its work of repression and retrogression.

The difference between Cuban children and those of the rest of Latin America is that, after 1959, they were able to escape the web of poverty, lack of education, and more poverty. The Revolution made education one of its primary goals.

Allocating ten times as much of its budget on education as was spent before the Revolution, Cuba was able to increase the number of schools by 500 percent in the first ten years of the Revolution. The number of teachers employed increased accordingly. One out of every three Cubans — children and adults — is now in school.

How did all this come about? It certainly wasn't easy for a country with scarce resources to provide educational facilities for millions of illiterate children and adults.

The first step was to put into practice the suggestion of Cuba's apostle of independence, José Martí, that fortresses be turned into schools. Batista's military garrisons and barracks were converted into schools. As North Americans and the handful of wealthy Cubans began to flee Cuba for Miami, accompanied by the gangsters and corrupt politicians of the Batista regime, palatial estates and luxurious suburban homes were left behind. The Revolution quickly converted these into schools. For the children who lived too far up in the mountains or in regions too remote to attend school, a number of these homes and fortresses were turned into school-cities where children receive room and board, as well as clothing, books, and all their education free. Most of the plush Havana suburb of Miramar became a school-city; so did the Moncada Fortress.

Urban workers with large families and low incomes — most of Cuba's workers — found that many of the non-boarding schools also helped ease the strain on family budgets by providing meals and school clothes for the children.

Not only were the schools free — they were open to everyone: blacks and mulattos as well as whites; girls as well as boys. The first step of making Cuba a society of equals had been taken.

Understanding that the future need would be even greater, some of the school-cities were dedicated to training more teachers. To be assured that the teachers would be prepared — like the doctors

— to go anywhere to teach, the first teacher-training institute was located high up in the Sierra Maestra mountains, where the young students lived a rugged life of work and study.

The path towards education for the new generation of Cubans had been laid out — but what of the millions of illiterate Cubans who were already past school age at the triumph of the Revolution, or those older children who would be half-grown before enough schools could be built for them, or whose families didn't want them to leave their mountain homes to go far away to school?

At first, volunteer teachers tried to resolve this problem, going off into the remote mountain areas, setting up schools, living and working with the mountain people. But when the Revolution made education a top priority, the counterrevolutionaries made schools and teachers a prime target for their attacks. Schools were burned and bombed, teachers were shot. When a black volunteer teacher named Conrado Benítez was killed in the Escambray Mountains, his death became a rallying point for bringing education to the whole island. One hundred thousand youngsters took a year off from school and formed the Conrado Benítez literacy brigades. Joining another one hundred fifty thousand adult teachers, they spread across all of Cuba, carrying their lanterns and alphabet books, and taught the forgotten *campesinos* and *guajiros* (mountain peasants) how to read and write.

The literacy brigades had to overcome many obstacles. First was the reluctance of many parents to let their children go off by themselves into remote areas — an understandable fear in any case, but especially so when counterrevolutionaries were trying to stifle all attempts at mass education. When one of the young literacy teachers, fifteen-year-old Manuel Ascunce Domenech, was killed by counterrevolutionaries, many feared that the parents would rush *en masse* to call their children back. But the literacy brigades remained firm.

Soon the literacy campaign had an even stronger test — this time a test of the whole Revolution to withstand armed attack. In April 1961 — when the first childcare center was inaugurated in Ciudad Libertad, and the first literacy brigades were spreading out through the mountains and farmlands — CIA-sponsored planes bombed military installations, airports and public buildings — including schools and the new childcare centers. The air attack was

Literacy Brigade.

quickly followed by an invasion of troops at Playa Girón — the Bay of Pigs. Armed, trained and financed by the CIA, these exile Cuban mercenaries hoped to establish a beachhead, declare themselves a "provisional government," and call for U.S. help in their "civil war" against the Revolutionary government.

The Revolution already needed every hand it could get to carry out its work in the fields of medicine, education, agriculture and industry. But for a few history-making days those hands had to reach out instead for guns to repel the armed invasion.

The invasion had, if anything, an opposite effect from what was intended. Deceived by their own self-interest and the lies of the CIA, the counterrevolutionaries came to Cuba believing the masses of people were so unhappy with the Revolutionary government that they would be quick to join the invaders in a popular uprising. Instead, they found the masses of people turned out to protect their Revolution. The Cuban people were not even slightly inclined to join their so-called "liberators." An insurmountable class difference separated them. Most of the people of Cuba had only known poverty, illiteracy and exploitation before. Most of the attackers came from the class that had exploited them. Of the men captured at Playa Girón, there were:

> 100 latifundists
> 24 large landowners
> 67 owners of extensive real estate holdings
> 112 wholesale dealers
> 194 former military personnel and agents of the
>   Batista tyranny
> 179 hustlers, "playboys," and gangsters
> 35 industrial magnates
> 112 lumpen elements, etc.

What the invading force hoped to personally gain of their former possessions included:

> Nearly 100,000 acres of land
> 9,666 apartment buildings and houses
> 70 industries
> 10 sugar mills
> 3 commercial banks
> 5 mines, and
> 12 cabarets, bars and various other properties.

The revelation of these official statistics made clear the social and economic composition of Cuba's enemies. The training and financing of this invasionary force by the United States also made clear to the Cuban people who their friends and enemies in the world community were. When the invasion was successfully repelled, and the last of the mercenaries captured, Fidel addressed a crowd of a million Cubans — among them many of the students who were teaching in the literacy brigades. For the first time the prime minister of the Revolutionary government described the Cuban Revolution as a *socialist* revolution. Pointing to the history of domination, exploitation and subversion by their imperialist neighbor to the north, culminating in this latest and most flagrant attack against Cuban sovereignty, Fidel concluded simply: "And that's why we are socialists."

The students who took part in the literacy brigades learned more than just who their enemies were that year — they came face to face with the hard reality of life in rural Cuba. Students from the cities had a chance to experience first-hand what life is like without roads, electricity, or direct communication with the "outside world." When they went into the mountains and rural plains areas, into the swamps and forests, they went to live with the people and to learn from them as well as to teach them. They lived in peasants' homes, went out to work with them in the fields during the day, and taught them to read and write at night, by lantern light. When they returned to their homes and schools at the end of the year, they had received a profound lesson in what the Revolution was all about — and how much there was left to do.

At the end of the year, too — despite the numerous obstacles set up by counterrevolutionary attacks — Cuba had become one of the first countries in the world to eliminate illiteracy almost totally.

QUANTITY AND QUALITY

The emphasis in the first years was on giving all children access to schools and teachers (a revolutionary concept in an underdeveloped country). Transitional measures had to be adopted to meet this sudden increase in demand for education. Many of the first schools were makeshift and inadequate. But they were an improvement over no schools at all.

In addition, there was a serious shortage of qualified teachers (aggravated by the thousands who left the country). Having always served the children of the wealthy, or frightened by tales of impending "communist atrocities," many, like the doctors, chose to join the wealthy industrialists and landowners in Miami. This problem was met — and is still being met — by the massive use of student teachers who are often just a few grades ahead of their pupils. As in the literacy campaign, bringing education to the people involved the masses of the people in the process. The slogan was: "If you know, teach, if you don't know, learn." The goal was to make the whole country "one big university."

The task of building schools, training teachers, and teaching an illiterate population to read and write was only part of the battle. The Cuban Revolution was concerned about the quality of education as well as the material and quantitative aspects of it. The rebels who fought at the Moncada and in the Sierra Maestra wanted to do away with the poverty and degradation that had filled the short lives of the

Cuban people under capitalism. But they wanted to do more than that. They wanted to create a new human being.

Che Guevara expressed it: "We must . . . with profound zeal . . . arrive finally at the conclusion that almost everything we thought and felt in that past period ought to be deposited in an archive, and a new type of human being be created. If each of us expends our maximum effort toward the perfection of that new man, it will be much easier for the people to create such a person and let that person be the example of the new Cuba."

The childcare centers begin the process of educating children in the example of Ernesto Che Guevara. The schools try to carry this goal to its fulfillment. Their job is to transform human beings, to raise political consciousness of a people whose consciousness had been penetrated and deformed by generations of U.S. imperialism, so that they can better understand and more fully participate in the revolutionary process.

The motto of Cuban school children is: "We shall be like Che." It is only natural that Che should be chosen as their example. He not only wrote and spoke of the ideals of Socialist Man, he embodied these ideals in his life and work. When Cuban teachers look for a model of hard work, of selflessness, of dedication, of discipline, of collectivity, and of true internationalism, they have only to look at the words and deeds of Ernesto Che Guevara, the Argentinian doctor who risked his life on numerous occasions for the Cuban people, and died fighting for the freedom of Bolivia and the Latin American continent.

If the schools were to take on the responsibility of transforming the consciousness of the new generations, it was not enough to simply build schools and staff them with teachers who had been trained and educated with the old consciousness, who would teach in the old way. In the old society private and Catholic schools were predominant; the public schools, as we have seen, were few in number, understaffed and undersupplied, as a direct result of government neglect and administrative corruption. (Cubans say a job in the Ministry of Education prior to the Revolution was a guarantee of a fat bank account from all the money allotted to the schools which these officials pocketed.) The nationalization of the schools was inevitable, and took place in 1961. This allowed the government to unify the school system throughout the country, as well as seeing to it that every child had access to education.

The structure of the educational system remains fairly simple. Children may attend childcare centers from forty-five days to four years of age. From four to six is pre-school, which may be conducted in the *círculo* or in the primary school. From first to sixth grade children attend primary school. This may be a normal, or National, school, which children attend from seven A.M.to five P.M., returning home for lunch. It may be a *semi-internado*, or semi-boarding school, in which the children receive lunch and sometimes other meals. Or it may be an *internado* or boarding school in which the children live all week, returning home to their families on weekends. The *internados* are considered scholarship schools, or *becas*, and the students are often referred to as *becados*.

After completing sixth grade, students go on to secondary school (*Escuela Secondaria Basica*) which may be normal, semi-boarding, or the new School in the Countryside. Since this period (from seventh to tenth grade) is considered very formative, the emphasis is on building more and more secondary schools in the countryside or near other work-sites where students can combine work with studies.

The equivalent of our high school is the pre-university, from eleventh to thirteenth grades, and then students may attend four- or five-year university programs. At the high school level (and sometimes earlier) students may elect to go to special technological, pedagogical, or vocational schools, or may be chosen for the Camilo Cienfuegos Military School or the Lenin (advanced science) Vocational School. There are also school shops for thirteen- to sixteen-year-olds who drop out of school and wish to learn a trade.

At every level there are also specialized schools for sports, the arts, and language, as well as schools for mentally or physically disabled children.

Description of the structural aspect of Cuban education — the number and kinds of schools, etc.— doesn't tell us how these new schools and new teachers prepare the new generation. For that we have to go beyond lists and numbers, visit the schools, and talk to the students. This is what I did between 1970 and 1973.

Probably the most thorough, overall picture I got of Cuban education came first, not from a Cuban child, but from a North American child named Gregory (nicknamed "Goyo") whom I met for the first time in late 1970, when he had been living in Cuba for about two years. Gregory was eleven years old at the time of this taped conversation. Goyo's remarks are particularly helpful because they present the point of view of an American child learning to adapt to the Cuban system, with a basis for comparison to other systems.

Here are Goyo's words in 1971:

My name is Gregory, I'm eleven years old, I'm a North American and I study in Cuba — I live in Cuba. I want to talk about the *beca* where I study.

The *beca* is a kind of school where children live, the children live there with each other in a dormitory — they sleep and eat and study and play and do everything at the school. My school is a sports *beca,* and it has a semi-military discipline: you have to march, line up. We have a schedule for sports and for everything else. We also have a lot of interesting things, like the Cuban Pioneer Union. In the Pioneer Movement the children study and do a lot of other things; it's an independent organization. Before it was under the directions of the Young Communists, but now it's independent. One of the jobs is the Pioneer Correspondent; his job is to transmit all the news about what the children are doing through radio, television and the newspapers, so the people will know what is going on in this organization. The school is run by a *comandante* and by different companies . . . . Every day we work out in whatever sport we're in: there's swimmimg, gymnastics, basketball, tennis, lots of different sports . . . . That's so the children will be strong, and when they're grown they'll be prepared physically as well as mentally. There are also competitions held every year called the National Sports School Competitions, in which all the sports schools in Cuba compete.

Last year I was *comandante* of my school, and now I'm the Pioneer Correspondent for the area. One of my jobs is to do political work with the other children who have a bad attitude, so their attitude will improve. For example, there's a boy who sleeps in the same room I do, at the *beca,* and one of my jobs is to do political work with him. This boy had a good attitude before, but now it isn't so good. And we have to work with him politically so he won't continue the way he's going. I've done a lot of political work with him, showing him the correct way to treat other people, how he should be acting in class, and in school in general.

There's a kind of love that exists among the children at the *becas,* teachers teach us this love and it's called *compañerismo* (comradeship). This love makes us love each other a lot. We share everything because we live in a kind of community where we all study, we all

work, and we all practice sports together. One of the ways I feel this love, for example, for me, I experience this love on Friday afternoon — because we go home to be with our parents two days a week: from Friday afternoon to Sunday afternoon — and when I go on pass on Friday it's hard for me to leave the *beca,* because I feel like the *compañeros* are my brothers. It's hard for me to leave the *beca.*

Now I want to talk about another kind of education, not at school, but about the education in Cuba in the streets — like the voluntary work we do through the CDRs [neighborhood committees]. We've done big jobs like finishing the Latin American Stadium for the World Series, and lots of children took part in that too. It's a huge stadium and it was completely built by the masses. That thing about kids not being good for anything doesn't exist here — just the opposite: everything is for kids, for example: I love astronomy, and I didn't know there was any astronomy in Cuba, but someone told me there was an institute, and I went out there and now I'm involved in astronomy groups, starting an "interest circle" [about astronomy] in my school, and everything. Here they don't treat children like they do in other countries, like they don't know anything or anything like that . . . .

I think I've talked a lot, let's see, what else can I say? Well, in the *beca* I feel great, but it's only natural that sometimes I want to be in a better *beca* or have something special, more toys, etc. But I've got to keep on learning that I can't have special things or more toys because here in Cuba the Revolution gives the same number of toys to everyone. In the future the children will be able to have more toys than they have now because production keeps going up and Cuba will continue to develop.

In his brief tape Goyo touched on a wide range of subjects — so wide, in fact, that most of the rest of this book will be spent elaborating on these various themes, primarily from the viewpoint of the Cuban children, teachers and Pioneer guides who were Gregory's — and my — main source of learning.

SCHOOLS IN THE CITY

The Adelaida Piñeira School is located in an older section of Havana, where the streets are narrow and winding, and the buildings grayed with age. This is a section where *solares* predominate — courtyards surrounded by single rooms — often without plumbing — which house entire families.

Adelaida Piñeira is an important reminder that the single greatest problem confronting Cubans in their everyday lives is still underdevelopment. It is impossible to look at the Cuban school system, to understand the process of trying to create a new generation, if one only looks at the goals and desires of the educators, and ignores the material conditions which are constantly holding them back from attaining the norms they have set. Looking at these conditions you really begin to appreciate the stupendous job the teachers and educators are doing.

Fidel Castro talked about this problem at the first National Congress on Education and Culture, held in Havana in April 1971. Fidel explained that the educational problems facing Cuba were first of all "the problems of a country ninety miles away from the United States, threatened by its airplanes, fleets, millions of imperialist soldiers, chemical, bacteriological, conventional and all other kinds of weapons . . . . [a] country involved in an epic battle against that empire which seeks to sink and block us everywhere, . . . those problems which result from our being an underdeveloped country that must support itself under these difficult conditions." He went on to describe: " . . . the problem of the more than two million children and young people or students whom we must care for, supply with books, pencils, clothes, shoes, furniture, desks, black-boards, chalk, audio-visual aids, classrooms, installations and on many occasions food, since we have about five hundred thousand who eat in school . . . ."

In 1971, the problems Fidel Castro was referring to could be seen each time you walked into a Cuban school, where often a single eraser or a blade to sharpen pencils would be passed around the classroom to each student who needed it. It could be seen especially in the makeshift schools, the converted fortresses and mansions from another era which, despite inadequate facilities, were still serving as schools until enough new ones could be built.

At Adelaida Piñeira the hallways and corridors were dark and grey, the furniture old. No one had even dreamed of sound-proofing when those buildings were constructed under Spanish colonial rule more than two centuries ago, and the noise of students studying and playing mingled throughout the building, crossing the open court-yard from one room to another.

This is the school eleven-year-old Julia Carmen goes to. The third child (and oldest girl) of five children, Julia Carmen has always been a bright student and an active Pioneer. Now she is *Jefe de la Escuela* (equivalent to student body president), after having been chosen monitor and outstanding student numerous times. Julia Carmen told me about herself and her school:

"My father drives a truck, carrying construction materials. Some times he's away from home for a long time. But when he's home he plays with us a lot; he teaches us things and takes us places.

"Mama works at one of the hotels in Vedado. She cleans the rooms of the hotel guests. Sometimes the people there are honey-mooners. Sometimes there are revolutionaries from different countries.

"At our school we have very high spirit. Most of the students are Pioneers, and we have a pretty good promotion rate — although it could be better," she admitted.

"Sometimes we don't have enough of the things we need; we could use more of just about everything. But what we have, we share, everybody alike. In our school everybody shares — students, teachers, everyone.

"The *padrinos* (sponsors) help a lot too," Julia Carmen told me. "Our *padrinos* are the men from the furniture factory. That's really good, because they come and build shelves and cabinets and things for us. They even helped with some electrical wiring. See all those bookshelves over there? They built those for us.

"When we visited their factory they showed us how they make our desks and chairs and tables and all the things we use. We saw how they do it just starting from pieces of plain wood. Our *padrinos* are really dedicated revolutionaries," she added proudly. "They always win the Moncada banner and all the emulations."

Without the system of national education which exists in Cuba the Adelaida Piñeira School could be like many ghetto schools in the United States. Located in what was clearly a poor working-class neighborhood before the Revolution, it would have lacked the financial resources to hire top-rate teachers and allocate sufficient educational materials to keep its students on a par with those of the more wealthy areas. But at Adelaida Piñeira the quality of teachers and allotment of resources are the same as those you find in any part of Cuba, from Miramar to the Sierra Maestra.

Raulito Castillo — chubby, black, talkative — is a fifth grader at the Bernardo Domínguez School in Vedado — one of the newer, richer sections of Havana, where the big hotels are located. Every day he watches foreign guests from the Hotel Riviera walk past his schoolyard. When he can, he engages them in conversation.

The school was once the lovely, old Spanish-style mansion of a wealthy family. Its colors are lighter, its rooms and corridors brighter and more spacious, than the schools in Old Havana. A small fenced-in yard and a large grassy mall in the center of the avenue in front of the school provide room for the children to run and play.

But, like the Adelaida Piñeira School, this house was not made to serve as a school house. Sounds carry clearly from one room to another. The director's "office" is the front lobby, with children and teachers wandering through it on their way to classes. This lends an air of informality to the school, but better design would probably facilitate studying.

It was at the Bernardo Domínguez School that I spent most time. I was living at the nearby Hotel Riviera, and found myself getting into conversations with the children whenever I passed by. One day I went in to talk to the young *directora*, Elsa, who invited me to sit in on classes whenever I wanted. I began making the school a regular part of my daily activities.

It was at the Bernardo Domínguez school that I really began to see how Cuba is defeating underdevelopment and taking the first long strides towards creating the men and women of the future.

In many ways education in schools like this one is surprisingly "normal." Children sit in rows at desks, teachers stand in front of the room and write on blackboards. Standard textbooks (re-written since the Revolution, of course) are read in all schools, tests are given, grades received.* Within this context, some students appear "brighter," more articulate and outgoing, get better grades, assume leadership positions. Others seem slower, or more reticent, don't excel — some don't pass. Discipline is maintained for all. Children wait in lines, study given subjects at regular hours, are expected to be quiet except when asking or answering questions in class, be respectful toward their teachers and classmates.

What is "revolutionary," then, about these schools?

My first morning at Bernardo Domínguez I arrived when all the children were lined up on the side veranda, which ran the length of the house. One young student was reading excerpts from the daily newspaper. The others listened with interest as she read about a new Soviet achievement in space; an article about black protests in the U.S. armed forces; another on CIA intrigues in Latin America; and one on the world economic situation. I realized that these were first, second and third graders who seemed so fascinated by international news, not squirming or fidgeting (although occasionally throwing sideways glances at me). Then a little boy began reading the national news: the commemoration of a martyr in Cuba's historic struggle for independence; the beginning of discussion by the CDRs of a proposed new law; activities of the High School Student Union in Las Villas province. He concluded with two short sports and cultural items.

I tried to remember what we had studied in our *Weekly Reader* when I was in grade school. Nothing came to mind. But I knew we had never learned so much about what was going on in the world outside our country — or even cared to know.

---

*In 1975 this was already undergoing some change, as the Ministry of Education began experimenting with a new system which not only eliminated grades, but kept children from first through fourth grades together with one teacher as a collective unit. After fourth grade students begin studying specialized subjects with different teachers.

Karen Wald (center) eventually became friends with children of Bernardo Domínguez School.

By now the children's curiosity about this strange visitor was boundless. Most stared — curiously or shyly — while those who already knew me from my walks past the school smiled and waved. Elsa, the *directora* of the school, began to introduce me to the students. I thought she would simply say "We have a visitor today," but instead, she told them I was from the United States. This apparently required some further explanation, because she then went on to say that I was a friend of Cuba, that I opposed my government's war in Vietnam, and "she is one of those Americans who are opposed to racism in her country, because she believes, just as we do, that all people and all races are equal." Later, when I learned how intensely concerned Cuban children are about the treatment of blacks in the United States and the war in Vietnam — which they saw, heard, and read about extensively in newsreels, TV, radio, magazine and newspapers — I understood why this elaborate introduction was necessary. Once I was so defined, however, I had no trouble befriending the students, who talked and asked questions quite openly. In fact, as I found when I traveled around the island, most children made that assumption naturally, just from my presence in Cuba. "An American in Cuba is a friend of the Revolution, because the Yankees have all been kicked out" — that was the way one little girl explained when I asked why she wasn't afraid I was one of the "bad kind."

After the reading of the morning news the children filed into their respective classrooms. Again, the mixture of the "normal" and the "unusual." Cuban children are graded chronologically, and move ahead year by year (except when they fail), just as they do in our schools. In the fifth-grade class I entered, the teacher was at the front of the room, writing on the board, and the children were sitting more or less quietly in their seats. Order was maintained by monitors and "unit chiefs" or "Classroom chiefs" chosen by the students themselves through their Pioneer organization. (Like Work and Study, the Pioneers are such a key part of Cuban education that the next chapter will treat them separately.)

The boy at the front of the room was giving the fifth graders a biology lesson. He had a leaf and a branch, and was teaching the children about terminal and lateral buds. He explained their different functions, and talked of the practical application of this knowledge in cutting and grafting different branches to produce better fruit or tobacco.

The atmosphere in the classroom was very informal. Two *responsables* or *jefes* of the classroom, a boy and a girl, were in charge of keeping the kids orderly. During the first five minutes or so they did this diligently, reprimanding those who were making noise. But after that they let things slide, and children chattered to each other as they explored the buds and branches. Group monitors were in charge of distributing pencils, one to each pupil, and magnifying glasses to study the leaves — one to each group. They also took charge of making sure each student found the points he or she was supposed to study.

The students were expected to write short summaries of their observations. At this point the collective nature of their learning stopped: each was expected to write his or her own summary. When the chattering reached a certain level, the teacher who was standing in the doorway reminded the students of this.

In Cuba, I found learning is always a mixture of this individual and collective effort. The goal is to provide an integral education so each person can become a complete human being, developing all of his or her full creative potential. Everyone is supposed to work together to produce this end; but each child ultimately has to acquire the skills and knowledge taught. So in most schools there are still individual exams, homework and grading, even though there is a strong emphasis on collective effort to achieve certain goals. (I will say more on this in discussion of emulation in the Pioneers chapter).

Since there are grades and individual rewards (like being chosen as monitor, *jefe,* or "vanguard"), I wondered to what extent the Revolution was progressing in teaching the children to place the collective good above individual advancement. When the noon recess began I joined the children as they filed out to the lunchroom, and engaged them in conversation. Many of my questions were aimed at trying to find out if these children thought primarily individually or collectively.

"What do you think when another student stands up to answer a question and doesn't know the answer, but you do?" I asked.

"I think that he or she hasn't studied, or hasn't prepared the lessons, or wasn't paying attention to the teacher," replied one little girl slowly.

"If it's a difficult question, we try to help him find the answer," suggested another, and several children voiced their agreement.

No one suggested that they would feel smarter than the child who didn't know the answer.

Next I asked several children, individually, "Now, I want you to think seriously about this for a moment, and then tell me what you really feel. OK? Which way do you feel better; when your school wins in an emulation, or when you are chosen vanguard?" Almost every child told me that he or she thought it was more important to win an emulation than to be vanguard, although several were torn and said they would like both to happen.

I tried asking the question another way: "Would you like to be the most intelligent student in the class, or would you like everyone to be just as smart as everyone else?" The responses were again in favor of collective rather than personal achievement. "We just don't think that way," explained a thin black girl with short straight hair. "No one would want to be the *most* intelligent. We don't believe in individualism, in individual privilege. What we have has to be for all. We do better that way."

A red-headed boy continued on the same theme: "We work together, we all cooperate, and then we all share what we get. Everyone helps each other. If we do things individually, not everyone does as well — some are worse off than others."

It's better that we all help each other," another voice chimed in, "so everyone knows everything, instead of one knowing everything and some not knowing anything."

"If you don't win an emulation, how do you feel?" I threw out my last question, looking at their faces to see their reactions. "We study harder" was the immediate chorus of responses.

The children's attitude was the same as I found in all schools, and at all grade levels, throughout the island as I traveled to different places during the next few years. Another aspect of the Bernardo Domínguez School that I was later to see repeated over and over again was the emphasis on health and cleanliness and the integration of these into the regular school program. As in the *círculos*, regular medical and dental check-ups are carried out through the schools. Every school has a clinic, staff nurse and visiting doctor. Larger school-cities even have hospitals. But even more impressive than this is the way health education is incorporated into the children's conciousness through their everyday school activities, conversations of the teachers and posters on the bulletin boards.

During my first morning at Bernardo Domínguez I heard a teacher ask the pupils to bring in urine specimens the next day. "Don't bring in a whole bucketful this time," she cautioned them with a smile. "This is just for study in our biology class, not for lab work." The children laughed. Later I learned that every student is asked to bring urine and feces specimens, and has blood drawn, at regular intervals, as part of the preventive-medicine program aimed at catching diseases in their early stages. I tried to imagine the reaction of American students — and many of their parents — if such a request were made in our schools.

My second day at the Bernardo Domínguez School, when I went into a third grade class, I saw one of the fifth graders I recognized from the previous day at the front of the room. He explained that he had signed up in the *guerrilleros de enseñanza* (teaching guerrilla) program. That meant he planned to study to be a teacher when he got older. The *guerrilleros* practice teaching younger students one day a week.

Watching this boy explain concepts and answer questions for the younger children, I realized that this wasn't just a game the adults were playing with the children, letting them be make-believe teachers for a day. This boy was really teaching! I began to feel tremendous respect for those educators who were far-sighted and had enough respect for their young students to allow them to develop their abilities seriously in this way.

Having grown up in a period when there were clear concepts in school about "boys' subjects" and "girls' subjects," I was very interested to see how this distinction manifested itself among Cuban schoolchildren. I knew their society traditionally placed men and women in very distinct roles, which their parents would be passing on to the children despite the Revolution. There were clear social differences between girls and boys, men and women. Out in the playground I could see that the girls and boys tended to segregate themselves naturally and play their own games.

But inside the classroom I could detect none of this distinction. Cuban children seemed more confused than anything else when I asked if there were some subjects that boys were better in, or others that were strictly for girls. Over and over again when I asked little girls what their favorite subject was, they told me "math"* (one of those I had been "taught" to do poorly in); the second favorite was generally "physics" (which Cuban children begin in grade school). In 1971, visiting an *internado* primary school in Marianao, I once saw girls go to a sewing class while the boys went to a separate room where they drew pictures and made paper cut-outs. But by 1973 this was far less frequent, and I never saw boys and girls attending separate classes, although there was separate work in one of the primary schools that combine work and study.†

The lack of distinction by sex in most subjects is aided as well by the program of *auto-servicio,* in which students are responsible for cleaning up their classrooms and school grounds, and helping serve and clean up in the lunch rooms. Here no sexual distinction was ever made.

It was not until 1974 — the year after my last visit to Cuban schools — that adult Cubans began seriously to attack the social bases of discrimination against women and the unequal roles men

---

*One of the recent innovations in Cuban education is that all children now learn New Math.

†These separate classes were abolished completely after the Women's Congress in Dec. 1974 and the enactment of the Family Code in March 1975.

and women were forced to play. At that time nationwide discussion was initiated on a new Family Code, which would mandate equal treatment of boy and girl children and charge male and female adults with equal responsibility for the work of the household. This was a thorny issue for most adult Cubans. While women were overwhelmingly in favor of it (typical comments: "Its long overdue!" "It's one of the most important pieces of social legislation of the entire Revolution," "It's a revolution within the revolution"), men were more hesitant ("Well, it's a very difficult question," "If that is what the Party says, it must be right, but I think I'm too old to change," "This time I think the Revolution has gone too far!").

Their children — especially those who lived in boarding schools and attended work-study schools, were way ahead of them:

Q. When you grow up, do you want to be a housewife, or work outside the home?
A. [Fifth grade girl] I want to work, of course. I want to serve the Revolution.
Q. [To a boy the same age] When you grow up, do you want to marry a woman who works outside the home, or one who will stay home and cook and clean for you?
A. I want to marry someone who works outside the home; someone who is revolutionary, who will be my *compañera.*
Q. Even if that means you have to share the work in the house?
A. Of course. If we're both working, we both have to help clean up.

At the Bernardo Domínguez School the only sex stereotyping I ever saw was when the children segregated themselves on the playground. Boys and girls were leaders in their classes, monitors, *jefes,* and girls and boys invited me to go with them and their parents to do voluntary work picking potatoes one Sunday.

I noticed slightly more difference in sex roles at the Manuel Ascunce Domenech *internado* in the suburbs of Havana. The classrooms and dormitories of this school were spread out through a number of modern one- and two-story homes that lined both sides of a quiet, pleasant street. Children lined up in their detachments or units to go to meals and classes, with separate lines for boys and girls. When they did their morning exercises, too, the teacher suggested slightly different exercises for the little girls when she felt the exercises were too strenuous. But the boys and girls marched, exercised and played gym together.

Inside the classrooms, again, I could see no differences in the treatment or expectations for boys and girls, although there did seem to be a slight tendency for boys to be more rowdy and playful and girls to be more serious and studious. (Several boys and girls got into a heated argument about this once when, after denying that boys were better than girls in any subject, some of the girls insisted they were better than the boys "because the boys like to mess around and then they don't pay attention.")

There are both similarities and differences between the *internados* where children live in all week (the *becas* described by Goyo in his tape) and the other schools. Like the National and *semi-internado* schools, many of the *internados* are housed in reconverted buildings, including the mansions of the upper classes who fled the Revolution. The *internados* are often in finer surroundings and more modern houses than the schools where the children don't live in. But they share with them the disadvantages of buildings that were not constructed to be schools. The new schools — *internado* and *semi-internado* — built by the Revolution are really the only ones that provide all the facilities to maximize learning conditions.

In the *internados* like the Manuel Ascunce Domenech school (named after the boy who was killed by counter-revolutionaries during the literacy brigades) you see boys and girls scrubbed and clean, hair neatly combed, dressed in identical clothes, clearly well-fed and in good health. The semi-military organization into units, detachments, etc. — aided by the *compañerismo* the children share from living as well as studying together — gives them a sense of orderliness and discipline. These children from poor worker and peasant families are a complete reversal from the street urchins, beggars and field workers, who slept in the streets or in dirt-floored huts, scavenged garbage dumps, and stole when they had to, before the Revolution.

But despite the discipline and order, I didn't find these children "repressed" in any sense. On the contrary, they were lively, aware, independent-minded, and very much children. When they marched, they sing-songed chants and rhymes — often about Che, or José Martí. One chant went "1, 2, 3, 4; 1, 2, 3, 4 El Che/Guevara/El Che/Cubano Argentino/Nosotros estudiantes seguiremos su camino/ El Che/Guevara/El Che" (Che Guevara, Cuban-Argentinian, We students will follow your example).

Other chants dealt with Vietnam, or the Cuban sugar harvest, or lines from songs like "Guantanamera." They were always performed spiritedly, often with hand-clapping. They seemed to be made up by the students and teachers of each school, since I seldom heard the same one at two different schools. When I asked them to explain any particular song or chant, a half-dozen children were quick to tell me what it was all about.

I spent several days at the Manuel Ascunce Domenech school, going to classes with the students, joining them at lunch and on the playground during recess, watching television with them at night. The notes that follow are from the "diary" I kept during those days.

Monday. This morning I went to visit a *beca* in Marianao. It was different from the schools I've seen in downtown Havana, since it was really made from a group of houses in what was obviously a very wealthy suburb before the Revolution. Since classes had already started when we arrived, we stopped to talk briefly with the *directora* of the school — a plump black woman with a warm smile — then hurried on to a classroom.

The first class we visited was the third grade. There were seventeen boys and girls, and it looked like more than half were black. Since *becas* are given on the basis of need as well as merit, I guess that reflects the effect of the economic deprivation which darker-skinned Cubans suffered before the Revolution, and which certainly must have carried over for a number of years after in terms of lower educational and skill levels.

It was still cool, and most of the children were wearing brown jackets supplied by the school. Each one had a blue-and-white Pioneer scarf. Most of them turned and gave me shy smiles and glances.

The teacher at the front of the room looked very young, certainly still in her teens. She was wearing a school uniform, too — a cream colored blouse worn loosely over a brown pleated skirt, sandal-type shoes and no stockings. As she handed out the pencils to her pupils she seemed slightly embarrassed that I should see the tiny stubs of pencils they were using.

I saw that this was a math class. The children were being asked to add columns of three figures. As they began the teacher handed out rulers and triangles that some enterprising person had cut from thin sheets of wood.

"How many students have finished the first problem?" she asked, and four black hands shot up into the air.

The teacher began to do the addition on the board, explaining it step by step. As she wrote the final number there was an outburst of remarks from the students. "Oh, teacher, that's what I got!" exclaimed one little girl happily. Several echoed her remark.

Each student who goes to the board to work out a problem is asked to explain out loud, step by step, for the benefit of those students "who haven't yet mastered the problem."

Heads bent down to work out the next set of problems. I saw the teacher go over to a little girl with curly blond hair who was having difficulty with the addition. She explained patiently, encouraging the child. Finally the girl looked up, smiling happily. As the children worked, the teacher walked up and down the rows, checking their notebooks, making sure to praise the students who seemed more hesitant about their work. The notebooks were also improvised, made from folded lined paper covered with the harder paper from the cover of *Bohemia* magazine.

10:00. — Recess and mid-morning snack. Some of the girls are sitting on the porch in front of one of the houses, playing "yacky." I look and realize it's what we called "jacks."

10:30. — The children have washed up, and now we go to a music class. Classes often focus on special historical dates in the world of music. This week is the anniversary of the death of Benny More, a famous black Cuban singer. The teacher alternates reading about him and playing a record of his music. The kids are listening with varying degrees of interest. They react to the livelier selections of his music with tapping fingers and toes, wiggling bodies. Sometimes the children look over at me and smile. But whenever I smile back their hands quickly shoot up to cover their faces in embarrassment.

Although Benny More died the year most of these children were born, they apparently know his music well, sing along with some of the songs.

11:15. — The morning has already become quite hot, and the children go back to their dorms to bathe and change clothes before lunch. They are more or less free now until two P.M. I go with the girls to the house that serves as their home away from home. One of the little girls collects all the socks that need to be washed while the rest are bathing, changing clothes, talking. Another hands out clean underwear. One of the women who works in the dorms is combing and braiding the girls' hair. Some of the older girls are combing and braiding the hair of the first and second graders.

12:30. — I joined the last group of students to go into the lunch room. They line up with their trays, and women wearing protective masks over their faces dish the food out. It's very quiet — no talking or shouting as the kids eat. The lunch is rice, a thick soup, fish, hard-boiled eggs, and milk. When they finish the children line up to leave, bringing their empty trays to other women on the way out.

The teachers eat with the children. When they are finished, teachers and student teachers from other schools without lunch-rooms come in to eat. At first I wondered why the children were so disciplined in the lunchroom. When I saw how many people had to be fed in a short space of time I began to appreciate the need for a no-nonsense attitude.

After lunch the children were free to run, play, talk, rest or watch TV. I wandered around to see what they did. A lot of kids were sprawled on the floor of the living room watching television. It was an entertainment program, with singers, dancers and musicians. The announcer was a black woman who walked among the children

Auto-servicio means the students do their own cleaning up.

in the audience as she spoke. I wondered whether specific classes or schools of children were brought to the TV studio each day, or how it was arranged, but no one there knew.

Out in the hall some boys and girls were reading the verses of José Martí that were posted on a bulletin board.

On the porch some kids were playing jacks, and I found out that no one had ever told Cuban kids that jacks is a "girls' game". Other kids were just sitting there quietly in the shade, watching some chickens out in the yard. A group of girls surrounded me, and I asked them about the chickens. They told me they belonged to one of the *empleadas* — the non-teaching staff who work at the school. This led to a discussion of who the *empleadas* were. I remembered that when I went to school workers who weren't teachers — the janitors, kitchen workers, etc. — were invisible. We never talked to them, never knew their names, were barely aware of what they did.

The girls described the different kinds of work the *empleadas* did, especially those who worked in their *albergues* (houses that served as dorms). "They don't just work here, they really love us a lot." the girls explained. "They bring us ice cream, and take us to the zoo on weekends" added another. "They are like *madrinas*, like our mothers or aunts."

All the children expressed great affection for the *empleadas*. A few children indicated that the *empleadas* were warmer to them than their own parents. One little girl from a poor home said that she was happier at school than at home. Everyone agreed that they had better physical conditions here than at home, most of them pointing to the open space and large playgrounds for them to run and play in. Most said that they ate pretty well at home, too, and a number of them had televisions at home or at neighbors' homes that they could see. But several said they didn't have indoor plumbing and showers in their homes.

I asked them who built these fine schools for them, expecting them to say "the Revolutionary government" — and was somewhat surprised when they answered quickly: "The workers."

When I asked them about what it meant to be revolutionary, what it meant to be a communist, they answered me by explaining what it was like in Cuba before. "Before most of the people were poor. They didn't even have shoes to wear." Some of the children began recounting the history of Cuba, beginning with the Indians, then the black slaves brought in by the Spanish. At each stage they told me how the people lived poorly, and were killed.

One little girl interjected: "Was Columbus good or bad?"

Someone said he was good, because he discovered Cuba.

"No, he was bad," several quickly corrected him, "because he killed a lot of Indians."

I asked the children whether life in Cuba was better now than it had been before. "Yes" they chorused. "Before the people were poor, they didn't have anything." "No food." "No clothes." "No shoes." "No doctors." "Before, only the rich went to the clubs, to the beaches. Now we all go."

"Before we couldn't go. We didn't have money. They didn't let us. Now the workers go."

"I went to Santa María beach."

2:00. — I returned to afternoon classes with the same group I accompanied in the morning. The teacher was new. Since the teachers are also full-time students, they teach for half a day and study the other half. This teacher looked about sixteen and, like the morning teacher, was wearing her cream-and-brown school uniform, with bobby sox and sneakers.

The class was "expression," a reading and grammar class. As the children read aloud I listened for the dull monotone I used to hear in beginning readers. But intonation, pauses — even expressive gestures — seemed to be part of reading for Cuban children.

After they read the passage the teacher asked them questions about the story, then about the grammar used.

When the children began writing a single-edge razor blade was passed around the room as a pencil sharpener, and a small piece of eraser.

4:00. — *Merienda*. Snack time again.

4:15. — The boys and girls split up, the girls going to a sewing class in which they made little stuffed animals. The boys went to a drawing class. I wandered around looking at their pictures. There were several boats, a cowboy, a Cuban tank shooting down a U.S. plane "because the plane drops bombs on Vietnam."

I wondered why the boys and girls had separate classes, since it seemed like both subjects would have been of interest to both sexes. But the women teaching the sewing class simply couldn't imagine little boys learning to sew. They insisted little boys' fingers aren't as dexterous as little girls', and that boys don't have the patience for that kind of detailed work. [Classes separated by sex were abolished in 1975.]

5:00. — The boys and girls are together again now for a "story hour". A young teacher is telling a story very expressively. She doesn't read from a book, but talks, gestures and acts out the story. The kids apparently already know the story, and join in telling it, add their own comments after it's finished. Then a child tells a story. Afterwards they all drew pictures of the parts of the story they liked best.

6:00-6:30. — Dinnertime passed pretty much the same as lunch.

6:45. — I went with the girls as they went back to their rooms to wash up and brush their teeth. One girl brings the toothbrushes, another holds the tube of toothpaste and squeezes the right amount onto each brush.

When we got downstairs many kids were already seated in front of the TV. (I could hear another group of youngsters out on the porch and in the front yard, singing.) Television seems to be a mass participatory spectator-sport. The kids jump up and down, yell in delight and encouragement when there's a confrontation between "good guys" and "bad guys". They know all the characters by name, and carry on a running commentary about the plot and characters. Several took it upon themselves to explain to me, pointing out the good guys and bad guys and outlining the general plot. It was clear that they saw this make-believe adventure as representing the real thing. "Look at Tania! Look at Tania!" they called out as the woman guerrilla fighter appeared on the screen in the program called "Rebellion." The character in this TV serial had another name, as did the male guerrilla fighter, but every child in the room knew they were supposed to be Che and Tania, the Cuban-based internationalist guerrillas who died fighting in Bolivia. When shooting broke out on the screen a little girl told me that the guerrillas were killing Batista's troops. *"Tania mató a uno! Eha!"* Gleeful exclamations of joy as good guys killed bad guys.

But a note of sympathy was struck for the bad guys when the rebel doctor in the serial (Che?) took care of the wounds of a captured soldier.

After the program, instead of commercials advertising toys or household detergents, there was a brief announcement about the need to take care in avoiding fires, and another that simply projected the slogan "Clik." The children explained that this was the symbol to remind people to turn off lights when not in use, to save electricity. "We need to save electricity so we won't use up so much petroleum," one boy elaborated. "Yeah, 'cause people in other provinces don't have as much petroleum as we do," volunteered another.*

8:00. — The younger children have gone up to bed, but some of the older ones returned to their classrooms for a review session for exams they are having tomorrow.

In the grammar review the young male teacher had written on the board: "Camilo fought to the death." "Fidel cuts cane." He began to conjugate "I fought, you fought . . . . " One child called out eagerly: "We will fight!"

Tuesday. There were some young women from the Ministry of Education visiting the school on my second day, and I spoke with them for a while about the advantages — and disadvantages — of the *becas*. Remembering Goyo's remarks, and the conversations I'd had with the children here the day before, I felt that it was a totally positive experience. The women from MinEd weren't so sure. "Actually, we don't think this is the best situation for children so young. In the future, probably only those children who have to will go to schools where they live in before they're twelve or thirteen years old.

"Children this age need a lot more affection and attention," one explained. "They need to be able to run and shout and play.

"But when you're living in a collective of other little children, your chances for doing this are limited," she told me. "You can't run and shout when others are studying, or sleeping.

"We've found, in fact, that children who return to their parents every night do better, at this age, than those who are in school all the time. They study better and behave better when they have to account to their own parents each night. The Revolution is building more and more junior high schools in the countryside," she concluded, "and some day probably all students that age will live collectively in school. But as that happens, fewer and fewer of the younger ones will live away from home."

---

*Nearly all of Cuba's energy comes from oil, shipped from the USSR because of the U.S. economic blockade.

The schools that I visited throughout Cuba — national, *semi-internado* and *internado* — were amazingly similar in most ways. In 1971, however, the most "revolutionary" aspect about them was still their very existence: providing teachers, schoolrooms, books, and materials to educate an entire population. It was revolutionary for all the children of working people, of all colors, of both sexes, to be attending school. It was revolutionary for them to learn a sense of pride in being Cuban and Latin American,* in being the future workers and builders of their country. The content of their classwork, in many instances, was clearly revolutionary. But the structure of the schools themselves had not changed greatly from the traditional model. And in fact I found in some schools, like the Manuel Ascunce Domenech, that there were still carry-overs of the old ideas about what boys and girls should study.

By 1973 the schools themselves were changing in a revolutionary way. Several of the new primary schools constructed in rural areas developed extensive *huertos escolares* — large fruit or vegetable orchards — for the children to work in. Boys and girls worked side by side in the fields, participated in sports, shared all classroom activities, and performed *auto-servicio* cleaning up their dorms and classrooms. The only carry-over of the sex-role differential I encountered during this period was in the workshop at the Tupac Amaru primary school, where some of the jobs were divided by sex. Here third through fifth graders packaged and assembled toys, Cuban artisanry, herbal teas and handicrafts. Most of these activities were shared by boys and girls. But when it came to embroidery and sewing, adult males drew the line. "We just can't have little boys sewing and crocheting," the Minister of Education affirmed. "The parents would never accept it."

But some of the teachers felt there would be no problem in this. The director of one school told me when she was teaching classes prior to assuming this position she always taught all the children to sew. "Boys have to learn, too," she explained in a no-nonsense manner. "When they go to the School in the Countryside,

---

*The African heritage of many Cubans was also taught, but was not stressed in the same way as the Latin American identity until 1976, when Cuba responded to the request of the new government of Angola to send troops, technicians and arms. This involvement in the African continent stirred many Cubans to take a new look at their African roots and to begin to identify themselves as "Afro-Latins."

or later into the Army, what are they going to do — send their torn clothes back home to Mama?"

It was clear all along that revolutionary change in the roles of women was easier to accept when it meant women engaging in activities previously prohibited to them than when it implied that men should carry out activities formerly designated to women. The final hold-outs against these changes were swept away only with the institution of the new Family Code in 1975. Once it was considered a man's revolutionary and legal duty to share all the work of the household, the rationale for giving boys separate activities from girls — except in cases where there is a real, biological necessity to differentiate — became obsolete.

Other changes were visible in 1973, too, mostly the outcome of the Congress on Education and Culture held in late April 1971.(I will discuss this in more detail in the section on that Congress.) But the Congress itself has to be seen in the context of the increasing *proletarianization* of the Revolution, the deepening of working class and revolutionary consciousness among all the people, and the institutionalization of the Revolution that became possible as a result of all this. The greater sense of collectivization, of workers' (people's) decision-making responsibility at the base, of *Cubanismo* (being Cuban and Latin American), all had their effects on the schools.

In a practical, structural sense you could see this in a number of ways. Some examples:

Cubanacán, the arts school which trained Cuba's future artists, musicians, dancers and actors, had formerly inadvertently served to prolong the stage of the artist and intellectual as an elite or privileged sector within the Revolution. After the Congress, the Revolution began constructing new arts schools in each province, and the students from each province who went to Cubanacán were expected to return and teach in these provincial schools in addition to their other artistic activities.

Four new high-school-level schools were built to train the workers in the childcare centers. Although initially the great demand and need for childcare had led the government to allow even women who did not have a sixth grade education to perform this work (providing they had the other qualifications and took a brief training course), the Revolution by the 1970s had reached a stage where this was no longer considered necessary or acceptable. If the *círculo* workers were to be charged with bringing up a new generation with a socialist consciousness, these educators would have to have a revolutionary training themselves.

There was another kind of difference in the schools by 1973, too — a difference which also reflected the changes in the whole society. Aided substantially by economic assistance from the Soviet Union and increased productivity at home, the Cuban economy was able to provide more goods and services of all kinds to its people. This could be seen in the schools, which had more, newer and better equipment. I saw more paints and brushes, clay, toys, educational aids (especially scientific and technical equipment) and sports facilities in 1973. The scarcity of pencils and erasers was a thing of the past. Educational needs were still great, but the most basic ones seemed to be on their way toward being met.

By 1974, Cuban educators were already beginning to talk concretely of raising the level of all educational work in the country; increase the age of mandatory education (which assumes a greater number of schools and teachers), and make education at all levels more efficient and comprehensive.*

---

*The details of this program go far beyond the scope of this book. They are available in issues of *Juventad Rebelde* from Dec. 1974, and from the Ministry of Education.

7

The Young Pioneers

If you were to ask me what was the single most striking factor that makes Cuban schools and Cuban school children different from all others, I would have to say the Union of Pioneers: the mass children's organization through which Cuban children organize and direct their lives.

I came into contact with Pioneers regularly from the first time I was in Cuba, but I never quite realized what the organization was all about, or how important it was to the children and to the life of the country, until I began learning about its structure and functioning in 1973. Until then, I simply knew that many or most primary-school children belonged to some kind of organization like the Scouts, that they wore blue and white neckerchiefs, and that they engaged in a variety of extracurricular activities.

Talking with Pioneers was impressive — in the way that talking with almost any Cuban children was impressive. The first group of Pioneers I met consisted of about a dozen first graders from a school in Santiago, who were visiting the motel I was staying at, on a hill overlooking the old city and the Santiago Bay. They were gathered around the motel's swimming pool, fully dressed, and distinct from youngsters vacationing at the motel by their blue and white scarfs. I wandered up to the pool and began talking with them.

"What does it mean to be a *Pionero?*" I asked one little girl. She blushed shyly, looking down at her toes.

"It means you are a communist," offered one of the other children. "It means to be like Che."

"Are you all communists?" I asked them. "Do you all want to be like Che?"

They nodded their heads enthusiastically.

"I'm gonna be like Tania," chimed in a little girl.

I smiled. "Who was Tania?" I asked.

"She fought in Bolivia with Che," several voices told me. "She was a guerrilla. An internationalist."

"Why did you join the *Pioneros?*" I asked a freckle-faced boy.

"To defend our country," he told me seriously.

"What do *Pioneros* do?" I asked the group in general.

"We study."

"Behave well at school."

"We're respectful toward our teacher."

"We help our teacher."

"We study more."

"We learn a lot and study."

"Not to be absent from school."

"We participate in all the activities of the Pioneers."

In the beginning, I thought the activities of the Pioneers consisted solely — or mainly — in trips to the zoo and other places of entertainment, educational excursions to historical sites, museums, and scientific centers, and participation in political-cultural performances.

As I spent more time in Cuba, I began to learn of other things the Pioneers do (mostly from reading the reports about these activities in the daily newspapers and national magazines). In this way I found out about the Pioneers' re-creation of historical events, like the assault on the Moncada, and activities such as the Pioneer Correspondents.

But it was only when I attended the *Encuentro Nacional de Jefes de Escuelas y Destacamentos de la Unión de Pioneros de Cuba* (the National Meeting of Heads of Schools and Detachments of the UPC) in May 1973 that I understood that the Pioneers run the schools.

Not that the children decide on curriculum, appoint teachers, or take on similar tasks that would clearly be beyond their scope. But an enormous number of the daily tasks and activities of a primary school are considered to be within their scope. The Pioneers are therefore asked to analyze their school work and activities, set goals and standards they want to reach, and organize and direct themselves in reaching them. They are aided in accomplishing the goals they set out by their teachers and Pioneer guides.

HISTORY OF THE PIONEERS

The Union of Pioneers did not first come into being with the triumph of the Cuban Revolution. Most socialist countries have a Pioneers organization (although in many, the Pioneers are in their early teens, and are considered vanguard students who will eventually be Young Communists and then Party members). In Cuba the Pioneers existed briefly during the period of the 1930s struggle against the dictatorship of Gerardo Machado. The Pioneers League, as it was called then, was created and directed by the Youth League of the Cuban Socialist Party. Since all such parties and groups were illegal under Machado, the Pioneers League remained a small group of children of militant workers, mostly centered in working-class areas in and around Havana.

The Pioneers — who generally ranged in age from ten to fourteen — took part in after-school games, excursions and other children's activities. Within the schools they tried to organize by presenting basic demands — such as for school materials, breakfast for the children, etc. — around which other children could be rallied.

The first Pioneer League succumbed to the general repression of the thirties and was not revived until after the triumph of the Revolution. It was reborn on April 4, 1961 as the Union of Rebel Pioneers, directed by the Association of Rebel Youth, the forerunner of the Young Communists. Its limited activities included campaigns to collect bottles and newspapers, productive work, and acts of solidarity with children from other countries.

But the next year, when the Rebel Youth became the Union of Young Communists (UJC), the Rebel Pioneers became the Union of Pioneers of Cuba (UPC). Although its activities were increased at this time, it was still a selective organization in which the best and most politically conscious students prepared to become Young Communists. In keeping with the nationwide trend for revolutionary Cubans to define themselves as socialists and communists, the new slogan of the Pioneers was "Pioneers for Socialism, Always Prepared!"

Since it was not yet open to all students, the Pioneers activities were all extracurricular, carried on outside the schools. This meant that the Pioneers did not in any way focus on scholastic activities.

The first major change in the character of the UPC came about as a result of a meeting in 1966, in which it was decided that the Pioneers should be open to all Cuban children. Ricardo García Pampín, Director of the Pioneer's weekly magazine, spoke of the reasons for — and implications of — this action, during a conversation on the porch of the elegant old building which serves as Pioneer headquarters in Havana:

"The organization grew, first of all, from the experiences of the socialist camp. But once formed, it began to set out its own tasks, just like any other mass organization in our country. The Pioneers organization comes not just from the experiences of other countries, but out of our own experiences."

Pampín described the initial tasks of the Pioneers as aimed simply at organizing the extracurricular life of the students.

But the Union of Pioneers soon became more than this; it became a vehicle for engaging in the ideological struggle that was going on inside the country:

"We were in a process in which everyone had to define himself: they were either on the side of the Revolution or they were not. The school had its own role to play in this process. The participation of children in revolutionary activities at times aided in their parents' definition of their own roles."

Pampín said that the Pioneers forced the parents to decide on their own commitment to the Revolution in two ways. In a society that was just starting to define itself as socialist after generations of virulent anticommunism, parents were confronted with the decision as to whether or not their children could belong to an openly communist organization.

But even more than this, according to Pampín, the children often exerted pressure on their parents.

"We could talk of many interesting experiences of children who have transformed the conduct of their parents. For instance, a doctor was planning to leave the country, and his son was a Pioneer. He committed the error, from his class point of view, of allowing his son to be a Pioneer. Then the son, when it came time for them to leave, told his father that he was a Pioneer, and that Pioneers don't betray their country. The decision was made by the child; the father stayed. This is perhaps one of the exceptional cases — but by no means the only one — that demonstrates how the child's interrelation with the organization has an effect on the parents."

I wondered whether in fact the Pioneers were creating a class distinction between children and parents who were not incorporated in the Revolution, and who wished to leave. Pampín believed this was not generally the case — that for the most part Pioneers were the children of revolutionaries.

At any rate, by 1966 socialism was pretty well accepted by the masses of people in Cuba as the goal of their Revolution. An organization aimed at forming children as socialist men and women now could be seen as appropriately belonging to all the children of Cuba, not just a select handful. With this change the Pioneers organization was able to become more directly linked with the schools, and to take on a variety of new tasks and activities. Some of the more important national activities of the UPC, initiated at that point, include the Children's Week of Victory, a symbolic assault on the Moncada on the 26th of July, Children's Cultural Festivals and celebrations (*Jornadas*) in Homage to the Revolutionary Armed Forces and the Ministry of the Interior. These activities, as we'll see later in a more detailed description of the Pioneers' assault on the Moncada, are designed to incorporate today's children more fully with the past, present and future of their Revolution.

HOW THEY RUN THE SCHOOLS

Even more important than the national extracurricular activities initiated when the UPC became a mass organization was the way it began to relate to the schools. The structure of the Pioneers, developed more fully two years later at the National Plenary of the UPC in August 1968, became totally intertwined with the schools, from the classroom to the School Council. The *detachment* (*destacamento*) became the organism through which children related to all their school and extracurricular work. The Pioneers Council became the way in which all children could participate in decision making.

The structure looks something like this:

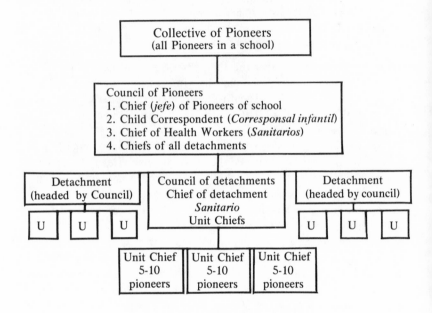

At the simplest level Pioneers are divided into *units* of five to ten children, all in the same classroom. Each unit has a unit chief, or *jefe*. Several units (all the units in a classroom) form a *detachment*. Each detachment is headed by a Detachment Council consisting of all the unit chiefs, a student in charge of health and hygiene in the classroom (*sanitario*), and an elected chief of the detachment (chosen from among the unit chiefs).

The chiefs of all the detachments form a Council of Pioneers, along with a Chief of Pioneers of the School, a Child Correspondent responsible for gathering and disseminating information for and about the Pioneers, and a Chief of the *Sanitarios*, all of whom are elected by all the Pioneers. The Council of Pioneers is responsible for basic decision-making, superseded only by the Collective of Pioneers, which means all the Pioneers of the School meeting as a body.

EMULATING The way this structure comes to life, on the simplest level, is through emulations. An emulation has often been described as a socialist form of competition. This is partly accurate, since there is certainly a sense of competitiveness about emulations, but to call it a competition largely misses the point. To most Americans, a competition means somebody wins and somebody loses. An emulation is not designed to produce losers.

To win an emulation is to complete a series of tasks. These tasks may be in terms of school work, productive work, or extracurricular activities. The individual or group that wins an emulation is considered to have set a standard — a standard that every other student can, and hopefully will, meet.

The emulations are most often carried out between detachments, but with the focus being on fulfilling the goals set out, not on "beating" the other detachments. If all detachments fulfill all the tasks or meet all the goals, they all win, and no one feels that they have been cheated of their "prize." In fact, Cuban school children over and over again told me that the best thing that could happen would be for everyone to win.

The key toward producing this attitude is that the goals and tasks the Pioneers are trying to fulfill are ones set out by the students themselves. Since 1969, Pioneer delegates from all the provinces of Cuba have been meeting at the national level to discuss the scholastic and extracurricular tasks of the Pioneers and their organization.

At these national meetings the Pioneers set up various areas in which to emulate (activities, organization, work, etc.), and four time periods in which the students would emulate. Pioneers can win three badges and a star by winning all the emulations, that is, by fulfilling all the goals set out for each time period.

Emulations combine individual and group incentive in a number of ways. For a detachment to win an emulation, 85 percent of the members of that detachment must receive three badges. An individual student will be proud to receive a star, to be chosen as "vanguard" or "monitor" for her/his efforts in school. But if the rest of his/her detachment doesn't do equally well, the greatest prize — winning the group emulation — is lost. This encourages students to help each other.

Many Pioneers described these thoughts, attitudes and processes.

In an *internado* primary school in Marianao I visited a girl's *albergue* (a house that serves as a small dormitory). The *albergue* was a modern, suburban home, like so many of the buildings that now house scholarship students. When we came in several of the girls were sweeping the front room. Soon a number of girls, a teacher, and two *tías* ("aunts": the women who work in the *albergues*) were sitting on the comfortable sofa, several chairs and the floor as we talked. I was asking what were the things a student does to be chosen "vanguard."

" . . . it's getting to class on time, being present in class, keeping the dorms clean . . . ."

"it means that the student's conduct is the best possible . . . ."

"having the best qualities, studying hard, good discipline . . . ."

They went on to explain that there is both house and class-room discipline, that is, a mode of desired behavior and routine, which all students are expected to follow. Each Friday night the students in each *albergue* meet to analyze the various points of discipline and how well they have been carried out. These points are added up for the *albergue* as a whole, and compared with other houses the following morning. The *albergue* that is "best" (fulfills most of the tasks and points of emulation) for the most Saturdays during the school term is named the best house of the year: it has "won" the emulation.

A young girl told me: "The point of the emulations is so that the *albergues* all follow each other's example, so that one that's not so good follows the example of the other that won the emulation, and so that they all better their discipline, their conduct, and get to be like the vanguard houses, so they can win the flag or emblem, and at the end of the year they make an example of all the *albergues* that are vanguard."

The students themselves, together with the teachers and the *tías* choose the vanguard students, both in the *albergue* and in the classrooms, which have a similar, weekly meeting to choose the best among themselves.

On January 1 each year (the anniversary of the triumph of the Revolution) all the students who have passed their grades and had good conduct all year are awarded the January 1 pin in a special assembly of the whole school. These pins are given out by the revolutionary government to all schools and work centers to honor the best workers and students.

In this *albergue* five or six of the girls had been chosen vanguard a number of times. I asked each of them which meant more to her: being chosen vanguard, or having her whole house win the emulation. In each case the answer was the same: "When my *albergue* wins . . . . " "Qué va! It means more to me for my whole house to win, because that means we're all vanguard, not just me alone . . . . "

Although the girls in this house described the qualifications to win an emulation as simply good conduct and discipline, it became clear from other conversations that this entails far more than we are used to thinking of in terms of "conduct" and "discipline" as obeying orders. Cubans constantly stress that discipline must be internal if it is to be meaningful, and Cuban Pioneers' participation in setting up the standards they are to live by goes a long way toward seeing that this is true.

But it is more than a question of discipline. By "conduct" Pioneers mean the way that students relate to and help each other. A student who always does exemplary school work but makes no effort to help other students learn that material would never be chosen as vanguard. On the contrary, such a student would be considered a "problem" student, whom the more politicized Pioneers would have to work with and help to develop a better attitude.

PIONEERS BECOME INDEPENDENT

As the Revolution developed and deepened, so did the Union of Pioneers. At the National Plenary of the UPC in 1968, the slogan of the Pioneers was changed once more, this time to: "Pioneers for Communism, We Shall Be Like Che!" — which remains their motto to this day. In 1969 the first national meeting of Detachment and School Chiefs was held, organized and directed entirely by the Pioneers themselves. And in 1970 the Union of Young Communists, which until this point was still directing the activities of the Pioneers, held a National Meeting on Education, in which it was decided that the UPC should become entirely autonomous.

Pampín recalled:

> The children were living in an environment in which everyone else had their own particular organization to belong to: the farmers have ANAP, the women have the FMC, workers have their trade unions,

students have middle-level and university student federations. All these, plus the CDRs, the militias, the Party and the Young Communists . . . . It was only natural that the children should want an organization of their own, one that really belonged to them, and that corresponded to their own particular needs.

I could understand from the children's point of view why they would want to have their own organization. But I wasn't yet clear from the Revolution's point of view why *the government* felt it was necessary to create a special organization to help mold the citizens of the future. Why not just do this directly through the schools?

Pampín's answer to this question — which I had posed early in our interview — was to review the history of the Pioneers and elaborate on their current activities and responsibilities, always placing everything in the context of the underdevelopment which still holds Cuba back at every step.

Why do we have an organization? Well, look at what we are trying to do. We are trying to form future communists. We want a complete person, a communist in practice, a person with an integral education, not just a technician or scientist or artist. To achieve this, we couldn't just leave the children's formation to spontaneity.

The schools alone can't satisfy all the objectives that we have set out for ourselves. We've been trying to supply simply enough schools and teachers and books to fill the huge gap we inherited when the Revolution took over the responsibility for educating our children. Our teachers have enormous responsibilities. It just would have been out of the question for them to take on all the extra activities which the children carry out through the Pioneers.

With the Pioneers, the children have two adult guides, who are not teachers, plus a teacher, a worker, a member of the FMC and the CDR who all relate to each detachment in some way.

When we lack materials for special activities — like instruments for a children's marching band, for example — we need to invent, create, use whatever materials are available. It would be impossible for one teacher to take on all this added responsibility — especially since in many cases teachers are still students themselves.

But Pampín made it clear that it was more than just the physical limitations of the schools and teachers that made an organization like the Pioneers necessary.

The Union of Pioneers is better structured than the schools for creating the kind of characteristics we want to see in our young people. We want independent, creative children capable of leading themselves and giving direction. That's hard to foster in a school situation where a great deal of the time must be spent absorbing information. The Pioneers provides an organization and a set of activities which the children can direct themselves, giving them first-hand experience in this.

The Pioneers also help develop a sense of collectivity in the children, first of all by their sense of being part of an organization that exists all over the country — in big cities, remote mountains, state farms, little fishing villages. Every Pioneer in the country wears the same blue and white scarf. It's a way of sharing experiences.

Pioneers work, study and play collectively. They emulate collectively. The organization itself is a collective body. And today 94.5 percent of the children in the country are members of this organization.

On a day-to-day basis collective leadership and initiative are carried out primarily through the detachment. The detachment council makes plans for various activities, including extracurricular ones like going to the zoo; creating a commission of students to visit a student who is not attending school, or one who habitually arrives late; talking to parents who don't want to let their child be a Pioneer. Pampín explained that children who aren't Pioneers are generally allowed to participate in Pioneer activities — if their parents don't prevent them. The 5.5 percent of children who are not Pioneers are almost always children of people who have political or religious differences (e.g., Jehovah's Witnesses) with the Revolution, and it's felt unfair to punish them for decisions of their parents.

THE KIDS TAKE CHARGE

The Pioneers do more than engage in friendly competitions between classrooms and organize extracurricular activities. The children elected by other Pioneers meet at sectional (municipal), regional, provincial and finally at the national level, to set out the goals and standards for the Pioneers each year. At the local and provincial meetings the Pioneers prepare working papers for the various commissions in which they will meet at the *Encuentro Nacional.* The commissions include Activities, Organization, Propaganda, *Divul-gación* (dissemination of information), and *Capacitación* (the process by which one's knowledge, skills and abilities are upgraded).

At Pampín's invitation I attended the *Encuentro Nacional* held at a scholarship school on the outskirts of Havana — in what was once apparently a boating resort and marina — in the summer of 1973. The building had towering ceilings, walls facing the ocean lined with floor-to-ceiling windows that opened onto slate verandas, and a large winding staircase leading to the rooms upstairs. What was once a ballroom served as the meeting hall for the plenary sessions; during the rest of the time the Pioneers were spread out throughout the building. In the evening the Pioneers were taken to nearby houses that served as dorms for scholarship students now on vacation.

I felt a little overwhelmed as I walked into this impressive building, and could hear and glimpse children bustling around or deeply involved in conversation and debate. But I was quickly greeted by several Pioneer Correspondents, whose duty it was (besides gathering and broadcasting the daily news of the event to the other students) to receive all visitors and members of the "adult" media, and see that they got all the information they wanted. The correspondents were my escorts, companions and confidants for the rest of the *Encuentro.*

Through them — boys and girls ages nine to twelve — I learned who was present at the event, what special guests attended, which special activities were engaged in by the Pioneers aside from their work in the commissions, as well as complete reports of the outcome of each commission's work.

They also taught me a little about the history of their organization, to make sure that I placed everything in its proper context.

A CHILD'S-EYE VIEW OF HISTORY

Maricela del Carmen, a student at the Republic of Chile primary school in Ciudad Libertad (Freedom City) was a Pioneer Correspondent at the municipal level, and a member of the Press Bureau for the Third National Meeting of Pioneer Chiefs. I asked her whether she thought it was possible for a children's organization like the Pioneers of today to function before the triumph of the Revolution.

Work sessions at the *Encentro* combined high spirits and enthusiasm with serious attitude.

"Of course not, because before it wasn't an organization respected by everyone, the way it is now."

"Do you feel that this is your very own organization?" I asked.

"Sure, because we made this organization ourselves; it's ours because for a long time, even though we didn't pick up guns, there have been kids like Paquito González [a martyr of the thirties] who fought and died for it."

She told me how the Pioneers organization had first been led by the youth (meaning older students, like the Young Rebels and Young Communists), but little by little the older kids had to move on to other work, and the younger ones "had to learn how to lead ourselves."

And now we see *compañeritos* who can stand up in front of six hundred seventy pupils in our school, a leader of the school capable of standing up before the whole school, before the teachers and directors, and maintain discipline.

Before the organization wasn't as widely respected as it is now, because now we Pioneers even speak over the radio, and we tell our *compañeros* about the important news.

WRITERS, REPORTERS AND NEWS ANNOUNCERS

For me (perhaps because of my instinctive identification with these young journalists), the correspondents were one of the highlights of a generally impressive event, and I spent a great deal of time talking to them.

I had already learned a lot about the Correspondents Movement from an article in *Bohemia* magazine interviewing Julio Machado, the man responsible for the children's press service in the Central Havana region of the UPC, and Carmen Solar, head of children's programming at Radio Progresso.

Julio Machado explained that the main task of the children's press service was to gather reports and information of interest to children, and transmit them to the various organs of the press. By 1973 every school had a Pioneer correspondent, who gathered such information in his/her school and sent it to the Pioneer Press Bureau. There the information from all the schools is compiled, edited and prepared for presentation in newspapers, magazines and radio programs.

Asked how the children were trained and prepared for this work, Julio responded:

> . . . we begin by giving them a seminar led by *compañeros* from the Union of Journalists of Cuba in coordination with the UPC, through which they learn to edit, and to evaluate the news. We also organize visits to museums, work centers, factories, shops, learning centers and historic sites. We pay special attention to visits to the organs of the press.
>
> These visits are oriented toward accumulating knowledge they can later apply in their job as correspondents. After these activities, teams are organized through which they can exchange the experiences they've had among themselves. This helps develop good individual and collective work. We've had very good experience with this system since the little works that they then compose enable us to evaluate their power of observation and their ability to capture what they've seen.

Although the great majority of articles written by the children deal with their activities in school, they also focus to a considerable extent on cultural, patriotic and military events, and on promotion, attendance and the emulations in the schools.

Machado tried to make clear in this interview that the object of this work was not to simply have the children document accurate reports of their activities. The Pioneer (adult) leadership hopes through this program to stimulate creativity on the part of the children by encouraging them to write their own poems, stories and tales.

> Besides, among the duties of each correspondent is to maintain his own personal little library of his favorite books, and always to have a book to read, since we try to awaken in them the habit of reading.

Carmen Solar went on to detail the work of the Pioneers in the radio station.

> . . . Once the material has been edited, we divide it up among the correspondents and meet together for what we call "preview reading" in which all the material is re-read and any possible changes or additions are made. We always try to see that the material has content, that they understand it, so that they know how to make the message reach the listener. That's why it's so important that they don't just read it on the spot, so we always tape-record it.
>
> This guarantees a perfect transmission and assures the kids that they can correct any mistake they might make. They are very responsible about this program, about its quality, they worry a lot about that.

Carmen stressed that the children's participation in the radio program wasn't meant as a form of entertainment, or just to have the kids speak into a microphone and then go home.

> We try to see that they evaluate the content of the material, that they feel it, and that they know how to make it reach the children who are listening.

I had feared at first that the children were simply asked to read over the radio material that had been prepared for them by the adults. Carmen Solar made clear that the children themselves are involved in the preparation of the material, from the school correspondents who send in reports, poems and stories to the sectional or regional correspondents who read them over the air. The youngsters who work on the program have the job of re-writing or adding to inadequate material, correcting mistakes, and putting in details — like the correct name and location of a school, which may have been left out in the report — which help clarify the material.

In addition to the letters and other materials submitted by Pioneer correspondents, the Pioneers also choose material from their weekly newspaper *Pionero* to read over the air, since the scarcity of paper in Cuba prevents them from printing enough copies for every child to have one. In one way or another, all the material they use is by and about children.

In this particular program — which was begun at the end of 1969 — thirty Pioneers from the Central Havana Region participated, alternating days in small groups. Throughout the island, wherever there are radio stations, similar groups of Pioneers participate.

INTERVIEWING AND BEING INTERVIEWED

The Pioneer correspondents and I spent some time interviewing each other. The interview they conducted with me went out over the evening news program broadcast to the participants in the *Encuentro Nacional* over the PA system. My interview with them became part of my tape file, to be transcribed later on. The following are some excerpts from these interviews.

Karen Wald: Why are there children correspondents? Wouldn't it be better to have adult journalists, who are more experienced and capable, do this work?

Pioneer Correspondent: The journalists are better trained, but we're given courses in locution, exercises in how to speak correctly, etc.

PC: We're also given this work so that we'll take an interest in it and in the future be able to become journalists.

PC: Another thing is that children are less embarrassed with children correspondents since we're the same as they are, we belong to the same organization and we know each other, so they have more confidence in talking to us.

KW: How were you chosen as correspondents?

PC: First we had a meeting in school where they talked to us about the work of the correspondents. Those of us who had done well in other Pioneer activities were chosen. First they select us at the school level, then the sectional, and then regional. The selections are based on our work and academic records, our grades, and our discipline.

KW: What characteristics should a correspondent have?

PC: You have to have good discipline. You should help those who need it. For example, if there are *compañeritos* in your detachment who don't understand something, as correspondents and as friends you should explain it to them.

We have to speak with and direct the rest of the Pioneers in our school, guide them in the three stages of the emulation: The first stage is from September to January First. The children who complete all the requirements for that period are given the January First — the Triumph of the Revolution — badge.

The second stage is from January to April 4, which is the anniversary of the founding of the UPC, and those who win this emulation get the April 4 badge.

The final stage ends in June, on the birthdate of Antonio Maceo and Ernesto Che Guevara (only they were born a century apart), two figures who are closely linked as brothers in our history.

The children who complete the emulations for all three stages receive a star.

KW: Does the work of the Pioneers continue during school vacations?

PC: Yes, during the vacations we correspondents participate in the activities of the Vacation Plans organized by the Pioneers. We help lead these activities.

COVERING A NATIONAL EVENT

The poise and self-confidence exhibited by these Pioneer correspondents at the National Meeting wasn't surprising given their already broad experience. One of the Pioneers, a blond-haired girl named Ana Lidia, told me her responsibilities as a school correspondent also included welcoming foreign and other guests to their school, along with the *Jefe* of the Pioneers of the school and members of the Pioneer Council. "I've already received ten delegations, including one of Chilean women, and other members of the committee preparing the May First Celebration."

After the correspondents gave me a general background of the Pioneers organization, they brought me up-to-date on the *Encuentro.* "What kinds of things have been discussed in the previous *encuentros?*" I asked.

"We talked about whether we needed to take on new responsibilities to make the organization function better, if we should get rid of some of our old rules and put in new ones," they told me.

"What kinds of things have been discussed in the commissions that have been going on this morning?"

"The Commission on Organization discussed the definition of the UPC — how we want to define ourselves," answered one.

"The Commission on *capacitación* talked about how to teach Pioneers to carry out their activities. One response was that a *capacitador* would be in charge of this, with a team of helpers.

"They also agreed that Pioneer *capacitación* should be carried out as an extracurricular activity, after school hours. They also decided that it's necessary to know something about the organization before joining it. One *compañerito* proposed that there be a special *capacitador* who can prepare the children who are not yet Pioneers." This thorough explanation was given by a dark-haired boy named Israel, who looked down at his notes several times as he was talking to me.

The correspondent from Matanzas Province interjected to tell me that the preliminary provincial meeting in Matanzas had come up with proposals for the National Meeting calling for a world meeting of Pioneers, and another stating that Cuban Pioneers were ready and willing to participate in the reconstruction of Vietnam.

Escorted by some of the correspondents, I then went to sit in on some of the commissions that were still discussing their working papers. A Pioneer named Olga Lidia told me that the working papers had been prepared in each province based on questions, problems and topics suggested in the Pioneer meetings at each school and in each region. She handed me a ten-page mimeographed booklet with a printed cover reading in large block letters: *Encuentro Nacional de Jefes de Pioneros de Escuela,* and bearing the UPC emblem. The first inside page bore the title "*Comisión de Divulgación*" and a drawing (apparently done by an adult) of two little boys, one sitting on a make-shift go-cart which he was using as a desk to write about his school, while being pulled by another Pioneer

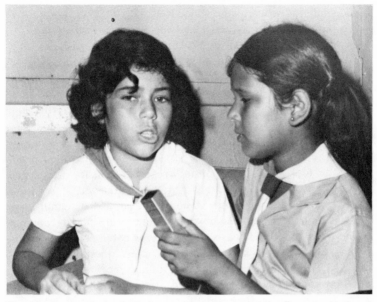

Pioneer corespondents did their own news coverage at the *Encentro National.*

on roller skates carrying a bullhorn! Under the drawing were the words of José Martí: "Children know more than you would think, and if you let them write what they know, they would write great things."

The questions raised in the booklet appeared to relate to specific sections of the Code regulating Pioneer activities. The first question posed was: What is the Pioneer emulation called? The sole response offered was "Three badges and a Star."

The second question — with fifteen possible responses — was "What are the requirements of the Pioneer emulation?"

Some of the answers included:

— To be punctual and not to miss school unjustifiably.

— To study and do your homework every day.

— To take care of social property and school materials.

— To participate in school and extracurricular activities with discipline and organization.

— To pass your grade.

— To study individually and collectively.
— To participate in productive and socially useful activities.
— To maintain good hygiene.
— To maintain good relations with the *compañeros*.

At its worst these sessions could be designed simply for the Pioneers to mouth approval of these already-laid-out tasks, goals and questions and answers. Since they were formulated after long discussions at the local level, one would think there would be a tendency for this to happen almost naturally.

But the Pioneers hadn't come just to read and nod their heads. Each one took his/her responsibility very seriously. There were long discussions in the meetings I attended over what the various points meant. Different interpretations were argued out until everyone was satisfied. Changes or amendments were not uncommon. In the daily report offered by the *Pioneros* correspondents on the second day there was a listing of how many questions had been analyzed, how many modified, how many accepted or rejected, and how many new ones presented. In each commission, there were at least two or three modifications; in one, there were ten. Only one commission had failed to come up with any new proposals; the average was two or three (out of a range of six to eight questions discussed!).

In the first commission I was attending (*divulgación*), there was disagreement about the inclusion of a newly proposed emulation-point: "Sixth grade students should participate in the *Guerrillero de La Enseñanza* movement." "Teaching guerrillas" are sixth graders who have decided — more or less taken a pledge — to become teachers (which are still in too-scarce supply). As preparation for their chosen careers they help out with a variety of tasks at school — including practice teaching. But as one student pointed out, even though teachers are badly needed by the Revolution, it doesn't make sense to encourage every sixth grader to become a teacher. "Not everybody has the vocation, the aptitude to be a good teacher," he reasoned. "We should only encourage those who *do* to become '*guerrilleros de la ensenañza*'."

After some discussion, it was agreed to modify this point.

In general in the various commissions I attended all questions were discussed, rather than just voted up and down. Even when there was complete agreement, one or two Pioneers usually talked a little about why he or she agreed with that point, or what it meant.

Each commission had a *jefe*, and two secretaries to take notes on what was carried out at each session. The *jefes* and secretaries seemed to be equally divided among boys and girls. In fact, the leadership of the entire event was also evenly divided, with half of the members of the National Council (elected on the first day on the basis of brief biographies of the candidates posted on a central bulletin board) being boys and half girls. The *Jefe Nacional* was a twelve-year-old girl from Camaguey named Xiomara.

The only place I noticed the division to appear unequal was among the correspondents who, probably by chance, were almost all girls.

Although the Pioneers were very serious about the task before them, the meeting was far from all work. Periodic outbursts of enthusiasm, singing of children's songs, handclapping and running around reminded you sharply that these were very much *children,* not "little adults," despite all the maturity they showed in their work.

Since this summer was the twentieth anniversary of the assault on the Moncada, it was not suprising that one of the guests who came to address the Pioneers was one of the survivors of that rebel attack. What was a little surprising to me was the level and the tone of the questions the children asked him. Mixed in with the questions that reflected a typical child-like curiosity were those which indicated a great deal of thought. Some of the questions I noted down were:

— How did you feel during the assault? How did you feel while you were riding in the car away from Siboney to the Moncada? How did you feel afterwards? How do you feel now?

— Did the soldiers at the Moncada suspect that something was going to happen?

— When and how did you get a chance to practice with guns for the assault? Under what conditions did you train?

— How long did the whole assault take?

— What were Fidel's objectives in attacking Moncada?

— What did you think about Marxism-Leninism before the attack on the Moncada?

— Before taking the step of assaulting the Moncada did you attempt more peaceful means of changing the situation in Cuba?

— How did you get the blueprints or floor plans of the fortress?

Other guests appeared before the plenary sessions of the meeting, too. In addition, on some days the Pioneers were taken on visits around Havana, including to a military base, where they met and talked with soldiers and officers from the Revolutionary Armed Forces.

Finally, the various commissions began to report that they had completed their work. The Organization Commission (which, perhaps predictably, was very, very organized in its work) concluded after ten hours of sessions in which, they said, a "critical spirit" was prevalent. As they read off the points to which they had agreed, Pioneers broke into loud cheers and handclapping to indicate points they were in particularly strong agreement with.

When the report was concluded, *Jefa* Xiomara asked for the approval of the entire body. When it was given unanimously, the Pioneers from the Organization Commission reacted very excitedly, jumping up and down, hugging each other, amidst a lot of handclapping.

Slowly, each commission read off its report. Half were accepted unanimously. Questions were first raised after the *divulgación* report, when one boy suggested that, although their work was generally good, the *compañeros* had failed to be particularly creative. "They really didn't add too many new ideas," he criticized, contrasting them to some of the other commissions. (Most of the questions concerning this commission had to do with the form, contents and quantity of school bulletin boards, the Pioneer paper, and information about the emulations.) Their one innovation — a message of solidarity with the people of Uruguay (who were then on general strike in protest against their dictatorial regime) — he criticized as being incomplete: "It should be generalized to all countries of Africa, Asia and Latin America, perhaps using Uruguay as an example," he suggested.

Later in the plenary the Pioneers did decide to send a message of solidarity to all the revolutionary and struggling peoples of the world.

The other commission which provoked most discussion was "Activities #1." (This commission had been broken up into two groups because it included so much work.) Within the commission itself there had been considerable discussion, argument and debate.

For example, in a section asking which activities would the Pioneers like to carry out with the Revolutionary Armed Forces and Ministry of the Interior, the suggestion of doing guard duty at military units was criticized and eliminated on the basis that "we don't have the preparation to do guard duty." The proposal to pay homage to those who fell in two particular battles was modified when several Pioneers pointed out that homage should be paid to all martyrs, not just those who fell in those battles.

But the question that aroused most serious debate concerned the participation of Pioneers in voluntary agricultural work. No one was opposed to voluntary work. But one boy brought up the question which must have plagued members of the Ministry of Education and Central Committee, and have been the subject of very serious debate at that level: the extent to which students should participate in this type of work, at the "expense" of normal school work.

The proposal called for participation in the Sugar Harvest Plan, requiring a considerable amount of time spent at agricultural work. The Pioneer who opposed it suggested that work in school gardens would be sufficient, and that it was unrealistic to assume that all schools (e.g., those in the cities) could engage in fulltime work-study plans. "We're students, with our whole future ahead of us," he argued. "We have to prepare for that future, when technicians and scientists will be needed to move our country forward. We should be dedicating ourselves more to study than to work at this stage."

A girl from Oriente province stood up to oppose him. She stressed the importance of combining work and study in terms of the formation of the individual as a worker and communist. The great majority of students agreed with her position. But another boy stood to back up the first argument. "We're an underdeveloped country," he said. "Instead of picking up a machete to cut sugar cane we should be developing new technology to mechanize this work."

The meeting went on record as favoring the combination of work with study — a decision that was similarly reached at the Ministry of Education, although they were moving more slowly with this at the primary school level than with upper grades. At MinEd they told me that there had in fact been serious debate over this; that many feared time taken away from classroom study would hurt the

students scholastically. What they found after several years of experiment, however, was that the schools that combined work and study
invariably had a better promotion and scholastic record than those
that did not.

The students also tackled another thorny problem of the Revolution: the question of material versus moral incentives. One of the
proposals had called for giving material incentives, such as pencils
and note-books, to students and detachments who did outstanding
work. A Pioneer objected to this, "because our organization is opposed to material incentive." He suggested instead that the incentive
offered could be group participation in trips to historical or interesting places and various non-material rewards. After some discussion,
the Pioneers in the Plenary session agreed to use *both* types of incentive.

Interestingly enough, this was the kind of decision that Cuban
workers were arriving at during the same period. Although leaders
of the Cuban Revolution had always mentioned the importance of
combining both moral and material incentives, the overwhelming
preference was toward eliminating material incentives and relying
on moral ones. Thus, no overtime work was paid, and workers were
urged to do productive work on Sundays and increase their production solely on the basis of the knowledge that they, the working
people of Cuba, would be the ones to benefit from all this.

At the thirteenth congress of the Cuban trade unions in the fall
of 1973 (several months after the Pioneer meeting), the representatives of the workers and Fidel Castro expressed the need to reeval-
uate this policy, and to assess more realistically what stage of development they were at in their road toward building a socialist and
communist society. Communism is defined as a period in which
all workers produce according to their ability, and receive according
to their needs. But socialism — a transitional stage toward communism — stipulates only that workers receive "according to their
work" — taking into consideration that not all workers will have
reached the level of consciousness whereby they would, with no other
stimulation, produce to the fullest extent of their ability. In the stage
of socialism, then, there must be norms and regulations regarding
work, and material as well as the moral rewards for accomplishing
that work.

In Cuba many had believed that the "material" rewards were
there, in that the working people were the ones who received the

schools, hospitals and other goods and services built by the proceeds of their work. But this was clearly too abstract for many workers to understand. So the decision was made that, while productive work would still be encouraged, and everyone would work toward building that consciousness in all workers, material rewards for work, including pay for overtime, would be the current policy.

It is impossible to tell to what extent this discussion and debate among adults, which surely must have been going on for many months prior to their congress in October, was seeping down to these youngsters and influencing (probably unconsciously) the themes and direction of their own debates. Certainly they were aware of these discussions on a certain level, from reading newspaper and magazine articles, and hearing conversations at home and on the streets. At any rate, for whatever reason, the predominant questions concerning adults at that time, and the decisions as to how to resolve them, were reflected in the debates of these primary school children as they met in their national organization.

There could be no better example of the extent to which the Union of Pioneers does in fact prepare the children to become the future workers, creators and leaders of their country's revolution.

Because they are still children, however — or perhaps because the Cuban Revolution doesn't believe that all work and no play should be the lot of anybody — the *Encuentro Nacional* ended with songs, cheers, laughter — and an evening bonfire and street carnival, complete with costumes, floats and fireworks.

MORE THAN JUST A CHAPTER

Journalistically speaking, it would be appropriate to end the discussion of the Pioneers at this point. But the Pioneers aren't just a chapter in the life of Cuban children: they are a thread which winds its way through their lives from the time they "graduate" from the childcare centers until they reach the junior high schools, and whose influence continues to affect the children's lives as they grow older. So it is worth appending some more observations on the Pioneers at this point. Since there are so many ways that Pioneer activities fill the children's lives, I've chosen two topics through which to focus on the UPC: the Pioneer newspaper, and their annual re-enactment of the July 26th Assault on the Moncada Fortress.

LEARNING TO WRITE FOR CHILDREN

As I learned when I tried to investigate various aspects of children's culture in post-Revolutionary Cuba, it has not been easy to fill the complete void which previously existed in children's literature, art, music, theatre and dance. This, despite the fact that Cuba had a rich literary tradition during the period of its struggle against Spain (the second half of the nineteenth century) which included José Martí's writings for children.

With the emphasis on youth — and children in particular — that came with the Revolution there was a strongly felt need to make up for this lack, to recapture the roots in Cuban history that made children important and, therefore, considered writing for children an important occupation for adults.

The weekly magazine *Pionero* started as early as 1961 — the second oldest publication created by the Revolution. (The only magazine initiated by the Revolution prior to this was *Verde Olivo*, the magazine of the Revolutionary Armed Forces.)

Ricardo García Pampín, one of today's editors of the *Pionero*, talked about the reasons for placing so much emphasis on creating a revolutionary children's magazine.

> A child isn't an isolated phenomenon within this Revolution; we don't see the child as a receptor, an empty vessel to receive information. We think of the formation of the child as something in which the children participate. History isn't something which they memorize, it's something they live. That's why we have the re-enactment of the assault on the Moncada, the marches along the paths of Camilo and Che, etc. The creation of a national children's magazine was basically for the same reason as the creation of a national children's organization: so that children can participate in their own formation and development in some organized way.
>
> Children need their own publication just as they need their own organization.

He also talked of the problems involved in trying to develop such a magazine.

Cuba had no recent tradition of children's publications, aside from a few isolated, semi-commercial efforts. So there was no one with experience in this when the Revolution triumphed. There was a great underestimation of children's literature and those who worked in this field by cultural sectors. Famous writers and artists looked down on it as something for "lesser" artists and writers.

The lack of skilled, experienced writers who could create revolutionary literature for children was only part of the problem the Cuban Revolution faced. The other part was the effect of cultural imperialism on children's media. Pampín recalled:

Cuba was inundated with comic books written in the United States and printed in Spanish in Mexico. These were reactionary in content, and distorted our history in accord with the North American viewpoint. Comics not only had a pernicious effect on Cuban consciousness; they also kept down any possibility of developing Cuban comics, since Cubans couldn't compete with the 10 cent price of the comics offered from the U.S.

The resulting lack of experience in this genre had several effects. One of these, as Pampín pointed out, was that during the first year of publication of the periodical there were "good intentions but bad results."

It was a lousy children's magazine. It had a bad design and layout. No one had ever done this before; no one knew how to lay out a children's magazine. The text, everything was badly done.

But, Pampín added with a smile, the ideology was good. And the people working on putting out the *Pionero* learned to overcome their original mistakes fairly rapidly.

The children, he said, were always receptive to the magazine — even when it was bad — because it was *theirs*. No one was being very critical at that stage. The *Pionero* developed slowly, through a natural process of improvement, plus comparison with similar works put out in other socialist countries, and some professional criticism. In a little over a decade of its existence it went from a circulation of eighty thousand monthly copies to one hundred forty thousand weekly.

As the Pioneers grew, the demand for the magazine grew too. It was then sold not just to Pioneers, but to anyone who wanted it, distributed through different state organisms, and publicly. Cubans were used to having a comic section in the local papers prior to the Revolution, so picking up on this tradition the *Pionero,* which is printed largely in comic-strip form, was distributed with the newspaper *Hoy,* a radical-progressive daily. When *Hoy* was replaced by *Granma* and *Juventud Rebelde* (*JR*), the organs of the Communist Party and Young Communists, respectively, *Pionero* was distributed as a supplement of *JR.*

But distribution was bad for a number of reasons. When it was part of *JR* (after 1965), the magazine was received in many places where there were no children, because adults liked it, and not always in every place where it was needed for the children. Transportation problems also meant it sometimes didn't reach remote areas. Scarcity of paper meant there were never enough copies to satisfy all the demand.

By 1973 several steps were taken to deal with these problems. The *Pionero* became completely independent (in keeping, too, with the independence of the UPC from the Young Communists) and was distributed independently, solely to Pioneers. Each *destacamento* (equivalent to each classroom) and the library of each school receives a copy. Better transportation and coordination meant it reached every province, including the most mountainous regions. "It might come a little late in some places, if a truck breaks down or something," Pampín admitted, "but it's generally received at the same time in all places, not just in the cities."

Listening to the description of just the technical and logistical problems of bringing literature to masses of children made me realize how much more there was to this problem than we could ever imagine, living in an overdeveloped economy where transportation is taken for granted, technical skills are abundant, and tons of paper are wasted in a million ridiculous ways every day. But the most interesting aspect of all this was the unique way the Revolution related to many of these problems.

After telling me how the magazine is distributed to the children through their detachments and school libraries, Pampín went on:

> The collective use of the magazine is to make up for the fact that there isn't enough paper to print one for every child. Before, some children didn't have a dime to buy a comic book. Now every child has got a dime — but we don't have the resources to print that many. But anyway, it's a good experience for the children to share them. We won't have abundance here for a number of generations,

and our children have to be prepared for this reality. We have to satisfy basic needs, using collective means when necessary, within the economic reality of our country. So the youngsters learn to share, and to save. Just as they learn that food is scarce, so you don't throw out food you don't want, you save it for later.

Despite this positive attitude toward the sharing of the children's magazine Pampín admitted that they don't have as many copies as they would like. "We'd like to see one copy for every five or six children of reading age, and we'd like to have separate magazines for the older and younger ones." At the current time, he indicated, the magazine was really oriented primarily to fourth through sixth graders. But since there was nothing else for the younger children, the same magazine was issued to all.

By now it had become apparent to me that the *Pionero* served as more than just an entertaining comic strip for the children, although this certainly was considered a legitimate function. I asked Pampín what he — and the UPC — considered the primary objectives of publishing the *Pionero*.

One of the fundamental objectives, as you can imagine, is to entertain the Pioneers. We want to provide something they like, of high enough quality and form so that the children want to read it. Without this, all the correct ideology in the world would be worthless. You could print the Communist Manifesto and be wasting paper. Once you achieve this, you are in a position to achieve the second objective.

This second objective is to aid in the integral formation of the child. In one sense this is political — but not just political, because a complete person can't be only political. Within this context we try to give them a sense of history, of internationalism, a hatred of imperialism — remember, Che talked about how hatred for the enemy is as important as love. Love for peace includes a hatred of the enemy of the people.

But because this formation isn't just political, we also want to have literature, science, art. The new human being needs to appreciate poetry, music, art, etc.

We also want to reinforce the *individuality* of the child, which is something quite separate from *individualism*. We want every child to have his/her own criteria by which to judge things. We want them to be interested in bettering themselves in every way. But that individual is always seen as part of the collective, so he/she wants

Assault on the Moncada.

to be better, but not at the expense of others. We want children to take on responsibility, but not as a means of getting privileges. We want them to feel that they want to be useful to society. Work should be like eating or breathing to them — a normal, necessary part of life. (We understand work as a transitory stage, but at this moment it is certainly necessary.)

We see the magazine as an organizer, a vehicle to help create all these ideas and attitudes in the children.

Pampín then gave me some concrete examples of how they try to use the magazine to foster these attitudes. The content of the various stories and poems was one obvious example. Not so obvious were the pages that need to be cut out, folded, and pasted, to create something. "This is to encourage the children to participate, not just sit and absorb. If you tell children that water is made of H_2O, that's not as good as giving them hydrogen and oxygen and letting them combine them to make water. The same reasoning applies to the Pioneers' assault on the Moncada, although that's a little more obvious than having children cut things out and put them together."

ASSAULTING THE MONCADA
MAKING HISTORY COME ALIVE

Each time I visited Cuba, wherever I went, I noticed one singular characteristic among all the Cubans I met and talked to: they were always ready to admit mistakes, criticize themselves, express concern for problems they were facing. Fidel once succinctly expressed this in a speech describing the many economic problems growing out of mistakes made during 1969-70, when the country had just failed to achieve its goal of harvesting ten million tons of sugar cane. Although recognizing that Cuba's enemies would certainly rejoice at the admission of problems and mistakes, and use them to shame the Revolution, Fidel insisted that all the economic data should be made available to all the people.

This same attitude was apparent when talking to teachers, educators, Pioneer guides, Party members and numerous other Cubans concerned with the future development of their young people. It also surfaced in reports, analyses, and discussions in the field of education — reports which were available to the public. In all of these, an air of self-criticism, a readiness to admit mistakes and talk about problems, was prevalent.

It was because of this attitude that I learned of a concern facing Cuban leaders and educators that went beyond the enormous, but relatively straightforward problems of schools, teachers, books and supplies. This was the question of how to instill a revolutionary spirit in a generation of children who have not known suffering and hardship, not lived with racism and sexual discrimination, and have not fought in the battles to overcome these.

Ruth Sidel, in her book *Women and Childcare in China,* tells how the Chinese encourage elderly people in each village or commune to spend time with the youngsters, telling them stories of what life was like in "the bitter past." Although there is no such organized program of storytelling in Cuba, parents and grandparents generally do tell their young what it was like before.

But this only begins to touch on the problem. Cuban youngsters generally know — in their heads, if not in their flesh — about hunger, illiteracy, degradation. They understand why it existed before, and that people had to fight to make things the way they are now.

But the children themselves did not take part in this battle. They can appreciate what has been done for them; they can dedicate themselves to work hard and study hard to continue developing their country, so it can never fall back into the misery that existed before. But where are they to get that revolutionary spark, that spirit, that total dedication that comes from having fought and risked your life for an ideal?

It's not a question that is answered easily, or in only one way. The problem applies to students now in college as well as those just beginning school. And the Revolution, while it does not yet consider itself to have the definitive answer, has been experimenting and innovating with a number of techniques.

The Union of Pioneers' contribution to all this is in part to try to make that history come alive for the youngsters by allowing them to re-enact it, while at the same time letting the children know that they are a very vital part of the ongoing Revolution of today.

The most dramatic aspect of this re-living of history is the Pioneers' Assault on the Moncada each July 26th. In 1973 the assault took on a special importance because it was part of the massive celebrations for the twentieth anniversary of the original attack.

A SPECIAL KIND OF SUMMER CAMP   Part of the responsibility of the Pioneers is to organize the children's leisure-time activities, and this becomes especially important during the summer vacation. Pioneers have arranged summer activities from street games to excursions to summer camps in each province and locale. Two of these summer camps are very special: the International Pioneers Camp at Varadero Beach, and the Assault on the Moncada Camp in Siboney, just outside of Santiago de Cuba. The two camps are similar in that both choose outstanding students to attend, and both are aimed particularly at fostering the kind of development the Revolution is striving for in its youngsters.

In addition to providing a meaningful way for the children to commemorate the action which launched their Revolution, the Assault on the Moncada camp also gives the youngsters a chance to meet Pioneers from the other provinces and regions of Cuba, and to have a good time while they are learning.

In 1973 each province except Oriente chose its best detachment of Pioneers (based on the criteria set up by the UPC in the previous year's national meeting) to attend the camp at Siboney. In Oriente individual children were chosen from throughout the Province, based on biographies submitted for each child. Several hundred children participated.

Several of the youngsters at the *Encuentro Nacional* had told me that their detachment was going to the camp at Siboney. They were all excited about it. Pampín, too, had mentioned it several times, and encouraged me to try to go to it if I could. I was nearly six months pregnant by this time, and at first the people I asked about arranging the trip thought I was crazy. But by this time I really had the fever: I wanted to go to camp with the Pioneers.

But the day before the Pioneers were supposed to leave, I still had not received an invitation to attend the 26th of July celebration in Santiago as a journalist (which would have more or less guaranteed my transportation there), and I hadn't been able to arrange any other transportation. Every car, bus and train available was already booked up with all the invited guests from scores of countries who were there to attend the twentieth anniversary of the start of the Cuban Revolution. In despair, I called Pampín at the *Pionero* office and told him I didn't think I'd be able to go.

Later that afternoon I got a phone call. It was Pampín. "If you can get your things ready and be at the Pioneer headquarters first thing tomorrow morning, you can go on the bus with the children from Havana or the Isle of Pines."

The bus ride he was talking about was sixteen hours long, partly over mountains and country roads. But I didn't think twice before assuring him I'd be there. I was going to camp!

ON THE ROAD Children were lined up or sprawled over suitcases all over the long porch which ran alongside the National Headquarters of the UPC when I got there next morning. Some of them had been waiting there several hours. Most of them seemed quiet and maybe a little sleepy. Certainly they seemed much more orderly than I would have expected from a group of girls and boys on their way to camp.

When I mounted the porch I was greeted excitedly by several children who recognized me from the *Encuentro Nacional*. They began telling me about the selection process for the camp,* and talking about what we would be doing there.

"The camp we're going to is a brand new one," Pedro told me. "Workers from the Young Communists (UJC) have been working 'guerrilla' to finish it in time for the assault. 'Guerrilla' work is when you volunteer to form work brigades and work day and night to finish a certain project," he explained in response to my questioning look. María Luísa, whom I'd met at the *Encuentro,* added, "The camp is alongside the *granjita* at Siboney, the little farmhouse where Fidel and Abel and the other rebels met to plan the attack. We'll be living there for the two weeks we're in camp, and we'll visit the *granjita.*"

"I was there once! I was there once!" chimed in a little boy, and he went on to describe the little white farmhouse with its red roof, and to tell how the rebels hid their guns in a dry well out back.

"We're going in the Girón buses," an older boy told me. "They're not imported — we made them ourselves here in Cuba."

Ana Lidia, who had been a correspondent at the *Encuentro,* told me that the symbolic assault this year would not be at the Moncada itself, since the people of Santiago were preparing the grounds of the Moncada for the tens of thousands of visitors who would be attending the main celebration there on the 26th. We'll be attacking the Palace of Justice," she said, "which was one of the other targets on that day. And another group from Oriente will be attacking the Fortress at Bayamo at the same time, just as the rebels did."

Just then the buses we'd been waiting for from the Isle of Pines pulled in, with the children inside loudly singing "La Isla! La Isla!" The children poured out of their buses, and lined up on the front lawn together with the Havana Pioneers, who were scurrying to get their luggage together and form into detachments.

While we were getting in order, the Pioneers kept talking to me about the camp and the reasons for the assault.

"The assault is a really important thing," a little girl named Maires assured me, "because the *compañeros* who attacked the Moncada gave everything to free Cuba."

---

*Because of different selection procedures, it was possible for a Pioneer to be chosen as an individual to attend the *Encuentro Nacional*, and also be part of an outstanding detachment chosen for the Assault on the Moncada camp.

A shy little boy named Luís added: "A lot of Cubans died at the Moncada, so we could be free, so we could have the things we have now. My papa and mama tell me they didn't have any of the things we enjoy today — schools or clinics or even enough food or clothes. That's why we study hard, we work hard, today. We have to be ready all the time. We can't ever let anyone take this away from us."

Then Pampin and several other leaders of the UPC were addressing the children, giving them last minute instructions about the bus ride and the camp — and introducing the "foreign guest" who was going to be riding along with them. Soon we were in the buses and heading toward the suburbs of Havana.

Although they'd been traveling for hours already, the children from La Isla were full of spirit, chanting and singing, popping in and out of their seats. They seemed to be encouraged strongly in this by their guides, two women and a man in this bus, all about eighteen to twenty years old.

Eventually, as the day wore on and the heat mounted — alleviated only slightly by the shade provided by the bus and the air coming in the open windows — the children began to nod in their seats, and fall asleep, heads on shoulders and laps of those beside them.

There were stops for gas, bathroom breaks and lunch — the longest one being at the Pioneer Palace in one of the middle provinces during the heat of the day — and again for dinner. Most of the provinces were just beginning to draft plans for building modern Pioneer Palaces like those in the other socialist countries, and these looked more like country summer camps than the pictures I had seen of such Palaces in China, the Soviet Union and Korea. But in each the buildings were clean (except the outdoor bathrooms in one province) and the food was good and plentiful. I noticed with surprise, though, that the kids were given soda pop instead of milk at the meals. I wondered if this was a special "treat," or poor planning on someone's part, but there was no one around to ask.

At the lunch break there had been some mix-up as to where we were to go, and the people in the city weren't prepared for us, so after scrambling out of the buses, the children had to wait in lines for a long time while someone went to find out what the problem was and straighten it out. While we were waiting two of the little boys — tired and irritable from the heat and the long bouncy ride, got into an argument, and soon one was crying, while the other one stood there, indignant, with his arms across his chest and his lower lip jutting out.

The other Pioneers — who had been waiting patiently — agreed that the boy who was crying had more or less provoked it, but that the other one had hit him unnecessarily hard. The aggressor just glowered: "My papa says if anyone messes with you, you have to fight back," he insisted angrily. A male guide and several of the Pioneers tried to explain to him why that wasn't the best behavior. In the end the two children were simply separated by sending them to different parts of the line.

As we entered more rural and mountainous zones we picked up and let off several passengers on a couple of occasions — once a young man in military uniform, another time a woman with a young baby trying to get to the provincial hospital. The bus was already a little overcrowded, but children tripled-up in their seats to make way for the passengers, and I heard no complaints.

At two in the morning we rolled through the gates of the Assault on the Moncada Pioneer Camp, and the sleepy Pioneers roused themselves to sit up and enter the camp singing and chanting the songs from their province at the top of their lungs. There were several guides waiting to direct us to our bunks; all the other buses had arrived much earlier and most children were asleep.

CAMPING CUBAN STYLE   When we got up the next morning there was activity all over the camp. We tidied up our bunks, got dressed, and found our way to a long building filled with rows of toilets, showers and wash basins. Everyone had to wait his or her turn, but there was no pushing or shoving, no cutting ahead or rushing to use the facilities out of turn. When we finished, we headed toward a building in the center of the camp which housed the kitchen and a large, screened-in dining hall. Pioneers were serving food and cleaning tables. (I later learned that each detachment rotated this duty.) Pioneers entered the mess hall in detachments, sat quietly during the meal so they could finish quickly and make way for the lines of children waiting outside. During the first few meals I didn't realize the children were supposed to eat without talking, and I spent the meals asking questions of the Pioneers I sat with. Finally one of them explained to me:

"We're not supposed to talk during our meals. We can't all eat at once, because there isn't enough room, and other Pioneers are waiting. If we talk during the meal, it takes longer. So we should talk after the meal is over."

I learned another lesson during these mealtimes. Among the Pioneers at this camp were a number who had participated in the *Encuentro Nacional* in Havana, some as members of the Council that led the meeting. But yesterday's national leaders were just Pioneers in this camp. Xiomara, the *Jefa Nacional* in Havana, waited on tables of other Pioneers along with the other members of her detachment. I began to realize that some of the humility I encountered among the children, their lack of a sense of "superiority" or "elitism", was probably due to this constant interchange. Children chosen as "outstanding" on any level were still expected to study, work and carry out all of the tasks that every Cuban child carries out.

After breakfast some Pioneers went to help unload pillows and blankets from some trucks and carry them into the bunks. Others organized themselves into squads to clean up the camp grounds. Most formed small groups to play games, sing and chant. I wandered among them with my taperecorder, recording the songs they were singing. Most of them were songs everyone sang in chorus, or where one child took the lead and others chimed in. Most of them were humorous, but with a distinctly Cuban tone.

All of the songs were sung with great spirit, in part because the children apparently enjoyed them, but also because singing was part of their emulation: to see which group showed the greatest spirit. I noticed, however, that whenever I approached a group there were a lot of sideways glances and more-than-curious looks.

Finally a counselor approached me. "The children would like to talk with you. Frankly, they're a little worried about what you're doing in their camp."

I realized that except for the children who rode with me in the bus from Havana, none of them knew what I was doing there. Any strange adult visiting a children's camp would arouse curiosity anywhere. But here, in a Pioneer camp in Cuba, the children were understandably concerned about the presence of someone from "enemy territory" in their midst.

We talked for over a half hour. I explained to them that I was there to write a book about the Cuban Revolution, and that I expected most of my material to be by and about the children who had been born since the beginning of the Revolution. In response to their questions I indicated that I was strongly opposed to my government's war against the people of Vietnam, and that I had always tried to fight against racism in my country. Our talk ranged across many subjects, including Richard Nixon, the CIA, socialism and capitalism. After some time I began to feel that I had convinced them I was not there as an enemy.

"Is there anyone else who's still concerned about why I'm here?" I asked. "Yes," came a chorus of replies, and only then did I truly understand the degree to which Cuban children have learned to be both cautious and analytical. One little girl expressed their lingering doubt: "If you're really a revolutionary, or at least have expressed your agreement with our revolution, why is it that Nixon, or your government — the bad ones — why do they let you leave your country to come to Cuba?"

While the children were forming into detachments and getting into the buses (which took a while, because things were a little disorganized this first day) I wandered around inspecting the camp. The children's bunkhouses were made of a corrugated material, painted pink, green, brown, orange and blue. There were separate bunkhouses for boys and girls, but they all were built alike. Separate buildings housed the boys' and girls' bathrooms. Some guides slept in each bunkhouse with the Pioneers, but there was also an additional bunkhouse for other guides, and one for administrative personnel. A little house surrounded by tropical plants and trees served as the administration center. Nearby was the infirmary, which had two fulltime nurses and a doctor. The dining room, which I'd glanced at through sleepy eyes during breakfast, was light and pleasant, with all walls made of screens and brightly colored table cloths on the tables.

Trees and plants abounded throughout the camp grounds, but to make sure, workers were planting rose bushes and other shrubs in areas that had been cut down while they were building the camp. Behind the bunks was an outdoor amphitheatre. The backdrop of the stage had large multicolored balloons painted on it.

The buses were lined up along the driveway which wound its way from the road along one edge of the camp. Almost all the

children were aboard the buses by the time I got there, so I entered
the first bus I saw, and began making new friends.

Singing was a favorite pastime on the bus for these Pioneers,
too, who were from Oriente. One of the songs was aimed at teasing
the driver for driving too slowly. But each time they sang this one,
the Pioneers would quickly follow it with a chant: *"Oye, chofer,
no se mortifique, porque los niños nacen para ser felices"* — which
essentially was saying: "Don't take us too seriously, we're just having
a good time with you." Later on, when emulation between provinces
became too heated and seemed to border on outright competition,
I heard the children catching themselves at times and chanting
this to the other provinces.

The trip to Santiago was a short one, because after lunch the
Pioneers had to get down to the serious business of choosing their
leaders and setting up emulations for the two weeks they would be
in camp.

National Council of Pioneers. Xiomara, the President (2nd. from right),
later waited on tables at the Assault on the Moncada Camp.

CHOOSING LEADERS, MAKING RULES After lunch some of
the Pioneers sat down with me to explain how they were chosen
for the camp, and how they in turn would choose the leadership
of the camp, and set up their emulations. "Each year we take
part in the symbolic assault on the Moncada Fortress, as a way of
showing our respect for those who fell in that action, and as a
way of linking the past with the present," a blond-haired, blue-
eyed Pioneer from Camaguey began.

> The detachment . . . or in some cases individual students . . .
> who come out first in their province in terms of promotion, revo-
> lutionary attitude, activities, etc. are chosen to take part.

To my question of how outstanding detachments are chosen, he
responded:

> The points of emulation are set up each year at the *Encuentro
> Nacional*, based on suggestions coming from each school and prov-
> ince. Some of the key ones are discipline, initiative, enthusiasm,
> and good participation in all school and extracurricular activities.

The Pioneers explained that even the best detachments are usually
lacking in one or another of the emulation points. The guides at
the district and provincial levels keep albums showing the activities
carried out by their best detachments, and these are compared to
select the ones which will take part in the assault.

Just as in the school, the Pioneers needed a *Jefe*, a *Sanitario*
(medical or health worker) and a Correspondent for the camp.
Representatives from each province met at the administration building
to discuss how these would be chosen. These same Pioneers formed
the Camp Council, who would set up the emulation goals for the camp.

They decided that each province would propose a candidate
for each position, and would prepare biographies of their candidates
so that all the Pioneers could make their selection in a mass meeting.

The points of emulation were worked out in conjunction with
the guides, who suggested the broad categories. They suggested
two kinds of emulations: between bunkhouses (which were not always
synonymous with provinces) and between detachments (provinces).
In the bunkhouses the Pioneers would strive to have everything
neat, clean, orderly and "aesthetic." The detachments would be
judged by their discipline, enthusiasm, initiative and work (maintenance of the area of campground assigned to each province).

With these basic decisions made, the Council members moved outside to join their detachments, which were lined up in one area of the camp to begin the selection of leaders, and to talk about the over-all plans of the camp. Many of the detachments were singing and chanting as we got there (in an apparent attempt to outsing and outchant each other).

After some initial confusion, it was decided that the candidate from each province would stand up and give her/his own auto-biography. As they stood up one after another, I noted with some surprise that five out of six candidates were girls. Only one of them, Rafael, the candidate from Camaguey, was someone I recog-nized from the *Encuentro Nacional.*

I kept brief notes on some of their presentations.

My name is María Luísa. I'm from La Isla [the Isle of Pines, renamed the Isle of Youth after the Revolution]. I began school at six years old. I've always been a good student, a vanguard. I've had various responsibilities. In third grade I was *Jefe de unidad,* in fourth grade I was *Jefe de destacamento,* in fifth I was a monitor and was on the regional committee of monitors. In sixth grade I was *Jefe de destacamento.* I led my detachment in various activities that made it one of the best in the region. I want to be a teacher. I was a delegate to the *Encuentro Nacional.* I've received visitors from various countries at my school, including the *compañeros* from Vietnam, Angela Davis and Billy Dean Smith.

My name is Mayra. I'm from Pinar del Rio. I've always been a good Pioneer, a good student. I participate in all the activities of the Pioneers. In second grade I was a monitor and *Jefe de destaca-mento,* in third *Jefe de unidad.* I've always won the three *sellos* (badges) of the emulations. I was also the *jefe* of a study circle, and helped students who had lower grades. I've had 100 percent promotion and 98 percent attendance. All my *compañeros* won *sellos* and my detachment won the provincial emulation and was chosen to take part in this historic assault.

The rest of the candidates were more or less similar. Ana Mar-garita from Havana had also been monitor and *Jefe* many times, had good grades, and had participated in provincial and national meetings, as had María Carmen from Matanzas. The candidate from Las Villas, Aida María, in addition to these qualifications had also been chosen to attend the Lenin Vocational (science) school (for which the top 5 percent of the class is chosen), had taken part in last year's Assault on the Moncada, and had been chosen to sit on the platform with Fidel on May Day.

Rafael, the Pioneer whom I recalled from the *Encuentro Nacional* and the only male candidate, had met with the Vietnamese delegation when they visited Camaguey. He spoke of work he had done in various work centers, like the Coppelia ice cream parlor and a local pharmacy. And he had been chosen to play the role of agricultural technician in their provincial carnival.

Maurice, a Pioneer from Oriente, also spoke of working, and her role in maintaining the discipline in her unit and detachment. "My students and I were always vanguard" was the way she expressed her school record. In addition to being chosen *Sanitaria* and *Jefe* of her school chorus, she was a *guerrillera de enseñanza,* a member of a radio and library interest circle, and had been chosen as one of the Pioneers who went to visit the Pioneers in Bulgaria.

It was easy to see from the impressive list of qualifications that any of these Pioneers could probably have carried out the role of *Jefe de Campamento.* It was also apparent in the voting that followed the reading of each child's autobiography that each province was voting for its own candidate. Since some provinces had larger delegations than others, that proved a less-than-satisfactory method. It was finally decided to let the candidates decide among themselves who was to be *Jefe.*

While they went off behind a bunk to meet and discuss this question, the voting went on, in similar vein, for the Pioneer Correspondent and the *Sanitario.* The candidates for *Jefe* had given rousing political speeches in addition to their lists of qualifications; the correspondents also did this to some extent, talking about the importance of the Assault, and the revolutionary actions of their schools and the country. The candidates for *Sanitario* — most of whom had been *sanitarios* in their schools, seemed somewhat less articulate than those who ran for *Jefe.* They primarily stressed their efforts at keeping their schools clean, participation in medical seminars, keeping medical information posted on the bulletin board, etc.

I wandered over to where the *Jefe* candidates were still discussing. It seemed to be mostly between Rafael and Mayra, the girl from Pinar del Rio. At nine years old Mayra was one of the smallest

Pioneers in camp, with short brown hair and soft eyes. But her speech had been a fiery one, full of revolutionary zeal. Blond-haired, blue-eyed Rafael was tall, thin, serious. I remembered him from the *Encuentro* as being very organized and efficient, and quite articulate.

In the end, the Pioneers chose Mayra. Throughout the remaining ten days of camp it was this tiny little powerhouse who presided over the morning flag-raising ceremonies and detachment reports, camp meetings, and work activities. She welcomed and addressed the various dignitaries, heroes and guests who visited the camp. Long after her voice had been worn hoarse she was urging on the Pioneers to greater spirit, more discipline, better work. In all this she acted as though she had been born into it and had been doing it all her life. At no time did she seem to lack the respect of the other older, bigger and sometimes more experienced Pioneers.

BEACHES AND TOMBS, MUSEUMS AND CARNIVALS   In a mass meeting at the amphitheatre that night the guides, directors of the camp and Pioneer leaders told the children of the activities planned for the remainder of the camp. The list included visiting all of the Revolutionary sites in the area: the little farmhouse alongside their camp where the assault on the Moncada was planned; the cemetery where martyrs of the War of Independence were buried; the former home of Santiago revolutionary martyrs Frank and Josue Pais (who'd been active in the urban underground) and a meeting with their mother; a trip to the Revolutionary museum in Santiago and the photo museum at the Moncada. In between these activities which were focused on teaching the children about their history were to be trips to the beach, the zoo and the Santiago carnival, as well as sports and cultural activities in camp.

On July 26 the Pioneers were to awake before dawn and leave the camp at 4:00 A.M., for an authentic re-enactment of the attack on the Palace of Justice. And on the last day of camp those Pioneers who were still physically able were to hike and climb fourteen miles, along the route Fidel followed when he escaped to the mountains following the failure of the assault.

Accompanying the Pioneers on these trips was probably the most profound educational experience of my life.

It gave me a chance not only to learn about the history of the

Cuban Revolution, but to see how that history is intertwined with today's generation of Cubans. This was the only occasion on which I was able to eat, sleep, learn and play with Cuban children over an extended period of time. If my opinion of them as a generation of a new type of human beings was considerable before, my respect, love and admiration for them — and the process that created them — was infinite by the time we re-entered the buses that were to take us to Havana.

"HAY PROBLEMAS, HAY CONTRADICCIONES" This is not to say that everything about the camp and the activities of these two weeks was idyllic, that nothing could be improved. A journalist once quoted Fidel as saying of the revolutionary process: *"Hay problemas, hay contradicciones"* ("There are problems, there are contradictions"). Of course there are problems and contradictions in any process. A country which has had little more than a decade to try to fight its way out of an underdevelopment imposed over centuries is bound to make mistakes, to suffer setbacks. "No one ever said socialism is Utopia," one of the camp counselors remarked to me one evening, while we were discussing some of the minor incidents that had upset me. "We're an underdeveloped country. We don't have all the things we need, much less all the things we want for our children. We're trying to create a generation with a new consciousness, but we were raised with that old consciousness. We came from a dog-eat-dog world, a world dominated by Catholicism, anticommunism, fear, and cultural backwardness. At every step of the way we have to try to overcome that heritage, to try with all our might not to pass it on to our children."

The things that bothered me ranged from questions of diet to apparent vestiges of "old style" behavior: a kind of fierce competitiveness that existed at times between provinces, and some old-fashioned male/female relations being carried on by the children.

The meals served the children were generally both ample and well balanced, with meat or fish, vegetables and starch available twice a day. But although fruit juice was available, neither milk nor yogurt was. I particularly noticed their absence since I had been having both regularly in the hotel in Havana. It wasn't really ever clear to me if the lack of this protein source for the children was due to a scarce supply of milk this year (or in this province), or simply because those planning the camp menu hadn't thought about it sufficiently to see that those supplies were on hand. No one at the camp seemed to know.

Knowing the Cuban preoccupation with proper nutrition for the children, I tended to doubt that this could have been an oversight. I had heard rumors that the milk supply wasn't what it should have been that year, but there was still the nagging feeling: why should the Havana Libre (and presumably other hotels) have the milk and yogurt, rather than the children, if there weren't enough to go around? In the overall rationing, children, old people and pregnant women have first priority for the milk. Every child gets one liter a day. So it seemed strange for them not to have it in camp.

Another concern was the amount of time the children were asked to stand in formation, under the glare of the hot sun, when it seemed to me that this was not really necessary. There were never any complaints from the children; but then there wouldn't be — not from these children. On three or four different occasions Pioneers were standing under the blazing tropical sun for a half hour to an hour, when shade was available nearby, and sitting in formation under the trees would have presented just as orderly (if not as "militant") an appearance.

I was starting to feel that some of the Pioneer guides were being somewhat over-exuberant, and pushing the children too far. But I felt very alone in this feeling, and too much of an outsider to bring it up — when some of the camp nurses brought it up instead. At the first planned visit to the Siboney farmhouse, there was a long unexplained delay outside. The Pioneers were lined up along the path leading to the front door from the road outside. The lawn all around the farmhouse abounded with trees and shade-giving tropical plants, but the children sweated instead under the hot sun. Apparently renovations and other preparations for the 26th of July celebration weren't complete, and the workers didn't want the children to go inside that day. Instead someone stood on the steps of the farmhouse and told the Pioneers about the preparations for the assault. Minutes stretched out to over a half hour as this was being discussed. Finally a camp nurse began arguing with some of the camp directors, pointing out the absurdity of making the children stand in the hot sun when shade was available, and eventually they were allowed to retreat to positions under the trees.

Some of the problems I noticed had to do with the carry-over of old habits to the young. Everyone washed his or her own clothes in the communal sinks. But there were only one or two irons in camp, located at one of the counselors' bunkhouses, and people took turns using them. While I was waiting my turn one night — along with about ten girls and two or three guides — I was amazed to see some of the boy Pioneers bring their shirts in for the guides — or their female classmates — to iron. "Why don't the boys iron them themselves?" I demanded. A guide (who couldn't have been more than eighteen or nineteen herself) told me, "Boys don't know how to iron." "Well, then why don't you teach them, instead of doing it for them?" I insisted. Several of the girls thought this was a good idea, but I never saw it happen while we were in camp. It was the only instance I saw where there was not a completely equal sharing of work and responsibilities.

(A year later dissatisfaction among women workers over just this question — the amount of housework that fell to their lot because their husbands claimed inability to do it — had reached sufficient proportions that it became one of the main themes both in the Family Code and the resolutions of the Second National Congress of the Cuban Women's Federation. One of the proposals of the Federation was that boys as well as girls study home economics in school, so they would be able to implement the provision of the Family Code calling for equal sharing of all housework.)

The last *contradiccion* I noticed dealt with the question of collective spirit. Although this was manifested in the children in a number of ways, the emulation between the provinces often seemed to take on a very competitive note. "Spirit" was understood to include singing and chanting. But instead of joining together to sing, or wait till one group finished singing and then try to sing better, the groups would virtually try to drown each other out — resulting in many hoarse voices by the second day of camp.

When some of the Pioneer correspondents from the camp interviewed me (turnabout is fair play, as far as they were concerned, and interviewing a foreign guest is always interesting), they asked me what I thought of the camp. After telling them how impressed I was by almost everything I saw, I mentioned this apparent contradiction in their behavior, this aspect that seemed like outright competitiveness to me. I'm not sure whether my comment was picked up on and later discussed, or whether their own self-analysis and criticisms would have led to the same result, but in any case, the next day much of the competitiveness seemed to have diminished. One of the more popular song-chants, says (more-or-less) "Shoulder to shoulder, hand in hand, the Pioneers of _____ are sure to Win." On the first days the tendency had been primarily to insert their own province in the blank space. After the third day they frequently sang "all the Pioneers" or some other collective refrain in that spot.

Since almost all of my experiences and impressions of the Pioneers were overwhelmingly favorable, I didn't really spend a great deal of time focusing on these various aspects that concerned or upset me. I include them primarily because there is sometimes a tendency — at least there was in my case — to become so impressed by the extent to which the Cuban Revolution has transformed the con-sciousness of its children, that you expect them to be perfect little beings. And of course they're not. They're little boys and girls, on their way to becoming men and women.

THE ASSAULT Throughout the camp there were always reminders about the main purpose of our being here: the twentieth anniversary of the assault on the Moncada. On several days Melba Hernández and other combatants came to the camp and spoke with the Pioneers. Several afternoons were spent going over the preparations for the attack. Local and national newspapers carried news and feature articles about the camp and the symbolic assault. When we went into Santiago one night to witness a massive political-cultural pre-sentation put on by thousands of the people of Santiago — including hundreds of local Pioneers — I could sense the eagerness of the children to be carrying out their own *acto.*

The night of the 25th the Pioneer leaders were up late, meeting and discussing. Many of the other children couldn't sleep because of the excitement. There was a lot of last-minute rushing around: get-ting "uniforms" of red berets, white printed tee-shirts and blue or red pants or shorts ironed. There was a last-minute frenzy when one detachment couldn't find the berets that had been assigned to it, and another was missing the emblazoned tee-shirts reading "Assault on the Moncada." I was given a tee-shirt, but my belly was too big, so I wore a maternity blouse instead.

At 3 A.M. the camp was all a-bustle. A small group of Pioneers was to ride into Santiago in pre-1953 model cars, the exact replicas of those used by the rebels. The others traveled in buses, leaving earlier so they could be lined up in the wings of the Palace of Justice when the principle actors in this special drama arrived.

When we got to the Palace of Justice we found that thousands of citizens were there waiting for us. All these nights were ones of carnival (that's why the 26th was chosen in the first place, so the rebels could go undetected in the confusion); so the *santiagueros* simply went from the carnival to the *Palacio* without stopping to sleep.

The Pioneers included a small detachment of youths whose fathers had participated in the original assault.

All the Pioneers carried large wooden rifles, shovels, machetes, and pencils. As they were waiting a man in a nineteenth century uniform, representing José Martí, rode by on a white horse. Fidel had always referred to Martí as the "intellectual author" of the assault on the Moncada, because he had always believed in and fought for Cuba's independence.

Finally the cars pulled up. They screeched to a stop in front of the *Palacio*, and the Pioneers rushed out, "guns" in hand. At a signal, the hundreds of waiting Pioneers rushed at the building, some converging on the first floor, others making their way to the second floor. Lights flashed on and off. Children yelled mightily. The people watching from the sidewalks cheered.

When the assault had ended, a participant in the original assault spoke at some length to the children and the crowd that had gathered there. Then everyone went home — or to continue the day's work, preparing for the mass celebration and Fidel's speech at the Moncada that evening.

For the Pioneers, the raison d'etre of their being there was past, but the excitement remained. That afternoon they were to spend long hours at the Moncada, awaiting Fidel's speech. And on their last day at camp, before heading back to their respective provinces, they still had their fourteen-mile hike along Fidel's escape route into the mountains.

As for the foreign journalist, I spent most of the rest of the time in camp. Big belly, swollen feet and general exhaustion had overtaken me. But I, too, had been swept up in the excitement of the assault, the fun and the seriousness of the past ten days. I decided this was a very, very good way to teach history.

8

Those Who Can, Teach

A NEW WAY OF TEACHING

When you talk about a whole generation of children who are radically different from previous generations, and from children in other parts of the world, an important aspect to consider in figuring out how they got that way is the teacher. It would be logical to expect a very complete chapter on teachers, teacher training, teaching methods, and teaching aids in a book of this type.

But when I went to Cuba to gather material about the new generation, I focused almost exclusively on the children. It was only toward the end that I had more than incidental conversations with adults. I did no research on teachers, have no current statistics, and can only relate bits and pieces that fell my way in the course of getting to know today's Cuban children.

I hope someone else will go back and do a book all about the teachers. They certainly deserve it, and we can probably learn a great deal from such a study. But until then, I hope these random observations will prove useful.

TEACHERS ARE VERY IMPORTANT PEOPLE

The respect Cuban children almost invariably pay their teachers is enormous. In part, I think, this reciprocates the respect that has been paid to children by adults since the Revolution, and in part it flows naturally from the admiration of teachers that most Cubans feel and pass on to their children. But I think it is also earned: in my experience, teachers, Pioneer guides — all people who work with children — are among the best, most qualified, most dedicated revolutionary cadres that the Revolution has produced. And this is no accident; the Revolution constantly seeks to find its best members and give them the responsibility of forming the next generation.

Cuban children not only respect their teachers — they *like* them. For many of their teachers, who are only a few years and grades ahead of their pupils, the students feel the kind of warm affection you have for an older brother or sister, or a good friend. Towards the older teachers, the children generally express a deep love, often close to the love they feel for their own parents. And they have no doubts that their feelings are reciprocated.

Over and over again, Cuban children told me how much their teachers cared for them, what great confidence they expressed in the students' ability to get ahead, to study and work hard, to contribute to the development of the Revolution. This plays an important role in the sense of self-confidence the children feel, especially in schools for the handicapped, or centers of re-education for those who would be termed delinquents in the United States.

THE "BEST" MAY NOT BE GOOD ENOUGH

To say that the Revolution seeks its best, most qualified members to teach the young does not mean that the Ministry of Education has always been able to provide teachers with an optimum level of training. In the beginning — and even to some extent today — the tremendous need for teachers so much exceeded the number with sufficient background that many were pressed into service who had scarcely more education than those they were teaching. In 1958, because the Batista government was unwilling to allocate sufficient funds to education, and because corrupt officials in the education ministry pocketed a great deal of what there was, there were over twelve thousand unemployed teachers in Cuba. Since the Revolution, there have consistently been more posts than could be filled.

In contrast to the situation of the childcare workers, Cuban tradition has not militated against recruiting males into the teaching profession, and there are probably an equal number of boys and girls going into the field. One argument for continuing with an all-female staff in the *círculos* is that men are still needed in the jobs that require hard manual labor and have not yet been mechanized. If this were the only argument for not recruiting and training men for the childcare centers, it would presumably carry over to the schools as well. Apparently the Cuban belief that women are better prepared by nature to care for young children is still the dominant factor in staffing the *círculos*. It will be interesting to see whether this changes as a result of the profound revolutionary changes taking place in Cuban society today among women, and in the family structure.

In looking for teachers, the Revolution has sought first of all women and men who are dedicated to the Revolution and what it is trying to carry out. Someone who worked with the 26th of July Movement, who aided the guerrillas, or who was active in the trade union movement might thus be considered better "qualified" to teach the young than someone with a college education but a bourgeois upbringing that prevented him or her from being able to identify totally with the goals of today's education.

This sometimes caused and causes painful contradictions. Once, at a public discussion of the Cuban Revolution held in California, I was introduced to a small, middle-aged woman who had left Cuba only a few years before. She was puzzled (not hostile) by the speakers' clear enthusiasm for the Revolution. She explained that she loved her country, had hated the graft and corruption of the Batista dictatorship, and was not opposed to the Revolution. But there was no place for her in it. "I was a teacher," she told me, "and all I wanted to do was teach. But they wouldn't let me. They closed my school." She was clearly asking for an explanation of what had happened to her — and at that time, I was unable to give her one. I hope she reads this book.

The woman had been a teacher in a private, Catholic school: the kind that taught the children of middle- and upper-class Cubans. The school wasn't a "bad" school as schools went in those days. It even gave scholarships to enable children of peasants and workers to attend.

But the school was totally enmeshed in the system that existed, and the teachers didn't know how to do otherwise than to teach within that system — and thereby perpetuate it. Some teachers who were younger, or had more political consciousness, or had come from a peasant or working-class background themselves, or were simply more adaptable, made the transition (not without considerable struggle). Others — like this sad woman — were simply left behind. They were not attacked or persecuted by the Revolution, the government just did not want them to influence the minds of the new generation.

Another experience showed me that it wasn't simply a matter of firing all the non-revolutionary teachers, or watching them leave the country when members of the upper class left. Among older teachers in today's schools, there are still contradictions, difficulties in adjusting, even if they have been able to commit themselves totally to the Revolution.

I saw this in a teachers' meeting at a primary school in Old Havana, which the *directora* of the school had invited me to sit in on one day. The teachers were discussing which of them should be given certain merit awards for those workers who perform in the spirit of the "Moncadistas": — the rebels who fought at the Moncada. All the teachers were asked to stand and explain why they felt they had earned this distinction.

In general the teachers got up, listed their work performance and anything outstanding they had done, or explained why they had been unable to do outstanding work (most often due to family pressures or illness). After each teacher spoke, the others had a chance to comment, positively or critically. There was little dissension or discussion until one elderly woman, who was teaching the pre-schoolers (kindergarten) told why she felt she should get the award, citing very regular attendance even when she had an injured leg, her years of duty, and her careful attention to her work.

A young woman with short, straight black hair and an outspoken manner stood up to oppose her. *"Compañera* X is a good teacher," she said, "and very dedicated to her children. But she does not know how to work with the collective of teachers. Although her children are always well cared for, she never contributes to the school bulletin boards or other collective activities. And when another teacher had to be absent last month, she was unwilling to take on that teacher's class as well as her own."

The older woman was clearly hurt and somewhat indignant. She had been taught that her job as a teacher was to do the best she could with the children entrusted to her. She was devoted to the Revolution, did her share of militia duty, stood guard at the school when it was her turn, took part in the activities of her neighborhood CDR. "But little children like mine need a lot more individual attention than the older ones," she explained. "You have to do everything for them — help them get their coats on and off, see that things are put away properly. I don't have as much time as the teachers of older children to take part in extra activities, and still give my full attention to the children under my care.

"If I had taken in that other class," she went on, "I would not have been able to care for them properly. It would have been incorrect to do that."

I felt very torn listening to this conversation, feeling sorry for the older woman and seeing some of the justice on her side. But I could also understand the argument of the younger teachers, when they answered by pointing out that the Moncada award was for people who had given outstanding service to the Revolution, just as the rebels at the Moncada had taken an outstanding position. "She's a good teacher," concluded the young woman who spoke first. "But she's not a *moncadista*."

TOMORROW'S TEACHERS

The young people who become teachers in Cuba today know that they will be expected to perform "above and beyond the call of duty." Initially, this was reinforced by having the future teachers receive at least part of their training in the remote mountain school at Minas del Frio in Oriente Province. Now there are teacher training schools in all parts of the island, but teachers are still made aware — by a rigorous program of work and study — that theirs will be a very demanding job, and a very rewarding one.

The inducement to become a teacher can be seen and felt all over Cuba. You see it in billboards, newspaper and magazine articles TV and radio programs. A typical billboard featured a proud father saying, "My son has decided to become a teacher." Newspapers like *Granma* and *Juventud Rebelde* regularly devote whole pages to the teaching profession. Teachers in Cuba receive the kind of respect and admiration of the whole society that is generally only reserved for doctors, lawyers, engineers and corporate executives in our society.

One of the main organizational forms of recruiting future teachers is the *Guerrilleros de Enseñanza* Movement: teaching guerrillas. Primary school children interested in a teaching career are incorporated into this movement; they visit teacher training centers and are told about the program carried out in them.

Some of the children in one school told me what the *guerrilleros de enseñanza* do:

> Well, we all have decided to become teachers, because that is one of the tasks the Revolution needs most right now. Some of the things we do are, if a *compañera* in your *albergue* has some weaknesses in some subjects, the *guerrilleros de enseñanza* help her to improve her work. And in the classroom if you can help someone else, you do.
>
> One day a week a student is chosen to carry out the job of the teacher, and actually gets up in front of the class, and learns how to teach and help the other students develop.

I asked some of them why they had decided to become teaching guerrillas:

> Because here in the school and in the whole country we need to help our *compañeros* who are behind us in our schoolwork. By helping them we also help our teachers. And this also puts us forward in our own schoolwork because while we are helping our *compañeros* we are also learning more ourselves.

Next I wanted to know why teaching is important in the Revolution.

> Teaching is important so the country can be more developed in terms of education, so there won't be any illiterates like there were before the Revolution. After the Revolution there was a literacy campaign to eradicate illiteracy. Even eleven- and twelve-year-old pupils went to the mountains and the plains to teach the *campesinos* how to read and write.
>
> This is important for the development of our country because we all have to learn, we shouldn't let anyone remain illiterate; because when we're grown-ups we have to do different kinds of work. We won't be able to do it if we don't learn. If we're going to work in a

factory we have to know how to count the number of products we make in a day, so when the next emulation comes we can say how many we will try to make next time.

The students who remain interested in teaching as a career apply to attend one of the provincial teacher training schools. These are *internado* scholarship schools, and only the best students — politically and morally as well as academically — are chosen. The prototype for today's teacher training schools was the Makarenko Institute, where young Cubans were taught the basic teaching theories and methods of the noted Russian educator, Anton Makarenko.

Although some of his methods have had to be adapted considerably to fit into the Cuban context, his theoretical framework is still heavily relied on. The importance placed on teaching by the Revolution can be seen by the fact that teachers are even recruited out of some of the elite scientific or technical training schools such as the Lenin School. At Lenin I ran into a number of youngsters who told me they had planned to become engineers, or biophysicists, or other scientific technicians, but had decided instead to become teachers, "at least for a while, because that's what the Revolution needs."

TEACHING IS A FULL-TIME JOB

Today, the young men and women who study to become teachers form part of the Manuel Ascunce Domenech Pedagogical Detachment. The teacher training institutes in each province try to recruit a set number of new students each year. They generally overfulfill their quotas.

Not that teaching is an easy job in revolutionary Cuba. On the contrary, it is perhaps one of the most exacting and time-consuming of all tasks, and bears a tremendous weight of responsibility. Those who bear this responsibility do so, according to one journalist who interviewed a number of the young teacher-trainees, with an impressive "maturity, concern, power of analysis, honesty, and enthusiasm."

In some of the boarding schools I visited I saw members of the teaching detachment who, in addition to their full load of studies, were teaching classes — and going home at night to an *albergue*,

Monitors who excel in their work help those who need it.

where they cared for thirty or more boys or girls. This of course in
not an ideal situation, but an outgrowth of underdevelopment, a
teacher shortage that seems never quite to catch up with the increasing number of children in Cuban schools (in addition to the
great number of adults who are now studying full- or part-time).
There is clearly too much strain on the teenagers who are asked
to carry this kind of load. But they carry it amazingly well, with a
fierce determination to perform whatever tasks the Revolution sets
out for them.

Despite this determination, the situation has serious drawbacks
for the young student teachers and their charges. It would take a
super-human being never to feel the strain, never to become short-
tempered, irritable — or simply worn out. Perhaps this is one of
the reasons behind the proposed cut-backs in the number of full-
time boarding students at the grade school level.

Teachers are expected to be exemplary, to be models for their
students to follow at all times. This is also sometimes asking a
great deal of a young teacher, who must become the New Man or
Woman while trying to form new men and women. It was probably
especially difficult in the early years when too often teachers had
little educational background themselves, and were ill-equipped to

deal with more than basic reading, writing and 'rithmetic. Among the *círculo* educators this problem was recognized and taken into consideration in planning the preparatory courses for the training schools to include psychology, pedagogy, social or political science, and a whole array of high school courses. Women with peasant or working-class background, for instance, generally felt embarrassed and unable to answer children's questions about sex differences. Now they learn how to answer such questions during their four years of teacher-preparation.

Similarly, the original teachers were learning about socialism through practice; none of them had any education in Marxist theory, or political economy. Today all students study political education — so of course their teachers must too.

THE MANUEL ASCUNCE DETACHMENTS: LEARNING WHILE YOU TEACH

One of the best ways to learn about Cuban teachers, the ways they are different from yesterday's, and how they are preparing for tomorrow, is to talk with the members of the Manuel Ascunce Domenech Teaching Detachments. Since I spent all my time talking with children (in some cases almost ignoring their teachers), I had few such discussions. But Alberto Landa, reporter for *Juventud Rebelde* newspaper, interviewed a number of young men and women, ages sixteen to eighteen, who had already had several years practice at becoming New Teachers. This is what he reported:

THEY WOULDN'T LET ME LEAVE THE GROUP Blanca Valencia is sixteen and is a member of the UJC. She had dreamed of being a pediatrician, but her role as a student leader led her to the conclusion that it was her obligation to become a teacher. Still, she felt a certain conflict at first. She first started feeling really good about her decision "when I saw that my attitude motivated many others, who hadn't wanted to become teachers at first, either." Today Blanca teaches math to eighth grade students. She recalls that "on the first day of classes, a year ago, I didn't even know what to say to the kids." It felt so strange teaching students two years younger than herself. To help her overcome her nervousness she decided to spend time with pupils of all different grades, except her own. With more and more experience, she says, she gained confidence in herself "and then I was able to relate to my own students, too. I was part of all their groups. Later, they didn't want me to leave them." Whenever they had any kind of a problem, they told me about it like they would to a friend. I saw that they always respected me.

Blanca believes that this combination of friendship, trust and respect that exist between her and her students helps raise the spirit and level of work in her class.

WITHOUT TEACHERS, THERE WOULDN'T BE A FUTURE
. . . Lázaro Mesa is a tenth grader who wanted to be a Naval Engineer. Of the fact that he's now teaching instead, he observed:

> It was a matter of conscience, of understanding that this is my trench in the battle against underdevelopment, of feeling myself necessary on this front.

He said his experience as a monitor in his history class made him decide to become a teacher.

> Besides, a Revolution without teachers would have no future. The teacher is one of the most important bulwarks of Socialism.

A NEW TYPE OF TEACHER APPEARS   Vincente Molina is seventeen years old, and nine of those years have been spent on the Isle of Youth, which he now regards as his home. A member of the UJC and vice president of the student union at the Heroic Vietnam Junior High School in the Countryside, he was also a member of the first Manuel Ascunce Detachment. When he was interviewed, his enthusiam and the words came pouring out of him.

> I have a lot to say because what we are doing here is communism. With us, a new type of teacher appears. I think that before the creation of the School in the Countryside, three years ago, a certain pattern existed in student-teacher relations. False concepts of respect, trust, predominated. The guide that we follow now is one of closer relations with the students. The pupils feel closer to us, because we share their problems, instead of just giving an order we explain what we want and why something should be done that way. So then they understand that we aren't making them do something, we aren't

imposing our will on them, we are orienting them — within the broadest sense of discipline — because we have more experience, more maturity.

And you know, we are helping ourselves at the same time. Look, I'm seventeen years old, and by leading students I learn at the same time to disclipine myself. In practice this contributes to the elimination of the clash between the leadership and the led.

Besides, they look at teachers from the Detachment as part of themselves, because they know that we come from the student body — and continue to be a part of it. And for their part, in the very near future that is almost upon us, they will join the ranks of the teacher training institute, and we'll be fellow workers. Because this movement will have to keep getting bigger every year.

Another important factor is the closeness in age. This helps us become natural, not imposed leaders. The students understand that we don't make demands on them just because we are teachers, but rather that another kind of relationship has been created, more legitimate and lasting.

What's more — and this is very important — we feel that our relations with older and more experienced teachers has become closer. On the one hand we've learned a lot from them, and on the other, we've brought to them our ideals, our concepts and criteria, and they've seen in practice our results. Because of this, as time goes on, our love for our profession takes root, grows deeper, and becomes ingrained in oneself.

Although he was both insightful and excited about the new kinds of teachers being produced by the Revolution in the Manuel Ascunce Domenech teaching detachments, Vincente was also aware that many students are not initially attracted to the teaching profession.

THE DIFFERENCES ARE SUBTLE

This stress on the new kind of relationship that exists between students and teachers which the Manuel Asunce Detachment members point out is important, because in many ways teachers in Cuba don't seem very different from those in other parts of the world. If you just walk into a classroom in Cuba, you will see a teacher standing in front of the room, or writing on the board, or going up and down rows checking students' notebooks. If that

were all you saw, you would think that education hadn't changed a great deal in Cuba.

The differences are often more subtle. You see them in the ways teachers and students speak to each other; in the kind of friendship that exists between them. It is also in the commitment to a common goal, a goal that is seen as beyond either of them, a collective goal.

Spending more time in the schools, you can also see some not-so-subtle differences. Like teachers going out into the fields and working alongside the students. Like janitors and kitchen workers participating equally with the teachers in school meetings (workers assemblies for workers in the field of education), forming the same units of the Cuban Communist Party at their work center, which is the school.

The stories that could be told about teachers, and teacher training schools, are numerous — yet they wouldn't be sufficient to answer all the questions educators in other countries must certainly have. That awaits another book.

9

Parents Still Count

A much-discussed   topic in Western circles is the role of the family in modern-day child-rearing. Many people feel that socialization of childcare is a step toward the destruction of the nuclear family. Those who regard the nuclear family as sacrosanct view this situation with horror. In fact a number of families fled Cuba in the early years of the Revolution because of the false rumors that the government was going to take their children away from them.

On the other hand, many "progressive" educators see the nuclear family as destructive of human development, and view its elimination as a positive step.

The Cuban Revolution believes that the people as a whole — embodied in the structure of the state — bear a basic responsibility for caring for all of the children as well as guiding their education and development. It does *not*, however, view this as a step toward breaking down the nuclear family. In fact, most Cubans believe the family still plays — and should play — a vital role in the raising of children. This interaction can first be seen when children begin to attend childcare centers.

Except in rare circumstances (such as death, illness, imprisonment or other serious family problems) children spend weekdays in the *círculo* and evenings and weekends with their parents. When a young child is first brought to the *círculo*, a parent stays with him or her until the child is accustomed to the new surroundings. In some *círculos* the parents come in with the children each morning, change them into their *círculo* clothes (usually bright-colored shirts and shorts or overalls). This provides a kind of transition from the home to the center. But this is by no means the extent of parent participation in the *círculos.*

Every *círculo* has monthly meetings of the Parents' Committee. The meetings include a brief, educational discussion by a speaker from the Children's Institute, the *círculo,* or someone active in some field of child development. Then there is a period of questions and answers, and general discussion. The staff of the *círculo* may suggest ways in which the parents can help with some particular problem faced by the *círculo* (ranging from the need for certain building materials, to help in preparing a collective birthday party or some other celebration). Parents are strongly urged to participate in these collective celebrations.

The Parents' Committee has an Executive Committee made up of a president, an organizer, the director of the *círculo,* a secretary, a member of the Union of Young Communists from among the *círculo* staff, a member of the Women's Federation section which sponsors the *círculo* (every *círculo* is sponsored by a section of the FMC as well as by a work center) and a representative of the *padrinos* from the work center.

The Executive Committee plans an educational program which helps educate the parents, and which emphasizes the importance of coordinating the home-life of the children with their lives in the *círculo.*

At the Children's Institute I was told that the parents are urged to schedule feeding and nap times according to those of the childcare center, and to try to develop habits in the children consistent with those they practice in the *círculo.* The "terrible Mondays" sometimes spoken of by childcare workers in this country are also encountered in Cuba. "We notice, sometimes, that some of the children have a certain behavior on Mondays, distinct from the way they act the rest of the week. In that case we know the parents are creating a very different environment for the children on weekends. Then the Parents' Committee talks with the parents concerned. We also talk in general about certain parental habits that can affect the children, so that their conduct won't hurt their children. For example, we might mention the importance of not interrupting a child's regular sleeping schedule to go to a late movie. We'll also talk about what kinds of foods are good and bad for the children. We tell the parents to avoid scary programs on TV that might frighten very young children.

"We always encounter situations where the children won't do at home what they do in the *círculo*. We try to make sure the parents know what their children are doing at the center, and each time they learn something new, so the parents can start doing that with the child at home. If there are problems we try to show the parent how to get the child to behave at home the way s/he does with us."

Although individual progress reports are made to each parent separately there are also group progress reports at these meetings.

In addition to the monthly meetings, special meetings with the Parents' Committee are called whenever the need arises. The director of one *círculo* explained:

"At the end of the year, when pre-schoolers are going to go to school the next year, we meet with all the parents of this age group to prepare them for this change, to give them evaluations of their children and their readiness for the school experience, encourage them as to how they can best help their children make the transition.

"When new information is needed from the parents, we might call them all in, discuss the problem, maybe have them fill out a questionnaire.

"Sometimes, too, the *padrinos* take on the responsibility for making or doing something for the *círculo*, and find out they need more help. So we arrange a meeting between them and the parents, so they can ask the parents to help out on weekends or evenings."

I attended one of the regular meetings of the Parents'Committee of a *círculo infantil* in Miramar in July of 1973. The *círculo* was located in what had formerly been the suburban home of a wealthy family which left Cuba after the Revolution. A glass-walled, patio-type room that led into the back garden was the scene of the meeting. A number of parents were already seated in chairs placed in rows facing a table at the garden end of the room. Most of the parents were mothers, with a sprinkling of fathers present.* At the front table sat the young woman who was going to lead the educational discussion, the director of the *círculo*, a nurse from the *círculo*, myself and Elda, the *compañera* from the Children's Institute who accompanied me to the meeting.

---

*It will be interesting to see whether this ratio changes as a result of the provisions of the new Family Code, which calls for the sharing of all household and childcare responsibilities between both parents.

When the fifteen-minute educational talk was concluded, many parents began asking questions and making comments. One mother asked, "What if your child comes home from the *círculo*, already fed, and sees you eating and says 'I'm hungry'?" The *educadora* responded that parents should worry more about the content of the child's food than the quantity. The food in the *círculo* provides all the nutritional content a child needs. "You should check with the *círculo* to see if your son ate well that day. If they say yes, give him some milk and distract him with toys or games or some other activity."

When the questions seemed to slow down, the *educadora* asked the parents questions based on her lecture, to see if they had understood everything she'd said, and to get them to repeat some of the basic ideas. This then stimulated other questions.

Other mothers began to cite their experiences — both positive and negative — with children's eating habits. As one woman would recount her problems, you could see other heads nodding familiarly.

The questions raised were generally similar to ones raised by parents throughout the world: the child who refuses to drink milk, problems of nap time, children who develop different patterns of behavior for home and school. The answers given by the *círculo* staff were also similar to those provided by psychologists and progressive educators in this country. What is unique, perhaps, is that in Cuba parents have a collective way to discuss and deal with the problems that come up in so many families.

When the meeting broke up, one mother in her early forties commented to me that she could see the difference between raising children before the Revolution and now, because she has several older children and a three-year-old who is now in the *círculo*. "My three-year-old can feed and dress herself. She's much more independent. My other children couldn't do those things at her age."

The childcare centers are trying to function within the Revolution to create new kinds of human beings. They recognize this process as an integral one in which all parts of the society participate. The family, far from having a diminished role now, is seen as having new and more responsibilities. Rather than replace the families, the *círculos infantiles* try to educate the families to help in the child's development. The parents in turn, are expected to actively participate in education and socialization of their children, both through teaching and example at home, and by active participation in the Parents' Committees.

Although the collectivization process continues and increases as children get older, with many children actually living at school for extended periods of time, the Revolution still assigns a key role to parents in the upbringing of their children. I could see this both in the literature put out by the Revolutionary Government, Children's Institute and Ministry of Education, and in the families I came to know. A typical example is that of Margarita, a little girl I met in a primary school in Old Havana, and her family.

MARGARITA'S MOTHER

At eight years old, Margarita is like many Cuban children: olive skin, dark hair and eyes, blue and white Pioneer scarf tied carefully around her neck. She's a good student, a monitor in her math class, and a member of an after-school interest circle that studies fish and oceans. Modest and polite when greeting adults, she also has that very *latino* brand of warm hospitality that I encountered everywhere in Cuba, which is most often expressed in the phrase: *Mi casa es su casa* — My house is yours. Over and over again children I met in schools, summer camps or recreational activities ended up by telling me their address and inviting me to come visit their homes. In Margarita's case, I accepted the invitation.

The section Margarita lives in is old, but the Spanish style homes and apartment buildings are more spacious and less run-down than the *solares* I had seen in Old Havana. I could tell nothing from the flat, concrete facade of the building as we approached her front door. But on either side of the footpath was a tiny (perhaps five foot square) plot of soil, in which brightly-colored tropical plants and flowers had recently been planted. This was part of the CDR's program to beautify the neighborhoods, Margarita told me.

Margarita's mother greeted us at the door as we went in, leading us into a living room that contained an old couch, a big stuffed chair, a television set, and a dark wood table with four chairs. Pictures of Fidel, Che and Camilo Cienfuegos, clipped from various magazines, were framed and hanging on the walls, along with what appeared to be several awards and certificates of merit made out in different names. One of them was inscribed to Beatriz Suárez Novoa. I asked if that was her, and she smilingly nodded her head.

"That's for being a '*Madre Combatiente*'" she told me. "The FMC has organized women who aren't working outside the home to provide assistance in the schools. They're called '*Madres Combatientes por la Education*' (Militant Mothers for Education). I haven't been able to work at my old job — I was a textile worker — during the past year, because I had to have a kidney operation, and I still can't be on my feet a lot. So I've been doing a lot of voluntary work, and helping out in the schools. We try to do a lot of things through this movement: fight absenteeism and drop-outs, get parents to attend school meetings, participate in mass activities at school, plan programs of recreational activities for the children, help keep the school clean and attractive, visit sick children and bring them their homework, and replace absent school workers and teachers when necessary. The *Madres Combatientes* movement is really important," she continued, scarcely pausing to catch her breath, "because otherwise the teachers have to do everything, and then they can't pay so much attention to their teaching. And when a teacher gets sick, there's no one to replace her, or him."

I hadn't realized until I had attended the teachers' meeting in Old Havana that there simply aren't substitute teachers in Cuba. I had never stopped to ask what happens if a teacher got sick. In the U.S. I took for granted the fact that a number of teachers who are unemployed, or only want to work part-time, are put on lists of substitutes to be called in case of illness of some staff member. In Cuba with the continuing shortage of qualified teachers, everyone who can teach is doing so. There are no lists of substitutes. If parents hadn't begun to take on this responsibility themselves, classes would simply be doubled up whenever a teacher was sick.

I asked Margarita's mother (she asked me to call her Beatriz, but somehow "Margarita's mother" has always stuck in my mind) to tell me about the ways that parents participate in their children's education. Her response took up most of the afternoon, interrupted periodically by her serving us cups of sweet black Cuban coffee, the ringing of the doorbell by a neighbor who wanted to discuss a community meeting, and the comings and goings of her three other youngsters. (Margarita sat with us and took part in the conversation.) This is some of what she told me.

"IF YOU DON'T CARE, YOUR CHILDREN'S SCHOOLWORK WILL SHOW IT"

Parents have a great responsibility to their children, and to society. We have to set examples for our children of the kind of people we want them to be. We can't just expect to tell them: "Be this way, do that" if they see us being something different, not living up to what we tell them.

If they see us sitting around the house on a Sunday, for example, instead of going out to do voluntary work with the CDR or our work center, what are they going to think? How will they be motivated to do more than just what is required of them?

We help our children become better students — and better citizens — in lots of ways, big and small. It may sound obvious, but one way is simply making sure they attend school every day, and on time. There are still too many parents who don't bother to do this. If the child doesn't feel like going to school one day, or has a slight sniffle, they say, "OK, stay home today. You can help me with the wash, or run to the store." They don't realize they are hurting their children's school work, and their future development. The child loses respect for school and sometimes for the teacher, when the parents let it be known that they don't think it's very important to go to school every day.

And children who are absent a lot can't keep up with their work; they don't know how to answer the questions in class, they're embarassed — so they stay out more. If they fall behind a grade,that reduces their incentive even more. So they drop out of school, or misbehave while they're there.

There are a lot of other ways parents can help, too. We take turns doing guard duty at the school. We help supervise extracurricular activities. If the school needs any kind of materials or repairs, the teachers or principal tell us at the parents' meeting. Then the parents bring it up at their work centers, to see if there's some way they can help. If some of the parents are carpenters, or electricians, for instance, and some shelves need to be built, or some wiring fixed, they see if they can do it.

We have regular parents' meetings, and we try to encourage as many parents as possible to come. We concern ourselves with the internal problems relating to the formation and education of our children. When new laws are being discussed — like the Family Code — we talk about it at these meetings. If we see a child, even though not our own, who is doing something wrong outside the school, we tell the school personnel and the parents at the meeting, so they can do something to correct it.*

I asked how good attendance at the parents' meetings was. She frowned. "It's not as good as it should be. There is always a good number of parents at each meeting; but the ones who should be there the most, aren't. By that I mean that you often see that children who have problems in school, are falling behind in their work, are absent a lot, or have trouble with other children — these children whose parents *should* be at the meetings — often they're not. And on the contrary, when you see a child doing outstanding work, being chosen vanguard consistently, passing every grade, taking part in the activities of the Pioneers — that child is likely to have parents who attend every parents' meeting faithfully, who take a real interest in their child's education."

The *Madres Combatientes* program is just for women. "Is it primarily mothers who attend the parents' meetings, too?" I wanted to know.

"That varies a great deal," she told me. "Conscientious fathers, like Margarita's, take part in as many meetings as they can." She smiled at her daughter, and Margarita smiled back proudly. "But there are always some obstacles, some contradictions — for women as well as men — and that is the great number of tasks that confront people in this society. We have responsibilities to our work centers, to our CDRs, to the Militia, to our Trade Unions, to the Party if we are members, or to the Women's Federation. And all of these have meetings. Sometimes there are just too many meetings, and you can't go to them all; you can't be at two or three at the same time.

"Families like ours, we try to divide it up. One night I'll go to a meeting and Raúl — that's my husband — will stay home with the kids. Or sometimes we'll both go, and my sister or a neighbor will babysit. But when no one can watch them, we take turns: I go one time, he goes the next."

---

*In 1976 this process was expanded even farther with CDR-sponsored Schools for Parents. Operated on a neighborhood level, these Schools for Parents were designed to answer such questions as "How can parents help their children in their schoolwork?" and "How may parents cooperate with the school in the formation of good habits among the children?"

"Of course," she admitted, "there are also problems of fathers with old-fashioned ideas, fathers who think that everything that has to do with the children is part of the woman's responsibility, so they don't want to go to these meetings. But that idea is changing, it's fading out. In another generation there won't be anyone left who thinks that way.

"Even within revolutionary families, the carry-over of old patterns, old ways of doing things, still has some effect. For instance, before, it was mostly the man who went out to work, the woman who stayed home. Even if the woman worked, she was still expected to be the one to take primary responsibility for the house and the kids. So it was generally the man, not the woman, who had all these other meetings: trade union, work center, Party. So the woman would end up at the school meetings. Now that's starting to change, too. But what it means is that women as well as men have a lot of other meetings to go to. So we have to find some way to adjust our time."

"Most of what you do as parents in connection with the school is involved with helping make up for some deficiency," I pointed out, "Like substituting for a sick teacher, or bringing in materials. Are there also ways in which you as parents help affect the kind of education your children receive? Do you ever have a chance to question what goes on in the classroom?"

"I should have explained," she told me, "that the parents' meetings are very much a two-way thing. We go there to see how we can help, and we also try to learn about what our children are doing, how they are being educated. The principals give us very detailed reports from the teachers about all this. Our discussions aren't just technical, they're political. But you must understand that here we are very united: we know what we fought against, we know what we are trying to build. Sure, at times we have different ideas about how to go about building it. We discuss those differences, we struggle to bring out the best ideas. But there is a mutual respect, a confidence — even a love — between the parents and the teachers that perhaps you would find hard to understand, since I don't think it exists in your society."

I realized that what she was saying was true. Talking to parents of pre-school and school-age youngsters in New York and California, what I found most often was a serious class and cultural conflict between the parents and the teachers, especially when the teachers were white and middle class, and the parents were poor and of a different race or culture. In this case, the educators often manifest an air of superiority, of "knowing what's best" for the children, blatantly disregarding the culture and traditions of the parents. In Cuba, when educators feel they should begin a process that is different from what the parents have grown accustomed to over the years, the matter is first discussed with all the parents. It is only when they understand and agree with the new approach that it is implemented.

Before I left Margarita's house that day, her mother showed me a scrapbook in which she had carefully pasted clippings from the newspaper regarding school, home, family — anything about the raising and education of children. "Everyone here is concerned that the parents maintain an important role in the lives of their children," she said, flipping through the pages. "The society has taken on a great number of responsibilities: schooling, medical attention, even recreation. But we are still their parents, and parents are very important in the formation of children. The family is still the basic social unit of our society.

"Look at some of these articles," she stopped to glance through them. "This one describes the typical morning activities of the youngsters in school. It's written so that you will know what your child is doing every day at school. But it's not just a matter of curiosity. Here they tell you how the child takes part in the flag raising, hears a reading of national and international news, and any questions concerning school activities, before going to classes. Why do they tell you this?"

She answered her own question. "It is so you will know why it is important for your child to arrive at school *on time:* for you to understand that the activities of these first fifteen minutes are important, and so you will then see to it that you don't allow — or cause — your child to be late."

She turned to another page. "This article describes in detail what the school notebook of your child should look like, how it is constructed, what your child's responsibilities are in keeping it neat, clean, together, and with the homework assignments recorded properly. You might think it's silly to go into all that detail over a notebook, in a daily newspaper. But we think it is the parents' responsibility to see that children take good care of their school materials, and use them properly. If parents don't know exactly what is expected of their children, they can't do their job of seeing that these expectations are fulfilled. So our newspapers see to it that we are informed."

Margarita interrupted then. "Tell her about not spanking, Mommy," she suggested with an impish grin. Her mother looked perplexed at first, then turned red. Finally she showed me a clipping entitled *"Un Método Ineficaz"* — "An Inefficient Method." It was a well-reasoned presentation of why parents should not use corporal punishment when their children misbehave, but instead should find other means to guide them toward correct behavior, or to punish them when necessary. I had often seen columns in *Juventud Rebelde* called *"Mini-siquis"* ("Mini-Psyche") which dealt with a wide range of personal and interpersonal matters, but I hadn't seen this article, which apparently had been written in response to readers' questions on the matter.

"I try to be revolutionary, and to bring my children up in accord with the Revolution." Margarita's mother told me, her face still a little red. "But you know, I was brought up in another time, and my parents saw things differently from how some of our educators and leaders see things now.

"We learned as children that if we misbehaved, that we had earned a spanking, and we were going to get it. We weren't bad children, and our parents didn't whip us often. But when it came, it came.

"And I applied the same rule to my children. They don't get spanked just on a whim, or because I'm in a bad mood. But I always thought, if they earned it, they should be spanked.

"Now," she sighed, "the people in charge of molding our children have studied this question, and they tell us it is not the right thing to do. Here it says:

> In effect [corporal punishment] causes an immediate halt to the undesirable behavior, but what happens is that this effect is later seen as transitory, and the old behavior reappears. Corporal punishment stimulates aggressivity and destroys the child's respect for the adult, the child will hate the person who punishes him or her, and the place where he or she is mistreated, and will also learn to fear, lie, hate and deceive to avoid the punishment.

"What did you do after you read this?" I asked.

"Well, my husband and I talked it over. Then we talked to some of our neighbors, because we weren't quite decided. We discussed it at our next CDR meeting. And we talked to our children about it too."

Margarita was smiling broadly now.

"Finally, we decided that the Revolution has been right in most things up until now; that we trust our leaders to be trying to direct us along the best course; and that the reasoning of this article makes sense. I think my parents raised me all right, and I don't criticize them. But we're going to try this. We're revolutionaries, and we're capable of change."

FAMILIES CHANGE, BUT THEY'RE STILL FAMILIES

As I left Margarita and her mother, standing smiling and waving good-bye at the door, I thought a lot about the changes families were going through in the Revolution. How hard this period of transition must be for the older folks! But certain points were now clear in my mind that had been in doubt before. So many "authorities" have stated that the nuclear family will (some say "should") fade away in a socialist society, as the state takes on more and more of the responsibilities formerly reserved for the family, that I had pretty much expected to see the Cuban family dissolving as a unit. Margarita's mother simply put into words what I had been seeing over and over again in Cuban homes: that the family is still alive and strong in Cuba, and that the Revolution expects it to stay that way. It is not the same family it was a generation ago: some duties have disappeared, new ones have been added. It is a family that is undergoing drastic changes, and sometimes these changes do put real strains on the old relationship. There has certainly been a tremendous increase in divorce since the Revolution cut women loose from their economic bondage to their husbands. But those who believe socialism means an end to the family unit are in for a surprise in Cuba.

A year after my talk with Margarita's mother, all of this became clearer as Cuba came closer to putting into law the new Family Code which she had mentioned in our conversation. In 1973 — the last time I was in Cuba — the Family Code was just beginning to take form, and only a few sections of it were being passed around for discussion. By 1974 the entire bill had been drafted, and was the source of some of the most heated discussion in Cuba in years.

INSTITUTIONALIZING THE REVOLUTION

"I think it's about time. We've been needing this kind of social legislation for years."

"This is one of the most important, fundamental changes the Revolution has made. It's a revolution in the Revolution."

"I support it 100 percent. We all do."

"Well, I don't know. It's a very complicated question."

"If Fidel and the leaders of our Party say this is the way things should be, I guess that's right. But I really don't see it."

"Of course we'll go along with it. We're revolutionaries. Revolutionaries have to make sacrifices."

"This time the Revolution has gone too far. I can't accept this. I'm forty-seven years old, and I'm too old to change my ways."

The above were responses to the question, "What do you think of the new Family Code?" posed to random men and women in stores, street corners, work places. As you might surmise, the first series were the responses of women; the second group, men. The varied reactions have to do with the fact that the new Family Code is indeed a "revolution in the Revolution" as far as male-female relations are concerned. In clear, unequivocal terms, the Code stipulates total equality of men and women in all aspects of Cuban life, *beginning with the family unit.* After defining marriage as "the free and voluntary union made between a man and a woman," the code then goes on to state that: "All the norms relating to marriage rest on the principle of the absolute juridic equality between men and women, of reciprocal duties between the one and the other, of mutual obligations with respect to the children and in the contribution to the maintenance of the home and the realization of domestic duties."

The Revolution already has control over the major institutions — school and work place — in which people enter into social relations, and it might have been felt that the state could have worked to abolish discrimination that persisted against women after the Revolution through these institutions. It is an indication of the continued importance the Revolution places on the family unit that it was felt necessary to make specific efforts within the family to speed up and institutionalize this process. Blas Roca, president of the juridical commission charged with rewriting the old Cuban laws, explained this in an introduction to the Family Code Project which was circulated all over the country:

> The project renovates and perfects the juridic norms regarding the family, according to the realities existing in this country and those socialist principles — including the promotion of the equality of women.
>
> The 1889 Civil Code made the family an institution based on the humiliating inferiority of the woman, on her submission and that of the children to the absolute rule of the father of the family, on discrimination against children labeled as illegitimate, on the protection of the concentration of wealth. The modifications that were introduced during the course of the years, including the precepts of the 1940 Constitution — many of which were won by the mobilization and lobbying by women and other popular forces — somewhat attenuated the archaic and regressive family concepts which were the base for said Civil Code.
>
> Even with the changes that we have briefly mentioned and weighing the new realities and practices introduced by the Revolution — like the massive incorporation of women in the social work force, both in services and production, increase in childcare centers, extraordinary increase in the number of women who are studying — there still persist discriminatory and obsolete norms in family legislation. In that legislation, discrimination is perpetuated against the children, in the inequality of the marital relations. Marriage is considered to be a civil contract with a certain property acquired during the marriage and a predominance of the patrimonial aspects of the institution.
>
> In formulating the project we have sought, without losing sight of what has been gained, to harmonize the juridic norms regarding the family with the realities existing in our socialist society with a view towards impetuously and constantly forging ahead in all those respects.

With that in mind, the Family Code Project begins with the fundamental consideration that the family is an entity in which are present and intricately tied social and personal interests in that, on the one hand as a fundamental cell of society it contributes to its development and serves important functions in the formation of new generations; on the other hand, as a center of relations in the daily life between man and woman, between them and their children, and amongst all their relatives, it satisfies deep human and social interests.

A society that is determined to raise a new generation of a "new type" of human beings cannot allow schools and teachers to continue to function in the same old way. It must also try to bring the family structure into line with the new concepts. This would not be true if Cuban leaders felt the family was "on the way out." It is a tribute to the permanence of the family within the Revolution that they have seen it necessary to institutionalize these new family relations along with so many other aspects of Cuban life.

It is easy to see how some of these matters directly affect children: for instance, institutionalizing the statement made by Fidel Castro in the first year of the Revolution that "there is no such thing as an illegitimate child. A child who is born is legitimate."

Not so obvious, but just as important in the Cuban concept of the New Human Being, is the way in which a society's treatment of women — inside and outside the home — affects the children. A major impetus for the new family code can be found in Blas Roca's simple statement depicting the old laws: " . . . In that legislation discrimination is perpetuated against the children in the inequality of the marital relations."

The Family Code was enacted into law on March 8, 1975 (International Women's Day), after being ratified by an overwhelming majority of the voting population (virtually everyone over sixteen years of age). Nevertheless, the heated discussions that took place prior to passage of this new law has shown that the changes will not come about easily or suddenly. From my experience with Cuban children, I would guess that their new consciousness will have an effect within their families as the law begins to be implemented. But, if they are not able to convert their elders' consciousness totally, at least the new Family Code may help prevent this generation of parents from passing on the worst vestiges of the old society to their children.

10

George Washington and the Cherry Tree

As a primary school student in Pittsburgh, Pennsylvania, and the suburbs of New York City, I learned a great many myths and facts about the heroes of America's Revolution and growth to power. Not surprisingly, most of these heroes were presidents. But they all had very endearing human traits, characteristics we all could admire. George Washington, when confronted with the fact of a mutilated cherry tree, produced his little ax and boldly admitted: "I cannot tell a lie; it was I." I was led to believe that, for his courageous act of honesty, little George went unpunished. He grew to be a man to be admired, and eventually helped free us from the tyrannical rule of King George.

Others of my heroes were Abraham Lincoln (the rugged country boy who grew to be president; who loved to read, was very self-sacrificing, and freed the slaves); Daniel Boone (who helped conquer the wilderness); Thomas Jefferson (for the Declaration of Independence); and so on. I don't recall any women on the list; I'm certain that there weren't any blacks or other "minorities."

But while I was growing up, I was very uncritical of this rather limited scope of heroes. After all, they did all have admirable traits that one would do well to emulate. Given this, I wondered what role heroes play in the life of Cuban children.

Even if I hadn't wondered, you really couldn't help finding out. Whenever you talk with Cuban children, heroes, martyrs, and the leaders of yesterday and today are an integral part of the conversation. In fact, that's one of the biggest differences between our treatment of heroes and theirs. Ours were always remote figures out of story (*history*) books; theirs are real-life, flesh-and-blood men and women of the people. Some (though not many) of them are women; many are black.

There are several different kinds of heroes in the lives of Cuban children. There are the heroes of the War of Independence against Spain. The best known (and most talked about) of these seem to be José Martí and Antonio Maceo. Maceo's mother, Mariana Grajales, is sometimes included.

Of the recent Revolutionary War, children most often speak of Fidel, Camilo Cienfuegos and Che Guevara. Others who participated in the assault on the Moncada, especially Abel Santamaría and his sister Haydee, and Melba Hernández, follow close after these, along with those who landed with Fidel in the *Granma*, notably Raúl Castro and Juan Almeida. Frank País, assassinated while leading the underground 26th of July Movement in Santiago, is also a favorite among the children.

International heroes also top the list. Probably foremost among these are Ho Chi Minh and Tania *la Guerrillera* (the woman who fought and died with Che in Bolivia); but most Cuban children frequently sprinkle their conversations with references to other heroes and martyrs from Vietnam and the struggles taking place throughout Latin America and Africa. Even the United States is included: a few years ago most Cuban children knew something about the Black Panthers; later it was Angela Davis.

All of these heroes who lost their lives in the struggle or are currently imprisoned are honored by days and sometimes weeks of commemoration of their birth or death.

Perhaps the most interesting aspect about Cuban heroes is that they are not limited to famous warriors and leaders as we have come to expect. Workers are heroes in today's society; there are National Heroes and Heroines of Labor chosen every year, and Cuban children are intensely conscious of this. In fact, this caused some moments of confusion once in a conversation I was having with two seven-year-olds. I was trying to find out if heroes and leaders in Cuba receive any kind of monetary reward, or simply get the recognition and love of the people. One thought that there was no reward, but when the term "millionaire" came up, the other insisted that some heroes were "millionaires." It took a while of untangling for me to realize that *macheteros* [cane cutters] who cut a million *arrobas* [1 arroba = 25 lbs.] of cane became work heroes, and that these heroes were often referred to as "millionaires."

Children have also been heroes and, on too-numerous occasions, martyrs. All of the children's hospitals, and many other Cuban institutions, are named after such children. Among the best known are Manuel Ascunce Domenech, who was killed while participating in the Literacy Brigade, and William Soler, a messenger for the 26th of July Movement. Youngsters who fought in the Sierra Maestra struggle against Batista, and at Playa Girón (Bay of Pigs) are also well known.

HAS ANYONE TOLD YOU ABOUT OUR MARTYRS?

Since the way I began conversations with children was, frequently, to ask them to teach me something about Cuba, the response was often: "Do you know about Camilo? . . . Che? . . . Maceo? . . . Let me tell you about them."

It is tempting to include here all of the children's comments on their country's heroes and martyrs, but since these often ran into very lengthy biographies, it would be somewhat impractical. Add to that all of their references and observations about international heroes, you could easily come up with a book just on that subject.

So to stay within the realm of this book, I'm including here children's comments on two of their best known heroes: Fidel Castro and Ernesto Che Guevera, and one youngster's reaction to the death of a revolutionary in Chile.

WHO IS FIDEL?

This simple question was put to some students in a boarding primary school in Havana, and to others of the same age at the 26th of July School in Santiago. Here are some of their responses:

— Fidel is a revolutionary.

— Fidel is a strong, brave, honorable man.

— He's tall, he has a beard, he's — well, not fat, but . . . .

— Fidel is the Chief of the Revolution!

— Fidel is our greatest leader, who attacked the Fortress together with his *compañeros,* who were Juan Almeida, Abel Santamaría, Haydee Santamaría, Pedro Marrero and others.

— Fidel is the revolutionary who participated in the attack on the Moncada Fortress, he wanted everything for the people, for the good of all, today he is *Comandante* of our Republic, who guides us and makes possible all the things the martyrs wished for.

— Fidel is the guide of the Revolution. He knew how to defend his country as every Cuban should.

— Fidel is our greatest leader, our greatest guide, he guides the Cubans in the struggle to untie the bonds that oppressed us, absorbing our riches, and it is he who now guides us in the work we must carry out and who fills us with revolutionary ideas.

— Fidel is a man who with his mind was able to liberate Cuba. Our *Comandante,* a man of fantastic ideas. A man who was able to get the impossible with his mind. Fidel has taken Cuba from capitalism to socialism, and he'll get it out of underdevelopment.

— Fidel is the one who showed us the road to freedom.

— Fidel is a great revolutionary who brought freedom from those distant mountains.

— Fidel fought in those high mountains.

— Fidel is a revolutionary man who loves his country and its inhabitants; he doesn't care about race, the only thing that matters to him is the well-being of the people. He came down from the Sierra Maestra with a group of revolutionary Cubans to free Cuba from the Yankee oppressor. Today he is our commander in chief whom all Cubans love and adore like a father and like our country.

— Fidel is our *Comandante-en-Jefe* who was the leader of what took place here [at the Moncada] and who in his trial uttered these words: "Condemn me, it doesn't matter, history will absolve me." And we will never forget those words.

— Fidel is a great revolutionary who fought and was a prisoner for our happiness, and that's why all the children of this center love him as though he were our father.

NO PERSONALITY CULT

Before readers get the wrong impression, I should make it clear that at no time did it seem that the Cuban people have built a "cult of personality" around Fidel, Che or any of the other heroes and martyrs whom they speak of with so much love and admiration. Although Cuban children often refer to Fidel, it is generally in the context of a conversation about something in which Fidel took (or takes) part. They don't attribute everything that is positive in the world to Fidel; don't ascribe to him miraculous powers or wisdom. They simply credit him with the actual contributions he has made and continues to make to the Cuban people.

Cuban children see their heroes and leaders as real men and women, made of flesh and blood. Youngsters thought it just as important to tell me that Fidel was fat, or had a beard, as that he was the *Comandante-en-Jefe* of the Revolution. No one thought he or she was being disrespectful by doing so.

Once I was talking with a group of primary school students about the idea of "thinking with your own head," which is what they had told me Fidel says all revolutionaries should do. "If Fidel or some other leader of the Revolution came to your school to talk with you, and you didn't agree with some of the things he said, would you

tell him?" I wanted to know. All of them nodded their heads, as I looked in vain for signs of doubt in their faces.

"And what would Fidel do?" I pursued.

"If that's how everyone thought, he would have to accept it," replied one little boy.

"But what if everyone else thought the way he did, and you were the only one who thought differently," I went on, addressing a thin black boy with dark curly hair. "Would you still tell him, and try to convince him of your idea?"

"Yes," he replied confidently.

"Here, everyone has his or her own ideas," explained an older girl. "No one has to think alike."

THE DOCTOR WITH THE GUN

Ernesto "Che" Guevara is as much a part of Cuban children's lives as Fidel Castro, although most of them are too young to remember him. The children of Santa Ana, a tiny pueblo in the Sierra Maestra mountains, don't have any memory of Che except what comes from the conversations of their parents, teachers — and from the Sierra itself. But when you ask them to speak of him, to tell you something about him, to write down what image they have of him, Che bursts forth immediately as if they had seen and known him all their lives.

This is the mountain children's image of Che Guevara:

— Che was a very brave patriot. He walked around the Sierra, he had a beard, a shotgun, a revolver. He had a mule, too. He traveled with Camilo and Fidel. He was killed in Bolivia, and he appeared dead in all the newspapers.

— I saw a photo of him and he was a man who was laughing, with hair on his face, riding a burro, sort of strong, and with a shotgun and a pistol behind him.

— Che was very good with the people and very bad with the troops and rural guard.

— Once he came to my house and he brought *la cachimba* in his mouth [he was smoking a pipe]. He gave injections. He was a man who sat down at the table with you.

— Che was Argentinian and Cuban. He fought in the hills, the rivers, wherever there was war.

Che Guevara with his first child, Hildita.

— Che didn't have blue eyes. He had other-colored eyes.

— He was a short man who carried a shotgun on his back. He smoked cigars — some big cigars! — he rode a burro, and he fought against the Batista tyranny.

— He fought against the rural guards. He fought against Batista's pigs. He was very good in this zone; he pulled teeth, cured wounds. My papa says Che had asthma.

— Che was a fighter who, from the time he was a little child, thought about freedom.

— He hurt his leg. They cut off his hands. He was a revolutionary.

— He loved Cuba. He sang songs.

— He fought to liberate Cuba. Che liked to play volleyball.

— Che was very patriotic. He passed through these hills and other hills. He was wounded near here and was limping for some time. His ideals were the same as those of Fidel and the other patriots of the Sierra.

— My father says he came to fight but that he also helped babies to be born, pulled teeth, and a lot of other things.

— The teacher told us in class that Che was very good with children. The teacher cut a picture of Che out of a magazine and pasted it on the wall.

— Che was tall, he had a lot of hair and a gun with a 'scope, and a *Comandante*'s uniform. It was he who fought so that we could have this school.

Many of the children told long stories or humorous anecdotes about Che. Through all these, certain characteristics stood out: they all saw Che as a modest, humorous, down-to-earth man, a constant, dedicated soldier and worker for the Revolution, willing to do whatever necessary and go wherever needed by the Revolution. Children in the cities in addition described him as a tireless, exemplary worker, a man who shunned all privilege for himself and his family. A typical example they gave me of this referred to one time when Fidel was leading a guerrilla band in the mountains. Rations were scarce, and one of the fighters wanted to give Che an extra portion of meat, since he was their leader.

"And then Che answered: 'Let's share it among everyone, because here the *jefe* and the troops eat the same.' "

WHEN A *COMPANERO* FALLS

It is easy to see why Cuban children, loving their patriots, martyrs, and others who fought for their freedom and well-being, would feel as they do about Fidel, and about Che, who though Argentinian, shed his own blood on their soil. Less easy to understand perhaps is how deeply they feel for heroes of other struggles, in Asia (Vietnam), Africa and Latin America. Yet whenever I spoke with Cuban youngsters, Ho Chi Minh and Nguyen Van Troi were always a part of the discussion of the war in Vietnam. Heroes of African and Latin American liberation struggles formed part of their understanding of the fight against imperialism. They expressed a deep sense of loss for fallen fighters whom most North American children (and adults) have never heard of.

This doesn't happen in a vacuum, of course. When an international liberation fighter dies, Cuban government, Cuban press, Cuban parents and Cuban teachers all speak out, react in some way to express their sense of loss. Still, the extent to which Cuban children incorporate these feelings is startling.

Cubans had, for example, developed a very strong sense of kinship with the people of Chile during the Allende years; they mourned his death and opposed the military coup with massive demonstrations and open arms for Chilean refugees. When a year later Miguel Enríquez, the leader of Chile's Revolutionary Left Movement (MIR), was shot and killed, I received in the mail a poem which one youngster had been moved to write. It was dedicated and titled 'To *Compañero* Miguel.'

> To say struggle is to say sacrifice
> and in struggle you expose your life.
> To commit an error is to leave an opening
> through which the soul escapes entirely.
> And although your life is impeccable,
> the general was never so kind
> as to leave a fighter alive.
> *Compañeros* must die
> to give life to the trampled nation
> to give life to the nearly dead nation
> And in the future:
> To give life to the liberated nation
> to give life to their own lives.
> When a *compañero* falls,
> and with his fall, a hundred fall lifeless,
> it is necessary that what he did in life
> must not be lost with the loss of the *compañero*.
> The path to the future must be illuminated
> as thousands of voices bid him farewell
> and millions bid welcome
> to the great example of his struggle and life.

The boy who wrote that was fourteen years old. He had clearly accepted into his consciousness the oft-repeated Cuban maxim: "to die for your country is to live." And he had no difficulty in translating that to death in any liberation struggle, inside or outside of Cuba.

Cadets at the Camilo Cienfuegos Military School. Frequent attacks mounted from the United States have made Cubans regard military defense as a necessity. They try to integrate military training and preparedness with the normal educational and productive activities of the country.

11

The Littlest Gusana

All of my experiences on my second trip, in the cities, the mountains, the countryside, in schools, in parks and in the streets had confirmed, over and over again, the first impression I had of children in Cuba. The lack of selfishness and individualism, the sense of companionship among the children, the patriotism combined with a broad and deeply felt internationalism, the concept of work and study in a working-class society, the belief in sharing — all these characteristics that I had encountered in the first children I met in Cuba continued to crop up in children wherever I went.

So I wasn't prepared for the child I'll call Juanita.

She was eight years old, with black hair wrapped tightly in two pigtails. Her brown skin and kinky hair would classify her "Black" in the United States; in Cuba she's one of a countless number of mulatto children. Her sleeveless white blouse was ripped in several places, and the tan pants she wore had seen rough play. Her face was given an owl-wise aspect by the grey-rimmed glasses she wore. At first glance you would pick her out as talkative and intelligent.

I met her by accident, in a *barrio* near old Havana, where the streets are narrow, and the houses still the old, dark, overcrowded semi-slums left over from pre-Revolutionary times. In Cuba, during the first years after the Revolution, the emphasis was on the countryside, the area that had suffered most before the Revolution. What scant materials and resources there were for building went first to the provinces, to bring electricity, plumbing and real houses to the people who had lived in mud and palm-leaf *bohíos*. In the cities, too, there were slums, but before, *everything* had gone to Havana and a sense of fair play meant that, though these problems also needed to be solved, they would have to come later.

I didn't think about any of this as I wandered through the narrow streets. There were schools, clinics and parks for the people of this area, I knew, and new housing going up on the outskirts of Havana. Things here weren't great, but they were getting better. Children were playing in the street; it looked like a normal Cuban scene.

I came to this part of town because a photographer I knew had taken some pictures here the previous summer, and had asked me to give copies to the kids in the pictures. All I had to go on was some street names, but it wasn't hard. Armed with the pictures, I went to the area the photographer had designated, and asked some kids in the street if they knew any of the children in the photos. They began taking me from house to house.

One of the pictures was of Juanita's ten-year-old brother. I climbed some narrow stairs leading to an apartment the children pointed out, and explained to the woman who answered — the boy's mother — why I was there. She welcomed me in. Sitting on an old stuffed couch, in a living room filled with plastic flowers, pictures, and knick-knacks, I met Juanita.

She giggled a lot when her mother said she was very talkative. Mrs. P. was a proud and somewhat pushy mother. When I told her I was writing a book about Cuban children, she urged Juanita to answer my questions, to sit properly, to be polite. It was Mrs. P., not Juanita, who told me the little girl was a *Pionero*. The mother and an older sister went out of the room, then proudly brought back Juanita's *Pionero* membership card.

"What does it mean to be a *Pionero?*" I asked Juanita the question I had posed to children all over Cuba. It was then I got my first indication that there was something different about this child.

"The *Pioneros* go to the zoo, and the beach, and the park, and the movies . . . . " She eagerly described all the delightful recreation in which *Pioneros* take part. I waited for her to list the responsibilities, then prompted, "What do you have to do to be a *Pionero?*"

"You have to have a card," she stated simply, and with an air of finality.

"And don't you have to behave yourself well?" I asked, since that was one of the first things most *Pioneros* told me. She giggled, and agreed. But she didn't elaborate.

"Are you a foreigner?" she asked.

"Yes," I admitted. "It's pretty obvious, isn't it?"

She told me she could tell by my leather sandals. Then she asked, *"¿Tiene chicle?"* — the traditional child's request for chewing gum which in 1971 had almost, but not quite, disappeared in Cuba.*

I was surprised at her question, and a little disappointed. My reaction showed on my face, as I told her I thought *chicle* was a trick, because it lost all its flavor after a few minutes, so you always had to buy more and more. She didn't comment.

Juanita didn't seem to embody all the characteristics I'd gotten used to in Cuban children, but she was alert and talkative. I asked if I could come back again, with a tape recorder, one evening or weekend after school. She and her mother agreed.

As I got ready to leave, she came over and put her arms around my neck, kissing me good-bye. Again I was surprised; Cuban children are generally shy with strangers, and it's usually the parents who push unwilling children to kiss a guest good-bye.

Juanita followed me out into the hall, and as I began to descend the dark, narrow stairway she reached her arms around my neck, and this time whispered, *"¿Tiene medias?"* Her question caught me unprepared, and at first I didn't understand. She repeated her request, pointing to her socks. Flustered, I told her I didn't have any socks for little girls, but would see what I could bring her when I came back.

I went out, but once in the street she was with me again. Walking along beside me, she began commenting on my clothes. "There are a lot of nice clothes in your country, aren't there?" she asked, more a statement than a question. She asked the same question about toys. I told her there were a lot of fine clothes and nice toys, but added that they weren't for everyone. "It's not like here," I pointed out, "You have to have money to buy everything, and if you're black, and poor, you might not get any." She ignored

---

*I've been told by more recent visitors that the new influx of tourists has, unfortunately, revived this old refrain.

this comment, focusing on the existence of many fine things.

"I'd like to go to your country. People are happy there," she told me. I tried to explain, in simple terms, about the contradictions within the U.S.: that being black and Spanish-speaking, she would very likely be unable to buy all the nice things she saw in the stores. "Or you might have nice clothes, but not enough food. You might be hungry. And if you get sick, you might not have enough money for a doctor."

She was unimpressed. She had food, medical care, a good school. The lack of these things was an abstraction to her. The reason you don't have something is because there isn't any in the stores; if it's there, you can have it. What she *didn't* have was fine clothes, lots of fancy toys. She could not conceive of the possibility of having clothes and toys and *not* having enough food, or medical care, or not being able to go to a good school.

"When I grow up, I'm going to your country." She wasn't daydreaming, she was very serious. I tried again to argue with her about the difference between the myth and the reality of the U.S. "Who told you these things about the U.S.?" I asked in exasperation. She smiled, tilting her head and pointing one finger at her forehead. "I think, I notice things," she told me sagely. She didn't, as I had expected, tell me her parents said so. "Does you mother know you think this way?" I persisted. Juanita said she did. "Does she want to go to the U.S., or stay here?" The little girl admitted her mother wanted to stay in Cuba, but explained it by saying, "She has to take care of my grandmother, who is sick."

Totally unaffected by my negative attitude, Juanita urged, "If I wanted to go with you to your country, would you take me?"

"No," I told her, "because the only people who go to my country are *gusanos*."

"I'm a *gusano*, then," she replied, not upset at the idea, "because I'm going."

All the ideas I had been forming about children in the new society had received a tremendous jolt from Juanita. I knew there were adults in Cuba who weren't for the Revolution, or, feeling neutral about the Revolution, still retained many of the old attitudes and behaviors of the pre-Revolutionary society. But I had never imagined that a child — with parents who were not *gusanos* — growing up

Sections of old Havana are still crowded and run-down. The children are given adequate food, clothing, education and medical care, but the Revolution still has a long way to go in providing good housing.

within the Revolution might not adopt the new values, might focus on material things, consumer goods, and place these above the communal benefits brought by the Revolution. I had never encountered a child like Juanita in Cuba before. Although I had told some other people in the *barrio* that I would visit and talk with them later, I decided to leave and head back to my hotel.

I wanted just to forget this one aberration in my neat vision of Cuban children. But — luckily — the people of that *barrio* weren't about to let me do that. A young *mulata* woman who had expected my visit saw me leaving, and called out to me. I finally told her why I was going. She encouraged me to come back, to get to know her *barrio* better by talking to more children, to learn that Juanita was neither unique nor typical. I went back.

The narrow sidewalks of this old section of Havana are walled by concrete buildings, interrupted by grill-covered windows and scarred wooden doors. Many of the doors, instead of leading to apartments, open into *solares*. A *solar* (like the Mexican *vecindades*) can best be described as an alleyway, with a number of doors opening off it on either side. Each door marks a room — sometimes two — which houses an entire family. At the end of the alley can be found a water-pipe and latrine. These *solares* are still home for many of the families in the older sections of Havana, although the Revolution is working with increasing speed to eliminate this type of housing and replace it with modern new apartment buildings.

Carlos, age eight, lives in one of these *solares.* He attends the Antonio Maceo school nearby. This school isn't *semi-internado;* he receives no meals there. The time Carlos isn't in school is spent in the *solar,* or playing in the streets with his friends. Carlos doesn't like school too much, complains about his teachers, says everything else about school is just "OK." According to Carlos, the other kids pick on him; and when he gets into fights, he is always the one who gets in trouble. The school is named after a famous general of the War of Independence against Spain. When I asked Carlos why this was, he explained, "Because all schools are named after either a patriot or a country or something: Antonio Maceo, José Martí, Republic of Venezuela . . . "

Asked to tell who Maceo was, Carlos replied by spinning a long, fantastic tale about the Cuban hero, which bore no faint resemblance to anything I had ever heard about Maceo. I asked Carlos whether he liked learning about the martyrs and patriots.

"Well, I'm still a little boy," he replied cautiously, "and I don't know if I like politics or not."

Carlos is one of many children in this *barrio* who have divided loyalties to the Revolution, at best. He, like many of his friends, has family who have "gone North." Now he is torn, between his mother, whom he lives with in Cuba, and his father and two brothers who are living in the U.S. Cuban exiles living in the U.S. frequently write back to their friends and relatives, glorifying their new lives, describing all their new possessions, etc. (It was from letters like these — heard about in the street and in friends' houses — that Juanita probably got her impression of life in the U.S.) But counterposed to this is the prevailing Cuban attitude that anyone who leaves is a traitor to the country, a *gusano*. Contrasted to the exiles' glowing descriptions of their new home is the constant image portrayed in Cuban schools, books, television and films of the United States as an imperialist power that exploits other peoples around the world, a racist country that brutalizes black and brown people within its own borders. For a child caught in the middle of these opposing descriptions, there is a tremendous ambivalence. They know the bad things that are said about the U.S.; they are unlikely to defend their Northern neighbor, but neither are they willing to join in the attacks. A criticism of the U.S., to Carlos, is also a criticism of those members of his family who went there. This became more and more evident in his answers to my questions.

I had begun by asking Carlos the typical questions, about school, toys, friends, family. He was nonchalant about school; asked what he studied, he replied "Whatever the teacher gives me." What he likes most about school is math . . . "What I don't like is the *directora* [principal] of the school, because she's very bad, because she spanks the children whenever she feels like it," he told me. Then he quickly seemed to contradict himself by adding, "But the other day they wanted to take her away from the school and we told them that we wouldn't let them take the *directora* away."

His teacher, too, met with little favor in Carlos' eyes. "Well, she's just OK, because sometimes she gives us snacks and sometimes she doesn't, because when the children don't behave themselves she gets angry and instead of hitting us she gives us multiplication tables or gives us tasks to perform. That's why she's just OK."

Asked whether any of the teachers in the school were better, Carlos answered: "Well, there all the teachers have to be just OK because they all laugh and fool around with the kids but when we don't behave they punish us."

Carlos, by his own admission, has been punished numerous times for misbehaving.

We also talked about toys. It was a week after Children's Day, and I asked what toys he had received. He and his brother had been given "A big airplane, a soccer game, a helicopter, a mouse" and several others. But, although he was "satisfied," he didn't really like the toys he got. He wanted "a sheriff game and a little truck" instead of the airplane and the mouse. Carlos hadn't gone with his mother when she went to get the toys, but he knew the ones he wanted had been all sold out. Still, he said, "I'm satisfied with what I've got — I couldn't ask for more."

The subject of visiting other countries brought forth the contradictory emotions in Carlos once again. At first he talked excitedly about visiting Spain and seeing the bullfighters. But when asked if he'd like to visit any other countries, Carlos hesitated, then said, "Well, my father is in North America." He hasn't seen his father for two years, and clearly misses him. "I'd like to stay with my mother," he explains, "but if I could go and come back, I'd go. But as I wouldn't be allowed to return, I stay with my mother, who is better.

"It's not like I love my mother more than my father," he went on, "I love them both the same, but I couldn't stand to live without my mother. If I went there to visit my family, then the Revolutionary Government wouldn't let me come back here, and I would have to stay there. So I'd rather stay here with my mother.

"You see, I don't know my father's address — all I know is that it's very cold where he lives . . . And I'd have nothing to do there. If I had to stay there I would miss Cuba . . . . "

Later in the conversation, I asked him what he knew or had heard about the U.S. Carlos hedged, felt uncomfortable about answering. "Well, I can't really know much because I'm here and not there, but the teachers say there are bombings there, that Nixon is there. I don't really take notice of bad things, and I never repeat the bad things people say or anything."

Carlos was, at eight years old, typical of a large number of children in that old section of Havana: children whose families were split up, who had relatives in the North, who were living in dark, overcrowded *solares* and venting their energies in school and in the streets by scrapping with each other. They were the kind of children Juanita played with and learned from.

But I found out they weren't the only kind of children in this neighborhood, and that the biggest difference was made, — at this stage — not by the house or even the school, but by the parents.

Reinaldo is nine, and lives a few blocks from Carlos and Juanita. Like them, his apartment is old, and needs some repairs. Unlike them, Reinaldo comes from a family where both parents work, both are very dedicated to the Revolution, and both spend a lot of time with their children, teaching them the realities of the new Cuba and the differences since before the Revolution.

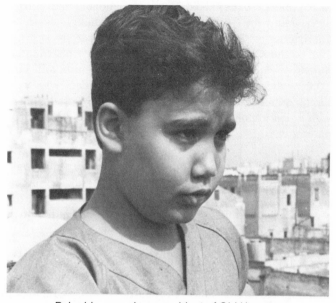

Reinaldo, age nine, a resident of Old Havana.

Reinaldo's father is a truck driver, and sometimes takes his son with him on long trips, talking to him along the way. His mother works in a nearby school. His sister, baby brother and grandfather live in the small apartment with Reinaldo and his parents.

Because both of Reinaldo's parents work, the school he goes to is *semi-internado*, meaning he gets his meals there. But it still suffers from the plagues of underdevelopment endemic in Cuba, notably in overcrowded classrooms. Still, Reinaldo's attitude is typical of most Cuban children: he likes all his teachers, and all his subjects (especially math and Spanish), he's a Pioneer and everyone in his class is too — in fact, everyone he knows is a Pioneer. He loves to read stories, and go to the movies; his favorite television program is the cartoons.

Talking to Reinaldo, I forgot for a few moments the conversations I had just had with Juanita, Carlos and other children in the same barrio. Reinaldo could have been any child in any part of Cuba. His comments on Vietnam, the U.S., school, Fidel, Che and Tania, the role of men and women in the Revolution, were similar to those I heard in the mountains of Oriente, the plains of Camaguey, the scholarship schools in Miramar. It was clear that living in a poor neighborhood, and daily exposure to families who had members in the U.S., and perhaps talked of leaving, did not necessarily turn children against the Revolution. Even Carlos, though clearly torn by the ambiguities in his life, and somewhat obstreperous, still basically adhered to the ideals of the Revolution and loved his country.

But the memory of the conversation with Juanita still bothered me. Where did a child like Juanita, with parents who were not apparently counter-revolutionary, who went to a Revolutionary school, get such a fixation on material goods? And what did the Revolution do about a child like that?

I decided to visit Juanita again. One sunny Saturday morning found me again climbing the steps to her apartment. I knocked on the door and asked for Juanita. A tall, thin brown-skinned woman told me she was taking Juanita to school. "We don't want her to be an *ausentista*" [truant, absentee], she said, rather seriously. I had forgotten that children go to school half-days on Saturday.

The young woman took Juanita by the hand, and as they headed out the door I asked if I could walk with them. When we got to the school a few blocks away, she sent Juanita to her classroom. I asked if she were the girl's sister, or aunt. "No," she told me, "I'm the principal of this school."

My initial surprise gave way to a flood of other thoughts — about what it meant for the principal of a school to take so much interest in each of her students that she would go to their homes to insure their attendance. Then, it occurred to me that perhaps this woman could help me understand the phenomenon of Juanita.

From our first conversation, I learned that many of my initial impressions of Juanita were correct. She is, in fact, exceptionally bright, and does very well in school. She does not express in the classroom her preoccupation with consumer goods, nor has she ever mentioned a desire to go to the U.S. But when I repeated my conversation with the little girl, the principal did not seem particularly upset.

Juanita, she told me, is the youngest child of a large family. As the baby of the family, she is very spoiled. Her parents let her do pretty much whatever she wants; she spends a lot of time out in the streets when her parents don't know where she is. If she says she doesn't want to go to school, her parents don't want to "force" her.

But, the principal went on, Juanita's parents are not counter-revolutionaries. They are not leaving the country. "That's why I'm not worried about her," she explained in answer to my confusion at her apparent lack of concern over what Juanita had said to me. "She will stay in this country. She will go to a Revolutionary school. Her teachers and most of her schoolmates are revolutionaries. In time, she'll change."

The principal's confidence was reassuring, but I still wasn't absolutely convinced. Then she told me:

"Several years ago we had a little boy in the school like Juanita — even worse. His parents were *gusanos*, and were waiting to leave the country. They wouldn't let him be a *Pionero*, and only talked about how wonderful life in the United States was. He was in second grade when he came to our school, and he talked just like his parents.

"But after a year in the school, he began to talk differently. In another year, he had changed still more. By the time his parents left the country, he was twelve years old, and he decided not to go."

The first day I had talked to Juanita, I had returned to my hotel feeling very depressed. I met a Cuban friend there, and we went to sit on the Malecón, the sea wall that for centuries has kept the waves of the Caribbean from tearing away the outskirts of the old city. I told him how sad and confused I felt at encountering a child like Juanita in the midst of the Revolution.

He understood my disappointment, although my story didn't seem especially to surprise him. "You have to write about this, too, you know," he told me. Then, observing my long face, he suddenly asked, "How long do you think the sea has been trying to destroy this wall?"

I looked down at the jagged rocks and worn patches of concrete at the base of the wall, and quickly estimated, "About a hundred and fifty years?"

"More," he said, then smiled. "And it hasn't been able to do it, has it?"

Talking with Juanita's principal, I suddenly understood why my friend had been so confident that nothing was going to destroy or erode this Revolution that the Cuban people had struggled for so long to build.

Before the Revolution poor children survived any way they could. *Bohemia* magazine printed these pictures in 1952. A little girl selling chiclets on the streets of Havana at night. *Bohemia* commented: "She already receives propositions from men. Later she'll be a prostitute."
Below, a young street urchin picks pockets for a living.

12

Juvenile Re-education

As can be seen from the examples in Old Havana and the comments of other children, not all children in Cuba — because of family influence or reasons of their own — are totally incorporated into the Revolutionary process.

For some of those children on the margins of the Revolution, attending revolutionary schools is sufficient to change their attitudes. For others, the solution involves more intensive work on the part of teachers and the Pioneers — who make a special effort when they see a child is diverging — in order to adapt that child's consciousness and behavior to that of other revolutionary children.

But Cuba is a society made up of human beings and, as in any society, there are children who will not accept the norms and values of that society for a variety of reasons; children who are habitually truant from school, who steal, who engage in illegal activities, are sometimes arrested, or brought to the attention of school, parents and eventually government authorities.

What happens to these children in a country like Cuba? Are they punished? Expelled? Or has the Revolution found some way to re-educate and reintegrate them into the process of the Revolution?

The answer to these, as to so many other questions, had ultimately to come from the children themselves.

CHANNELING REBELLION

"Does this say what I think it does?"

Bob Cantor, a lawyer from New York, had come into my hotel room in the Havana Libre holding the evening edition of *Juventud Rebelde,* opened to the sports page. The headline announced: "Third Festival of Re-education," and three columns the length of the page were filled with descriptions of the events and pictures of the participants.

I skimmed through the article quickly. It first described a variety of activities engaged in by young student-athletes participating in the Festival: a trip to the new Lenin Park, a huge entertainment and amusement complex, complete with a rodeo, aquarium, train and pony rides, movies, including Marlon Brando in *Burn!*; and activities with the Young Communists.

The program was similar to that engaged in by the outstanding Pioneers from each province; these must be the best athletes from the various junior and senior high schools, I thought.

But then I looked back at the headline. "Festival of Reeducation." The Re-education Centers are schools for juvenile delinquents. Were they really holding a national sports festival, complete with top headlines in the sports pages, and trips to all of Havana's most famous entertainment spots, for juvenile delinquents?

The answer — as we learned from the rest of the article, and those that appeared on the following days — was yes. The reason why was explained by Angel Boudet Gómez, second-in-charge of the Bureau of Juvenile Affairs from Camagüey Province, who accompanied one group of athletes. He told *Juventud Rebelde:* "In this way we educate these young people in the sense of collectivity. We want to change the basic pattern of their conduct, which has been one of individualism." He went on: "The attitude of these kids has been magnificent! They've received a tremendous stimulus, merited by their own improvement in their behavior. When they take part in this type of activity they feel like they occupy an important place in society. We try to maintain this idea of not marginalizing them in every situation."

In these few words, Boudet Gómez had pointed out what are probably the most important elements of juvenile re-education (rehabilitation, we would say here) in Cuba — the aspects that most differentiate the Cuban program from what is found in the United States. First, instead of making the youths feel alienated from their society, they are made to feel that they can have an important role to play within that society, that in fact they can contribute to the Revolution and the development of their country. Second, they are made to understand that their individualistic, selfish behavior is not in the interest of the Revolution or themselves; that the way that all will progress is to work together for the common good.

The Sports Festival contributes to this development in a unique way. To take part in it, the student athletes have to have made good progress within their respective re-education centers, as students, as athletes, and as people relating to other people. Thus, the Festival itself provides a very strong incentive for these teenagers to do well at school. But more important is the conduct of the Festival itself. The Festival awards aren't for athletic prowess alone. The competition is conducted like any other emulation in any school in Cuba, and the students' attitude, behavior and discipline count as much as their athletic ability. In 1972 and 1973, Matanzas Province won first place in the Festival, although it placed fourth and fifth, respectively, in the sports competition. In 1973 the head of the delegation from Oriente Province had a long face, although his province had placed first in the sporting events. When asked why, he replied:

"We weren't the winners in discipline, which is the most important, the thing we wanted most in the Festival. Although our results in the sports events were the best, we can't feel satisfied."

Points lost for "indisclipine" could come from such simple infractions as leaving sports equipment lying around instead of returned to their proper places; leaving dorms messy and beds unmade, or failing to arrive at the Festival with the same number of competing athletes as each Center had committed itself to bring. This latter could be due to a prospective competitor failing to keep up his or her good work at school, and thus failing to qualify to take part in the Festival. But it could, ironically, also be due to the opposite: the head of the Matanzas delegation pointed out that they had lost several of their best athletes because the youngsters had improved so much that they had gone home already.

A commission of young people from the Young Communists (UJC) was in charge of the emulation. It was they who decided when an individual or a team lost points for "indiscipline." But they stressed that their main purpose was to educate, not punish. "We don't report a boy or girl for committing some indiscipline just so that they'll lose points," commented one of them. "We explain to them why it was a fault, and why it is important not to do that."

When the tournament ended — after daily massive coverage in the sports pages of Havana's newspapers — a political-cultural event was held in the Mella Theatre, often the scene of some of the most important political and cultural acts of the Revolution. Seated on the stage with the national and provincial leaders of the re-education program and organizers of the Festival were the two out-standing athletes: Manuel Díaz and Rafaela Veliz. Their pictures, too, appeared in the newspapers, wide smiles and modest words sounding typical of the revolutionary children I'd met all over the island. Of the plaque he received, Manuel commented: "I'm going to bring it to my center, and dedicate it to my teachers, the re-educators." Rafaela told how her mother had come to the Sports Stadium every day to see her compete, and had "jumped up and down with excitement whenever I won."

In the United States I had known young people who had spent time in juvenile detention facilities, and had seen the shame and bitterness experienced by their families. The idea of sporting events between the inmates of such facilities was unusual; that their pictures would be published in the daily papers, and their families happily attend such events, unheard of. To be sentenced to a reformatory is a disgrace; the names of such youths are kept hidden by law to protect them and their families from being subjected to the humiliation and discrimination that almost inevitably follows.

But there is little more than superficial similarity between juvenile law and rehabilitation in the United States and in Cuba since the Revolution. The differences are what makes a Sports Festival for Re-education Centers a commonplace in one and an impossibility in the other.

USA: KIDS IN TROUBLE, KIDS IN JAIL

An article in the *San Francisco Examiner* on April 7, 1974 pointed out that "more than 100,000 children will spend at least one day in an adult jail this year. "Nearly 500,000 others will be confined in juvenile detention facilities."

The article quoted a report by Rosemary Sarri, co-director of the National Assessment of Juvenile Corrections. In her report Professor Sarri points out that the majority of such young prisoners have not committed any major crime, but are being detained for such "non-crime" offenses as truancy, curfew violation, running away and promiscuity — offenses for which no adult would be put in jail.

In fact, only about 20 percent of those who spend some time in juvenile detention or jails have committed major crimes, and the bulk of these are drug-related (marijuana possession) and burglaries (which include such things as breaking into a schoolyard or gym to play basketball).

The greatest number of youths so penalized — 40 percent — have committed what would be termed misdemeanors if they were adults, with penalties limited to fines or six months in jail. Yet youths can spend five or six years in reformatories — or worse yet, in actual prisons — for such minor offenses.

The saddest statistic of all is the third category: 35 percent of the boys and girls who are remanded to juvenile detention facilities have committed no crime whatsoever, or have done nothing that would be considered a crime if they were adults. Most of them are there because they are "out of control," meaning their parents are unwilling or unable to take care of them. Over 80 percent of teenage girls confined to youth facilities are in this category. Such children may spend up to six months in a juvenile detention facility while the courts are trying to decide what to do with them.

Professor Sarri points out that the arrest of young people for non-crimes such as truancy or curfew violation often results in children sharing cells with adults charged with more serious offenses.

"The beatings, rapes and suicides that take place under such conditions are all the more tragic," she notes, "when the victims are not dangerous to themselves or to society."

A survey by the National Council on Crime and Delinquency in New York revealed that 43 percent of the children held in local jails were not charged with a misdemeanor or felony. They were allegedly "persons in need of supervision," Dr. Sarri reports, "and local officials claimed there was no place else to put them."

Normal activities are encouraged at the centers.

CUBA: PUTTING KIDS ON THE RIGHT PATH

There are certain superficial similarities between juvenile justice in
Cuba and the United States. Proceedings against minors accused of
committing a crime are not open to the public, but are limited to the
authorities and families involved. Young people can be sent to re-
education centers for an indefinite period of time. As in the U.S.,
this "indeterminate sentence" is imposed with the view toward rein-
tegrating the youth into society and therefore keeping him or her
under the control of the State until it is felt that reintegration has
been achieved.

But the similarity ends there. Courts proceedings for juveniles
are not public in Cuba because "the youth's personality and family
background are on trial,"* not because there will be likely humiliation and discrimination following such proceedings. In fact, as

*Robert Cantor, "New Laws for a New Society," *Cuba Resourse Center Newsletter,*
Vol III, no. 5-6, December 1973.

seen by the tremendous public attention paid to the young detainees during the Sports Festival, having made a mistake, having "taken the wrong path," is not a source of shame in Cuba as long as the former delinquents have worked to overcome their early mistakes. Rather, it is a source of pride to have done so (not to have made the mistakes, but to have overcome them).

The appearance of "similarity" is even more misleading in the case of the indeterminate sentences which can be handed down to juvenile offenders in both systems. Although the theory is the same in both cases, the practice is very different. Nowhere can this be more clearly seen than in terms of the recidivism rate: the proportion of delinquents who return (repeatedly) to juvenile detention facilities following their release, or simply graduate to adult prisons.

In the U.S. the great majority of men in prison have previously spent some time in juvenile rehabilitation facilities. In California, 50 percent of the youths who are detained by the California Youth Authority are re-arrested within three years after leaving the CYA facility. Interestingly, several studies, including one conducted in Flint, Michigan,* indicate that youths who have committed crimes and *not been caught* or, having been arrested, were *not detained,* have a much lower percentage of re-arrests or repetition of crimes than those who have spent some time being "rehabilitated."

In contrast, there are very few repeat offenders in Cuba's juvenile system, and almost none who go on to become adult criminals after passing through the re-education program.

What this means is very clear. In the U.S., there is no real "rehabilitation" going on. In Cuba, apparently, there is. Why?

The Cubans would answer as follows:

In a capitalist system, laws are made by the dominant class of property owners, and an overriding concern is the protection of property. Although that system proclaims universal equality, it does not provide the economic or social conditions for realizing its achievement. In the U.S., a handful control the wealth; the majority have far less access to goods and services. Not surprisingly, then, the majority of those who come before the courts for violating laws come from the lower economic strata.

The people who make the laws, sit in judgment, and hold the prison keys are part of, or represent, a class (and generally a

---

*Martin Gold, vol. 3 *Perspectus,* a juvenile law research journal.

race) different from that of the people judged and confined. That does not go unnoticed by those who violate the laws, even the very young. They see themselves as oppressed by a system which they did not help make, and which does not give them the same opportunities or rewards that it gives to others. Since this is an objective reality, there is little the juvenile reformatories can do to change this view, to "reintegrate" the delinquent into society. At most, it may make the juveniles fearful enough of the consequences to refrain from repeating the activity that put them behind walls. More likely, it will simply make them more cautious. But since the social and economic cards are stacked against them even more heavily when they come out of the reformatory, their chances of ending up back inside are all the greater.

What does Cuba do that is so different? That can be answered both in general and concrete terms. The general refers to socialist legality; the concrete to the everyday practice of re-educating juvenile offenders.

SOCIALIST LEGALITY   In a recent article analyzing Cuba's legal revolution, Bob Cantor describes socialist legality as a system of laws and legal institutions (including the popular organizations) that protects the interest of workers and peasants — as compared to protecting the wealth and property of a small handful of bourgeoisie.

> Under a socialist system all individuals are entitled by and at birth to the basic necessities for full human development (food, health care, housing, education, etc.). Therefore, the people have a collective right and obligation to protect their socio-economic system and goals.

What follows from this is that no individual or group of individuals has the right (the "freedom") to take away any of these basic economic freedoms and liberties, as they do under a capitalist system.

Cantor describes three main principles of the Cuban legal system. 1. *Crime is caused by the individual's inability to acquire the basic socio-economic necessities. Criminal behavior can only be reduced when these necessities are satisfied on an equal, non-competitive basis.*

In practice this has meant working on developing the economy and seeing that goods and services get distributed as equally and justly as possible. It meant, in the first years of the Revolution, not just outlawing prostitution, gambling casinos, etc., but rounding up the prostitutes, the gamblers, the hustlers, even the shoeshine boys and beggars — and sending them, not to reformatories, but to school. If people don't have the education and training to be productive members of society, it was felt, it is impossible to eliminate criminal behavior. The results of this policy can be seen in the statistics: In 1959 there were 200,000 people convicted of all types of crimes in Cuba; in 1968 that number had been cut in half, to 100,000. And the reduction in major crime was even more outstanding. There were 2,650 homicides in 1959; 475 in 1968.

For juveniles, a major aspect of this policy was in building and staffing enough schools for all children to go to, then making attendance compulsory. Today, no Cuban youth can say he or she stole because s/he didn't have the education or training to get a good job. As we shall see, this doesn't automatically eliminate the problem; but it does change it significantly in terms of numbers, content, and treatment.

2. *People acquire an understanding and respect for law when they participate in its formulation and administration.*

This aspect of Cuban law is best known in terms of the People's Courts: popular neighborhood tribunals in which working men and women, rather than professional barristers, sit in judgment of their errant neighbors.

An even more significant way this policy is put into effect — especially in terms of the youth — is seen in the level of mass participation in making the laws, as well as discussion of and familiarity with all of Cuba's new legal code.

All major new laws (and Cuba's entire judicial system has been undergoing major revision in the last few years) are discussed, analyzed, debated and amended by all of the people in the country. This would be less relevant to the question of juvenile delinquency and rehabilitation if it were carried out only by adults. But the agency for these discussions is the mass organizations; and as we have seen, everyone in Cuba, down to the children in the primary schools, can participate in some mass organization.

Of course, the Pioneers do not play an active role in the formulation of new laws. They do become involved in the legal process, however, during "Traffic Week," in which all Pioneers study and learn all the rules of traffic, and then go out in the streets and help conduct traffic as crossing guards, etc. They symbolically guard the ballot boxes during elections. And they are also aware of the mass discussion of new laws, since they hear their parents' conversations as each new law is proposed, and see billboards, television programs and newspaper cartoons on the subject.

In 1969-70 the topic on everyone's tongue was the new law against *vagos* — able-bodied men who refused to work, or worked only sporadically, while still benefiting in terms of food, housing, clothing, etc. from the work done by everyone else. *Vagos* was often a theme of children's drawings I saw that year; the term cropped up frequently in their conversations.

The mass organizations — even those at the children's level — do more than just provide a formal way in which people can vote on new laws. They provide a structure through which people can run their own lives, on a daily basis. This applies to women through the FMC, workers through their trade unions, small farmers through the ANAP, people in general through the CDRs. But it also applies to children through the Pioneers (which as we've seen play a substantial role in running the schools), the FEEM, or Middle Level Students Federation, and the FEU, or University Students Federation. That sense of having some organized way in which you can run your life and make basic decisions is important in forming a consciousness of wanting to abide by the laws, regulations and social codes of your society.

Starting at the junior high school level, young Cubans take an active part in formulating the laws and policies which will affect their lives. At sixteen Cubans are considered adults under the new law, so sixteen is the voting age.

The sector most affected by each new law takes the lead in discussing it and amending it. Work centers were the main focus for discussion of the law against the *vagos*. Women from the FMC and women workers took the lead in discussing a law expanding maternity benefits for women workers. And students from the junior high schools, high schools and colleges led the discussion of a new social service law, which requires that all professional and skilled workers who receive their education from the Revolution (that is, from the people), pledge to put that skill and knowledge at the service of the Revolution, rather than use it for their private gain. Since young people studying in these various jobs and professions were the ones to be first affected by the new law, it was considered normal and proper for them to play a leading role in formulating that law.

It seems as though it should go without saying that people are more likely to respect and adhere to laws that they have been involved in making. In theory, we do that in the United States, through our elected representatives to Congress and state legislatures. But many people aren't even aware of the countless new bills that pass through these bodies each year; very few are ever consulted about them. In Cuba, the process is direct: the laws are passed by the people who will live under them.

3. *The rehabilitation of offenders is more important than mere capture or punitive isolation.*

This third principle of socialist legality is probably the one that most directly affects the everyday running of the juvenile Re-education Centers. As Cantor points out, "socialist legality stresses . . . that everyone can play a productive role in building a new society." He goes on to explain that in Cuba "rehabilitation is defined as preparing a person to rejoin society with the capacity to do productive work."

This is especially true of young people, and is one of the features that most distinguishes Cuban rehabilitation from what is found in the U.S. Despite the claims and wishes of even the most progressive penalists in the U.S., prisons and youth reformatories are not and have never been designed to educate and train young men and women to go out and get gainful employment when they leave. In fact, that's almost a contradiction in terms, because if this society *had* meaningful employment for all of its citizens there would be far fewer in its prisons and jails today.

In Cuba, there is no such thing as unemployment, and work itself has taken on new meaning. Once, Cubans worked under the threat of starvation, or in the hope of someday "getting rich." Today, most Cubans work to build up their country, to develop their economy, because they know they will all share in the fruits of their labor. There are not enough people to fill all the jobs that need to be done to get Cuba out from underdevelopment, so there is no fear in "overeducating" youthful offenders, no labor unions worried that these youngsters will come out and compete with their members for scarce remunerative jobs, no corporations who seek to maintain a "reserve army" of unemployed to keep wages depressed and workers in line.

JUSTICE FOR JUVENILES

How then, concretely, does the Cuban system of juvenile justice fit into the precepts of socialist legality outlined above?

First of all, as soon as a minor is arrested, he or she is immediately sent to a Center of Evaluation and Diagnosis. A team consisting of a psychiatrist, psychologist, doctor, lawyer, and often a teacher and social worker meet, talk with and examine the youth. A report is made, evaluating the youth's educational and work history, family background, psychological state and the nature of the offense. The report recommends a course of action, such as keeping the minor at home, sending him or her to a specific technical school, or placing the young offender in either an open or closed re-education center. The judges who receive these reports almost invariably follow their recommendations. While convictions of adults form a part of their permanent record, youth convictions do not, and future work places would be unaware of them, except in the cases where students at these centers have so excelled (such as in the Sports Festival) that they have come to national prominence. But in this case, as noted before, having been in a re-education center is really no social or economic stigma.

There are special courts and judges for minors, and a much more relaxed, informal procedure. But youths are entitled to all the legal rights that an adult will have, and prosecutors and defense counsel take part in every case. Guilt must be established beyond a reasonable doubt. But, in keeping with the concepts of socialist legalism, there is a further consideration: the desire to halt a process of social deterioration before that process has gone too far. A young officer from the Ministry of the Interior explained that youthful criminal acts need a wider definition than those committed by adults. As an example, he pointed out that stealing for an adult is defined as "using force to appropriate property which belongs to another, for one's personal gain." he observed. "A boy who steals a car just for the joy of riding in it doesn't have the same sense of 'personal gain' as an adult who wants to keep or sell it."

In practice what this means is that, with parental consent and the advice of the evaluation team, a young "pre-delinquent" may be sent to an open re-education center for an indefinite period of time — not as punishment, but as a means to guide that young person "on a better path." In this society, such an action would be greatly resented by the youths involved. That it isn't among the majority of youths who go through this process in Cuba is one more indication of how different the two systems are.

But there are a number of other ways of dealing with a "pre-delinquent state" short of sending the boy or girl to a re-education center. Although a child may commit any number of anti-social acts, including truancy, in the absence of the commission of any illegal act, that child would not end up before the juvenile courts (although parents could be sent to court in such a case for not taking proper care of their child). More likely in such a case, *Prevención Social* (Social Prevention) or the local school authorities would become involved.

Prevención Social is a commission within the Communist Party (and also within the UJC) made up of representatives of the FMC, CDRs, CTC (Trade Union Federation), Ministry of Education, Ministry of Justice, Ministry of Public Health, and the Young Communist League. Members of this commission would likely visit and talk with family, neighbors, friends, teachers and classmates in the case of a pattern of minor anti-social acts, trying to resolve the problem in this way. If the child goes on to commit illegal acts, or if the parents and school authorities feel they are unable to correct the situation, then the report of the commission is considered at the Center for Evaluation and Diagnosis in determining whether to send the youth to a re-education center or to recommend some other course of action.

The youngest a child can generally be sent to a re-education center is ten years old, although in rare exceptions there have been some eight-year-olds. Most of the young people I met and spoke with were fifteen to seventeen years old. Most of the centers today are small, with an average of one hundred students, although some have as few as sixty or as many as two hundred fifty. Most of them are "open" centers, without cells and located in rural settings. They are, by conscious design, much like the Junior High Schools in the countryside, and like these schools, have a split session of work and study. The few "closed" centers are for multiple-offender youths or those who have committed such serious crimes that they are considered dangerous to themselves or others.

A typical day in an open center consists of classes, productive work, sports, group meetings and activities, and cultural events. Many of these activities are coeducational, with centers for boys and girls in close proximity. There are approximately two teachers, called re-educators (never guards) for every twenty-five students. The teachers — many of whom are from peasant backgrounds — sleep, eat, work, study and play with their students. Although the Revolution hopes to have all such re-educators have a university education in the near future, at present there are few with this level of education. "We've had to sacrifice quality of education for quantity of teachers," an Interior official explained. "We don't want to have kids sitting in cells. It's better to have them in schools, even if the teaching isn't of the highest level." Re-educators attend a special three-month course before they begin their work, and many of them have been working in the Ministries of Education or the Interior prior to this.

BEING LOVED AND NEEDED

The program at the centers, the school-like atmosphere, and the society's attitude toward the delinquent youths — aimed at integrating, not isolating them — all contribute to making the re-education program work. But the fundamental aspect, the key to the program's success, comes in human terms. In each center I visited, all the youngsters I talked to spoke of the close rapport they felt with their teachers — even with the policemen who had arrested them. They unanimously described the re-educators as very loving people, "like parents, or like big brothers and sisters."

A re-education worker from the Ministry of the Interior in Camagüey once told me:

> Sometimes — most of the time — the children's problems are because of the parents. They are too busy, or not really interested in their children, and don't pay attention to them. In the school, we try to show them that someone cares about them, and help them to care about themselves.

Mixed chorus: Re-education center stresses coeducational activities.

We give the kids a lot of special attention. If they are interested in music, for example —guitar, piano or whatever — they can study and learn that. We provide sports events, movies, social events, as well as an education for them. They can learn a trade that is needed by the people of this country, and so they can learn to feel useful — needed.

This woman also pointed out that there are essentially two kinds of parents who "neglect" their children in this way (aside from those suffering the problems of broken families). Some of these are on the margins of the Revolution, or have a very low educational and cultural level, or simply don't care. In these cases, the Ministry of the Interior and *Prevención Social* try to spend a lot of time re-educating the parents. "Otherwise," she pointed out, "when the children go back home, they just fall back into the old ways."

But interestingly, the other category of parents who often fall into a kind of "benign neglect" of their children are those who are in a sense "super-revolutionary": the parents who are always going to meetings, working overtime, doing civic tasks. While both parents are at work, they think their children are in school, and don't know that they have been playing hooky, running around and getting in trouble, until a policeman or member of *Prevención Social* comes knocking on the door. "These cases are usually easier to remedy. The program in the re-education center is usually enough to eliminate the problem, once we've talked to the parents and explained their responsibility. Such children almost never repeat their mistakes."

In addition to the affection and attention the re-educators give to the young people in their charge, there is an organized program to provide them with the skills they will need to be useful, productive citizens. At the center I visited in Camagüey, boys were learning to make infants' shoes. A girls' center in Havana offered the students a chance to work in a perfume factory or learn TV and radio mechanics. In addition, every center has a *huerto*, just like the majority of rural and semi-rural junior high schools, where the youngsters from the center grow their own food. Each school conducts emulations, and students are chosen as "outstanding" by their teachers and fellow students in weekly assemblies, as in all other schools.

After they've been in the center for a few months (or as little as one month) most students are eligible to go out on "pass," to visit their friends and families. To spend weekends living like normal members of the society. They are given a great deal of freedom and responsibility in this: they are not "guarded" and it's up to them to behave correctly and return to school on time. The factories that most youths work in are not part of the center, but regular factories. The boys and girls go to and from their work centers themselves, and at these factories the other workers are their teachers. There are no guards.

During the week, and on weekends for those youngsters who don't go home on "pass," there are coeducational political, sports, social and cultural events. The Cubans cannot understand the concept of strict segregation of teenagers by sex that is practiced in most juvenile reformatories in the U.S. Since their aim is to have these young people play normal, productive roles in the society, they want them to remain as much a part of society as possible during these formative years.

This makes a great deal of sense. In a book of letters from prisoners* in California, a young male prisoner told how he was repeatedly denied parole by the prison authorities who cited, among their reasons, his homosexuality. This young man had been confined

---

*Eve Pell, ed., *Maximum Security* (E.P. Dutton & Co., New York) 1972

continuously since he was twelve or thirteen years old. He had never been with a member of the opposite sex in that time. Acknowledging that he might like heterosexual relations if he ever had a chance to try them, this poor prisoner could not understand how the prison system could keep him away from members of the opposite sex for his whole life, then refuse to let him go because he was a homosexual.

RE-EDUCATORS AND THE RE-EDUCATED

I first became aware of the re-education process talking with Olga Bueno, a middle-aged woman living in Camagüey, who had worked with juvenile delinquents through her job at the Ministry of the Interior. In the early years of the Revolution she had worked re-educating former prostitutes. Now, she said, there was no longer a school for delinquent girls in Camagüey, because there weren't enough delinquent girls! "The few cases we get now are sent to a school in Havana," she explained.

There was, however, a rehabilitation center for boys in Camagüey, and after a few phone calls, I was able to visit it. After driving through the streets of Camagüey City, we pulled up to some small, single-story houses alongside a busy factory.

Waldo Hernández, provincial director of *prevención* for the Ministry of the Interior, greeted me inside one of the small buildings which served as a classroom in this workshop center. He explained that this was not a full re-education center, but rather a workshop center linked directly to the factory. The men from the shoe factory had, in fact, built the classrooms and dorms for the boys.

Most of the youngsters in this center had had some kind of family problems: broken homes, etc., and in addition (or possibly as a result) were many grades behind in school. Rather than be given the normal primary school course work (most were studying first through fifth grade), they were enrolled in the Worker-Peasant School program, designed for adolescents and adults.

After four hours of classes, the students moved on to the factory, where the workers taught them to use the machines to make children's shoes.

"Part of the reason for this training," Hernández told me, "is to give us a chance to form new habits in these boys, eliminate the bad conduct they've acquired in another setting and give them a new pattern of behavior.

"But the program isn't just therapeutic. We're teaching them skills needed by the Revolution. When they finish here, they can go on in this industry, as skilled workers. The prospects for employment in this field are great in our country. There is an ever-growing need for children's shoes, and a low number of skilled workers in this field. Moreover, the general age of the workers is high, and many will be going into retirement soon. So the skills these boys are acquiring are very valuable."

Some of the boys, in fact, were being trained as specialists within the field. "Three of them are studying orthopedics," Hernández told me, "and one may receive a scholarship to study abroad in this field."

I asked what happened with a boy who decided he just didn't like this job, or who wanted to go on to study. Given the low educational level of most of the youths, Hernández was somewhat skeptical of their ability to go after a university education. He felt it was much more realistic for the Revolution to offer to train them as skilled workers. But if a student was persistent, and reached an educational level within the school that would enable him to go on to higher studies, he would be able to do so, and would be given a scholarship. If he simply wanted to transfer to a different kind of work, however, he would first have to "prove himself" by studying and working well in this center.

Despite the advantages of this type of program over a closed center, the boys were still not free to come and go as they pleased. I asked the director how the boys felt in this center. He told me to ask them.

MANILITO   Manilito was one of the youngsters I found studying in a classroom. He was seventeen years old, thin, pale and quiet. He was studying the fourth grade, and had been in this center for a year. He had apparently been involved with a group of boys who had been stealing and committing other crimes. Although he himself had not been involved in the thefts, he had kept quiet about his knowledge of them, and was remanded to this open center.

When I asked how he felt about being in the center, his response was "OK—so-so." His main complaint was that he missed his mother. He said she couldn't come visit him very often (parents can visit every Sunday, boys get a certain number of home passes each month) because he had an invalid brother, "She worries a lot about me," he confided.

Manolito said his secret ambition was to become a doctor, but he said he'd never told anyone about it because he was too shy. Since he was only in the fourth grade now, I asked if he realized how many years of study he had ahead of him to become a doctor. He said he did, but that he was doing much better in his studies since he'd come to this school.

> When I came here I was a mess. But then I analyzed things, I got set on the right path. I learned from experience. I thought about my mother, and what I could be in the future. I realized that I'm already a young man, and I want my children to have a good impression of me, to be able to respect me. So I've changed completely.

Manolito said he'd had family problems while growing up. "My family's separated, and my parents have been fighting since I was a little kid," he explained. So he began to hang around with other kids a lot, and refused to listen to anything his parents had to say.

Although he was sure he would rather live as he was now, instead of following the path he'd been on before, Manolito wished he could change the program he was in. "Instead of being trained to hold a shoe in my hand, I'd like to hold a needle and give someone injections — I'd like to be studying medicine."

Asked how he thought the other boys felt in this center, he said: "They feel OK, because they're not like me." Aside from the question of being a doctor, he said, "I think a lot about my mother. I exhaust myself thinking about her." He said the other kids ran and played a lot.

But when I asked him whether he felt like he was in a prison here, Manolito was quite clear. "No, this is nothing like a prison." In the quarterly evaluations conducted by teachers, workers and members of the Ministry of the Interior, Manolito had already been told he would be free to go home soon. Asked what he would do then, he replied: "I'm planning to work hard to study medicine."

Manolito apparently had emotional and psychological problems. But since I had promised the boys I spoke to that their conversations with me would be strictly confidential, I didn't ask the director what kind of current and follow-up treatment he was getting. Clearly, if he was being sent home, they felt that he could be treated much more effectively in his home setting than in this center.

RAFAEL   When I left the classroom I walked over to the factory where a number of the boys were at work making shoes. There I encountered Rafael. He was sixteen, with sandy blond hair, blue eyes and freckles. He looked straight out of the Midwest of the United States, and was in for the most typical of boyhood crimes: joyriding. Only Rafael had stolen a tractor — which he didn't know how to drive — and had ended up crashing it into a building.

Since this was the third time Rafael had appropriated a vehicle he didn't know how to drive, and had wrecked it, the authorities had felt it was best to send him to a rehabilitation center. Rafael seemed pretty relaxed about the situation.

Not at all shy or hesitant, Rafael told me he was studying math, geography and Spanish grammar and literature at the fourth grade level. "They sent me here so that I can work and study and be rehabilitated — so that I can learn to live with humanity. They brought me to this school so I can learn, and I've learned all I could and I'm already rehabilitated," he told me.

Q: Do you like this kind of work?

A: Yes, I like it.

Q: When you return home, would you like to continue in this field?

A: Yes.

Q: You like cars a lot, huh?

A: (with a grin) Yeah.

Q: Have you thought about becoming a truck driver or mechanic?

A: Yes. But I don't want to be a tractor driver. I just stole the tractor for a lark.

Q: You don't think you'll steal any more cars?

A: No — I've been re-educated, and I understand that you shouldn't take things that don't belong to you.

Q: What was it like when the authorities caught you? How did they treat you? Where you ever beaten or threatened?

A: No. They called me and gave me advice, and told me that I shouldn't have done what I had because the tractor wasn't mine, and that since I didn't know how to drive it I could have killed myself or someone else. They sent me here because if they had only scolded me I would have committed another crime the same or worse. So they sent me here so I'd feel good and not commit any more crimes, and know how good the Revolution is, and what one can do in it. They teach me the good way, what a worker and student can do in the Revolution.

Q: You were never beaten physically by anyone?

A: No. No one ever beat me when they caught me or since, no one pulled a gun or even pushed me. They only called me, and brought me to DOP [Dept. of Public Order] and filled out a form. Then I had a trial with my friend who I'd been with and they told us they were sending us to a re-education school till we were re-educated. No one ever laid a hand on me.

Q: Was there any time you were afraid they might beat you?

A: We wern't afraid because we knew that here they wouldn't beat you, even if you had killed someone, that they would only punish you. We knew that there is justice here.

Q: How do you feel about the policeman who caught you? Is he your enemy?

A: No. The policemen who caught me are my friends, because if they hadn't caught me I would have kept committing crimes, and might even have killed a family or been killed myself. So they're my friends, not my enemies; they're my *compañeros,* and I get along very wellwith them.

Rafael sounded so different from most boys I had talked to who'd been through juvenile detention facilities in the U.S. that I stopped to ask him: "Are you saying what you think you should say, or what you really feel?" He looked at me in suprise. "I'm saying what I really feel," he said firmly. "You're sure?" "Very sure."

We began to talk about how far behind he was in school. Rafael told me it was because he didn't like to study before.

> I didn't like school; I didn't like to write or study. Because I didn't see why I should study; I thought I wouldn't be able to do anything anyway. Whatever I could get out of studying would be far off into the future, and I didn't understand that. My thing was not to study, and I didn't.
>
> Then, when the Revolution took me into its hands, it taught me to like to study and work. So then I got myself on the right path —and I've stayed that way. I still don't know what's going to happen in the future, 'cause no one can ever know that. But now I know why I'm studying, and I feel good about it.

Rafael was the oldest of five children in an apparently tight-knit family. He received a lot of love and encouragement from his parents, and he clearly felt a sense of obligation to "straighten out and be good" for them. After listening to him talk about his family for a while I asked:

Q: Is everyone in your family revolutionary?

A: Yes.

Q: What does it mean to be revolutionary?

A: It means to be united to the force of this Revolution, to be with the Revolution, to help it in every way one can, so our Revolution will continue moving forward. Now we are in a stage of under-development, moving toward development.

Rafael said he had once cut cane with other young men and the workers and their teachers. Although the work was hard, he said he liked doing it, and had gone voluntarily, because "I feel happy cutting cane along with my *compañeros,* knowing that I'm doing it so the Revolution can come out from underdevelopment." He said he'd felt sad when he learned that they would not achieve the ten-million-ton sugar harvest that had been the goal that year, but he felt better thinking that "in the next harvest we'll do ten or maybe twelve million tons."

Since we had begun talking, indirectly, about the United States, I asked Rafael what sort of country he imagined the U.S. to be. If he had been at all marginalized by the Revolution, or simply spending time with people who didn't closely identify with the Revolutionary process, I thought that he would have heard a number of favorable things about the country to the North. But Rafael didn't identify with the United States or the people who wanted to go there.

I discovered that Rafael's concepts of life in the United States were exaggerated, but I could also see where that was coming from. Cuban newsreels and TV news reports, newspapers and magazines had frequently shown blacks in the U.S. marching and demon-strating, and sometimes being shot or beaten. Prison rebellions that occurred in the U.S. were front page headlines in Cuba, as in many other places. I wasn't surprised when I found black Cubans especially concerned about racial problems in the U.S., but it still took some getting used to to find light-skinned Cubans, who had never experi-enced racism themselves, so interested.

Because news stories of prison conditions in the U.S. almost in-variably dealt with the worst aspects of that situation, Rafael's view of this was, like his view of racism, slightly exaggerated. When asked what he thought would happen to a boy who committed a crime as he did in the United States, or in Cuba during the Batista regime, he replied:

In the U.S. he'd be killed, or, being a minor, he'd be put in prison, where he'd die in two months for lack of food, water and clothes. They wouldn't give him anything.

Here under Batista there was a rehabilitation center where minors and older people caught committing crimes were put. You knew when they went in, but not when they got out. Some who entered as boys didn't leave until they were old men. Sometimes they killed each other inside. There weren't enough beds, and they would fight each other for a mattress, or a piece of food.

Although Rafael's view of the situation in the U.S. over-emphasized the worst aspects of the system, his perceptions of the conditions in the Batista period was, from all historical accounts, quite accurate. An official from the Ministry of the Interior described Torrens and Aldecoa, the two pre-Revolution juvenile prisons, as "huge storage centers. There was neither school nor work for the youths who were confined there. Money meant for their food, clothing and health needs went into the director's pockets. It was true that a juvenile could get lost in that system, for no records or statistics were kept. No one in power cared enough.

In the 1950's the news-photo magazine *Bohemia* had frequent articles and editorials decrying the sorry conditions of children during the Batista regime. The photos showed the abysmal conditions in Havana slums, children working, begging, rummaging through garbage dumps, hanging out on street corners, stealing, and periodically landing in jail.

On August 31, 1952 the magazine editorialized against the Center for Youth Orientation (Torrens), calling it "The center of the most abject depravity . . . The University of Crime." But it pointed out that the prisons and jails were even worse, and that courts and jailers habitually ignored laws calling for the separation of prisoners by age, conduct and type of crime. "They throw together murderers and pickpockets, young and old, first-termers and repeat offenders."

The article was followed by another series of pictures, including one of a crowded jail cell with old and young prisoners jammed in together, and another of a group of boys — black, brown and white. Their arms were around each other's shoulders. The caption described them as "buddies — abandoned and looked down on by society, bonded together. They hang out together, grow up together, and maybe commit crimes together."

Since this was the way pre-Revolutionary magazines documented the treatment of juveniles under Batista, Rafael's description was not far off. It also made the next question obvious:

Q: Is your treatment here very different from that?

A: It's much better here. Here you're not murdered for a misdemeanor, nor put in prison. They want to take you and put you on the right path. They want you to understand your crime. They give us work in factories to see if we like it, so we can feel like Revolutionary Cubans, equal to all.

There aren't many delinquents here now. Many commit one crime to pass the time, or one day when they're feeling blue. Like me. And they said I'd have to pay for my crime, but what They did was to send me here till I'm re-educated.

GIRLS IN TROUBLE

Statistics show that 80 percent of teenage girls who are sent to juvenile court in the United States are there for being "out of control": runaways, truants, rebellious and disobedient. More than half of them are non-white; many of them are unwed mothers. They are placed in reformatories because the other institutions of the society have not been able to convince them to conform.

In Cuba the proportion of girls sent to re-education facilities is very low today, and I didn't meet any until I encountered a group of youngsters enjoying a vacation plan in Havana. Like the outstanding Pioneers, the boys and girls chosen as "outstanding" in each re-education center are rewarded by participation in a national summer camp, including a trip to historic sites, amusement centers, beaches, exhibits, and recreation areas. I met the group that was participating in this plan in the summer of 1973 as they were lined up at the Coppelia ice cream parlor across from my hotel. I spent much of the rest of that day and the next with them as they went to movies, the beach, and an exhibit for the twentieth Anniversary of the Assault on the Moncada.

After talking at length with many of the boys and girls in the program, I taped long interviews with two of the girls: Inocencia and Nancy. Inocencia was typical of most girls who end up in juvenile centers in the U.S.: black, a school drop-out, an unwed mother at fifteen, a youngster who liked to hang out on the street and wouldn't listen to her parents.

Nancy was a junior version of a Cuban counter-revolutionary, expressing her rebelliousness and her dislike for the communist system and Fidel by pulling telephones out of walls, and plotting to leave the country with a group of similar-minded teenagers who called themselves "hippies."

In the summer of '73, both girls had been so changed by their experience in the re-education center that they were among the vanguard of their center, and had been chosen to take part in the national vacation plan.

The following are the conversations I had with them.

INOCENCIA   Inocencia was seventeen when I met her. Dark black skin, short straight black hair, shy. She tried to hide behind some clothes that were hanging in her bunk when I took pictures — not because she was ashamed to be there, but because of her shyness, and because "I look a mess." But once she started talking she was quite open. I asked her how she had ended up in a re-education center.

— For disobeying my parents. So my parents, to guide me onto the right path, placed me in the re-education center, so I wouldn't be disobedient, so I wouldn't be an ignorant kid off the streets, but rather an educated and studious kid who could be useful to the Revolution.

Before all this, Inocencia had been a student at a Teacher Training School, but she had left school, not liking her courses, and had begun just to "hang out." At fifteen she gave birth to a son. She wasn't working or studying; her parents were worried about the crowd she was hanging around with, but she didn't listen to her parents. In her words, her parents simply didn't know what to do with her any more. They spoke to various authorities, and a decision was reached to admit her to the re-education center in Havana.

Now Inocencia was Secretary-General of the center, an outstanding student and leader, with the same bright prospects in front of her as any other girl her age. But I wondered what it had been like for her at first, an unwed teenager with a child, a school drop-out, a street kid, who was always getting into trouble and who wouldn't listen to her parents. (In this country the legal term is "Out of control.")

"UNFIT MOTHER" I remembered an article I'd read in the *San Francisco Examiner.* The headline was "Jailed Mom's plea to hold her baby."

> "My baby hardly recognizes me anymore," complained Carol Phelps, a 25-year old mother now serving a one-year sentence for theft at the Conta Costa County jail.
>
> Ms. Phelps filed a class-action sex-discrimination suit against the jail today. She said she is unable to see her 15-month old child without first obtaining a court order. She has been in jail one month and has seen the child once, while in court.
>
> If she is granted the right to see her baby, it will be through a partition, since female inmates are not permitted to hold children.

The article had sent chills down my spine when I read it, moving me to angry tears. The more I learned of the treatment of women, and especially of mothers, in America's jails and prisons, the angrier I got. In comparison to many women prisoners, in fact, the woman who filed that suit was lucky. In case after case, I learned, such women have had their children taken away from them permanently by the State, or have had to fight long, costly legal battles to regain custody when they came out. In the case of a minor, she would stand little chance of getting to keep her child unless she had the support of her parents — and a poor relation with parents is often the root cause of a girl's ending up in juvenile detention.

I was in the fifth month of my first pregnancy when I met Inocencia, and felt sharply what separation from your child could mean. Did Inocencia go through what unwed and imprisoned mothers do in the United States, I wondered?

> My son is with his grandparents, my sisters, the aunts — in general, with the whole family, 'cause everyone in the family is crazy about him.
>
> Whenever I need to see him or I'm worried about him I talk to the director of the center, and like the human person that he is, he gives me a pass. Or if not, he sends for him to be brought here — because I can't always go out on pass, I have to realize that I did what I did.

When I was sent to the re-education center my parents came to see me on the second day. They cried and I suffered a lot seeing how much they were suffering to set me on the right path. On the third day they brought my son, and we laughed and played and we were really happy. They spoke with the director to find out when I was going to be able to go out on pass, and how I was behaving. They left very happy knowing that my behavior was good, and that I followed the orders of the instructors.

I asked Inocencia if there had ever been charges that she was an "unfit mother," or attempts to take her baby from her.

Of course they said I had behaved badly, but no one would ever think of taking my son from me. This is my son. I want to leave here soon so I can take care of him, and so that in the future, when my son is a lieutenant or a captain in the FAR [Revolutionary Armed Forces] he won't have to say: "My mother was detained; my mother has done so many things that I would never do." I want my son to grow up to respect me.

In the school whenever I ask for permission to go see him I'm very thankful because they give me everything — even a car and driver, since I live in Matanzas which is pretty far from Havana — and they let me go there, and take him out and have fun with him.

Talking with Inocencia I found it pretty apparent that she had changed greatly from the apolitical street kid who had entered the center two years before. I felt sure that such drastic changes wouldn't have come about if they had treated her differently: made her ashamed of herself and her child, or kept her child from her. Cuba abolished the concept of "illegitimacy" in the first years of the Revolution, when Fidel declared: "There's no such thing as an 'illegitimate' child; if a child is born, it's legitimate." The new Family Code puts that policy and belief into law. So no special stigma was attached to Inocencia for have a child.

Inocencia was very aware of the change in herself.

My parents' decision to send me here was a very good one. They wanted to set me on the right path, they wanted what was good for me, and I'm glad now that they did it, seeing the great change in myself. I never thought I'd be this way. I never thought I could just freely talk with a teacher about anything, or that I'd be able to address myself to a decent person. I never in my life thought I'd be able to speak with Fidel, or pay tribute to the martyrs as we've done here in this center.

I've changed a lot in the center, since now I don't think the way I used to. Before I didn't pay any attention to my parents, and now I do 'cause I know they want what's best for me. I have good behavior in the center, I belong to all the student organizations, and I'm *jefa* in almost all the ones I belong to. I take the lead in discipline and especially in political work.

I asked her what she thought had been the most important factor in changing her ideas and attitudes. Her response surprised me, even though I could see how thoroughly she had been reintegrated into the Revolution.

The thing most important in changing my ideas is so that in the future I can belong to the Young Communists, to be able to sit up on the platform with Fidel, and so each time that delegations of foreign visitors, like Angela Davis or Miriam Makeba, come to Cuba I can sit up there with them and talk about the Revolution.

I have some good ideas and some good thoughts, because we study in political study circles. I read every book and magazine I can get my hands on, and I'm up to date on all the news. We talk about Fidel and all the other heroes who today are resting in peace.

What are the political events like in the center? What do you talk about, what do you study?

Right now in the study circles we're talking primarily about Che, then Camilo, and finally "History Will Absolve Me." Since this is the anniversary of the assault on the Moncada most of our political events are focused on this. We met and had discussions with some of the combatants, together with our teachers, and we saw that many of their ideas of the Revolution are the same as ours.

We also meet with the boys from one of the other re-education centers for political discussion groups. They're ahead of us in this, so they help us a lot. It's also nice to see how well they treat us, how courteously, to show how they've changed completely from the rude, uneducable kids they were before to the re-educated boys they are now.

Although I didn't ask her about it, Inocencia began telling me about one of the key elements in the re-education program: work. Since the Revolution is trying to educate the children as producers in a working-class society, there is an emphasis on combining practical productive work with education at every level. Most of the young people in the centers, although teenagers, are school drop-outs or far behind in their classes, so few have had the experience of attending a work-study school. The few primary schools which combine work and study have been developed recently, since 1972.

People from the Ministry of the Interior had already explained that there are two types of work the students engage in. One is the work at a shop or factory through which they learn a skilled trade. The other is productive work in a *huerto*, a large orchard or vegetable farm run by the school. The latter are patterned after the school *huertos* in many junior high schools and some primary schools. In them, the students grow the food needed to feed themselves and the school staff. Conversations with a number of students made it plain that they take great pride in this task. Inocencia volunteered:

> I want to tell you that we have one hundred fourteen girls in the center, and among them there are fifty-five who work in a *boniato* [a tuber type vegetable] plantation, where they plant *boniato*, and weed it, and later we eat it. We use it in our meals, fried, boiled or we make it into a salad with oil and onions.
>
> And our teachers are so happy and excited to eat the food that we've planted and grown.
>
> We also grow corn, make tamales, and we also make stew. And for the teachers who don't like stew or tamales we make a roast in the oven to please them.
>
> Since Cuba is underdeveloped there are lots of foods we don't have, and lots of ingredients we need to cook with we have to grow ourselves. So we plant onions, garlic, carrots, and chili peppers. There is one girl who is in charge of collecting them and giving them out. And no one can pick them without her authorization — not the director, nor a provincial or national visitor — because they are her responsibility. And if any of them are lost or picked before they're supposed to be the whole camp loses out, because that's not for one person to eat, it's for the whole camp, for everyone. So from the moment of planting no one is allowed to pick them, so when we eat we all eat together.
>
> "It's like the saying: "Those who don't work, don't eat," since here we all work and we all eat. And when there isn't enough we share.

Her eagerness in telling me about the farm work prompted an obvious question:

Then the work here isn't a form of punishment?

No, for us work isn't a punishment, it's part of the daily routine of re-education. One of the most important kinds of work we do is in the factory. And in our country there are twenty thousand persons "on the street"— civilians, not prisoners — who do this kind of work. And to work in a factory you have to be really integrated into the Revolution. Those of us who are being re-educated have this great opportunity that Fidel and the Revolution have given us of working in the factories: in perfume factories, bitumen factories, factories where you learn to make radios and televisions, artisanry factories where you make hats and caps that are exported to other countries that still haven't been liberated from the yoke of imperialism.

Her last remark led us into a discussion of other countries. She talked for a while about Chile under Allende, and the problems the Chileans were facing, comparing their struggle with that of Cuba. Like most other children, she talked with great feeling about Vietnam, and what was happening to the children there. Since she several times compared these other struggles to "Cuba before" I asked her what Cuba had been like before.

"WHAT THE CUBANS PLANTED . . . WAS EATEN UP IN THE U.S."

Like I told you, people of color couldn't do anything in Cuba, before. They couldn't relate to whites because they'd get beaten up. They couldn't walk out on the streets after nine P.M. because there was a curfew and they'd get beaten up by the soldiers. And Fulgencio Batista did away with a lot of people, who are the martyrs we pay tribute to today. Now we can get out of work at twelve o'clock at night and go anywhere and nothing happens — which is natural.

She also talked about "the capitalists and counter-revolutionaries who wanted to do away with the Revolution" and whom the "millions and millions of Cuban revolutionaries" have to watch out for and protect the country against.

Maybe they don't like this way of life where everyone is equal, and where we all eat the same; maybe they'd rather live in the United States, where they'd have things just for themselves and not have to share it with everyone.
   That's why there was exploitation in Cuba before the Revolution: because what the Cubans planted went into the hands of the imperialists and was eaten up in the United States. The U.S. has always been a super-developed country, and they've never wanted Cuba to be developed like they are. They want us to stay underdeveloped and today a lot of them, like Nixon, think that's the way things still are. They think that people here go hungry, and that the people who re-

educate us mistreat us, and beat us, and don't give us clothes or shoes or food.

If they could only know all the things that our Revolution gives us, that Fidel gives us! All the things the centers give us, good meals, good shoes, nice clothes — the kind that before you had to work much too hard to be able to buy and sometimes you still couldn't buy it. And we have the Cuban people to thank for this, and all those who fell fighting for this Revolution.

As she said this she looked at me intently. Then she asked, a little sadly, "Where you live, no one believes all the things that Cuba is doing?"

I told her that many people in the U.S. would find it hard to beileve that the juvenile re-education centers are the way they are.

Innocentia put her hand on my arm and said:

I wish they could understand! I wish they could see how Cuba is, through photographs, through our deeds. I wish they could see how Cuba has changed, and the kind of treatment that Cuba gives all its prisoners. We've seen in the newspapers how other countries treat their prisoners, beat them, let them starve, give them electric shocks until they destroy their minds. I wish they could see how different it is here in Cuba!

Students and teacher at re-education center relax during vacation break. (center: Inocencia)

NANCY: A LITTLE COUNTER-REVOLUTIONARY

Most of the tales Inocencia was worried about came from Cuban exiles or cuonter-revolutionaries based in the U.S., who tell tales of hundreds of thousands of political prisoners who they claim are imprisoned and tortured in Cuba. I had a chance on several occasions to see that no matter how disruptive, obnoxious or difficult a person might be, he would not be arrested unless he had broken some law. But the rumor persists outside of Cuba that people are arrrested for holding or voicing beliefs different from that of the government.

Most of the twenty-thousand persons in Cuba's prisons for counter-revolutionary acts have committed some form of sabotage, from burning public buildings like schools, communication centers, and government offices to destroying crops or industrial machinery, or they have been involved in actual attempts against the government. Nancy was a younger version of these counter-revolutionaries. Although the Ministry of the Interior refuses to use the term, she was what the other young delinquents referred to as a "political prisoner": she had been convicted of committing acts of sabotage against the State. "Little sabotages," she called them.

Anthony Platt, former professor of criminology at the University of California in Berkeley, and author of the book *The Child-Savers*, once commented:

> A lot of the kids that end up in juvenile court don't represent the "run of the mill" kind of kids who are engaged in trouble situations, but really represent the most recalcitrant, the most militant, the most primitavely political — and I say"primitively political" because it's not as though they had a full-blown political ideology. They're just "bad kids": they're into fighting back, they're into checking out the system and undermining it, they're into being rebellious.

What the schools and, finally, the juvenile courts and detention system are doing in the U.S. is to smash the rebelliousness, according to Professor Platt. The unique aspect of the Cuban Revolution and its juvenile education and re-education is that instead of trying to crush this rebellious spirit, it tries to foster it and channel it in productive directions. The leaders of the country are very conscious that their rebelliousness was what led them to oppose and eventually overthrow one of the most oppressive dictatorships in

Cuba's history. They would like to see all future generations manifest this same spirit of revolt against injustice.

The results, as in cases like Nancy's, are startling. At fourteen Nancy was a "hippie," a self-described counter-revolutionary. In large part Nancy had acted out her rebelliousness against her parents — dedicated and committed revolutionaries — through "political" acts against the State. But rather than try to crush this rebellious spirit, the Revolution had treated her with love and understanding, encouraged her to develop her many talents, and given her other outlets for her spirit and creativity. The Nancy that I met was a bright, articulate, imaginative and high-spirited young revolutionary.

Nancy was one of the teenagers I met outside the Coppelia ice cream parlor. Although most of the kids were a little shy about answering my questions, Nancy wasn't at all hesitant.

When I joined them later on at the school dormitory they were staying in while on their vacation tour of Havana, I again spoke with Nancy. They were dressing to go to the beach, in brightly colored bathing suits. When we decided to tape an interview, I arranged to come back and meet them after dinner. What follows is the complete text of my interview with Nancy.

Q: How old are you?
A: I'm sixteen.
Q: What's the name of your school?
A: Well, my school is a re-education center for minors, in other words in this country schools have been built to re-educate, that is what the country has done. It's a very pretty school, some really nice and friendly teachers go there. They treat us well, they try to teach us new things that we don't know, they give dance classes. We do exercises, we go on many fieldtrips, we have a lot of fun. On the weekends we put on cultural programs among ourselves and with the other re-education center of boys that's near our school. On the 26th of July, a very glorious date in our country, we celebrated the twentieth anniversary [of the assault on the Moncada] by doing a political program; the content was about "History Will Absolve Me."
Q: What grades are included in this re-education center?
A: Well, the grades included in our center, for girls, are first, second, fifth and sixth.
Q: And junior high school, isn't it included?

A: No, because now, at the beginning of the year in September when classes start the girls who are in junior high school will go to junior high schools outside the center; they go out by themselves to study. A lot of the girls are still studying primary school.

Q: What do you study?

A: I go out to a television and radio factory near our school. I go without any kind of guard or anything. There I have classes in electronics, so I can learn to be a radio-mechanic.

Q: Can you become a radio mechanic?

A: Sure, why not? As long as I stay interested in it.

Q: And have you already learned something about it?

A: Well, in the school we have a television set, and whenever it breaks I fix it.

Q: That's a lot more than I can do. Tell me something about the *compañeras* (guards or "re-educators") who are working with you.

A: Well, okay, I'm going to tell you a lot about that. When I came to this center I was completely anti-social, I was apathetic to everything around me, to the point of hating the whole world. And I created a kind of complex against society, because I was a prisoner, because I found myself here and it seemed like the whole world was falling down on top of me. But then I began inter-relating with the teachers, then they spoke with me about my problem. They tried to explain that what I had done wouldn't get me anything, and I got a lot of help from them. Not from my parents, though, because mine are the kind of parents who don't understand anything; they worry a little but not enough. And everything I've overcome is because of the interest I took and also because the teachers set out to help me and they succeeded.

Q: What are the teachers like? Are they like guards?

A: Well, they are guards, which is natural, but they treat us with love, as if they were our parents or sisters and brothers. And they like for us to be frank with them.

Q: And do you get respect from them, or . . .

A: Well, I understand what you mean, and I'll tell you they treat us really well, not like in some other countries over there. I think Cuba is one of the countries where re-education is really good. In our centers we have the same level of education as the schools that don't have this problem. We study and we do what everyone else does.

Q: Do they ever treat you as if you were inferior because you have committed some error, or are you treated just like any other worker or student?

A: They treat us the same as anyone. Girls go out from the school to work in factories — really interesting factories, like the one where they make perfume — and they learn all about how to make it, they work with the plants, etc. That is, we receive the kind of treatment no one could complain about.

Q: Do you have emulations, political discussions, *auto-servicio* and other things like other schools have?

A: Yes, we do. I'll tell you everything we do, in order. First, when we wake up, we wash up and have breakfast. Then each one goes to her factory. We go alone; no one has to take us. That's an opportunity that the Ministry[of the Interior] created. A bunch of girls go to the factory, and others stay to clean the dorm, or the outside areas (lawns). We painted the center ourselves — we got paint, posters — well, we felt like we were the same as any other girls. Also others go to do agricultural work, which is a very important task, because we're developing the economy of our country, and we feel useful doing this kind of work.

Q: How was it that you came to be in the center?

A: It's a little hard to explain, and I don't like explaining it so openly, but I'll tell you. At first I was "catalogued" as a complete anti-social, because I didn't like the ideas of Fidel, I didn't agree with the Revolution or communism. So I did sabotage — little acts of sabotage, against the state, like breaking telephones. [The government runs all utilities, like telephones, and all public telephones are free.] I even thought about leaving the country.

These were my own ideas. Sometimes other persons give you ideas, but I created these myself. Sometimes you feel things like that, and in that moment that's how I felt. I knew what I was doing, and I wasn't under the effect of anything, and I always knew what I was risking — that if they caught me they would send me to prison and if they didn't catch me, I was going to go the whole way.

Q: And did you do this with other kids?

A: Well . . . with some, yes. Here in Cuba there was a group of hippies — do you know what that means? [I told her I did.] And it was with a group like that that we did what we did. And I was going to leave the country with them, but when some of them left I was already in the re-education center, and I didn't have a pass and couldn't go out. That was in 1971. I had just entered the re-education center and I couldn't go, although they invited me to leave with them. They said that I'd gotten kind of weak-willed since I'd been caught, but I told them: What would I want to abandon all this for? Because in spite of all I'd done, I could change my ways and belong to a society and be a girl equal to all the others and nobody would repudiate me for what I had done, and nobody would point me out. Then they wrote and told me they had arrived very well, that they hadn't had any kind of problems. But I didn't even write them back. Since then I haven't received any more letters from them.

I was caught in February, and my conduct right after that was pretty bad. I didn't pay attention to the teachers, I behaved badly, I hated everything they told me, when there was a political study circle I didn't like anything I heard, when they talked about Fidel or anything. Before I was caught a lot of times I used to say bad things about Fidel.

As time passed I was called before the *dirección*, like when you first come in, and they spoke to me. I didn't understand because, well, at first you don't understand. Later I began getting the idea that I had to change. I began to change a little, but not completely. I was always in the worst group, not in the group of the best students. Each time my parents came to see me, the teachers said I'd improved a little.

Now I've been in the center two years; I have one year left. I'm taking part in the vacation plan [for the best students], and really I'm very happy because they treat us as if we were the same as everyone else. It's a really impressive plan! It's like the international vacation plans for all the children of the world, but ours is national. That is, all the re-education centers from all the provinces participate in this plan. Here there is no "superior," no "guard," we're all the same. The "guards" sleep with us, clean up the dorms with us. They always tell us we can overcome our errors, that we're not going to fall again, that we won't always be anti-socials, that we have to be something in this life, and I believe with all this I've changed a lot.

Q: Tell me something about the vacation plan. What is it and how were you selected?

A: First I'll tell you some of the points and requirements for the plan. You have to be in the center more than four months, not to have run away, maintain a good attitude and discipline, have good human relations with the other *compañeras*, inside and outside the center. To have maintained a magnificent and excellent attitude in the neighborhood where we live each time we go out on pass.

Now, the activities that we're carrying out: the first day we went to the zoo, the second day we visited Alamar, which the Revolution is building. That is, they are new apartments that the workers are building to put an end to those things the *campesinos* used to call houses; all of that is already being ended in Cuba and not only in Alamar but all over the country there are programs like this. Then what they call microbrigades are the ones who are building these great works which, although they are very hard work, in one or two years they've built a lot of buildings and they themselves make everything they need, the doors, windows, furniture — because the apartments and houses are furnished with really nice, fine furniture which specialists themselves say is very well made.

OK, I'm going to continue telling you about the vacation plan, 'cause I had forgotten . . . Then we visited, first Alamar, then we went to the National Aquarium, then we went to the dorms, bathed, dressed, and we went to see the Twentieth Anniversary Exposition. It's a very pretty work, which is about the struggles since 1895, about Maceo, Martí, about all those liberators who have always sought the freedom of our country, although they thought they had done it in vain because someone always tried to frustrate them. But they always stood out because they say that their ideals are what counts most. Then you see, in the same pavilion, how the country has been transformed since the Revolution. You see the splendid carnivals. You also see there on a screen the program of the twentieth anniversary in Santiago de Cuba, which was a very nice program, you see the fiesta in color. And although we're prisoners, we could visit that pavilion without anyone looking down on us. Everyone smiled at us, everyone was happy. We didn't go dressed like prisoners, because when the teachers take us out they don't like us to go out dressed like prisoners. We were dressed in skirts and blouses that the school gave us, very pretty blouses with lots of colors. The boys were in pants, sneakers or shoes and white pullovers. They looked really nice. Everyone thought we were scholarship students instead of prisoners, and that made me feel really happy!

Q: Do your parents still live here?

A: Yes, my parents still live here.

Q: How have your parents reacted, first at the attitude you had before, and to your evolution?

A: Well, my parents are revolutionaries. My mama belongs to Social Prevention, who are the *compañeros* who guard the zones, making sure that the *compañeros* who live there don't commit any indiscipline. They do guard duty at night in case any *gusano* tries to commit sabotage or things like that. But it's difficult for them [the *gusanos*] to do that because we've always got our eyes open. The people from Social Prevention are always cooperating in trying to reduce anti-social conduct, which has been eradicated somewhat in Cuba. The teachers and the other *compañeros* say that in the future, in the coming years, there won't be any re-education centers in Cuba — we won't need them any more.

Q: How were you caught?

A: Well, in those days we had just finished carrying out some of our mischief, and people had become aware that there were a lot of telephone cords cut, in Havana and in the interior of the province. That was in February 1971. They got some details about us, or some people had seen us, and at least I was captured. I was walking toward the Hotel Nacional and a *compañero* identified himself to me and told me he was from the Ministry of the Interior and asked if I would accompany him. And I said OK; at first I said no, I became rebellious and they put me in their car and took me to the *unidad* and later to State Security. At State Security most of the cases are political ones. They treated me pretty well there, they had a lot of patience with me, and I'm not sure why because at times I behaved a little rudely and I didn't want to answer their questions. When they asked where I lived I didn't answer; I wouldn't answer when they asked who I did these things with, and that tries one's patience, but . . . .

Q: And did they call your parents?

A: Yes. They let me talk with them. I was in the Security unit about one month. Then they took me to *Trece Paseo*, an evaluation center for minors, where they go over your conduct in the street before you were caught. While there they also take us to the doctors, the psychologists, to see if we have some kind of physical or psychological problem. They also take us to the dentist and fix our teeth, if necessary.

Q: Did you have a trial?

A: Yes, my trial was in *La Cabaña,* and it was pretty impressive because it was all military people there. Two *compañeros* from Security took me there from the *granja* [State farm. Sometimes used more loosely to indicate a correctional center]. The trial was kind of complicated for me.

Q: Did you have a defender?

A: Yes, we didn't ask for defenders, but they always give you a defense lawyer for your trial. Mine defended me a lot and pointed out my parents who were seated in the hall. The defender said that my problem was psychological and I said that it wasn't, that I hadn't done it emotionally or carried away by some ideas. I just had felt that way and when I feel something I express it, without fear of anything. Then the *fiscal* (prosecutor) came and I was sentenced to a re-education *granja* until I was twenty-one years old. I was fifteen at the time. Then the *compañeros* from Security took me to the re-education *granja,* or rather, the re-education center. I've completed two years there and, since I've had a good attitude, they've cut my sentence in half, and I'll leave next year.

Q: Did your ideas change a lot in the school?

A: My ideas have changed plenty. Now I have revolutionary ideas, ideas of the truth, and I express them without fear; and sincerely, I'd like to say to the North American sisters and brothers that everything that I'm saying is the truth. Here nobody makes me say anything, and you haven't told me to say anything except the truth, or anything like that. You just spoke to me and told me that you'd like us to make some recordings so people in the United States would know the truth about the re-education centers here in Cuba. I hope when they see the pictures and hear these recordings that people there will know what it's really like. And I hope some of you [North Americans] can come here like Karen, to visit Cuba, so you can see for yourself that everything we're saying is true.

  If anyone were to speak to me against this socialist government, I'd be the first to stop him and tell him "no," that he's wrong. This government isn't at all like the last one under Batista, with the capitalism that used to oppress us. Then we suffered from hunger, and the poor had to work awfully hard just to get bread to feed their children. As you know, there weren't any schools, no shops, or Secondary Schools in the Countryside like they're building now. And the re-education *granjas* were like death, because they put out the eyes of the prisoners, they pulled out their fingernails, they beat them and starved them. Now you can see the difference between capitalism and socialism, you can see how they treat us so well, how they give us good meals, and dress us in good clothes and shoes. They even give us money when we go out on pass, so when we go someplace we can pay for ourselves and our parents don't have to worry about it.

And now the *compañeros* from Re-education are planning to have the minors who are working in factories receive a salary. That's a really, really good idea. I'm in complete agreement with that idea. We feel really happy about that because that way we can help our parents, and feel useful to society. Now we feel like we are really forming the free Cuba.

Nancy and teacher on trip to Havana.

13

Culture as a Weapon

WHEN THE SUN COMES UP

A poem by Cuba's black poet laureate, Nicolás Guillén, is today a children's song called "Song of the Working People."

Cuando sale el sol	When the sun comes up
a la fábrica pronto	right to the factory
camino yo,	go I
cuando sale el sol,	when the sun comes up
porque soy el obrero	because I am the laborer
trabajador,	worker
cuando sale el sol.	when the sun comes up
Cuando sale el sol	When the sun comes up
las tierras de mi tierra	the lands of my land
cultivo yo,	I cultivate
cuando sale el sol,	when the sun comes up
porque soy el campesino	because I am the peasant farmer
trabajador	worker
cuando sale el sol. . . .	when the sun comes up. . . .

And it concludes:

Cuando sale el sol	When the sun comes up
a construir la vida	to construct life
camino yo,	go I
cuando sale el sol,	when the sun comes up
porque soy el pueblo	because I am the people
trabajador	worker
cuando sale el sol,	when the sun comes up
el sol,	the sun
el sol,	the sun
cuando sale el sol.	When the sun comes up.

These lines reflect one of the most important aspects of the new culture that is emerging in Cuba.

Another children's song, this one taken from a speech by Fidel, reflects working class morality, instilling a sense of collective responsibility for the welfare of all. Called *"Ricos y pobres, pobres y ricos,"* it goes:

Mi casa no es mi casa	My house is not my house
si hay quien no tiene casa	If there's someone without a house
al lado de mi casa.	Alongside my house.

calabaza, calabaza

La cosa es que mi casa	The thing is that my house
no puede ser mi casa	can't be my house
si no es también la casa	if it's not also the house
de quien no tiene casa.	of whoever has no house.

The shelves in libraries and classrooms are filled with books designed to reinforce what the children learn in class and from their parents, and the example of the Revolution itself. Since work is a central theme, stories try to create in the children a sense of the importance of work that the Cubans call the "need to care for the material goods created by the hard labor and efforts of our workers," and at the same time a love of work, "to encourage interest among the youth in professions which are of vital importance for the economic development of the country," and "to give social prestige to occupations vital to the national interest."

For the youngest children, stories are frequently about animals. Although the Little Red Hen is the clearest example ("if you don't work, you don't eat"), many of these stories have the same focus, encouraging the young kitten, duckling or chick to go to school, help with the barnyard work, etc.

Since Cuba is a working-class society, work becomes a natural theme in all kinds of writing. A typical grade school textbook, for instance, gives the following arithmetic examples:

> 700 workers are employed in a factory. After an extension of the factory, the number of workers is increased by 100. How many are there now?

> In the School in the Countryside the students have planted 100 coconut trees, 600 lemon trees and 800 orange trees. In all they must plant four times this number of coconut trees, three times this number of lemon trees, and twice this number of orange trees. How many will they have planted in all?

> At a beach resort there are 123 houses for vacationing workers. 100 are occupied by cane cutters and 6 by workers from a state farm. Think of two questions based on these figures and calculate them.

Although in some ways these examples seem like ordinary math problems, in fact they reflect real changes in Cuban society. Before the Revolution, when few but the wealthy could send their children to school, few students would have dreamed of soiling their hands by planting trees. That sort of work was for the children too poor to go to school. And the beach resorts, far from being vacation spots for Cuban workers, were barred to all except the very wealthy, white Cuban bourgeoisie and foreign tourists.

Love for Cuba and the Cuban people is well represented in children's books, many of which deal with Cuban history and the independence struggle. One of the most interesting books of this type is called *Así Vemos El Moncada* (This is How We See the Moncada). From its glossy paper cover through the entire book, *Así Vemos El Moncada* consists of children's drawings, done by the children at the National Library, and their accompanying descriptions. Beginning with José Martí, "intellectual author" of the attack on the Moncada, the book's drawings tell the story of the rebellion led by Fidel Castro in 1953, the capture and murder of many of its participants, the return of Fidel and the rebels in the Ship *Granma*, their struggle in the mountains, and their eventual victory. All of this is told in the simple words and brilliant pictures of children four to twelve years old.

But the Revolution doesn't want children who are simply nationalist. Cuba is raising a generation of internationalists. Love for your own people is seen as only the first step in generating a love for all peoples. Thus, a great number of Cuban children's books deal with peoples of other lands — from the Indians of North America to the peasants of Vietnam.

In the 1969-73 period, popular stories about Vietnam ranged from a small book of short tales about Vietnamese fighters and children called *The Little Shoeshine Boy of Saigon*, to a hard-covered book about the land and people of Vietnam entitled *Vietnam and You*, which describes the life of Vietnamese children, the clothes they wear, the food they eat, the houses they live in and a few words of their vocabulary. Describing the child-fighters who defend their fields and villages, the book concludes, "Not even the bombs can destroy their happiness."

Following both the line of giving children a voice in their own literature and that of internationalism, one of the most beautiful books put out by the *Gente Nueva* section of the Cuban Book Institute features a series of poems written by a thirteen-year-old Vietnamese boy, translated into Spanish and accompanied by colorful paintings of Vietnam. In one poem the young author is expressing his sadness at the death of Ho Chi Minh. "You have left us, Uncle," he addresses himself tearfully to the deceased president of his country. But he later concludes, "You have left us the future . . . . "

Although love of country, work and all peoples of the world are very important themes in Cuban literature, it would be a mistake to give the impression that all or even most children's books bear these themes. Armando Hart, a leader of the Revolution, once said: "We wish to see a rebel youth who think for themselves, who are capable of reasoning, eager to learn more, to investigate new fields, a youth free of biased simplification or dogmatic thinking." It is just as essential to the Cuban Revolution that its young people's literature be creative and imaginative as that it teach them class consciousness and international solidarity, and all of this is as important as teaching them math and science and grammar.

The Revolution has provided a variety of ways for the children to participate in creating their own literature, from recorded dialogues to poems and stories submitted to the *Pionero*, an education magazine called *Simientes*, and others. In addition, writing is often combined with other art forms, like music or drawing. At the National Library there is a regular children's program which meets twice a week. Children draw, paint, hear stories and lectures, and construct things out of paper, wood or any other available material. One activity is to have each child write a story and then read it aloud to the others. The other children then draw pictures to illustrate the story.

Despite the contribution to children's literature by the children themselves, the teachers and writers I talked to all spoke unhappily about the continuing lack of sufficient reading material. Even the children were aware of it. At the National Library one little boy mentioned that he had just turned ten years old. I asked him what he had done on his birthday. "We had a cake," he told me, "and some kids brought me gifts — some books. *Children of the Sierra Mestra, The Life of the Slaves* and some others."

He went on, "I like to read a lot, but there aren't many books left for me to read. That's why we have to get out from under-development — so we can have more books."

Although this youngster mentioned the scarcity of paper as one reason for the low number of books, the "colonialization of the mind" which some Cuban writers and educators talked of at the 1971 Congress on Education and Culture is probably as much to blame. The Revolution has had to contend with the inherited cultural ideas concerning children's literature and who should produce it. As the writer Eliseo Diego put it: "Today, in the midst of the Revolution, we still have to overcome an annoying obstacle: this scornful flippancy with which men of Latin cultures regard children's things, considering them the business of maiden aunts or grandmothers. Yet José Martí," he added reproachfully, "who was more man and more poet than the best of us, did not look down on writing for children, but in fact considered it an honor."

Since most of the people with the education and background

in literature and story-writing at the start of the Revolution were
men, this meant that Cuba could not at first count on the help of
its most skilled sector in producing material for the children. This is
changing in two ways, as more and more women are educated,
and take an equal place in society, and as the Revolution inexor-
ably works on the conscience and consciousness of the men to
abolish these vestigial notions. But meanwhile, today's children
could not wait for a new generation to produce literature for them. In
addition to having the children write some of their own literature
(thereby also helping develop their own creativity), the Ministry of
Education, the Union of Writers and Artists, Casa de Las Americas
Literary House and others offered contests and prizes, as well as
much public acclaim, for outstanding new contributions in the
field of children's literature.

   Although the situation seems to be improving, the initial results of
these contests were not as rewarding as many had hoped. Ricardo
Garciá Pampín, editor of the Pioneer newspaper, Luís Pavón,
president of the National Council on Culture and a variety of teachers
and writers all suggested the same reason: writing for children
requires a very delicate balance. On the one hand, you must write
simply, clearly and interestingly enough to capture the child's attention and keep it. But at the same time, you must not be talking
down to the reader, for even the youngest child senses this con-
descension, and quickly becomes bored or disinterested. Very few
had this unique ability. Many writers and a number of young
teachers who had not written before, but knew children through
their work, tried with varying success.

BREAKING THE CHAINS OF THE PAST

"We're talking about a policy or orientation of culture in a country
emerging from its colonial past and building socialism," observed
Luís Pavón. "The fundamental problem of culture in our society
is the struggle against the old concepts imposed by imperialism
and colonialism. For many years in Cuba there were values imposed
on us that weren't Cuban values, but were those of the bourgeoisie.
We had the falsification of cultural values, with the artificial ones
replacing popular culture. And this was done intentionally and

maliciously, first by Spain, then by the United States."

What North American textbooks call the "Spanish-American War" is viewed very differently in Cuba: as U.S. intervention in Cuba's successful independence struggle against Spain, for purposes of economic penetration and political domination. According to Pavón, this wasn't all.

> When the U.S. intervened in 1898, we were faced not just with economic penetration; the penetration was carried out in the cultural arena as well. The first measure of that intervention was a reorganization of the school system, imposing a U.S. model (in the name of "progress" and "enlightenment" — a kind of "civilizing the heathens"). During the first years of the pseudo-republic set up by the United States in Cuba, our teachers and students didn't study Cuban history at all. They were given a little bit later on, but this was deformed and distorted in favor of creating a positive image of the U.S. That is, the schools were used to create attitudes and concepts convenient to imperialist interests.

This cultural penetration, according to Pavón, touched on every aspect of Cuban life. Pavón, who is to all outward appearances what would be classified as "white" in this country, decried the imposition of white racist values on Cuba.

> After the U.S. military intervention one of the rules laid down was the prohibition of the playing of drums. This was aimed at the lower calsses, primarily the blacks. The pretext used was that the drum-playing festivals were the scene of noisy gatherings, but more profoundly, the Americans were trying to "civilize" those low-level Cubans. The banning of drums was linked with their overall disparagement and depreciation of Cuba's African culture.
>
> This is a flagrant example of the distortion and falsification of our forms of artistic expression. We're a *mestizo* nation. Naturally drums are an elemental part of our musical heritage. There had been a widespread popular tradition of Cuban music using drums which they were trying to crush.

But the resistance by the creole Cubans, "black" and "white," to this cultural onslaught by the North Americans was strong, and the attempt to wipe out African and creole culture failed. The popular traditions of rhythm and music persisted, and were eventualiy incorporated into all forms of popular music, from dance bands to symphonies.

This falsification of national values took place in terms of Cuban history, too. National heroes were rewritten in the U.S.-produced textbooks to appear as totally different characters. "They eliminated most radical aspects of these heroes, and gave them almost mystical overtones," the head of the CNC explained.

The mass media were used to spread these false images to the entire population. Comic books and movies aimed at children were especially subversive in this sense. As a rule they were solely commercial ventures, with no intent to educate — except when used to miseducate along lines convenient to their producers.

Cuban culture was in the hands of the capitalists, who used it to impose discrimination against blacks, against Indians, against Latins. And what they gave us was the sub-culture of imperialism, not even the real culture of the United States. Because we believe the people of North America do have a real culture, a valuable one, seen in writings of such men as Walt Whitman, for example. José Martí and other revolutionary Cuban intellectuals greatly respected what they regarded as true American culture. But we got Superman instead of Walt Whitman, Mickey Spillane instead of Ernest Hemingway.

African dances and music are an important part of Cuba's cultural reawakening.

A PEOPLE'S CONGRESS

The Congress on Education and Culture, held in 1971, was built from the grassroots up. Teachers in every school, and then cultural workers, held meetings and discussions concerning various themes suggested by the planners of the conference. Out of these discussions came new topics — especially concern for what the children were learning from the mass media. This resulted in the broadening of the Congress to include all aspects of culture as well as classroom education.

One of the results of this process was the formation of a new Cuban trade union: the Union of Workers in Education and Science. The country was beginning to move concretely from the concept of intellectuals as a privileged elite, to the idea of "intellectual workers."

Well over a hundred thousand workers in the field of education contributed hundreds of papers and thousands of recommendations at the regional and provincial level, before the national congress was convened. Drawing on the massive support for cultural independence expressed by these teachers and cultural workers, the Congress immediately set out a basic guideline stating that "in all forms of art, music and literature," efforts should be made:

1. To work on the development of our own forms and revolutionary cultural values.
2. To develop an understanding of the cultural values of fraternal nations of Latin America.
3. To assimilate the best of universal culture without having it imposed on us from abroad.
4. To develop educational programs for teaching the nature and origins of Cuban music.

The Congress declaration continued:

Culture in a collectivist society is a mass activity, not the monopoly of an elite or the decoration of a chosen few or the free franchise of those with no roots in society. True genius is to be found among the masses and not a few isolated individuals. The class nature of the enjoyment of culture has resulted in the brilliance of only a few individuals for the time being. But this is only a sign of the prehistory of society, not of the nature of culture.

In April of 1971, when I left Cuba, the Revolution was calling on all educators and cultural workers to take their abilities to the people — especially the children — and to share with them their knowledge and skills. When I returned two years later, in April of 1973, I was interested to see what effects the Congress on Education and Culture had had. I went to see Luís Pavón at the National Council on Culture headquarters in Old Havana. Pavón spoke first of the changes in the arts school, Cubanacán, and the development of amateur (*aficionados*) groups in all fields of art and literature. According to Pavón, the *aficionados* movement was set up to spread art among the masses — by involving workers, campesinos, young people and even children in the performance of art. The movement embraced all those who expressed themselves artistically, but whose main work is not an art form.

The *aficionados* movement was an immediate success in the schools, where large numbers of boys and girls formed theatre, music, painting and writing circles. In many societies, *aficionados* are the persons with a great, but passive, interest in art. In Cuba, *aficionados* are expected to participate in creating art — not to be mere spectators. This applies to the youngest children as well as to the oldest adults. But a mass movement needs instructors, and the art school hadn't focused on preparing instructors. It had not trained artists in the technique of bringing their ability to the masses of people. By 1973, admitted Pavón, there were still not enough cadres and instructors for all the schools and all the informal groups of young people who wanted to participate. "Artistic cadres aren't formed in just two years," he commented.

Those who had been professional artists before were called on to participate, and some of them formed artistic brigades to teach in the schools. Most of these were young artists and performers who volunteered two years of service — similar to other forms of professional service to the Revolution pledged by doctors, lawyers, and others.

But the biggest change took place in the development and training of new artists. According to Pavón:

> The most important change in the art school is in concept. We no longer train people to be traditional artists, but to learn how to carry skills, talents, and culture to the masses, to teach the masses

how to do it themselves. There are two forms of doing this: through teaching, and by bringing various art forms to the masses so they can learn from experience how to do it.

TAKING ART TO THE STREETS

Taking art to the streets and other places where it is not habitually found was not as simple as bringing it into the schools in a massive way. "First of all, we didn't have habitual places where people were used to congregating and where we could put on performances and exhibitions," Luís Pavón told me. The Cuban Film Institute ICAIC had moved on this very early in the Revolution, sending mobile film units to remote mountain areas.

The CNC also experimented by putting juvenile art in the Museum of Fine Arts, giving unprecedented public exposure to this movement of novice painters. The factories and agricultural centers also receive everything from art displays to symphonies, and they have been found to be as successful there as more popular art forms. This at first might seem unconnected to the culture of the children. But children in large measure have their interest in cultural activities awakened by their parents. Prior to the Revolution only a handful of Cubans had the opportunity to know and enjoy most forms of culture and the arts.

The integral education of all human beings means, to the Cubans, educating the parents as well as the children of the Revolution in the appreciation and participation in all art forms.

When Fernando Alonso, National Director and choreographer of the Cuban National Ballet (of which his wife Alicia Alonso is the internationally known *prima ballerina*), went into the countryside recruiting children for Cuba's national dance school, he found that most children didn't even know what ballet was. "We had to choose them by very arbitrary methods: height and size, ability to clap their hands in rhythm, etc." After a number of such children from peasant areas were given scholarships to the arts school, there were more problems. "Sometimes we had to convince the kids that it was more interesting and worthwhile to do dance exercises than to climb trees," Alonso recalls. There were other problems,

too: keeping the other little boys from calling the boy dancers "sissies." "Finally we had to take what I would have to consider a very un-socialistic measure," Alonso admitted. "I told them: 'The next time a boy calls you a sissy, I want you to punch him in the nose. And if you *don't,* I'm gonna punch *you* in the nose!'" Within a year, he states, no one was belittling the boy dance students.

Music has been an integral part of Cuban culture throughout its entire history, and survived the attempted repression by foreign powers and military leaders at the turn of the century. Nothing more powerfully evokes the African and Latin American heritage of Cuba than its music.

For Cuban children — like children in all societies where they are not repressed — song and dance are natural means of expression which youngsters use unselfconsciously from the time they are toddlers. The simplest songs are usually about flowers, animals, raindrops or "nonsense" songs, like those of children everywhere. But the political and social content appears very early. One of the first songs I learned in Cuba was from a friend's six-year-old daughter, who wandered around the house singing and humming *"Hemos dicho basta!* . . . " a song set to the words of Fidel's Second Declaration of Havana: "This great people has said Enough! And has begun to move forward."

The same little girl came home from school singing a song she said her teacher had taught her. Her mother referred to it as the "Fred Hampton Song." Earlier that year Cuban newspapers had carried big articles on the Chicago police raid of the home of some Black Panthers, in which Panther leader Fred Hampton had been shot to death while asleep in his bed. The words of the song reflect, I think, what many Cubans must have felt when reading about or seeing on television police attacks on civil rights demonstrators and antiwar marchers in the United States, and the killing of unarmed blacks. The song goes:

> Enough! marching for peace
> Enough! marching without guns
> You have to understand reality
> There has to be another Vietnam in the North (USA)
> So that no black man dies in his bed
> So that no black man dies in his bed
> Enough! marching for peace
> Enough! marching without guns
> Enough! marching without reason
> You have to understand reality.

The United States is very much on the minds of Cuban children. Repeated armed attacks on coastal villages by U.S.-based counter-revolutionaries, the families split up by members "going North," the television newsreels of life in the United States are a constant reminder. When Angela Davis was on trial, I heard children everywhere singing a song about her in which they call her trial a "farce," based on a "lynch law," and declare that "the children shout for Angela . . . and Cuba demands her freedom."

Some typical verses of a children's call-and-response song went:

Si un día me mataran	If one day they kill me
Por marxista-leninista	For being a marxist-leninist
Con mi sangre escribiría	With my blood I will write
Viva Cuba socialista!	Long live socialist Cuba!
Batista con cinco estrellas	Batista with five stars
No supo ser general	Didn't know how to be a general
Pero Fidel con uno sola	But Fidel with just one
Hizo la tierra temblar	Made the earth tremble

Si quieres comprar un burro	If you want to buy a jackass
Debes tener presente	You'd better keep in mind
Que sola a noventa millas	That just ninety miles away
Hay un burro presidente	There's a jackass for president*
Si Batista se muriera	If Batista should die
Que le entierren boca abajo	Let them bury him face down
Para si quiere salir	So that if he wants to leave
Qué se vaya más por abajo!	He'll go farther down!

Other songs dealt more lyrically or seriously with subjects such as Vietnam and Cuba. One particularly internationalist song (which I've been told originated in Spain) was called *Marinero*. The children sang it over and over again on the bus to the Pioneer camp and throughout the two weeks in camp. It starts out simply, addressing itself to a sailor leaving the shores of Chile, but concludes with the very Cuban lines:

En este campamento,	In this camp, in this camp
En este campamento,	Of Pioneers, of Pioneers
de los pioneros, de los pioneros	We are all happy,
Todos somos felices,	We are all happy,
todos somos felices	We're all brothers and sisters
Somos hermanos del todo	Of everyone in the world.
el mundo.	

FUN AND GAMES

"Children are born to be happy."

José Martí

As has been noticed by innumerable visitors to the Island, Cuba's children are the darlings of the Revolution. Every effort is made to see that they are not only well fed, clothed and educated — but happy as well. In a country where all resources are scarce, funds have nevertheless been set aside for parks, playgrounds, zoos, aquariums, circuses, outdoor puppet shows, etc.

But Cuban educators also feel that children's play can deform

---

*Referring to Richard Nixon in 1972 and 1973.

instead of develop if it is not correctly geared to the child's age, sex, abilities and other factors; if it is not properly directed. Vacation plans are organized during all periods when school is not in session so children are not left just to wander on the streets alone while their parents are at work (or, alternatively, to keep mothers from having to drop out of the work force when their children are on vacation.)

In 1971 Havana began experimenting with building Children's Recreation Houses, surrounded by large open areas and containing a variety of activities inside. These are to be available for children in all non-school hours, and include some educational activities as well as games and entertainment. Sports play an important role in these *Casitas.*

The summer vacation plans are more elaborate, involving taking children on trips and excursions to beaches, parks, zoos, and various historical sites.

In addition, certain days and weeks are devoted entirely to children. Cuba celebrates both International Children's Day on June 1 (with a week of activities), and a Cuban Children's Day. The Cuban event used to take the place of Christmas and was only recently moved from January 6 (the "Day of the Three Kings" which is celebrated in many countries) to the third Sunday in July, when it will correspond with the adults' period of carnival and festivities at the end of the sugar harvest.

To celebrate International Children's Day in 1973 the Pioneers carried out a week of parties in childcare centers, street fairs, excursions, drawing exhibits, sports meets and games.

In the schools of each region Pioneers prepared gymnastic and folklore tableaus, including dances from countries around the world. They also burned effigies representing imperialism and sent letters and post cards to the children of Vietnam with little mementos of Cuba, to demonstrate their love and solidarity. At the end of the week they had Friendship Bonfires at which were read compositions written by Pioneers in salute of the international event.

A major artistic spectacle was performed by the children in a theatre in the Vedado section on the final day, attended by Vilma Espín, President of the Children's Institute and member of the Central Committee of the Cuban Communist Party, along with the Ministers of Education and Public Health. Children as young as five years old took part in the dances, games, songs, skits, rhythm bands and puppet shows, many of which revolved around international themes or the assault on the Moncada. The next day the event was reported in the press with all the fanfare that would be accorded any major artistic spectacle.

Cuba's Children's Day has been moved from January 6 to July 6 that year, and it came at the end of the *Encuentro Nacional de Jefes de Pioneros*. Perhaps because of this, or perhaps just because of the seriousness with which the Revolution takes the organization of children, on that day leading delegates of the UPC were called to the Secretariat of the Central Committee in the *Plaza de la Revolución*, where they met with Fidel and a number of other members of the Central Committee and spoke with them for some time.

GAMES CHILDREN PLAY   It would be a mistake to give the impression that all is politics and seriousness for the children on Children's Day. Just the opposite is true. The same children who met with Fidel joined the other *Pioneros* on July 6 for a tour of the fabulous new Lenin Park — acres and acres of park, recreation areas, amusements, and entertainment.

Children's Day is when Cuban children get their toys, instead of Christmas. On that day, each child's parents are entitled to buy three gifts. The child may go with the parents to select the gifts. The Revolution doesn't believe in Santa Claus.

I frequently asked young children I was interviewing to tell me about Children's Day, generally feigning ignorance to elicit complete replies. One day I was talking to a group of young Pioneers in Santiago de Cuba. They knew I was a foreigner, although I had not told them which country I was from. Some of the littler ones — six and seven years old — were very shy at first, leaving the talking to the older or more outgoing children. But one shy six year old found her tongue when I asked about Children's Day. She patiently explained how each child gets three toys on that day. "Everyone gets three??" I feigned surprise. "Don't some get more and some get less?" She shook her head, repeating that everyone got the same amount. "That's very interesting," I told her, "because where I come from, some kids get fifteen or twenty toys, and some don't get any."

"That's because in your country there's exploitation," the tiny Pioneer informed me somberly, forgetting her shyness.

Pioneers explain Childrens' Day.

Changes have been occurring in the area of toys as well as all other aspects of children's cultural life, because toys reflect and transmit culture as surely as books, art, literature or music. A doll factory that inherited molds, dyes, and techniques to produce European-looking dolls has to make a lot of adaptations to try to produce Cuban-looking dolls. When I spoke with the director (a man) and head engineer (a woman) of the doll factory in 1973, they were still looking for new, better models.

Toys are a barometer of some of the social changes Cuban society is going through. In the years I was there, the toys parents could buy for their children on Children's Day depended on the sex of their children: the toys were listed as "boys'" or "girls'" toys. The growing consciousness about women's role in a revolutionary society finally led to the elimination of sexist distinctions in toys by the mid-seventies.

Toys and games also reflect Cuba's working class consciousness. In 1971 I discovered a board game called *Triunfo*, which looked like a socialized version of Monopoly. The board is divided into provinces of Cuba. Each province has two or three spaces with the same color, each marked with a different product produced in that province: cattle, nickel, sugar cane, etc. Each side of the board also has at least one square representing a regional office of the Agricultural Development Department and one space for the Ministry of Construction. There are also "Chance" squares entitling the person who lands there to pick up a "Chance" card. The four corners, instead of representing "Go," "Jail," "Court," etc. represent the Development Center — where you pick up your "resources" instead of two hundred dollars; a Meeting (equivalent to being sent to jail, unless you get sent there with the bypass explanation, "But only to bring coffee"), or Vacation. The board also includes one meat and one dairy cattle breeding station, and other industrial or economic centers.

Instead of money the players are allotted "resources" which have a certain worth. Tobacco is worth one hundred twenty, minerals one hundred, forestry one hundred. But you pay for them with other agricultural products or machinery. A tractor is worth twenty, a cane cutting combine one hundred, a cane lifter fifty, a truck five.

Although no player can buy or rent any of the squares, or build private houses or hotels on them, they can erect various structures useful to the Revolution — schools, sugar mills, etc.

The game as a whole is an exact duplicate of "Monopoly" geared to suit the reality of Socialist Cuba.

Not all toys have been so easy to adapt, however, and underdevelopment has played a major role in keeping the Revolution without all the toys it would like its children to have, both for fun and for learning. Although the allocation of three toys per child insures that no child will go without, it is still far less than they would like to have.

This is even more true in the childcare centers, where toys of all types are considered fundamental to the children's development. Earlier U.S. visitors to the *círculos* sometimes commented on the apparent scarcity of toys, or the zealousness with which the *asistentes* protected the ones they had from damage or misuse by the children. (This concern that toys be properly cared for was sometimes mistaken for an overemphasis on cleanliness. While I think that the preoccupation with cleanliness is typical in terms of frequent bathing, the scarcity of toys and the difficulty in replacing them were probably more responsible for the care with which toys were always put away.)

Sometime after 1971 the *taller didactico* — Didactic Shop, literally

— was developed. These are centers in each *círculo* region where toys and games are produced for all the childcare centers in that region. The *talleres* employ volunteer help from students, teachers and retired folks, and use any kind of scrap material they can find. The Children's Institute provides them with a specific list of the kinds of toys it wants for the development of the children, and each center or *taller* is responsible for producing them with the materials at hand.

I visited one such shop in the outskirts of Havana, and wandered around looking at the various toys and games produced there. There were twenty-one different types of toys that I observed (each in a separate cubby hole, box or table). They included toys aimed at developing muscular control, such as blocks, rubber balls, and clay (balls of which were stored in multi-colored egg cartons); and simple educational toys for very young children to learn colors, motor skills, space relations. This section included a cardboard house, a necklace, a telephone, and cardboard tube figures painted to look like people, each painted a different color. In the childcare centers three- to five-year-olds play various games with these figures and use them as puppets, while learning the colors.

There were also a number of musical instruments and noise-makers for a rhythm band, ranging from bottle caps on sticks to real toy pianos and guitars.

One section included traffic toys: street signs and a traffic light made of blocks that come apart.

A number of toys were dedicated to learning about nature. There were fish, plants, and other sea creatures made of paper, cardboard and shells to teach children about the sea.

In one area I saw brightly painted handmade boxes and baskets. When I asked what they were for I was told that it was for the children to collect things: leaves, pebbles, shells. Then back inside the *círculo* they would learn about the things they collected, and play games by putting them in order of shape, size, and color. It hadn't occurred to me before that in order to collect things children need something to put them in, and that "having things to put them in" doesn't come easy in an underdeveloped society.

Many of the toys were aimed at encouraging children's participation, creativity, and imagination. This ranged from "learning boxes" which develop tactile sensitivity, to handpuppets, masks and costumes.

One "learning box" was made to look like a circus lion cage on wheels. The plastic wheels were removable, leaving two large holes through which children could put their hands. They would then be asked to identify the objects they could feel inside the box.

The puppets, props and scenery for dramatizations were among the most ingenious creations there. A butterfly on a stick, for example, utilized a tube from an artificial insemination plant.

Other toys ranged from simple rattles and mobiles for the youngest infants, to elaborate farm sets, complete with little animals, fields, fences, and housing. There was also a blackboard and clothboard for the more explicitly educational activities.

Although I hadn't expected books to be among the things improvised in the *talleres,* these too were included. Volunteer workers had put together picture books, especially about nature, and folders of handmade pictures to illustrate stories that would be told to the children in the *círculos.* Many used pictures from magazines, carefully cut out and pasted. (I was told *Bohemia* magazine also helped in the production of these.) These picture books, along with cardboard, hand drawn puzzles, were prepared to coincide with the weekly programs planned for the childcare centers by the Children's Institute.

Seeing that even books had to be put together in this volunteer manner to assure that every childcare center throughout the island would receive the same supplies, reminded me even more strongly that toys and games, like art, music, and literature, are an integral part of the culture of Cuban children. From the classroom to the school vegetable garden, the city to the countryside, in all the arts, the children of Cuba are the *recipients* of a strong and vital historical tradition and revolutionary heritage as well as being the *creators* of a new socialist culture. They are the builders of a new life:

> When the sun comes up
> to construct life
> go I
> because I am the people
> worker
> when the sun comes up
> the sun the sun
> The sun comes up.

14

Working Their Way Through School

In school one must learn how to deal with the forces with which one must struggle in life. We should say workshops, not schools. In the afternoons, the pen, but in the mornings, the hoe.

— José Martí

Two mottoes have inspired Cuban education since the beginning of the Revolution. One is "Every worker a student, every student a teacher." The other is "Study, Work and Gun." Both of these are rooted in the concrete experience the Cuban people have had in trying to build — and defend — their Revolution in the midst of underdevelopment, blockade and armed attack. They are also a reflection of the kind of society Cuba hopes to build, and what Cuba will have to do to build it.

The socialist idea of work is different from the one we have in a capitalist society, where work is seen only as the necessary means to stay alive and feed your family. The socialist ideal considers work as the expression of a person's creative energies. Until this ideal can be reached — in a society without scarcity — work is also regarded as the people's *collective* effort to develop their economy and improve their lives. Cuba tries to create in its young people, as we have seen, this socialist attitude toward work. The Cubans do this not just through words and example, but through the actual combination of work and study in the schools.

Karl Marx described the purpose of combining work and education in a socialist society:

> Education will, in the case of every child, combine productive labor with instruction and gymnastics, not only as one of the methods of adding to the efficiency of production, but as *the only method of producing fully developed human beings.* [emphasis added]

In Cuba, Fidel Castro put it this way:

> In a collective society where material goods must be produced by all members of society, it is logical that work, training for work, the concept of work become an essential part of the education of the whole person. We must start creating the conditions for all human beings to envision work as the fulfillment of their aptitudes, their intelligence, their vocation, and their personality. And without any doubt, the more we do this, the more quickly we can change the idea people have of work.

The idea of relating work to study sounds at first like something we have heard before — something we still hear. As Americans we were taught the "Protestant Ethic" in grade school: "Work hard, study hard, and you'll get ahead." As we were growing up we were bombarded with the plea to "stay in school" so that we could get good jobs when we grew up. The American dream says if you study hard, get good grades, go to college and graduate school, you will have the whole world before you.

Along with this idea of higher education as a means toward status and wealth goes a negative attitude toward manual and blue collar work and working people. Education and work in a capitalist society are based on the social and economic class, race and sex of the participants and the needs of the capitalist economy. Those who are able — through wealth, family position, skill, education, etc. — to avoid engaging in actual manual labor, are looked up to and respected. Those who are forced to earn a living by their own sweat are looked down on, pitied — or ignored.

If this is the relation between "work" and "study" in a capitalist society — our society — then it is quite different from what is meant by "work" and "study" in a socialist society like Cuba. Socialist society changes the meaning of "work and study" because it first of all does away with separate classes of owners and workers.

In Cuba, everyone works, and no one is allowed to live off the work of other people without contributing in some way.

Since Cuba is not trying to reproduce a social system with separate classes, its school system is designed to make every person a student, a worker, a complete and creative human being. There is no "tracking" by race, sex or social class. All children learn to relate to work as a normal part of their daily life.

PARENTS, *PADRINOS* AND PLANTS

As we have seen throughout this book, attitudes toward work are created in the children very early. All Cuban children are the children of working parents, and most of them learn to respect work and working people at home. This respect is reinforced in the childcare centers, by teaching and by example. One of the most direct examples is in the *padrino* system, by which a factory, farm or office sponsors every childcare center. This gives very young children direct contact with workers and work centers which they might not otherwise have (although in fact many children do visit their parents' work centers, especially on Saturdays). Because the *padrinos* build and make and repair things for the *círculos,* children learn to see workers as friends and helpers. This bond of friendship is reinforced by the *padrinos'* participation in all major activities, holidays and events at the *círculos,* from the collective birthday parties to the annual May Day parades.

Most of the childcare centers I visited had little play areas designed to represent some interesting kind of work. These include service as well as agricultural or industrial jobs. In addition, working in their own little garden plots gives the children a chance to learn pride in their work, and the satisfaction of eating what they produce. This is done on a very small scale, but the five-year-olds I saw working in their *círculo* garden took just as much pride in their achievement as do older students who care for hundreds of acres.

Doing handicrafts at primary school in Alamar. Their products will later be sold.

STUDENTS ARE WORKERS

The attitudes children learn as toddlers are reinforced in the schools in a variety of ways. As pointed out earlier, the stories and even the arithmetic examples in their books reflect the values of a working-class society. Primary and secondary schools have work centers as *padrinos,* performing the same functions as they do in the *círculos.* Even more important, many children actually *work.* And this work is not divorced from what they study in the classroom; on the contrary, it is all part of an integral whole which is preparing them for life in their society. The examples given in school books help build respect for the work that others do. The actual participation in work takes the students on to the next step to becoming workers themselves.

This step is important because without it the Revolution, which provides free education for everyone, might fall into the trap of simply producing a larger stratum of purely professional and intellectual workers. Cuba still has a great need for manual labor and, as long as this lasts, the Revolution is determined to break down and eliminate the old barriers that separated manual and intellectual work. Long before they enter the labor force full-time, students are encouraged to incorporate physical work into their programs of study.

THE SCHOOLS GO TO THE COUNTRYSIDE

The Revolution experimented with a number of ways to put this theory into practice. At first some urban schools had small garden plots, and some junior high schools introduced a half-day of productive work into the school program. Then in 1965 the first major step was taken with the inauguration of the "School Goes to the Countryside" program.   Junior high school students and their teachers in urban areas went to spend six weeks in the countryside, dividing their day between agricultural work and academic study. Every urban secondary school student was expected to spend six weeks in this program each year (barring any physical handicaps).

At the same time an experiment was initiated on the Isle of Pines — renamed the Isle of Youth — in which teenagers would volunteer to spend from six months to two years helping with the agricultural development of the island. Prior to the Revolution the Isle of Pines was sparsely inhabited. It contained a Mafia-run gambling resort and the infamous prison where Fidel Castro was sent after the Moncada. But little, if any, attempt was made to farm the land or make it productive.

The Revolution of course could not afford this kind of waste. The inhospitable land had to be made productive. Cattle raising and citrus growing were decided on — but it would take a corps of really communist-minded workers to undertake this massive conversion. Cuba's youth — brought up in the ways of the Revolution — were the first to volunteer.

This was regarded as the first real experiment — although more symbolic of future goals than of current reality — in putting communism and a moneyless society into practice. Fidel commented on this in 1967:

> We observed an extraordinary phenomenon. Those young people didn't go there to work for money. They went with a deep awareness that their efforts were needed for the economic development of their country. They went there with the awareness that it was necessary for them to participate in that effort, not only as an economic need but also as an educational need.

The old prison was converted into a school. Many of the students who went for six months or a year volunteered to extend their stay. Some got married, and began raising their families on the Isle. Others moved in, and several new communities were built. The tiny island that had been a prison and a gambling resort was reclaimed by the Revolution. As with other areas of Cuba, the School went to the Countryside and made it prosper.

AND THE COUNTRYSIDE GOES TO SCHOOL

During all this time rural junior high schools were being built in the countryside for the peasant youth who had known no schooling before. The rural schools combined a general educational curriculum with vocational courses specifically related to agriculture and animal husbandry. The students — mostly from farming communities — work in fields adjacent to the schools, learn to care for the animals and repair and use the farm equipment provided by the government. By the mid-sixties there were over four thousand students (out of one hundred sixty thousand junior high school students) at these rural agricultural schools.

In the late sixties it was decided to expand the experiment which until that point included the School Goes to the Countryside Program and the Isle of Youth. A new type of School in the Countryside was inaugurated, different from the rural junior highs in that children from urban areas were encouraged to attend them. The students chosen for these new schools (called ESBECs: *Escuela Secundaria Básica en el Campo*) are considered *becados* — scholarship students. Students live in the schools all week in modern, brightly colored dormitories. Their meals, clothes, medical care and entertainment are provided by the school. The first such school, completed around the time of the 1970 U.S. invasion of Cambodia, was named "The Martyrs of Kent," after the four students who were killed by National Guardsmen at an antiwar protest at Kent State, Ohio.

ESBEC students have three hours of work each day in the fields, plus five hours of classroom activities, plus sports and cultural activities. Their work provides food for the students and teachers, and often enough to contribute to the supply of local hospitals or other communal centers.

Polytechnic schools in the countryside are also already under construction in sugar mill communities in Oriente Province. Plans call for these to be built near mills and factories all over the country. High schools and pre-university schools will be built near work centers, enabling all students to have some direct link to a factory, mill or farm.

The schools are coeducational, with boys and girls living in separate dormitories, each containing communal showers. They generally share one large co-ed dining hall. Farmwork is usually divided according to sex, with the heavier work going to the boys. But the girls are nevertheless engaged in work formerly reserved for men, such as planting trees and driving tractors.

By the mid-seventies the Revolution was building 150 ESBECs a year. The goal is eventually to have all junior high school students studying and working in the countryside or, if that is not feasible, in connection with some factory or work center.

Polytechnic schools in the countryside are also already under construction in sugar mill communities in Oriente Province. Plans call for these to be built near mills and factories all over the country. High schools and pre-university schools will be built near work centers, enabling all students to have some direct link to a factory, mill or farm.

WORK IS CHILD'S PLAY

In 1959, a few months after the triumph of the Cuban Revolution, rebel leader Camilo Cienfuegos visited the village of Meneses in a rural zone of Las Villas province. Camilo had led a bitter struggle in the region against the army of the Batista dictatorship. In the village of Yaguajay, only five miles from Meneses, his guerrillas had scored a major victory over Batista's troops.

So when Camilo entered the tiny village the people gathered around to welcome the "hero of Yaguajay." Camilo was much loved by the Cuban peasants for his personal warmth as well as his fighting prowess. The villagers wanted to greet and thank him for freeing them from the oppression they had suffered under Batista. But they also wanted to make known some complaints. One crudely written sign indicated that they were in need of a school.

Looking around him, Camilo observed that this would be a wonderful area in which to build a school. He asked the villagers to try to repair the local school house for the time being, but promised that the Revolution would build them a new and better school.

Camilo Cienfuegos died in September of that year when the light plane he was flying was swept out to sea in a storm. But twelve years later the Revolution kept the promise Camilo had made. The Hero of Yaguajay school that was constructed in Meneses provided modern new classrooms, spacious grounds, a library, sports centers, a laboratory, housing for the teachers and a kitchen and dining room to provide meals for students and staff. It was to be a model school of the future; as Fidel pointed out: "The school that Camilo promised would have to be one like this!"

But the Hero of Yaguajay didn't get its characterization as a model school because of its modern educational plant. There was something else special about this school. It was to be the first primary school to combine classwork with agricultural work on a regular basis, the first primary work-study school.

The school began with fourth through sixth grade students spending two hours a day sowing maize, cucumbers, onions, tomatoes and other vegetables. Soon the school was providing all the vegetables needed to feed the students and staff of the school. Within a year their surplus was being used to supply the workers' cafeteria in Meneses and part was being sold in the local market. The students took such pride in their accomplishment that visitors and journalists who went to the school all commented on the children's high morale and discipline.

Although some educators had questioned whether the youngsters would be able to keep up with their school work if they were devoting so much time to field work, the children's discipline in the fields carried over to the classroom. Attendance, grades and promotion were found to be above the national average at the end of the first year.

But just as this question was being resolved, another one came up. The kindergarten, first, second and third graders of the school began demanding that they, too, be allowed to go out and do field work! Somewhat taken aback, the teachers at first didn't know what to tell them. After consulting with leaders of the Ministry of Education, the teachers received authorization to let the little ones spend an hour a week in the fields. They did their work so enthusiastically and responsibly that, within a short time, they were allowed to increase to two and eventually six hours a week (for the first through third grades — kindergarten was kept to two hours).

The work on the vegetable plots is organized by a non-teaching staff consisting of a director, an agricultural technician and five workers who do the heaviest and most difficult jobs. They are supplemented by a student administration run by a student administrator, deputy administrator, and personnel chief.

The students are mainly the children of *campesinos* and rural workers, and have learned to respect work from their parents. The parents also participate in the work of the school, organizing volunteer work teams to help in the fields, especially when the children are on vacation.

Within a year after the Hero of Yaguajay school opened, another rural work-study school was inaugurated in the middle of the Niña Bonita dairy cattle center, and then a third in a new village for workers of another cattle center near Jibacoa in Havana province. The children of these two schools — Lazo de la Vega and Rolando Valdivia — also do field work two to ten hours a week, depending on their age. And like the school in Meneses, these schools have distinguished themselves for high scholastic work among their student workers.

LAZO DE LA VEGA

It took us a couple of hours to reach Lazo de la Vega from Havana, driving in one of the Friendship Institute's Cadillacs (which made me feel quite uncomfortable as we drove past the stares of villagers in dusty rural towns). By the time we got to the school many of the students were already out in the fields, so we stopped in to talk to the administrators first. From them I learned that half of Lazo de la Vega's students are *internados* who live in the school; the rest are *semi-internados* who eat in school but go home at night. Seventy percent of the children are those whose parents work in the Niña Bonita center.

In addition to the regular student body, the sixth grade classes are augmented by students who have attended rural primary schools through the first five grades, and then finish up their primary school career at Lazo de la Vega. Although the rural schools have certain periods when the children do field work, the work is not integrated into their education on a daily basis the way it is in the new work-study schools, and the level of teaching is apparently superior in the new schools.

All students study music and practice sports (including swimming in a new Olympic-size swimming pool) in addition to their regular classes and field work.

In this school, too, the youngest children had asked their teachers that they be allowed to work. The vice-principal of the school told me that they had set up certain norms based on the amount of work they expected the children to be able to complete in a given time, based on age — and that they had constantly had to raise these norms because the children were surpassing them.

I asked how they knew when the children were ready and able to do more work. She told me that this was determined by the children themselves through their work. When the teacher observed that the children who had been given two rows to weed were finishing early and beginning on a third and even a fourth row, it was time to raise the quota. Children also take part in production assemblies every two weeks (just like adult workers). They analyze all aspects of their work, discuss how they could improve it, what problems they've had. If they feel they've been working ahead of their quota, they can suggest at these assemblies that the quota be raised.

Discussions at the production assemblies are based in large part on the analysis sessions which follow each day's work in the fields. "Each day they evaluate their work, before leaving the fields," the vice-principle told me. "They decide if their work was good or if there were difficulties or deficiencies. Maybe two or three students didn't cooperate well in the work that day. The other students will point this out, discuss it, and suggest certain measures if necessary."

The emphasis is on quality not quantity of work. "They must look for the best tomatoes, the ones ready to be picked. If they pick ones that aren't ready, or overripe, then the fruit just goes to waste." The children are very aware of this responsibility, she said, and take their work quite seriously.

The administration was very proud of the health and scholastic record of the students. Since half of the students live in the school it is equipped with its own clinic and infirmary. But she said that, aside from one child with asthma and another with a "physical defect," no children had had to stay out of school or out of the fields

Field work is part of a normal school day.

due to illness. And scholastic records were equally impressive: 87 to 94 percent of each grade was promoted in 1973. "And all this tells us that the students have no problem with the relation of work with study."

Cuba, like many other countries of the world, had known the scourge of child labor at its worst before the Revolution. I wondered how Cuban parents had taken to the idea of their children working. But rather than encountering resistance in this sphere, I was told, the administration found that the parents of this region welcomed the opportunity to have their children combine work with their studies. This applied to the parents of little girls as well as the parents of boys. The vice-principle explained that at the beginning the parents are given a general vision of what their children will do in school, the education they will receive, and their problems. A relation is established between the parents and the school. Working parents apparently have no qualms about their children working, as long as they know that the health and educational needs of the children are being met, and the interests of the children are looked out for.

INSIDE, OUTSIDE; BOOKS AND HOES

One of the more interesting aspects of the school was to see how classwork and field work were connected. Was it just that the children did both, I wondered, or was there an effort to draw some direct link? The administrator I spoke with told me that in classes where applicable, the students are taught how their subject matter relates to the work they are doing. In science classes, for example, it is easy to talk about how plants need water for survival, the role of fertilizers, the necessity of weeding, and similar topics. At the beginning of each work session the teacher dedicates ten or fifteen minutes to talking about the work the children will do that day.

There was still time to catch the kids in the fields before they came in from the morning session, so (overcoming my embarrassment) we hopped back in the Cadillac and drove out to the fields. The fifth graders were moving up and down the rows, carrying large burlap sacks which they were filling with huge root vegetables that looked like turnips. I moved up and down the rows of deep red soil, taking pictures and occasionally stopping to talk with the youngsters. All too soon they had finished the morning's work. I followed them back to a clump of trees, where they sat down on the ground with their teacher and a white-haired *campesino* who directed their field work, and began to analyze their morning's work.

I listened to the discussion go on for a while and then, when it seemed they had finished, I began asking some questions. I asked them to tell me something about their school. They replied that the school was a commitment on the part of the Revolution "and our Comandante Fidel" to provide education for the youth of tomorrow, and a commitment on the part of the youth to educate themselves to work for the future development of the country.

Although knowing the answer, I asked them whether they worked to get money, or to enrich the wealthy people of Cuba. They didn't understand my question. Finally, after I repeated it in several ways, one boy answered: "We don't work for the rich, because there are no rich people in Cuba. We work for ourselves and for other schools as well."

"But isn't work a form of oppression?" I persisted.

"For us, in this school, work is an honor," the same boy replied.

"And apart from that, it's also a necessity, because our country is underdeveloped, and if we work we can help our country become developed."

A dark-haired girl in a bright orange scarf added: "When I'm working I feel really good, and proud that I'm working for our country, for our school."

A black girl standing next to her said: "Other schools receive what we produce in our *huerto*; primary schools and workers' dining rooms do, too." She stated this as though it were conclusive proof that work could not be seen as a form of oppression.

Still playing the devil's advocate, I asked: "Why do they receive the food that you grow? Don't they work?"

"Yes, they work," the girl in the orange scarf said. "But they don't have a *huerto* like we do. And we want them to have the fruit from our *huerto*."

I asked about the work discipline in the fields. Jesús, a chubby blond boy, answered:

> Discipline isn't a form of punishment for us. The discipline for field work is to come to the *huerto* without a lot of disorganization, to work and to fulfill the quota that we have set for ourselves.
>
> Discipline isn't imposed on us; it's explained to us why we should maintain a good discipline, it's explained how this carries our school forward, how this is very fruitful for our school.

At first I thought he had said the last line as a pun (the pun comes out the same in Spanish as in English), but when I realized he had done so unintentionally, I followed up: "What else does work mean to you, to your country?"

> For us work means something very useful, that shapes us as human beings. Our *Comandante en Jefe* once said that work forms the child, and that the child in turn is capable of bringing that education to his home. Children are being shaped through work from the time they're very little. And then those children, when they are adults, already know how to work, know what work is, and are useful people.

Although I didn't ask, Jesús went on to add:

> Before the Revolution in our country women didn't carry out the productive work they do today. Now the woman carries forward many tasks; there's an organization that brings together all the women and that has carried out a lot of tasks for our Revolution. This didn't exist before. Now the woman is just as important as the male worker in carrying our Revolution forward.

Wanting to test a little further their commitment to work, I half-teased: "Which would you rather hear your parents say on a Sunday: 'Let's go to do productive work,' or 'let's go to the beach?'"

A dark-skinned girl answered: "I'd feel better going to do productive work, because that way I'd be helping the Revolution and the country get out from underdevelopment." Then she added with a quick smile, "After I did the voluntary work, sure, I'd like to go to the beach."

Since this was one of the few primary schools that integrates work with study, I wondered how well the two were balanced, and if the children were learning to respect and enjoy each equally. In response to my questions several students told me how things they learned in the classroom were related to the work they do in the fields. They also, in the course of the discussion, indicated that there were separate bi-weekly assemblies for production (field work) and promotion (class work). Since I knew from conversations with students in other schools that children are periodically chosen as "vanguard" in these assemblies, I asked if some children could be chosen vanguard for their work in the *huerto*, and others for their work in the classroom. When they told me yes, I asked: "Who do you respect more, the student who is chosen vanguard in the classroom, or the one who is vanguard in the *huerto*?"

"It's the same. We respect equally the one who is vanguard in class and the one who is vanguard in the field."

"Which would *you* rather be, vanguard in class or in the *huerto*?"

"I'd rather be vanguard in both."

WORKERS IN A WORK-STUDY SCHOOL

In previous conversations with the administration I had gotten the notion that there was a particularly close relation between the students and teachers of this school and the non-teaching workers. The vice-principal had told me that all school workers, even those in the service department, are closely linked to the educational process. Each work department within the school "sponsors" or "adopts" a classroom, just as outside work centers act as *padrinos*. "These workers are familiar with every situation in the classrooms," she told me. "They know their problems, they help organize recreational activities . . . ."

Jesús, the Pioneer Chief of the school, in describing the many activities carried out in the school, had talked about all the things the workers were building for them — a huge sports area and an Olympic-size pool. I had asked him then what relation the students had with these workers, and he told me:

> The workers here are in charge of keeping things clean, the work of the *huerto*, and the construction of our sports field.
>
> We have a lot of relations with these workers. For example, now we are helping in the construction of the sports field. In addition, there are worker guides who substitute for the teachers at times, to take us on excursions, or for the work-orientation in the fields, etc.
>
> They also help mold the habits of our pupils. For example, they help the *compañeritos* in our evening study periods. And in the case of *compañeritos* who are already in sixth grade and have a higher educational level than the workers, then the student helps the workers. The workers attend Peasant-Worker Advancement Classes to raise their educational level.

When I was talking to the fifth graders who had just finished their field work, several of the older workers had been standing behind the circle of students, listening attentively. I wanted to draw them into the conversation, but wasn't quite sure how to go about it. Finally I hit on the idea of having the kids interview them. Passing my tape recorder to one of the students, I asked if they would help me get a clearer idea of the relation between the older worker and the students.

The girl I gave the recorder to held the microphone a little awkwardly at first, but spoke clearly into it, looking at the white-haired *campesino:*

"I'd like to know what opinion you have of the work the kids do in this *huerto*."

Taking the microphone in his wrinkled and calloused brown hands, the old farmer replied:

"It's incredible with what enthusiasm, with what faith, with what warmth the children here do agricultural work, especially since this kind of work is a little difficult — and yet they do it well. You can see, without a lot of explanation, what they have produced, and everything being produced here is done solely by the work of the children. There are just a few of us workers and we only do the heaviest work. We think that this is the most beautiful, the richest work that any revolutionary could have, working with the children who will be the men and women of the future. And when we work with these children, we see the new generation that Che spoke of."

One of the children asked the old worker how they had decided to work with the students, and he answered slowly:

"We wanted to teach you everything that we know, and all the things that we are learning day by day. And day by day we do this with more enthusiasm, and more affection toward you. And when we think about you, we think about all the children of Latin America and all the children of the world."

The girl in the orange scarf asked the worker if he believed the work-study plan would aid in the students' development.

"I'm convinced of it, that this work-study will fulfill its objective. Before when this didn't exist, we saw children who neither studied nor worked, and then they became delinquents. We see how all of your time is occupied in study and work and self-improvement. Each day you are more and better prepared for the future, in agriculture, in industry, or in whatever you do."

When I asked whether the children respected the workers, and if in turn the workers respected the children, one child answered:

"They respect us, for our work and for the way we treat them.

"In this society we respect people who work. The ones we look down on or dislike are the ones who live well without doing any work. Those are the ones who don't get our respect."

Although the answer seemed obvious from everything they had said so far, I asked one more question before we headed back to the school:

"If you could choose between studying here, or in a school in downtown Havana, which would you prefer?"

Jesús appeared to be voicing the sentiments of all the students when he declared:

"I'd rather stay here. For a lot of reasons. This school has a *huerto escolar,* it links work and study, there's a lot of enthusiasm. They don't have the formation there that we have here. Even if it were a very modern school in the center of Havana, I'd rather stay here."

Apparently there were many others who shared this feeling, for when we arrived back at the school there were several school buses pulling up in front of the main building: children from Havana coming to spend a day working in the fields.

BABIES IN THE FIELDS: "MY PAPA TAUGHT ME"

I went back to Lazo de la Vega on Wednesday afternoon, when the preschool (kindergarten) children go out to do their two-hour shift in the field. I'm not sure what I had imagined the scene would be like. I think I probably expected the giggling, squirming excitement of children out for an afternoon's lark in the countryside. I don't think I expected their serious dedication to their work, which they seemed to understand perfectly and which they treated as responsibly as a mature adult.

Their teacher was involved with some other activity, so the five-year-olds were being escorted to the fields that day by two fifth-grade monitors. The children were all dressed in work pants and old shirts, with straw hats to protect them from the hot Cuban sun. As we walked down the dirt road to the papaya field, I spoke with the two monitors. They told me that it would be their responsibility, once they arrived at the field, to explain the day's work to the children and see that it was carried out correctly. They expressed complete confidence that the youngsters would do their work well. "They like to pull weeds and water the little plants," the two older girls told me.

"But they're so little," I protested. "Where did they learn to work? Who taught them to have such a positive attitude toward their work?"

"I think it's because they've always seen their parents working," one of the monitors replied, "and now they can do it, and they feel happy about it."

The other one added: "Besides being fun, the work has already taught the *compañeritos* work habits; they're already used to working."

I spent the afternoon taking pictures, and before I knew it the two hours were up. The children formed a line at the edge of the field, talked about their work for a little while, then began the trek back to the school. There they would bathe, change clothes, and return to the classroom.

When we arrived at the school I went into one of the dorms with the youngsters and began talking to them. As our conversation continued, I saw that the older children were right about where the children had learned their attitudes toward work. Since field workers, teachers and older students were showing these youngsters how to weed, water and pick the plants, I expected them to name one of these groups when I asked:

"Where did you learn to work like that?"

But the first response I got was: "At home. My papa taught me." That led to the next series of questions.

"What does your papa do?"

"He works in the sugar mill. I've gone to the mill."

"What's a mill?"

"A place where cane grows."

I ignored his wrong answer, and went on:

"Would you like to work in a mill?"

"No, with horses."

"With horses?"

"Yeah. I want to be a cowboy. To take the cows to the pen, to put them in order, so they eat."

The conversation took several interesting turns, revealing other aspects about the children's lives, and that of their parents. Some of the best comments in this regard emerged from talking with a group of preschool girls. I was especially interested in the example that working mothers provide for their daughters. What I had overlooked was the fact that women who work outside the home are also more likely to be involved in other activities of the Revolution: in the

Women's Federation, the CDR, the militia, their trade union, and perhaps in the Party. Although I didn't ask about any of these things, their comments showed that this, too, was part of the children's reality.

"Angela, when you grow up do you want to be a housewife or a worker?" I queried.

"A worker."

"Does your mother work?"

"Yes."

"Where?"

"In the meeting."

I smiled and asked another girl:

"What have your parents told you about work?"

"To work hard and be a good girl."

"Haven't they told you why they work?"

"For the emulation."

"What's an emulation?"

"To behave yourself. To go to the meeting."

"And what do they do in the meeting?"

"Talk."

What emerged from our conversation was that most of these children's ideas about work had been formed at home, from their parents, and that most of their parents not only worked, but attended many meetings. Not everyone's mother was happy about the idea of working outside the home. This was in 1973, before the passage of the Family Code required men to share in the housework if their wives worked outside the home, so most working women were still on the "double shift." When I asked one little girl if her mama liked to work, she answered frankly:

"She doesn't want to work."

"Why not?"

"'Cause she has to wash a lot of clothes, and clean the house and everything."

When I left the little girls' dormitory I ran into the two monitors who had accompanied them to the fields. They had washed up and changed back into school clothes. I told them I thought they were right about the little children learning about work from their parents, and asked them what influence their own parents had had in forming their attitudes.

My parents are happy that I work well, because they know I've learned how in this school. They ask me if I like the work in this school and I tell them yes. They tell me that everyone in this country has worked a lot so that we could have all this.

As if to illustrate her point, she turned to a younger child passing by and asked:

"Have your parents explained to you why work is useful to you?"

"They tell me that they worked hard before the Revolution, and that they never want me to have to work the way they did then."

I asked what the difference was between the work that they do now in Cuba, and what the children had to do before, or have to do in other, capitalist, countries now.

"The difference is that the work that we do here isn't based on discrimination, nor on maltreatment. We do it as a duty and an honor. And in other countries children have to work from the time they're little, and they don't work with the same enthusiasm we have, because they don't have the same things we do. For example, they go about filthy, and poorly dressed. They work out of extreme necessity."

Since they felt that work was bad and oppressive to children under certain conditions, I asked under what conditions they considered work to be good.

"When children see that they're being mistreated, they don't like to work. But if they could have a revolution the same as ours, they'd be just as happy to work as we are. We start working here when we're five years old, but no one forces us to. We do it for the Revolution.

"And when we finish with our work, we sit down at the table and eat what we produced ourselves!"

CHILDREN IN THE SHOP

After these first very successful experiments, school gardens at the primary school level began to multiply, although few had such large acreage to care for as Lazo de la Vega. But, although Cuba is still heavily agricultural, it is unrealistic to think of combining all schools with agricultural work on a full-time basis. As Cuba industrializes and diversifies its economy, it must find non-agricultural work that students can link with their studies.

Education in Cuba is heavily oriented toward getting the Cuban economy out of the Dark Ages and into the modern, technological period. Many of the junior and senior high schools (*secondaria basica* and *preuniversitario*) are technical and vocational schools, training youths in the skills and methods of industrial work, agricultural technology, maritime skills, and advanced science.

The most outstanding of these schools is the Lenin Vocational School for top science students. This school grew out of a National Monitors Meeting in 1966, attended by Fidel. Cuba's prime minister suggested to the youngsters present that the country needed to create "a new kind of school," one that would serve as a model for the future schools of Socialist Cuba. The school — which is being duplicated in three other provinces besides Havana — has as its objective to develop a full range of vocational training oriented especially to the fields of science and technology most needed by the country. The school also encourages interest in and development of skills for research in scientific and technical fields, experiments with new teaching methods and provides new teachers for the coming generations of Cubans. To assure an integral education of these youngsters there is also emphasis on all aspects of learning, cultural development, a variety of sports activities — and a heavy schedule of productive work.

The modern, airy, multi-colored buildings of the Lenin School sit amidst sixty-six acres of green lawns and fields about fifteen miles southwest of the city of Havana. Classrooms, dormitories, labs, work rooms, staff living quarters, dining halls, as well as indoor and outdoor theatres, gardens, Olympic-size swimming pools, baseball diamonds, soccer fields, tennis and basketball courts and indoor gymnasiums, plus the fifty-bed infirmary and clinic, were built with some participation by the students themselves.

When the school was completed (classes were going on even while it was being built), the students turned their fifteen-hours-a-week work shift to other tasks: work in the citrus and vegetable fields, producing sporting equipment (uniforms, balls and baseball gloves), putting together radio and TV components and assembling complex computer components. Although the school is interested in having the students learn about these fields through their work there is nothing academic about it: everything produced must be of a quality to be used, eaten, sold or exchanged in the school and in the foreign and national markets.

The students are recruited primarily from the science and technology "interest circles" conducted in each primary school. Only top students, academically and politically, are chosen. In a meeting with two of the vice-principals of the school in 1973, they told me quite frankly:

> Our education is a class education; we're not educating our students apolitically. The education we give them corresponds to the needs and interests of our society; they're not being educated in isolation from these problems. Our students must understand their role in this society.

Basically, the school is looking for boys and girls who have already begun their formation as communists. The leaders of the school see this as no problem, however, since the children being recruited today have grown up entirely under the new system of education in Cuba. And, according to the educators, they are already conscious that the whole society — from their parents, daycare workers and teachers, to fellow students, and the workers who provide their food and clothes — have all contributed in some way to helping them acquire the knowledge, work and study habits to get to this school.

This is especially important because Lenin School is in many ways a reward (if only moral and psychological) for a good scholastic record, and it could easily fall into the trap of producing a new elite. Teachers and students alike felt that the students' consciousness of the collective effort to get them there — coupled with their heavy work and study responsibilities — keeps them from thinking of themselves as elites.

The Lenin School consists of about half boys and half girls. This was not true in the first few years, when nearly twice as many male students applied and attended. But in the next few years there were consistently more girls than boys recruited and accepted, until the percentage evened off. Coming as I did from a background where girls were assumed to be less interested and able in the fields of math and science, I thought it not at all surprising that there should be more boys than girls in a science-oriented vocational school. Certainly that would be true in the U.S., I thought. But when I spoke to the tenth-grade girls at Lenin about this, they seemed surprised. No, they told me, no one had ever suggested to them that girls don't do well in these subjects.

The Lenin School is new not only in its emphasis on teaching advanced science and technology aimed at speeding up Cuba's economic development; its teaching methods are new as well. Students receive no grades; rather, they are evaluated all of the time, in class, at work, in their living and eating units. This analysis is discussed at periodic general assemblies which include teachers, administrators, students, and parents. Although there are no grades and no exams, students do participate in emulations just as other students in Cuba. These may be individual or collective, but the students have a tendency to opt for collective ones.

The other way in which this school is startlingly different from others is that, from ninth grade on, the students stop attending formal classes as such, and instead do most of their studying through the various interest circles. The younger children are introduced gradually to the interest circles, which are designed to help develop the students' interest and understanding in various fields of science and technology (although there are some circles in the field of humanities). They are taken in small groups each week to visit a work or research center related to their interest, talking with the engineers, biochemists, and technicians. Students participate in their chosen interest circle for a year; if they remain interested, they continue. If not they may switch. Later they are taken to spend four weeks actually participating in the work of their interest circle. They meet with the workers, have talks, work sessions and engage in sports and cultural activities with them.

When the older students have chosen their fields of interest they meet in these circles for three-to-four-hour weekly theoretical and practical work sessions. Their activities are supervised by people from research institutes, factories, agricultural centers, and industries. In addition to the interest circles there are "area intensification groups" in six specialties — ranging from physics to ecology — whose purpose is to enable the students to delve more deeply into classroom work.

ACQUIRING NEW HABITS AND BRINGING THEM HOME

Although all the students at the Lenin School live in school all week, the directors of the school try to maintain a strong link with the parents, who are asked to participate in the periodic general assemblies. The weekend pass is never taken away from a student as punishment for an infraction, I was told. And it was clear, from talking with administrators, students and some parents, that the students are bringing many of the work and study habits learned at school to their homes. One teacher told me:

> Parents generally say that their children are more respectful, more responsible at home now that they are going to this school. They're more aware of the work their parents do, and what it means, so they help more at home.

One mother told me:

> Gregory's group was on the cleanup detail the whole first year. That means they were responsible for the daily sweeping and mopping of an entire building. This was his group's work shift — the same as working in the fields, or in one of the factories of electronics equipment or sporting goods.
>
> In keeping the school clean all the time they got a good understanding of what this kind of work involves and what it means to have to keep an entire building clean and hygienic. Anyway, by now after a whole year Gregory and his group know the ins and outs of cleaning a large building. And I often see the results of this knowledge at home on weekends, when he does his share of the housework.

THOSE WHO CAN, TEACH

One of the stories that most interested me at the school was how two-thirds of the tenth grade volunteered to train to become teachers in their fields, although none of them had come to this school with the idea of becoming teachers. These were the students who were selected to become the country's top scientists, researchers and technicians. What made them volunteer for teacher-training instead?

I remembered when I was in high school, and thinking of teaching as a career, I was taught an "old adage." It went: "those who can, do; those who can't, teach." Rather than a profession that was looked up to and admired, teaching was considered a career for those people not at the top of their fields. That is clearly reflected in the pay scale in the U.S., too. A doctor, engineer or architect can easily triple or quadruple the yearly salary of a teacher.

But in Cuba, the professions or jobs with the most prestige are those that are most needed by the Revolution. The students who came to the Lenin School — the most "prestigous" school in the country — were the top students in their fields. But also the most dedicated to the Revolution. So when they were told that the Revolution badly needed more teachers in their field, they massively signed up to become teachers.

ARE THERE ELITE WORKERS?

The Lenin School is impressive — in fact overwhelming — in many ways. But despite this, the same nagging question kept coming up: Is this school producing a new elite in Cuba, a stratum of workers who, through their superior education and abilities, would form a new kind of hierarchy? If not, what was keeping these children from developing the attitudes and habits of a privileged sector, since certainly they knew that they had been chosen as the outstanding students in their schools and in the country?

The administrators of the school tried to provide some of the answers. They pointed to the high degree of political consciousness of the students (including the already-mentioned understanding that they had arrived at the Lenin School through the collective efforts of many, many others). They talked of the concept that those who do best — like monitors in a classroom — and have the highest ability have the responsibility to help the others, not lord it over them, so everyone can benefit from this knowledge or ability.

"And these concepts are not taught to them as postulates," they told me. "The students learn them slowly through experience."

One teacher pointed out: "Once they get here, they're students like everyone else. Everyone at this school was a top student in primary school, so no one is a big shot. And everyone is expected to go out and do the same work. Sometimes that work means cleaning the toilets or pulling weeds for weeks and months on end. The same students who construct computer components also do that kind of work. So it's hard to get smug and think that you're better than anyone else."

The constant reminder of the agricultural and industrial needs of their country is also presented as a means of keeping the students oriented toward the idea that they are here not as a reward for past behavior (good study and work record) but as a way to prepare them to contribute more to the growing needs of Cuba.

In the end, of course, I realized that the only way to find out whether the Lenin School was creating a privileged class of elite students would have to come from the students themselves.

I met with a group of eleven monitors — three boys and eight girls. Since someone had suggested that perhaps children of Party leaders and professionals would predominate in the selection of students for the Lenin School, I asked them first to tell me something about their families. Five of them said their mothers worked outside the home, in jobs that ranged from teaching geography in a junior high school to the head of an electronic computation section in the Sports Institute. Their fathers' jobs included a maintenance worker in the food industry, a radio reporter, a national traffic director, a mechanic in a textile mill and a regional Party official.

Almost all of them expressed a desire to be doctors or scientists when they grew up, although several qualified this by saying they would be willing to work in another field if that was what was needed by the Revolution. Needless to say, none of the girls expressed a desire to be a "housewife," and all of the boys insisted the women they would marry would be *compañeras* who worked outside the home.

Here are some of their comments in response to my question about the "superiority" of students who attend the Lenin School.

> We don't think that we're better or superior to the students in other schools. We're here because we have certain qualifications that we think other *compañeros* — making a little more effort — can have too. We're here because we've met a certain standard, and by meeting that standard we show the others, not that we're better, but what they can do if they try.

> We didn't come to this school because we were born with a super-developed intelligence, but rather because we're students who have always liked to study and to push ourselves in our studies. We're also here because of our political conditions, our way of expressing ourselves, of inter-relating with others, and our trying to help those who have problems in their work. We're not here because we were born smarter, we're here because we tried harder.

> I think that our parents have helped in our development because they've known how to educate us, and to give us their experiences based on the shameful past they lived in. And they've taught us to be collective, and that socialism is a government that seeks the good of everyone.

The whole people help in the individual's development from the time you are very little; everyone in this society helps in that development, from the person who works in the food industry who sees that we get the food we need for proper nutrition, to the *compañeros* who work in the book institute whose work provides us with the books we use, to the construction workers who build our schools and the professors, and those who taught our professors.

That is, it's the Revolution in general that educates us. We didn't get the way we are in junior high school; it started when we were in the *círculos.*

Since I was unable to get from any of the monitors a sense of individual superiority, I turned my questions to the future. Wouldn't having this kind of education entitle them to special privileges, give them more power than other persons?

We don't think in terms of power, because what we have to do is help everyone, without being better than anyone. Some of us might become leaders, but being a leader isn't having more power, because here the ones who direct, the ones with the power, are the masses. We're not going to be rich, we're not going to live off the work of others; we're going to work to develop our country.

In our country there aren't going to be some people who are richer than others. If we develop ourselves in this school to be able to serve the needs of our country, what we're going to do is struggle so that the workers who are still working in the fields get the same material resources and the same living conditions as any other kind of worker.

Leaders here aren't ones who satisfy their own individual desires and their desire for wealth; they're the ones who put their abilities at the service of all the people.

Hoping to make me understand how different their school and their Revolution are from what I was used to, one of the monitors concluded:

Our school has a great sense of responsibility, not just in terms of helping develop the scientists and technicians for our economy, but a sense of responsibility toward the whole world. We have a lot of activities in solidarity with students of other countries. We try to always be aware of and feel the problems of people who are struggling everywhere. When we leave this school, we'll be workers; workers who have been trained to better enable us to help working people everywhere.

ALAMAR: WORKERS BUILD A CITY
AND CHILDREN SHARE THE WORK

Even if there were nothing special about the schools in Alamar, the experience of living and growing up in such a city would be a very powerful example of what life is like in a society run by working people. Alamar is a modern city that grew from nothing, created out of the will and desire of the working people who now live there. It lies on formerly barren land between the northern outskirts of Havana and the sea.

From rock and beach-grass grew multi-colored housing units; then a supermarket, a polyclinic, a pharmacy. Schools, childcare centers, laundry. Hairdresser and barbershop. Then factories, to provide work for the growing population of the city. Alamar — a city that is still growing — is being built by "microbrigades." Microbrigades are made up of groups of workers not from the construction industry, who take voluntary leave from their regular work centers in order to help meet the demand for more housing and other construction. In order to do so, the other workers at their regular work place must have agreed to take on the extra work that the absentees will leave, so production quotas do not fall.

The most interesting thing about Alamar is that just about everybody who is living in the city is involved in building it and running it. Men and women work on the construction crews. Others staff the stores, clinics, schools, *círculos*, and the new factories.

The second most interesting thing about Alamar is that the children of these workers are attending schools which also combine productive work with their daily life routine (which in the case of children, of course, consists of study, sports and play). These urban youngsters do not have fields that they can sow. So instead, they build, assemble and package toys and handicrafts. The schools of Alamar are the first city schools to combine work and study.

It was in the Tupac Amaru school in Alamar that I encountered my first "contradictions" with the system of work-study — and the best explanation given to me by any child about why they like to work.

URBAN GUERRILLAS

The Tupac Amaru school was named after a Peruvian hero, an Indian who had led the independence struggle against Spain in that country. He was the same hero that the Tupamaro urban guerrillas of Uruguay took their name from. The students of the Tupac Amaru school are quite consciously a new type of "urban guerrilla." They're struggling to build their future with their own hands.

I didn't spend much time wandering around the school: I had come to see the workshop that I had heard and read so much about. I found it in the center of the complex of new buildings and flowering gardens that serve as "school" for over five hundred of the young residents of Alamar. Large, light rooms, with tables instead of desks, and walls lined with the products of the children's work instead of blackboards. On the shelves were all types of toys, carefully assembled by the youngsters. Partitions divided the large room into different sections. Groups of fifteen or twenty students were engaged in various tasks.

In addition to assembling and packaging toys, some groups were packaging medicinal tea, and still others were making their own handicrafts. Within this latter group, a number of little girls were crocheting and embroidering small articles that would be sold to to tourists. Only girls. It was the second time I saw boys and girls given separate work not in any way related to their ability to perform the work.

The National Women's Congress that followed close on the heels of the discussion of the Family Code in 1974 recommended combining all home economics classes and shop classes in the schools. By now, hopefully, this has had its effect on the workshops of Alamar, so that students who are being prepared to be tomorrow's workers won't be learning that there is "girls' work" and "boys' work."

But aside from this one aberration, the student workshops of Alamar provide all of the education for a working class society that the primary schools in the countryside do. Children learn to take work seriously, to respect the products produced by their own and other people's labor, and to feel like useful citizens of their country.

And knowing how things are made, at what effort, they are all the more willing to share what they have. Over and over again chil-dren spoke excitedly of the possibility that some toy they had assem-bled might find its way into the hands of a Vietnamese child, "who had suffered the horrors of the Yankee bombardment."

The children were also aware that they were carrying out work formerly done by adult workers, and that those workers were now free to move into other fields, "to be doing other work that the people of our country need just as badly, or even more."

Work seemed to these children very much a family affair. "Our mothers and fathers are building this city," they told me. "Everyone has his or her job. And we do too. We're part of the work force of Alamar," they declared proudly.

I had heard over and over again, from children of every age, color and description, how important it made them feel, how useful to the Revolution, that they were now learning through their work to become productive citizens of tomorrow. But the children of Alamar gave one more reason why they were so happy to be carrying out this work. I stopped to ask one youngster, who was carefully counting out the correct number of red and black checkers before sealing them in a plastic bag, if he liked his work. Without pausing, he nodded his head affirmatively. "Why?" I asked him my much-repeated question. He looked up at me, very seriously, his hands never stopping their work. "Because to us Cuban children," he explained, "checkers are *very* important!"

". . . to us Cuban children checkers are *very* important."

WHAT DOES IT ALL MEAN?

The integration of work with classroom education is here to stay in Cuba. Everyone from the classroom teachers to the head of the Education Ministry is more than satisfied with the results so far.

By 1980, students combining work and study will cover the cost of education in the entire country through what they produce. This has tremendous significance for an undeveloped country that is commited to providing free education for everyone who wants it.

But the economic advantages of this system are by no means the most important factor. Combining work and study has many effects in terms of the development of the children. In the United States, children think food comes from the supermarket. In Cuba they know it comes from the ground, and that somebody planted it, weeded it, harvested it and transported it. They know this because they have taken part — even if in only a small way — in this entire process. Cuban children do not think that clothes, toys, books and household goods "come from the store" any more than they think that babies "come from the stork" or that their presents on Children's Day "comes from Santa Claus." They have seen how goods are produced, and have helped produce them.

This process also helps in building a sense of discipline among the students and a respect for the material things they have. The Cuban people have learned that they are the owners of their products and resources, and that it is now in their interest to protect and develop them. Children today are much less likely than before to drop out of school, miss classes, or misuse and destroy books and equipment. "Teach children to plant trees and nobody will will have to punish them for destroying trees," Fidel suggested. "We can teach respect for goods by teaching people to create goods."

Preventing school dropouts isn't a light matter in Cuba; the problem has been expressed with sreious concern by teachers, administrators, and even Fidel. In 1972 the matter was raised publicly at a meeting of the Young Communist Union (UJC). Although one would think that now that Cuba had made education free and available to everyone, the population would be eagerly taking advantage of it, this was not always the case. Especially in rural areas, where there was no tradition of going to school, families often kept their children home during planting and harvest time.

In a speech to the UJC Fidel pointed out that, of the children who entered first grade in the 1965-66 school year, only 21 percent had reached the sixth grade, and that of the junior high school class of 1966-67 only 13 percent made it to tenth grade. Many teenagers dropped out of school after that, without working or studying, and many more were repeating grades.

This problem was of utmost importance to Cuba, not only because the leadership of the Revolution feels that people can become more fully developed, and therefore happier, human beings if they have a complete education, but also because they become more productive human beings. Cuba simply cannot afford to have a sizable segment of its population living without contributing anything to the economic growth of the country. Despite the advances, much of the economy is still quite backward, with over three hundred thousand manual workers participating in the sugar harvest in peak years. Mechanization and technological development are considered vital to the growth and development of the economy. The scientists and technicians can only come from Cuba's schools.

Since the drop out and low pass-rate problem was raised as a burning issue in the spring of 1972 there has been a tremendous mass collective effort to remedy that situation. The UJC and the mass student organizations — the Pioneers, FEEM and FEU — have all launched campaigns and conducted emulations in the schools to assure greater attendance and higher promotion. The CDR's watch out for truancy as well as do propaganda work in the neighborhoods. And this has been accompanied by changes in the school programs — most notably the institution and increase of work study programs at all levels, making school a more real and vital part of the children's lives.

The results have been visible even in the first few years of this campaign. All promotion rates have gone up, with the Junior High Schools in the Countryside showing the highest rate: 95 percent.

The problem of dropouts and low promotion rates was also probably a contributing factor in the creation of the Centennial Youth Column, which later merged into the Army of Working Youth. The CJC was comprised of twenty-four thousand young people who volunteered in 1967 and the following years to do a three-year stint in the cane harvest of Camagüey Province. Economic necessity led to the call for the Youth Column: Camagüey is a very under-populated province with miles of canefields and many sugar mills. Before the Revolution men driven by hunger and poverty would flock to the Camagüey fields during cane-cutting time, looking for work. Once individual economic necessity was removed as a motivating force, the Revolution recruited and mobilized tens of thousands of industrial workers from other parts of the island. But this was always done at the cost of production in other areas. So the mobilization of thousands of young people who were not yet linked to other work centers and were not in school met a crucial need.

But aside from providing a significant solution to the economic problem in Camagüey, the Centennial Youth Column also gave an answer as to what to do with all these teenagers who were not in school or working. The young volunteers not only made an important — and highly praised — contribution to their country, but many of them also continued their education while they were at it — something they might not have otherwise done. Ten thousand out of the twenty-four thousand in the first contingent finished their three-year stint having learned skills and trades ranging from machine operators to teachers. And thousands upon thousands of them raised their grade level by studying at night after work in the Worker-Farmer Education program.

The experience with the CJC in Camagüey during its first three years led not only to its extension in Camagüey but in other provinces and other fields of work. The Youth Column of the Sea was organized to train future fishermen and maritime workers by letting the youngsters go out on training vessels in which they did a full share of work in addition to their courses.

And after five years, the CJC merged with the work units of the FAR (most of Cuba's Revolutionary Armed Forces, after receiving combat training, are involved in some kind of productive work) to form the *Ejercito Juvenil del Trabajo* (EJT, the Army of Working Youth). The EJT continues to provide a meaningful work experience which combines education with service to the Revolution for those young men and women who volunteer to join its ranks. For many who have been unable to relate to the academic school experience (especially those who haven't had the opportunity to attend a School in the Countryside), the EJT provides a means for them to feel part of the Revolutionary process, instead of like "dropouts", as they concretely assist in the building of socialism in their country.

Although the incorporation of dropouts and potential dropouts into these work columns has alleviated the problem a great deal, the fundamental answer is seen not in the column but in the combination of work and study in the primary and secondary school level. The Revolution hopes in this way to stop the problem before it starts. In addition, as has been mentioned before, educators see many other benefits in combining work and study.

For girls especially, the process of combining work and study means creating a whole new life. Women who share half the productive work of the country can no longer be expected to stay at home and care for the children while the men run the political side. Young girls growing up to take part in all collective work and all collective decision making are unlikely to be silent on these and other issues — as the voices of young women workers at recent workers' congresses has attested. The men — at least those who clearly identify with and support the goals of the Revolution — not only accept but welcome this change.

The combination of work and study is no longer just a plan in the minds of Marxist scholars and political theoreticians in the leadership of Cuba's socialist Revolution. It has already become ingrained in the minds of the new generation. They told me in a hundred ways: in drawings and compositions about work, in the ways they spoke to and about workers.

15

Children of Che and Uncle Ho

If the island of Cuba lay in a remote, undiscovered sea, or if it were the only country in the world, the Siboney, Taíno and Guanjátabey peoples might still be peacefully fishing off its coasts and extracting food products from its rich soil. There would have been no Spanish conquerors, no mercantile fleets, no Barbary pirates, no African slaves.

But the island of Cuba lay on the route to what many Europeans in the fifteenth century thought was the Indies, ninety miles off the shores of what was to become the richest — and in the opinion of many, the most exploitative — imperial power in the world. The people of Cuba fought for over a hundred years to free themselves from the political, economic and cultural effects of being a small, strategically located country with a fair amount of exploitable resources.

When Cuba finally threw off the last vestige of foreign control in 1959, U.S. hegemony over Latin America was being challenged for the first time since Pres. James Monroe declared that Latin America belonged to the United States. The U.S. response was quick and angry. The United States government set up an economic blockade and trade embargo, and financed various military incursions aimed at regaining control over the tiny island. Other countries which remained under the political control of the U.S. were forbidden to trade or have other relations with Cuba, thus effectively cutting the island off from almost all of Latin America.

In the face of this, Cuba began to look for new friends in the world community. The Revolutionary government found them among other small, oppressed nations — and among the socialist countries of the world.

The myriad effects of this new alignment — certainly quite opposite from what U.S. policy-makers had intended — have been of historic proportions. Cuba became, in its own words, "the First Free Territory of the Americas", and then — both cause and effect — the first socialist country in this hemisphere.

Slowly but surely, despite the blockade, Cuba began winning back friends and allies, trading partners and political supporters. Canada and Mexico never succumbed to the embargo; Peru, Argentina, Panama, and Chile (until the violent overthrow of the Allende Government) later rejected it, as sovereignty became more important to them than good relations with the United States. Even U.S. allies like England, France, Spain and Sweden engaged in limited commercial relations and growing political and cultural ties with the small island nation.

As the rising tide of nationalism that has been sweeping the world began affecting other governments of Latin America, one country after another began reassessing its obedience to the embargo imposed by the U.S. and the Organization of American States. Finally, in 1975, the OAS voted to allow its members to trade and maintain diplomatic relations with whomever they pleased. This was less an acceptance by the U.S.-dominated organization of the Cuban Revolution than it was a recognition of the growing independence of the member nations, many of whom had already demonstrated their willingness to break the blockade.

The Cuban people have been intensely aware of which peoples and governments caved in to U.S. pressure, and which stepped forth to help the struggling nation. They have seen concrete as well as moral help extended, not only from some of the more developed of the socialist countries like the USSR — which has been consistent and unstinting in its aid in recent years — but also from smaller and poorer countries. They have had a chance to experience assistance given with no strings attached, something that was unheard-of in their long history of domination by Spain and the U.S.

Out of all this, the Cuban people have come to rank among the most internationalist peoples on the globe. And nowhere can this be more clearly seen than among the children.

You hear it first in their names: children who bear the names of other peoples, other cities, other countries. Africa. My Lai. Lien. Yuri.

The children see it in the names of their childcare centers and schools. "Heroic Vietnam" Childcare Center. "Martyrs of Kent" Junior High School.

Internationalism — love and solidarity felt for all peoples of the world — is what Cuban children are taught from the time they are born. It is the reason most often given for their love and admiration for Che Guevara: "Because he fought not just for himself or his own country, but for all people. . . . "

Once, when I showed my "Children of Che" slide show at the parents' meeting of a childcare center, a middle-aged black man whose daughter attended the center (located in a working-class neighborhood in a small California town) wanted to know, "How do the children get to be internationalistic when they're taught so much patriotism? They learn about *their* flag, *their* heroes and martyrs, *their* revolutionary history. Isn't this a contradiction when trying to teach them about internationalism?"

For Cuba, there is no contradiction. Love for their people, their country, is not chauvinistic in Cuba; it's not done at the expense of other peoples. For Cuban children, love for your country is the middle part of the natural progression which begins with a sense of pride in yourself and leads to a love and respect for all peoples. Once Cuban children are taught to love and respect their flag as a symbol of the Cuban people and all the struggles they've engaged in to be free, their teachers then go on to explain that the flags of other countries represent the peoples of those countries, and that "we should respect their flags as we do our own."

Because Cuban children learn to respect themselves, to work collectively with all other people, and to love their country, they are more prepared to love and respect other peoples of the world than are children who don't have this sense of personal and national pride.

Internationalism is a part of the children's daily lives. It is taught conscientiously in the *circulos*, through song and dance and stories. It is taught in the schools, with acts of solidarity, compositions, visits by foreign delegations. The Pioneers make internationalism part of their regular activities, making love between peoples real through trips abroad and participation in international summer camps. Everywhere Cuban children go, they are surrounded by manifestations of love and solidarity with other peoples: in the billboards on the streets, in programs on TV, in the activities of their parents and neighbors, in newspapers, magazines and movies. It is so pervasive that there is almost nothing that you can see, do, read or hear about that concerns children in Cuba which does not in some way reflect their internationalist spirit. (Look back through all the chapters of this book.)

TEACHING CHILDREN TO LOVE

The teaching of internationalism begins on the simplest level in the childcare centers, where children are taught that the children of other lands "are just like you, but with different clothes, food, and customs." They are encouraged to dress up in the costumes of children from other countries, draw pictures of their flags and learn a few words of their language.

Young children are taught about other countries and peoples in relation to things they know about: in terms of the children of those lands, or in terms of the similarity to Cuba and Cuban history. They understand that people in Asia, or Africa, or Latin America are fighting because they are poor, oppressed and exploited — "like Cuba used to be." Whenever I asked youngsters why there was a war in Vietnam (or Guinea-Bissau, or guerrilla struggles in Bolivia or Uruguay . . .) they would invariably include among their answers: "They're fighting so they can have schools, and nice houses, and warm clothes, and good food, like we have now." Often they would say, "Because the U.S. wants to take away their land."

Their focus on children is especially clear when they are talking about or drawing pictures of another country in the midst of struggle. During most of my visits (between 1969 and 1973) children most often talked about Vietnam, which was still fighting against U.S. troops and bombs. "In Vietnam, the Yankees drop bombs on the children's schools," I heard over and over again. "Why does your government do that?" The caption of one drawing read bluntly, "Nixon, what have you done to the babies?"

By my last stay there in 1973, children were already thinking and talking a lot about Chile. The concern intensified after the September 1973 coup. When Cuba became directly involved in Angola's struggle for independence in 1976, attention focused on that African nation just as totally as it had on Vietnam a few years earlier.

Before the Revolution Cubans learned to view themselves as the inferior neighbors of the rich and powerful North Americans. Now instead they learn that they are part of Latin America, and share a common history with all the former colonies of Spain. They are taught to identify with all those peoples who are still struggling for freedom and independence. While Cubans are proud to have taken some major steps out of the poverty and misery in which other Latin American countries are steeped, they are also quick to share what they have with others.

Cuban children see their parents and teachers line up to give blood for earthquake victims in Peru or Nicaragua; they see teams of doctors and construction workers volunteer to help in any part of the world where they are needed. Cuba welcomed delegations of children and working people from Chile during the Allende Government, and has taken in many families of exiles since the bloody coup that overturned the *Unidad Popular* Government.

Cuban children also learn that part of their history lies on the African continent, that African blood runs through their veins. Because of this heritage, and even more from a deep sense of solidarity with all colonized and exploited peoples, the Cuban children have developed a strong feeling of comradeship for the peoples of Africa. The consciousness of their African heritage was greatly intensified when Cuba became directly involved in the African continent in a massive way through its aid to the people and government of Angola. Cuban identification with and participation in the liberation struggles in Africa had taken place earlier, but on a smaller scale.

In the period 1969-1973 Cuban children I met were aware that a number of Cubans fought alongside their African brothers against the Belgian and Portuguese colonialists in Africa — some giving their lives. There was a huge reception for a Cuban guerrilla fighter captured in Guinea-Bissau who was freed from a Portuguese prison following the left-wing coup in Portugal and the cessation of the wars in its former African colonies. Orphaned and exiled children of African liberation fighters have been given homes, medical care and scholarships in Cuba.

But when Cuban troops, technicians and medical personnel were sent to Angola this general interest and sense of solidarity escalated into a nationwide concern of great intensity. When I wrote to a Cuban friend in early 1977 requesting she send me some material demonstrating this, she replied: "I don't know how to respond to your request for 'something about solidarity between Cuban children and Angola,' because it's a constant!! There are songs, poems, there is this extraordinary consciousness on the part of the Cuban child as on the part of all Cubans. . . . " A Dutch educator, Kathinka van Dorp, wrote after her visit to Cuba in 1976: "Cuban children I met didn't know where Holland is, but they do know where Angola is. They have learned about that at school. They also know fathers who are there now." The children told van Dorp that their teacher had taught them about Angola from things she read in the newspaper, saw on television, and learned "from everybody, because we all talk about it."

In the small town of Santa Cruz, a child told her that Cuba was helping Angola because "we want to share everything with other children in the world who have less than we do." Asked how Cuban children helped those of Angola, the little girl replied, "In our schools children from every classroom have sent boxes with things like shoes and clothes, books and pencils, to the children in Angola. We made some drawings, and a picture of the map of Angola, and their flag, and of Cuban children. I wrote a letter. The Angolan language looks a lot like Spanish."

The girl added that she had written her first poem for the Angolan children. "It said that the children there will have as good a life as the children of Cuba, because now they're free. And it also said that we want to help them."

In Havana, the Dutch educator encountered other school children who said they were helping Angola. A fifth grader named Juan Carlos said he had sent his most beautiful book — children's stories by José Martí — to Angola. Asked whether they helped Angola in other ways, he and his friend Ignacio responded, "We study hard, we work in the school gardens, we play sports and we participate in music and theatre groups that carry out activities in solidarity with people who fight for their freedom."

"But do you help Angolan children in this way?" queried Kathinka van Dorp.

"Of course," was their reply. "If we learn a lot at school, and also afterwards, then we can go to Angola with that knowledge. And if we produce a lot, like in our school gardens, and like other Cubans do at work, we can give what we produce to the Angolan people. In the past we've also given sugar to Vietnam and Chile."

Solidarity activities between Cuban and Angolan children were initiated and organized by the Pioneers. UPC leader Ricardo García Pampín noted that the trunks of goods sent to Angola by the children were especially precious because they had come from the children themselves. Learning that 90 percent of the Angolan people are illiterate, the children organized to send books, pencils and other educational materials. "To meet their enormous needs in this area can't just be done by taking up collections," Pampín pointed out. "But what the children have done is tremendously important from a human standpoint. For us it would be much easier to go to a factory and send a ship full of pencils to Angola. But a pencil that a child chooses to send from among the few he or she has assumes a different, greater value than the quantities we could send from the factory." The Pioneer leader also pointed out that children had sent toys and clothes, items which are strictly rationed in Cuba to assure that the scarce supply is evenly distributed.

The weekly magazine *Pionero* during this period also reflected the extent to which Angola permeated Cuban consciousness. Each issue contained drawings, poems and stories about Angola and other countries of southern Africa. Some of the articles and photographs were provided by the adult editors of *Pionero,* but the rest came from the children themselves.

Van Dorp found that children spontaneously involved themselves in varied activities relating to Angola. She wrote of Gisela Olivero, "a girl from a traditional workers' quarter in Havana, El Cerro." Gisela had seen on television an Angolan woman performing a seventeenth century dance. The girl immediately made notes about the music, clothes and dance steps. Later, watching other movies about Angolan dances, she began to plan how she could perform an Angolan dance. Gisela spoke with some children from her school with whom she had done drawings, songs and theatre in their free time. The youngsters began rehearsing each afternoon after school, making replica African instruments themselves. Gisela made her African dress out of a table cloth. Because the children had very little paint and other design material, they painted the figures on the dress with boot polish and pasted on shiny cigar-bands.

Van Dorp said there was total silence followed by thunderous applause when Gisela performed her Angolan dance, first for the children of her school, later for the people from her *barrio*, for psychologists from the Ministry of Education who wanted to expand

Gisela practices intricate Angolan dance.

the work of this group to other schools, for the workers of Cuba's largest magazine, *Bohemia,* and finally for Fidel Castro, Angolan President Agostinho Neto and ten thousand Pioneers in the José Martí summer camp.

Gisela and her friends were not unusual in the depths of their feelings for Angola, although they certainly stood out in terms of initiative and creativity. By the time they're in their teens most young Cubans already have years of experience actively demonstrating their feelings of solidarity for other peoples.

For this generation of schoolchildren, that experience reached its height in the Fall of 1977 when Fidel Castro announced that one thousand Cuban high school students would travel to Angola as teachers. Fidel had earlier suggested the creation of an internationalist teachers brigade to meet the Angolan government's critical need for people to teach one million grammar school students.

Six thousand children studying for a teaching career responded to Fidel's request. The thousand who were chosen will complete their teacher training in Angola while teaching Angolan primary school children.

"WE'RE ALL BROTHERS AND SISTERS"

The Union of Pioneers plays a leading role in developing the children's love for other peoples in a concrete way.

At the *Encuentro Nacional* of Pioneer chiefs in 1973, I asked a Pioneer named Sonia what she liked best about being a Pioneer. She told me:

> What I like best is participating in all the Pioneer activities where you learn about the Revolution and about other countries. For example, during the summer vacation I traveled to Poland with the Pioneers. I liked that a lot because that way you learn how Pioneers live in other countries. We have meetings with Pioneers from all over the world who are visiting Cuba.

When I asked Sonia what "internationalism" meant to her, she told me: "It's that the Pioneers of Cuba are the friends of Pioneers from all the other countries."

Another Pioneer joined in:

> For me internationalism is the union, the solidarity, the fraternity of all the peoples of the world, and in this case, of all the Pioneers. It's that all of us Pioneers feel that we aren't divided by race or country, because we all belong to the same organization.

The Activities Commission of the *Encuentro Nacional* had listed two complete pages of "activities in solidarity" with other countries, asking the Pioneer delegates to name the ones they had carried out and liked best, and the ones they would like to carry out.

But lists are easy to make, even though these lists certainly included many activities which few American children would think of. It was what these children felt, and how they expressed it in their daily lives, that was so impressive — and so difficult to capture on paper.

Once I asked a child why it was that Cuban children talk and sing and think so much about the children of Vietnam. Almost angrily she responded:

> Because Vietnam was a country exploited by poverty and discrimination. Because of all the wounded, the murdered. We know how their country has suffered, and we give them all our love and try to help them in that way to make a Revolution like we have here in Cuba.

Her next words mixed anger with admiration, as she said:

> They were burned, their parents were killed, they lost their families — and they kept fighting so that their people could have true freedom.

In one interview after another, children told me that, although they knew it was difficult, they would go off to fight in other countries of Latin America or Indochina if the need should arise. "Ten-, twelve- and thirteen-year-olds fought in our revolutionary struggle," they pointed out. "And children even younger than that are fighting in Vietnam."

How do they know all this? Of their own revolutionary history, they have ample accounts in their history books, stories, poems, movies and personal accounts. What happens to children from other countries they learn, in addition to all this, from the children themselves. Among the frequent visitors to Cuba in this period were children from Vietnam. From them, Cuban children learned a great deal about life under U.S. bombs. When asked by some Pioneers how the children take part in this struggle, a little Vietnamese girl responded:

> Well, *compañeros*, our main task is to study, but besides that we participate in the struggle together with our parents and brothers and sisters. We take part in voluntary work, and we help the soldiers by carrying water and food. Sometimes we carry the ammunition boxes if we're big enough. We also cut branches of trees to camouflage the artillery, and we gather rags from torn clothes that people don't need so the soldiers can use them to clean the guns.

Cuban children have regular contact, through visits, meetings, parties and cultural acts, with adults and children from the various diplomatic missions and embassies in Cuba. But in addition to this, as indicated above, there are a number of children from other countries who, for one reason or another, have come to live in Cuba. What the children learn from them is often painful. But it makes very real what they have heard and been taught about peoples' struggles everywhere.

THE LITTLE EXILES   Cuba has a fairly sizable population of foreign exiles for a country so tiny. Many of them come from Latin America: the children of martyred revolutionary fighters from Brazil, Argentina, Uruguay, and Bolivia — or those whose parents are still fighting in those countries.

Chilean girls at an international Pioneer camp. Many of these children are now refugees or prisoners of the Chilean junta.

Serinha (not her real name) was twelve years old when I met her — thin, quiet, with dark skin, short brown hair and somber eyes.

She was born and lived in Brazil until she was ten, when police killed her father, who was involved in Brazil's liberation struggle.

Serinha's father had been imprisoned once before, but had been freed when other commandos from his guerrilla unit had kidnapped a foreign ambassador and demanded prisoners' freedom in exchange. Unable to accept the relative safety of life in exile, he had returned to join the clandestine struggle in his country, until he was shot.

Serinha told me: "My papa joined the struggle six years before he was killed. He joined because he saw the conditions in Brazil. Many people lived in the streets. Many died of hunger. He wanted to make Brazil a better country. Because you would walk in the streets and see people begging for money and everything. The poor gave them something — whatever they could — but the rich just passed on by without giving them anything. So my father decided to become a revolutionary. He talked with my mother and she agreed. So then papa spoke to some *compañeros*, and they began to give him some lessons. They taught him how things were, and what had to be done, and he learned."

Serinha recalls one day when her family was warned that police were coming to her house. "We just got out in time. We were turning the corner in our VW van just as the police rounded the other corner. The police ransacked the house, stealing our radios and everything of value."

Before coming to Cuba in early 1973 Serinha had lived with her mother and younger sister in Chile. When asked why she left Chile for Cuba, Serinha replied: "The situation in Chile is very complicated. There you have both *compañeros* and reactionaries, leftists and rightists."

Less than a year after Serinha's family left Chile, the bloody military coup in that land imprisoned, deported or murdered virtually the entire exile community in that country. Thousands of Chilean families were broken up by assassination or imprisonment, and hundreds of Chilean children found themselves, like Serinha, being offered the hospitality of the Cuban people.

Of the exile children in Cuba, Serinha's case is not by any means the most tragic. A number of children from the African colonies which fought for their independence from Portugal and which only recently won have also made Cuba their home — and a number of these were brought here for treatment of napalm burns. Although there was widespread protest in the U.S. against the use of napalm against the people of Vietnam, very few Americans were even aware that the U.S. was also supplying this barbaric weapon to the Portuguese for their war in Africa.

Other children — from Brazil, and more recently from Chile — were forced to watch their parents undergo torture in fascist military prisons, and some were subjected to torture themselves. The military regimes of these countries hoped they could force prisoners — men and women — to "talk" if their children were being beaten in front of them. "But if you don't know anything, you can do nothing but watch your child's agony, feeling as if you were being pulled apart inch by inch," explained a Brazilian mother sadly. Her husband had been killed, and an older son imprisoned for guerrilla activities. "But they never told me anything," she said. "I tried to make up answers, tell the police anything they wanted to know, but then they found out I wasn't telling them the truth. They wanted to know where the 'hideout' was, and when they tortured me, I just made up an address. When they found out I lied, they began beating my child."

Some parents faced an even more difficult situation: they *did* have information the secret police wanted. One such woman was asked how she could resist talking when the interrogators beat her child in front of her. "Seeing my son being beaten was very painful — more painful than anything they did to me," she replied. "But what if I had told them what they wanted to know, betrayed my *compañeros*? Others would have been imprisoned, tortured, or killed. And what would my son have thought of me — and of himself — when he grew up and learned that we bore the responsibility for the fall of those comrades? He would have to have lived with that knowledge his whole life.

"Besides," she went on, "past experience has shown us that torturers don't necessarily treat prisoners any better if they do talk. Sometimes they take this as an admission of guilt, and so punish you more. Or, having gotten what they want from you, they kill you."

Cuban pediatricians and psychologists have had to deal with the after-effects of children traumatized by terror, imprisonment and torture in their own countries. Children were brought to them who were unable to speak or play with other children, who were super-aggressive or afraid of anything that moved.

Doctora Elsa Gutiérrez headed a team of psychiatrists and psychologists at the Cerro Pediatric Clinic in Havana when the case of María and Ze came to her attention. The Brazilian woman and her three-year-old child had been imprisoned and tortured by Brazil's military police. The child was severely traumatized by the time they reached Cuba.

She said at first the medical team was not even certain it would be possible to return Ze to a normal life. "We didn't know if we could erase the terrible imprints left on his psyche by what he had lived through."

Doctora Gutiérrez described the months of intensive treatment, ranging from tranquilizers to reduce Ze's hyperactivity, to play sessions, and the phenomenal daily efforts made by Ze's mother, María. After three months they began to see some progress: Ze began to speak!

Slowly, he began to acquire normal habits of eating, sleeping, and playing. But Ze was still far from a normal child. "One of the most depressing things," *Dra.* Gutiérrez recalled, "was realizing that Ze didn't know how to defend himself. If another child tried to hit him — even in play — he couldn't defend himself. He was so used to being beaten by older persons that all he did was cover himself with his hands and let himself be hit."

When asked what would have happened to Ze if he had been left untreated, the psychiatrist explained:

"He would have died or become a monster. He would have been malnourished and prone to diseases, any of which could have killed him in the future. . . . And he would have been a child who didn't know how to laugh, who didn't know how to love; one who lived in a fantasy-world and who would have been retarded in all aspects."

Dra. Gutiérrez said she wrote about the case of María and Ze out of fury and indignation. While writing it, she said, she learned of the "plans by the fascist Chilean Junta to send the children of revolutionaries to concentration camps." This, she said, would repeat on a massive scale what had happened to Ze, "leading to the death of many children, leaving hundreds as traumatized as Ze, and some without any hope of recuperation." The purpose of writing about Ze, she said, was to "alert people so that humanity wouldn't be responsible for allowing the monstrous plans of the fascist Junta to take place."

Now, after seven months of intensive treatment, Ze was behaving normally and attending a childcare center. "Luckily, Ze arrived in Cuba while he still had some potential of recuperating," the doctor remarked. "We're happy about that — but it also makes us think with profound pain of how many children from Chile, Brazil and other countries have forever lost the hope of a normal and happy life."

Although "María" and "Ze" are not the real names of this mother and child, the facts of their life are real. Cuban children are growing up with youngsters like this today. Often they hear from the children themselves of the horrors they have been subjected to. All of this makes Cuban children's hatred of imperialism and the military dictatorships subservient to it both real and deep.

These African children visited Cuba when their country was fighting for independence from Portugal. Many were being treated for napalm burns.

ALL THE CHILDREN OF THE WORLD   In a song the Pioneers sing the children state: "We are the brothers and sisters of everyone in the world." At the International Pioneer Camp held in Varadero Beach each summer the children have a chance to put their song into practice. Pioneers from all over the world gather there to meet, exchange experiences, play, and engage in sports, cultural and political activities together. Most socialist countries have Pioneers organizations — although most of them begin at the age where Cuban Pioneers stop. In addition, other countries in the midst of struggle are invited to send small contingents of children to the camp. Since 1972, a small group of North American youngsters age nine to fourteen has participated in the international camp. Patterned after the Venceremos Brigades — people from the U.S. who travel to Cuba to express solidarity with the Revolution and take part in two months of voluntary work and travel there — the American children are called "Venceremitos."*

The first group of *Venceremitos* was made up of twenty-three

Venceremos meand "we will win." *Venceremitos* can be roughly translated as "little winners."

boys and girls — black, white, Chicano, Puerto Rican and Filipino — from New York, Chicago, Los Angeles and San Francisco. They lived in a camp at the formerly exclusive Varadero Resort area, and came to know children from Cuba, Vietnam, Chile, Guinea-Bissau, Bulgaria, the Soviet Union . . . children from all over the world.

When I asked one of the *Venceremitos* what she had liked best about the camp after she returned to California, she replied without hesitation: "The other kids." I found that was a universal reaction among the youngsters, many of whom continued to exchange letters with their new-found friends from other countries. Almost none of the children could speak any language other than their own. They were accompanied by translators, but the *Venceremitos* told me they often didn't need them. "We just sort of understood each other," one boy said with a smile.

The *Venceremitos* had been given a small sample of what Cuban children are exposed to every day. Each day they were in the camp was dedicated to the country of one of the delegations. There were photographic exhibits and displays, films, panels, seminars and presentations prepared by the youngsters of that country. When it was their turn the *Venceremitos* presented a skit portraying young people marching and peacefully demonstrating in protest of the war in Vietnam, and demanding an end to racism, and more jobs at home. In the skit a group of policemen came to break up the demonstration and arrest the demonstrators. "Imprisoned" behind the locked arms of their policemen-jailers, the demonstrators broke into song: "We want our freedom, we want our freedom . . . Stop the bombing . . . Revolution, Revolution."

The Cuban Pioneers for their part took great pride in teaching the visiting delegations about their revolutionary history. One of the excursions the children made was to Playa Giron — the beach where the Bay of Pigs attack was defeated. But the Cubans never lorded it over the Americans or made them feel uncomfortable. "We know you're fighting against imperialism too, and that your government oppresses you the same way it oppresses other people around the world," they assured the *Venceremitos*. "But don't worry. All the children of the world are your friends, and we'll help you. Your government can never win against all of us together."

16

Babies are Born Every Day

Books are supposed to have a beginning and an end. But Revolution is an ongoing process, and the story of the children of the Revolution is really just beginning. Changes occur every day. By 1971, observations I made in 1969 were outdated. In 1973, issues were being struggled through that hadn't even been conceived of in 1971. That process continues today.

The Revolution has already made major changes in the lives of the Cuban people. This is most visible in the children: in their health care, their schools, their activities, and their social and political formation.

The Revolution does not claim to have created a Utopia. Nor have all the problems facing the Cuban people been resolved. There are still not enough schools or teachers. There are still old concepts being handed down from parent to child. Many concepts of child-rearing are still under close examination. Methods of educating and training young people are being revised as some methods are shown through practice to work better than others. Educators and all those concerned with Cuba's future generations are constantly seeking new information, from all parts of the globe, to improve the childcare and education system they've already devised. At every step of the way, they are still being held back by underdevelopment and blockade.

Although the Cuban system makes no claims to perfection,

there are many ways in which it can serve as a model to others. Other Third World, underdeveloped countries can benefit from Cuba's practical approach to providing care and education for all its children through a combination of work and study.

Developed countries, too, can learn much from the Cuban example. Many of the values Cuban educators and parents seek to instill in their youth are ones parents and teachers around the world might want to emulate.

In looking at what the Revolution has been trying to create, we can say at this point that New Children already exist in Cuba, children who have been molded "in the spirit of Che." The Revolution has focused its attention on raising children who are free to grow up happy and healthy, to develop themselves in every way possible. It has tried to create children who work, study and play together collectively, without smothering any child's individuality. Through teaching and example, it has attempted to instill in its younger generation love and respect for work and working people. And it has attempted to produce in them a sincere feeling of identity with, solidarity and love for all the peoples of the world.

The children I met throughout Cuba already incorporated these traits to a significant enough degree that I was able to feel they are, truly, the "children of Che." But for a North American writer, educator or parent, this isn't enough. The question is raised over and over: of those traits Cuban's are developing in their children which we admire, which ones can we duplicate here? How can we go about it?

The answers to those questions are very complex, and can't be dealt with thoroughly in this book. When people ask, "Can we do it here?" the answer has to be both yes and no. Childcare and education cannot be separated from a society's values, or from its practice. Parents and educators could try to instill in their children some of the values being taught to Cuban children, such as a sense of collectivity and sharing, a love of productive work, a feeling of brotherhood and sisterhood with peoples of all countries and all races. Programs could be devised in particular centers or schools, adapting from the methods used in Cuba to teach these values. But the children would still live in a society whose dominant sectors have different values. Those children would still be faced with many conflicting ideas and attitudes in the streets, on television, in movies, magazines, storybooks and often from friends and families. Basic values can't be changed in children until the overall society changes. Where there is a relatively homogeneous view, as in Cuba since the Revolution, devising new ways of raising and educating children to new values is simplified. In a society as heterogeneous as that in the United States, the task becomes infinitely more difficult.

But that is not to say it isn't worth the effort. To the extent that progressive parents and teachers have input into the curriculum and practice of their childcare centers and schools, they could attempt in an organized way to incorporate some of the ideas presented in this book. But like the Revolution, this book is only a beginning. There are paragraphs which should be whole chapters, chapters which should be the subject of further investigations and new books. Entire sections had to be left out because of space considerations. All that's really presented here are some glimpses into the lives of Cuban children, a look at what it's like to grow up in Cuba today. When this book was first being written, the possibilities for expanding on this by further investigation were severely limited. But now, as the United States finally moves into the twentieth century in terms of its relations with Cuba, we may expect to see a complete end to the blockade of that island. Then perhaps more educators, parents, researchers and writers can travel to Cuba and bring back more in-depth information and evaluation of the many areas of childcare and education. This would greatly facilitate implementation of programs designed to achieve better quality childcare and education in the U.S.

We are not likely to see the dramatic results that can be found in Cuba. The working-class parents who most need the kinds of services offered to Cuban children are those with the fewest resources to provide them in this country. Liberal middle-class and professional parents who want to educate their children in a new way are likely to find opposition from other members of the same class, as well as from the conflicting barrage of different values daily imposed on their children. Ultimately, the children of Che will exist only in a society that has undergone a profound political, economic and social Revolution.

Index

Karen Wald is a free-lance journalist and has written for numerous magazines and newspapers. She worked for eight months as translator, editor and writer for *Tricontinental* magazine in Havana in 1969. She started gathering material for this book in 1970-71 and made two more extended trips to Cuba to complete it in 1972 and 1973. Her documentary videotape *Children of Che* has been shown on Public Television and her slide-lectures on Cuba's educational system have found large audiencies in California.

Ms. Wald holds a BS in Industrial and Labor Relations from Cornell University and has a California Teaching Credential, with a MA in Early Childhood Development from The University Without Walls, Berkeley. She now lives in Berkeley with her two children.

Hal Z. Bennett is an educator in alternative education and medicine and author of *No More Public Schools* and *The Well Body Book*. He is a consultant to Early Childhood Education Programs in Santa Cruz, Watsonville, Marin County and San Francisco and a consultant to the UC Berkeley Student Health Service.

The cover drawing was done by Albis Morejon, eight years old, who took part in the Summer art and reading program at the National Library in Havana in 1973. Albis said the drawing was of "a school where the *campesinos* go."
Back cover: A Cuban Pioneer addressing an international meeting of Pioneers attended by children from all the socialist countries.

DATE DUE

DEMCO 38-297